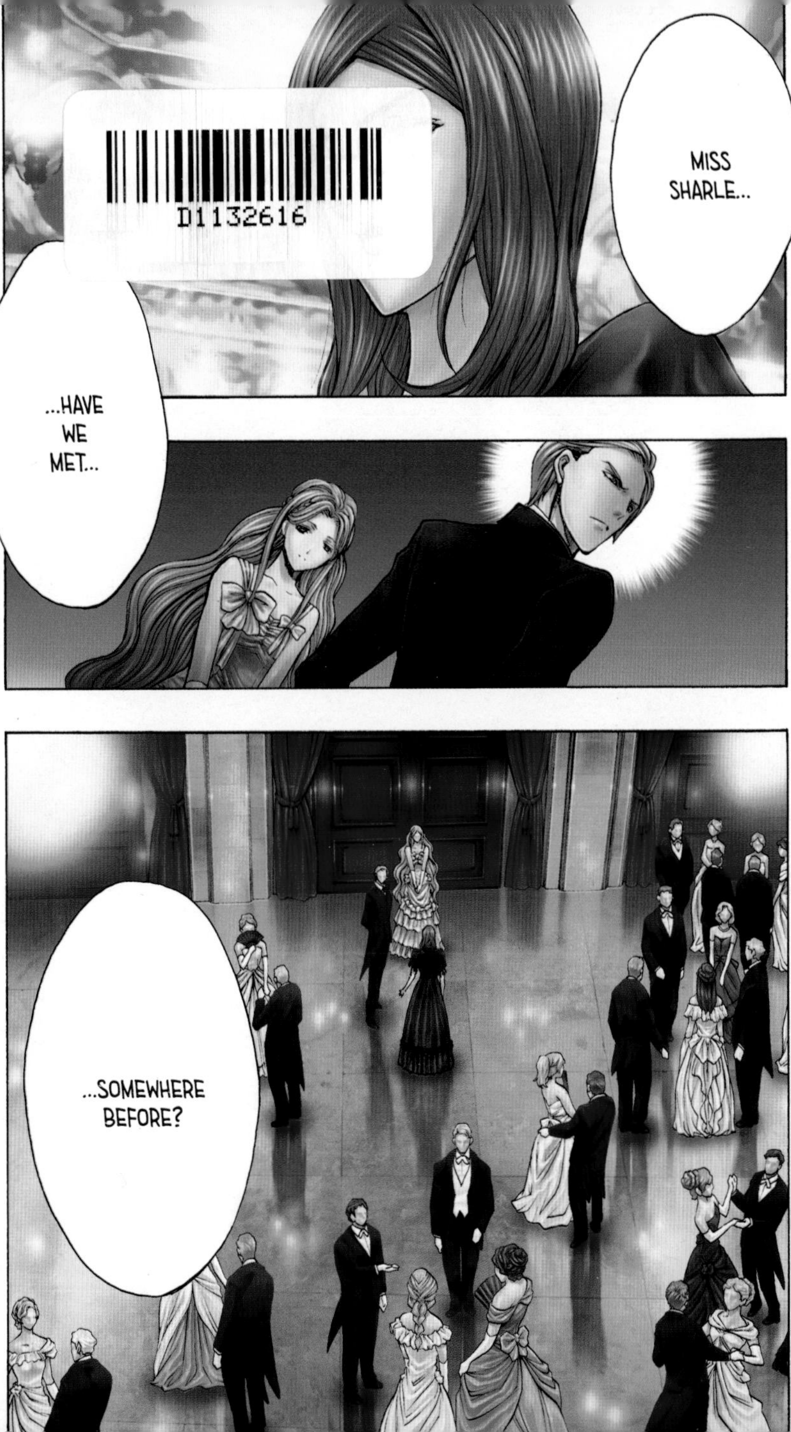
MISS SHARLE...
...HAVE WE MET...
...SOMEWHERE BEFORE?

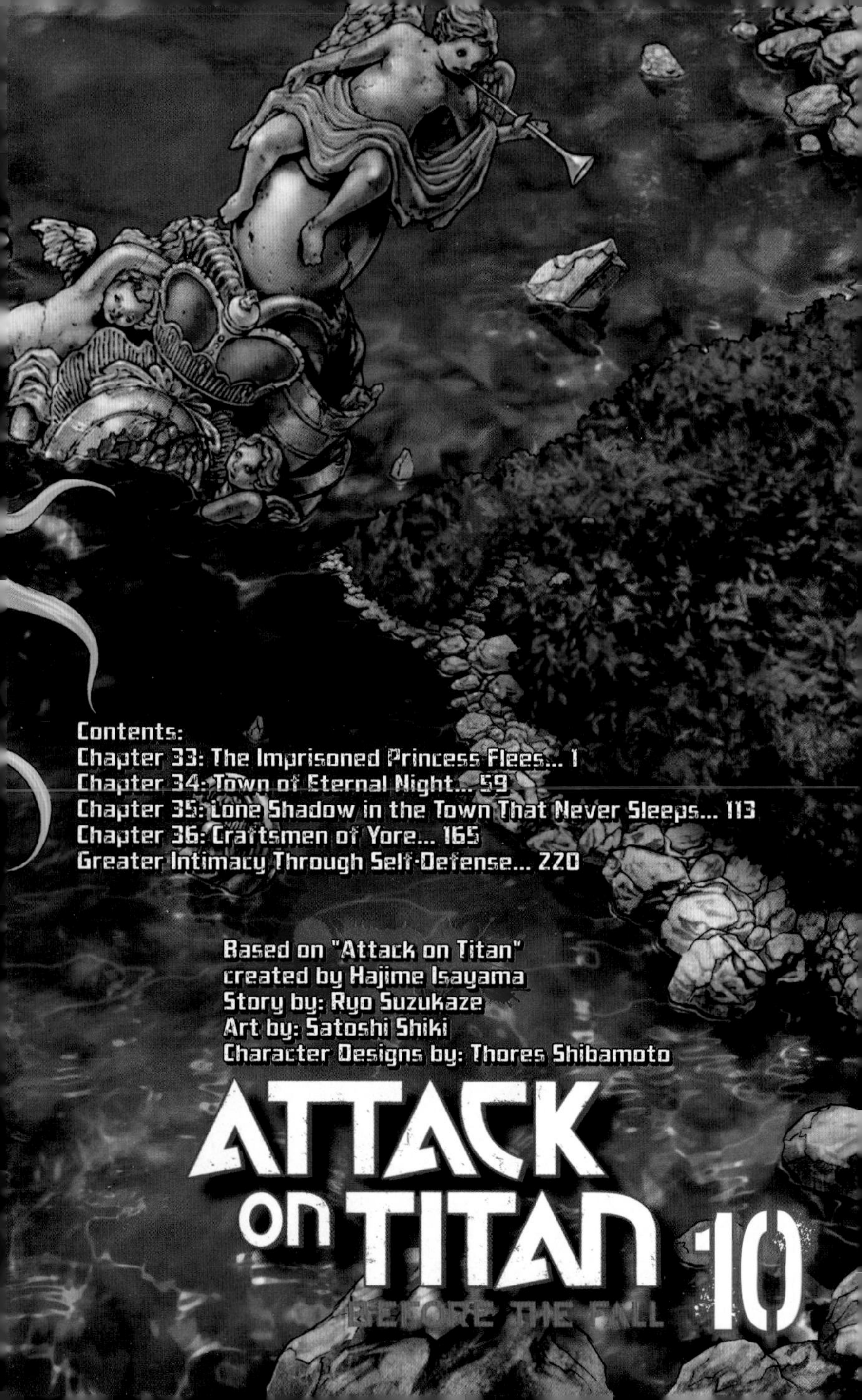

Contents:

Based on "Attack on Titan"
created by Hajime Isayama
Story by: Ryo Suzukaze
Art by: Satoshi Shiki
Character Designs by: Thores Shibamoto

ATTACK ON TITAN

BEFORE THE FALL

10

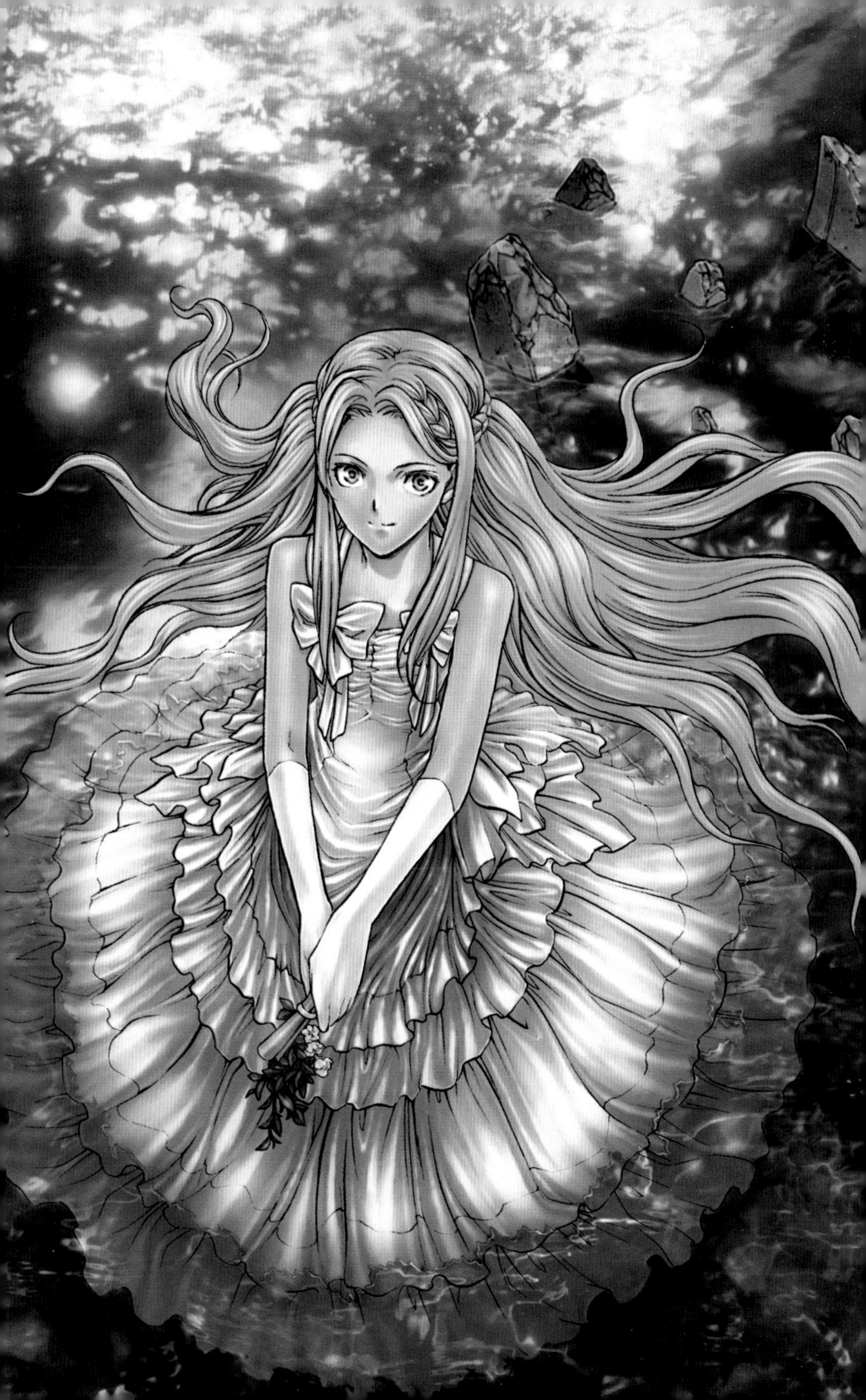

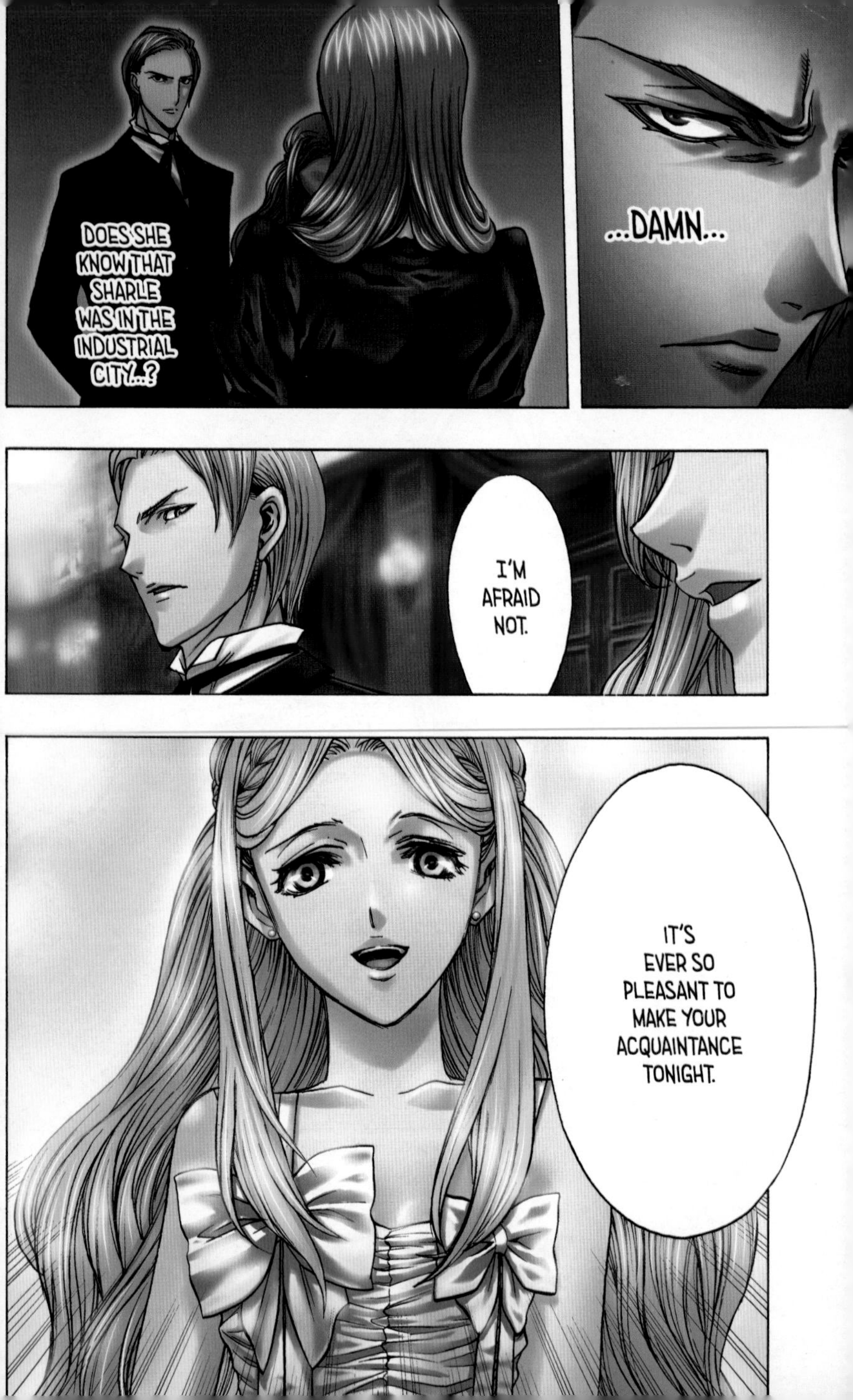
...DAMN...
DOES SHE KNOW THAT SHARLE WAS IN THE INDUSTRIAL CITY...?
I'M AFRAID NOT.
IT'S EVER SO PLEASANT TO MAKE YOUR ACQUAINTANCE TONIGHT.

Before the fall — Character Profiles

Kuklo

A 15-year-old boy born from a dead body packed into the vomit of a Titan, which earned him the moniker, "Titan's Son." He is fascinated with the Device as a means to defeat the Titans. The protagonist of this story. His current status is unknown, after he was defeated by Xavi.

Sharle Inocencio

First daughter of the Inocencios, a rich merchant family within Wall Sheena. When she realized that Kuklo was a human, she taught him to speak and learn. She trained as an apprentice craftsman under Xenophon in the industrial city, until Xavi dragged her back home.

Xavi Inocencio

Head of the Inocencio family and Sharle's brother. Member of the Military Police in Shiganshina District.

Cardina Baumeister

Kuklo's first friend in the outside world, and his companion in developing the Device.

Jorge Pikale

Training Corps instructor. A former Survey Corps captain who was hailed as a hero for defeating a Titan.

Carlo Pikale

Jorge's son and current captain of the Survey Corps. After they battled Titans together, he has great respect for Kuklo.

Xenophon Harkimo

Foreman at the Industrial City. He took over development of the Device from its inventor, Angel.

Gloria Bernhart

Captain of the Military Police in Shiganshina District. A powerful MP officer with a cold, tactical mind.

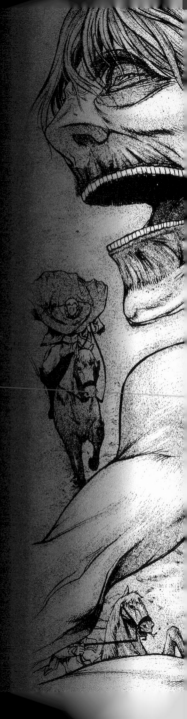

When a Titan terrorized Shiganshina District and left behind a pile of vomit, a baby boy was miraculously born of a pregnant corpse. This boy was named Kuklo, the "Titan's Son," and treated as a sideshow freak. Eventually the wealthy merchant Dario Inocencio bought Kuklo to serve as a punching bag for his son, Xavi. On the other hand, when she learned he was human and not the son of a Titan, Xavi's sister Sharle decided to teach him the words and knowledge of humanity instead. Two years later, Kuklo escaped from the mansion along with Sharle, who was being forced into a marriage she did not desire.

In Shiganshina District, the Survey Corps was preparing for its first expedition outside of the wall in 15 years. Kuklo snuck into the expedition's cargo wagon, but the Titan they ran across was far worse of a monster than he expected. He helped the Survey Corps survive, but inside the walls he was greeted by the Military Police, who wanted the "Titan's Son" on charges of murdering Dario. In prison, he met Cardina, a young man jailed over political squabbles. They hoped to escape to safety when exiled beyond the Wall, but found themselves surrounded by a pack of Titans. It was through the help of Jorge, former Survey Corps Captain and first human to defeat a Titan, that the two boys escaped with their lives. The equipment that Jorge used was the very "Device" that was the key to defeating the Titan those 15 years ago.

Kuklo and Cardina escaped the notice of the MPs by hiding in the industrial city, where they found Sharle. It is there that the three youngsters learned the truth of the ill-fated Titan-capturing expedition 15 years earlier, and swore to uphold the will of Angel, the inventor of the Device. Next, Kuklo and Cardina headed back to Shiganshina to test out a new model of the Device developed by Xenophon, Angel's friend and rival, but they failed to defeat a Titan with it.

As he recovered from his injuries, Kuklo heard ominous rumors about MP activity, and rushed to the Industrial City to protect Sharle. When he got to the gate of the city, he came across the stunning sight of battle between anti-establishment dissidents and the Military Police. Kuklo was able to slip through the chaos to rescue Sharle from the dissidents. But just as they started to celebrate their reunion, Sharle's brother Xavi arrived, and turned his sword on Kuklo. Xavi won the battle by inflicting a grievous blow on Kuklo, who fell into the river. Sharle was taken back to the Inocencio mansion, where she was forced to make her society debut for the sake of Xavi's political ambition. At the event, she suddenly came face-to-face with Captain Gloria, who had just finished quelling the uprising in the Industrial City.

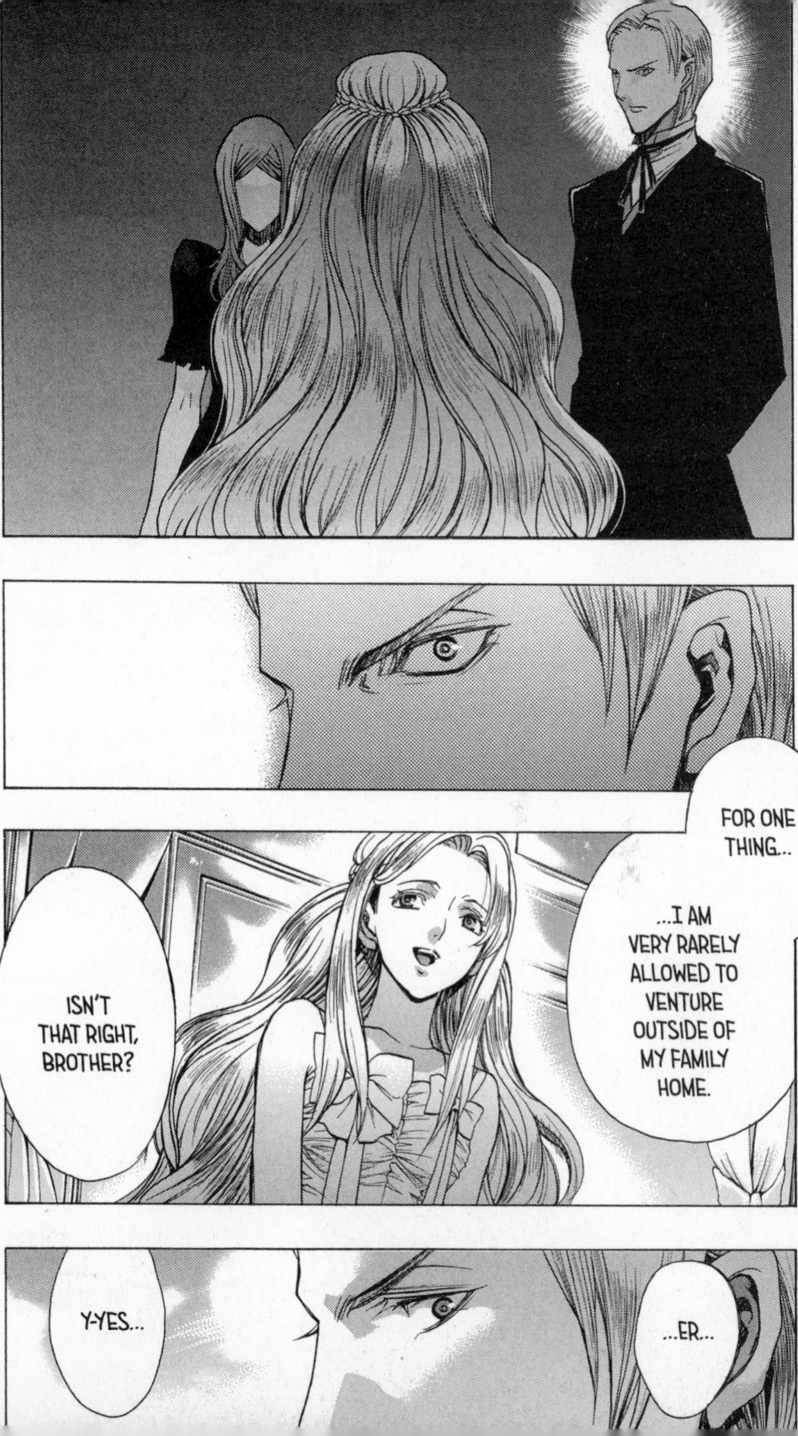
FOR ONE THING...
...I AM VERY RARELY ALLOWED TO VENTURE OUTSIDE OF MY FAMILY HOME.
ISN'T THAT RIGHT, BROTHER?
...ER...
Y-YES...

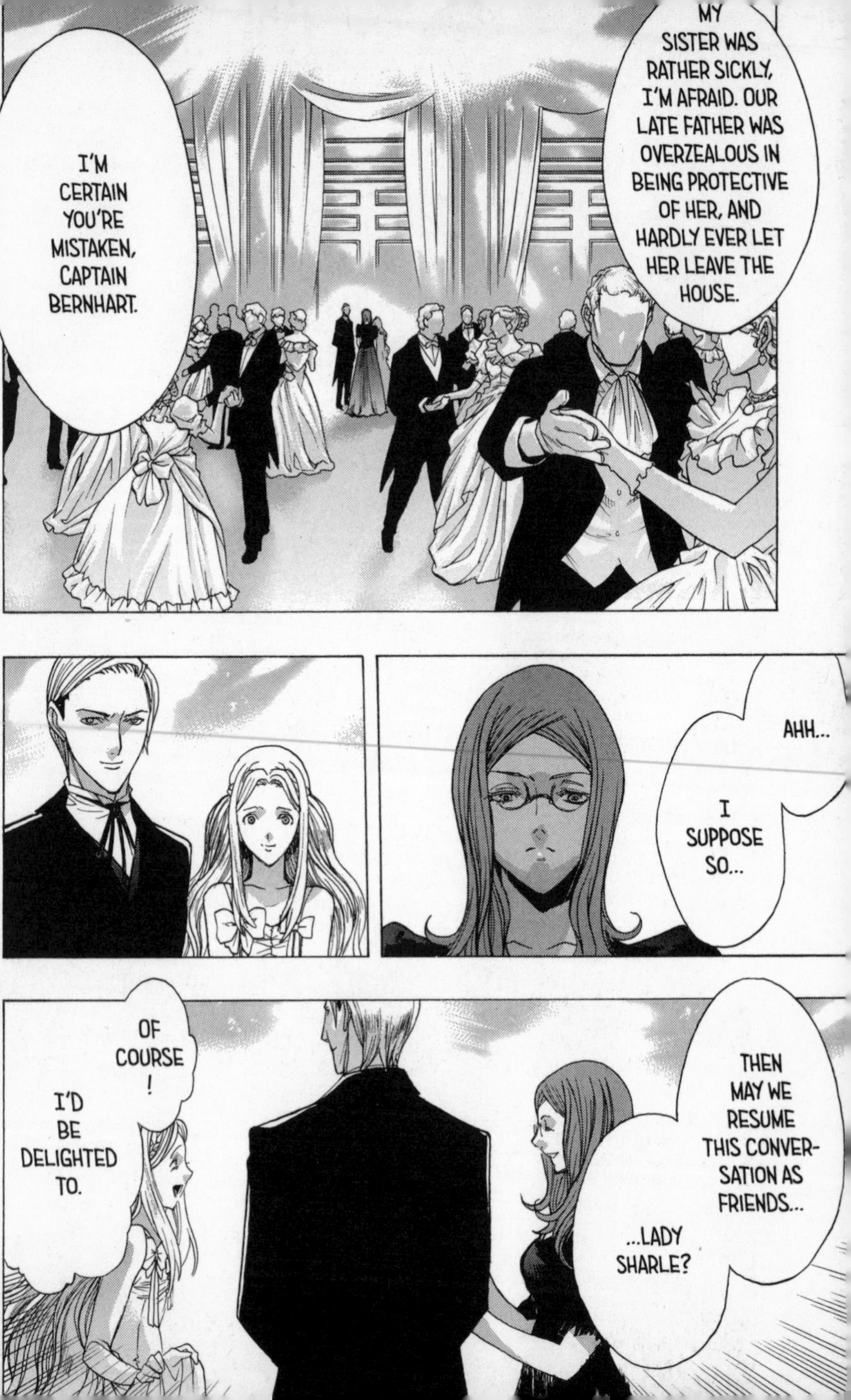
MY SISTER WAS RATHER SICKLY, I'M AFRAID. OUR LATE FATHER WAS OVERZEALOUS IN BEING PROTECTIVE OF HER, AND HARDLY EVER LET HER LEAVE THE HOUSE.
I'M CERTAIN YOU'RE MISTAKEN, CAPTAIN BERNHART.
AHH...
I SUPPOSE SO...
THEN MAY WE RESUME THIS CONVER-SATION AS FRIENDS...
...LADY SHARLE?
OF COURSE!
I'D BE DELIGHTED TO.

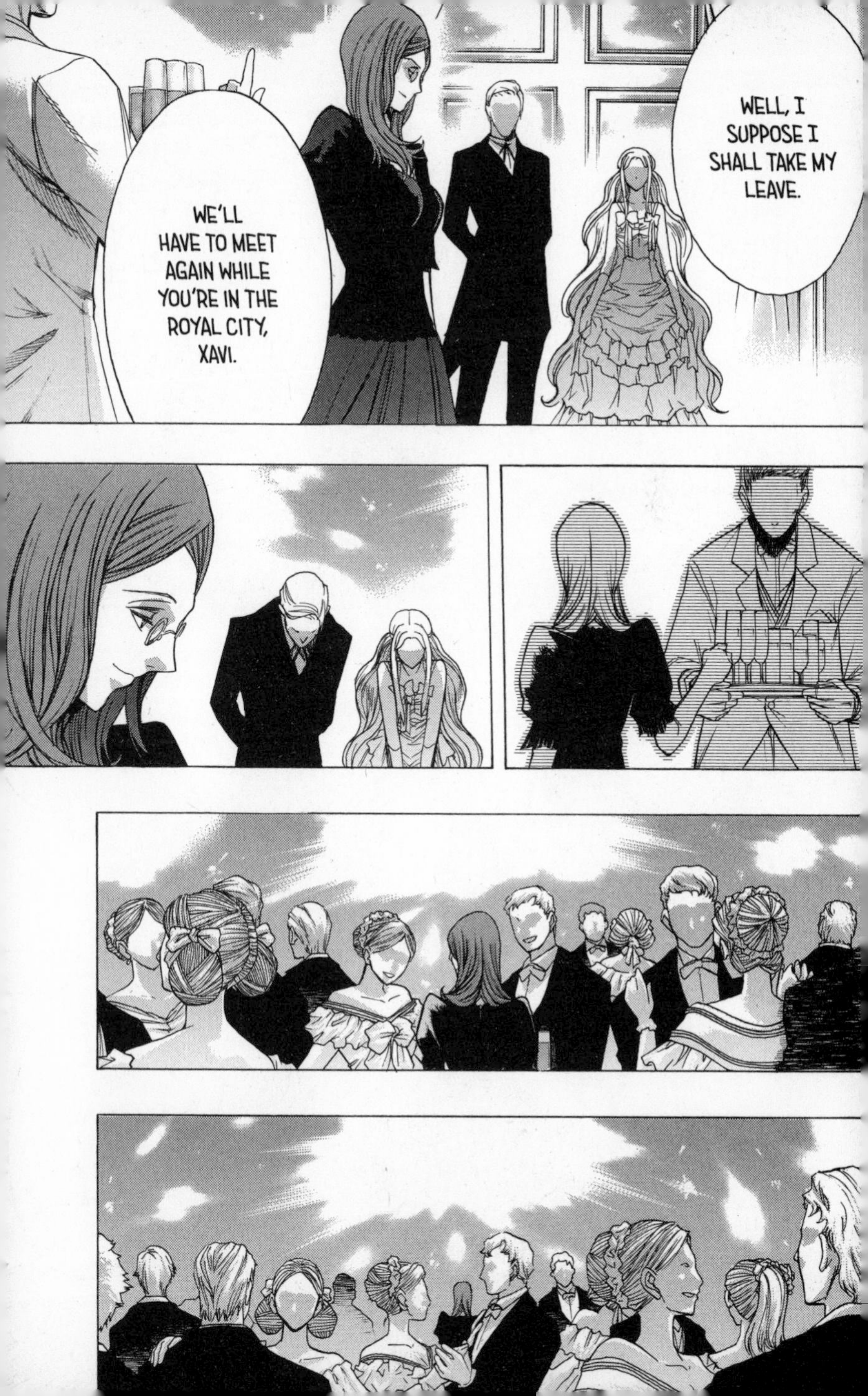
WELL, I SUPPOSE I SHALL TAKE MY LEAVE.
WE'LL HAVE TO MEET AGAIN WHILE YOU'RE IN THE ROYAL CITY, XAVI.

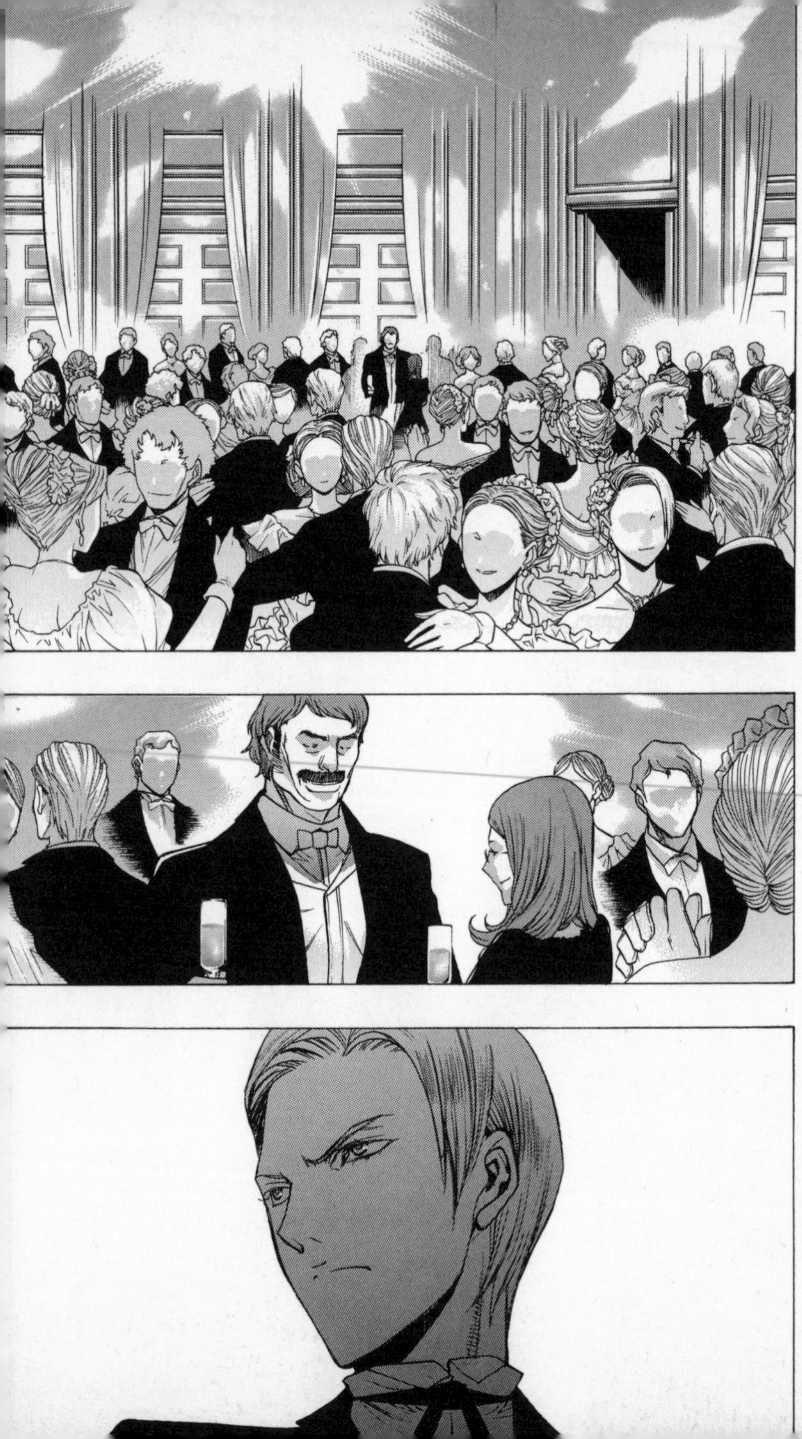

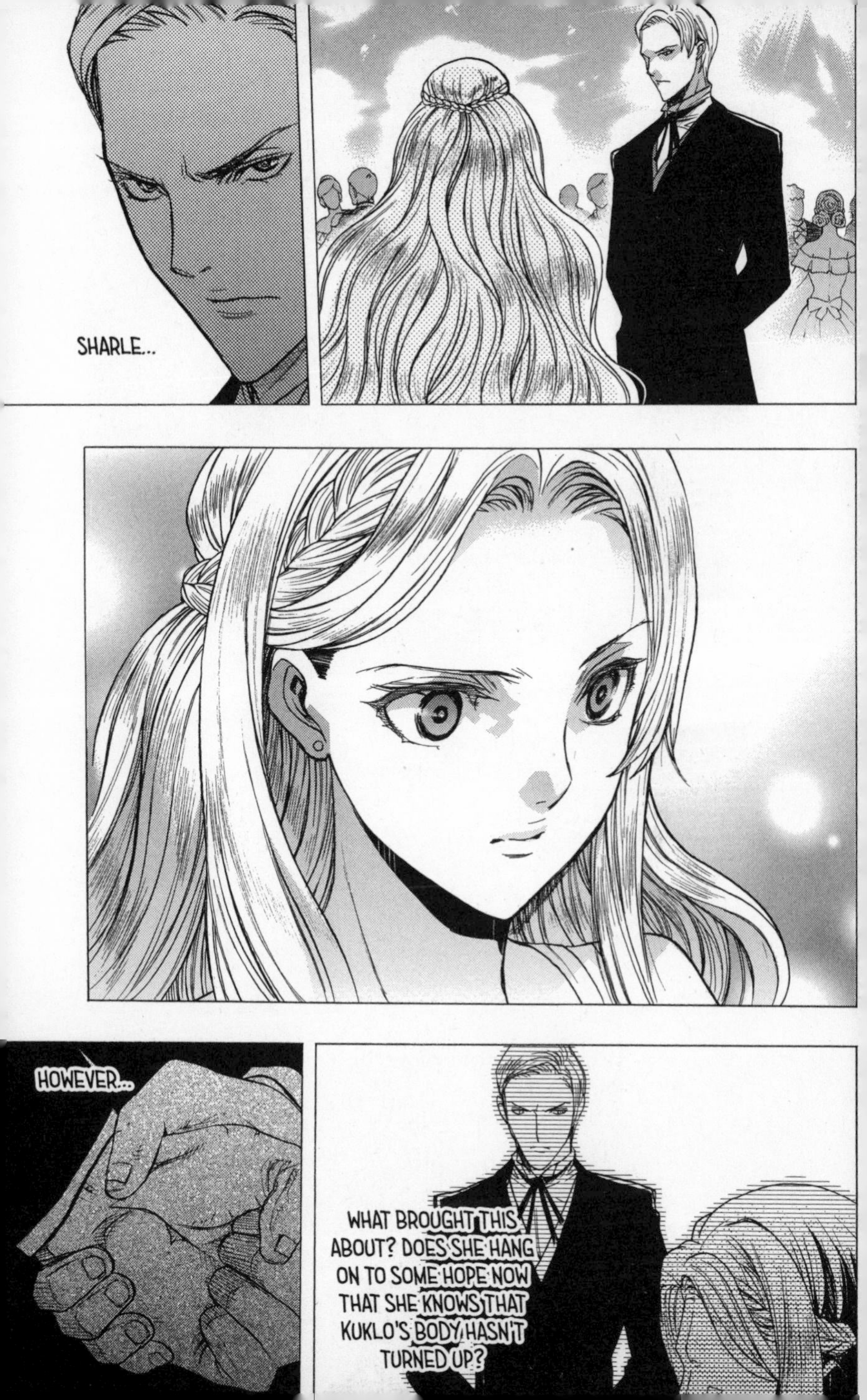
SHARLE...
WHAT BROUGHT THIS ABOUT? DOES SHE HANG ON TO SOME HOPE NOW THAT SHE KNOWS THAT KUKLO'S BODY HASN'T TURNED UP?
HOWEVER...

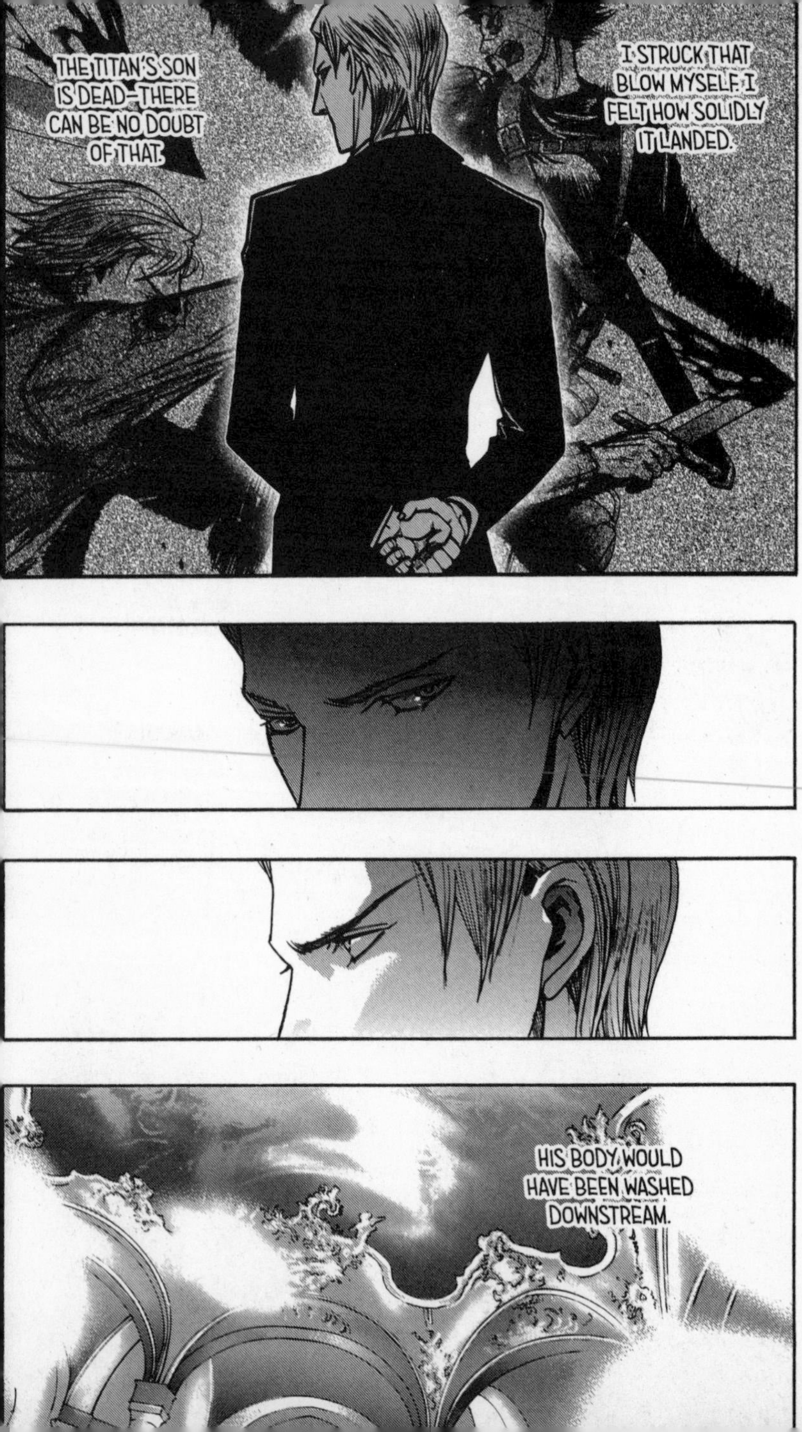
I STRUCK THAT BLOW MYSELF. I FELT HOW SOLIDLY IT LANDED.
THE TITAN'S SON IS DEAD—THERE CAN BE NO DOUBT OF THAT.
HIS BODY WOULD HAVE BEEN WASHED DOWNSTREAM.

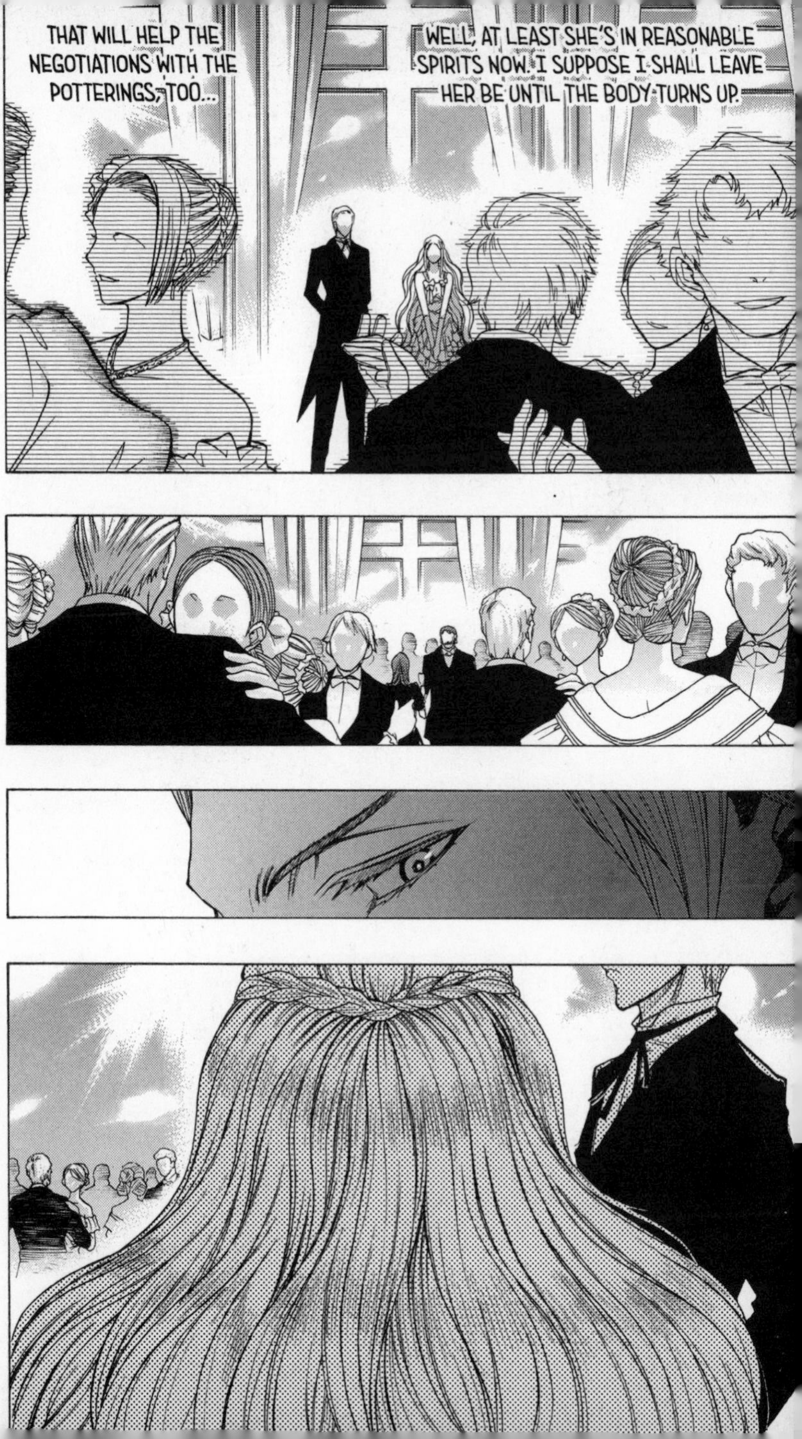
WELL, AT LEAST SHE'S IN REASONABLE SPIRITS NOW. I SUPPOSE I SHALL LEAVE HER BE UNTIL THE BODY TURNS UP.
THAT WILL HELP THE NEGOTIATIONS WITH THE POTTERINGS, TOO...

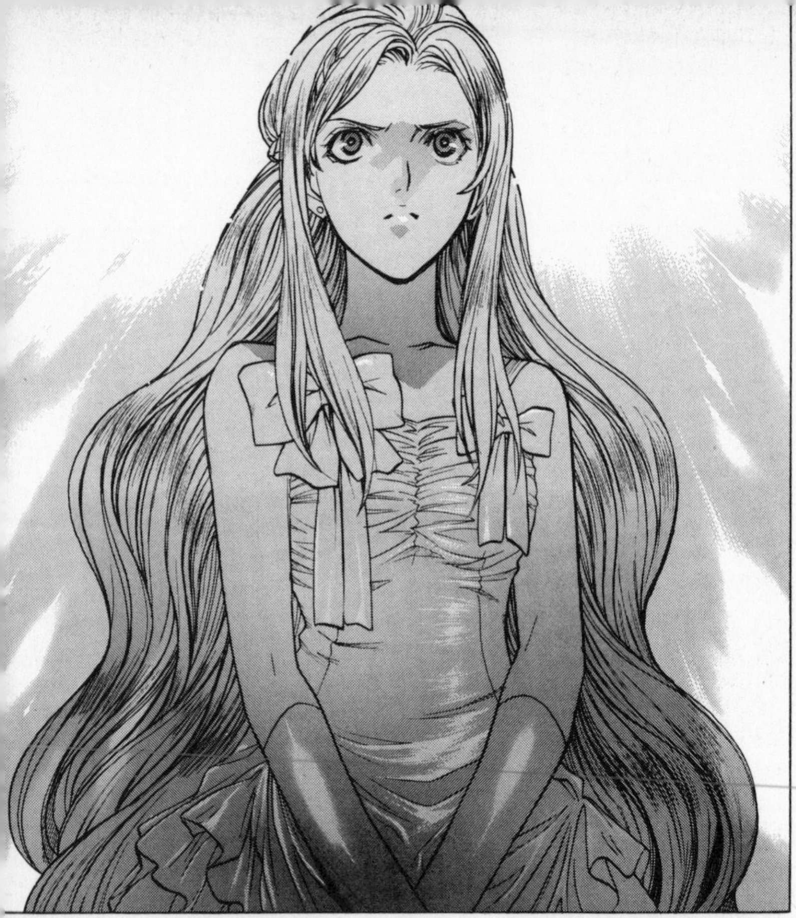
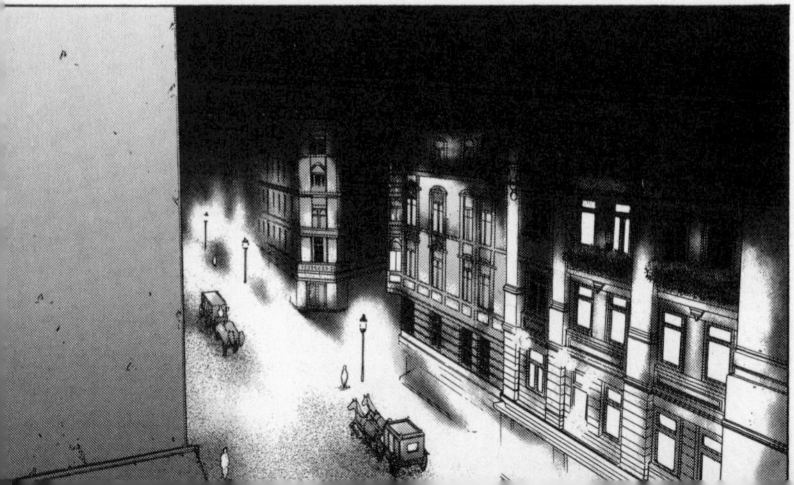

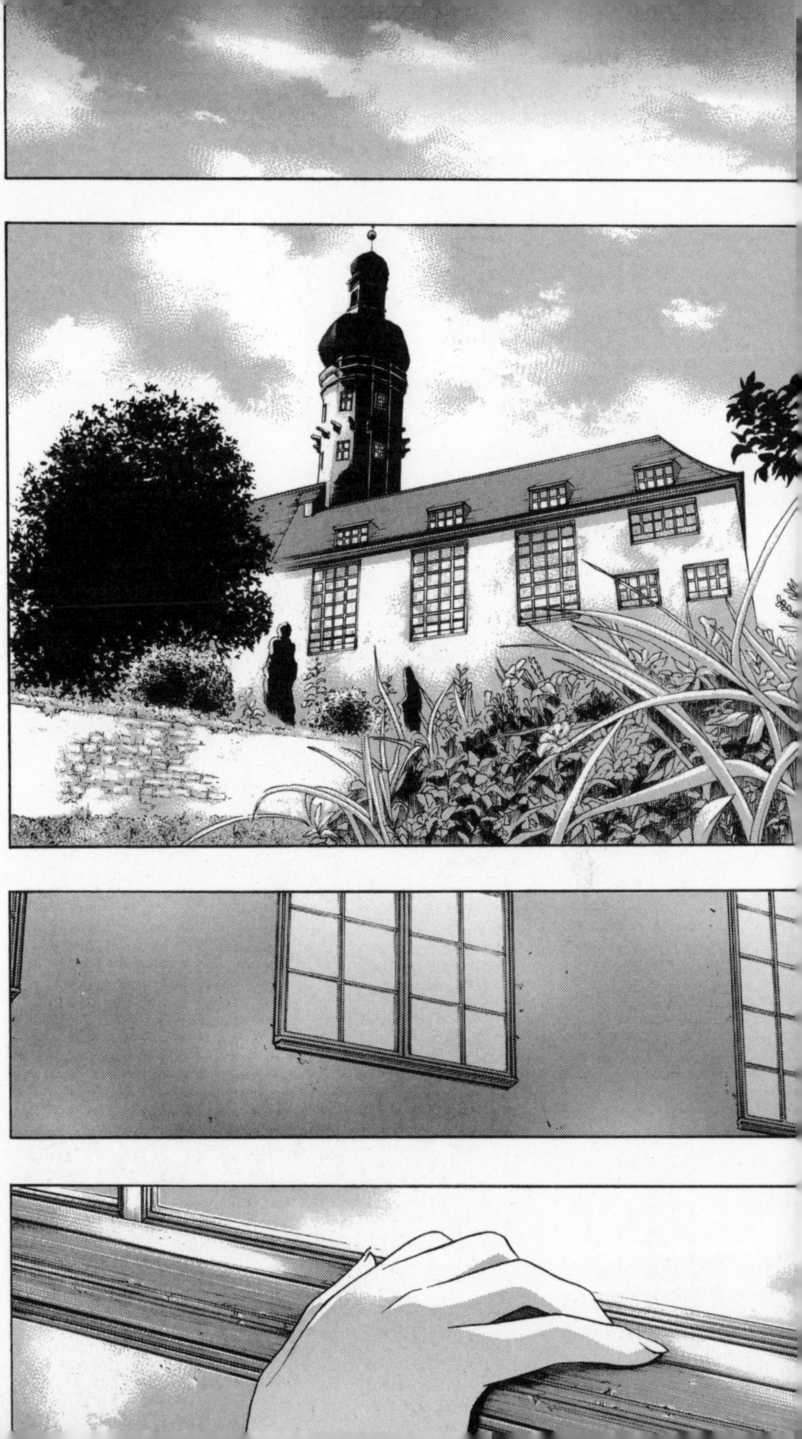

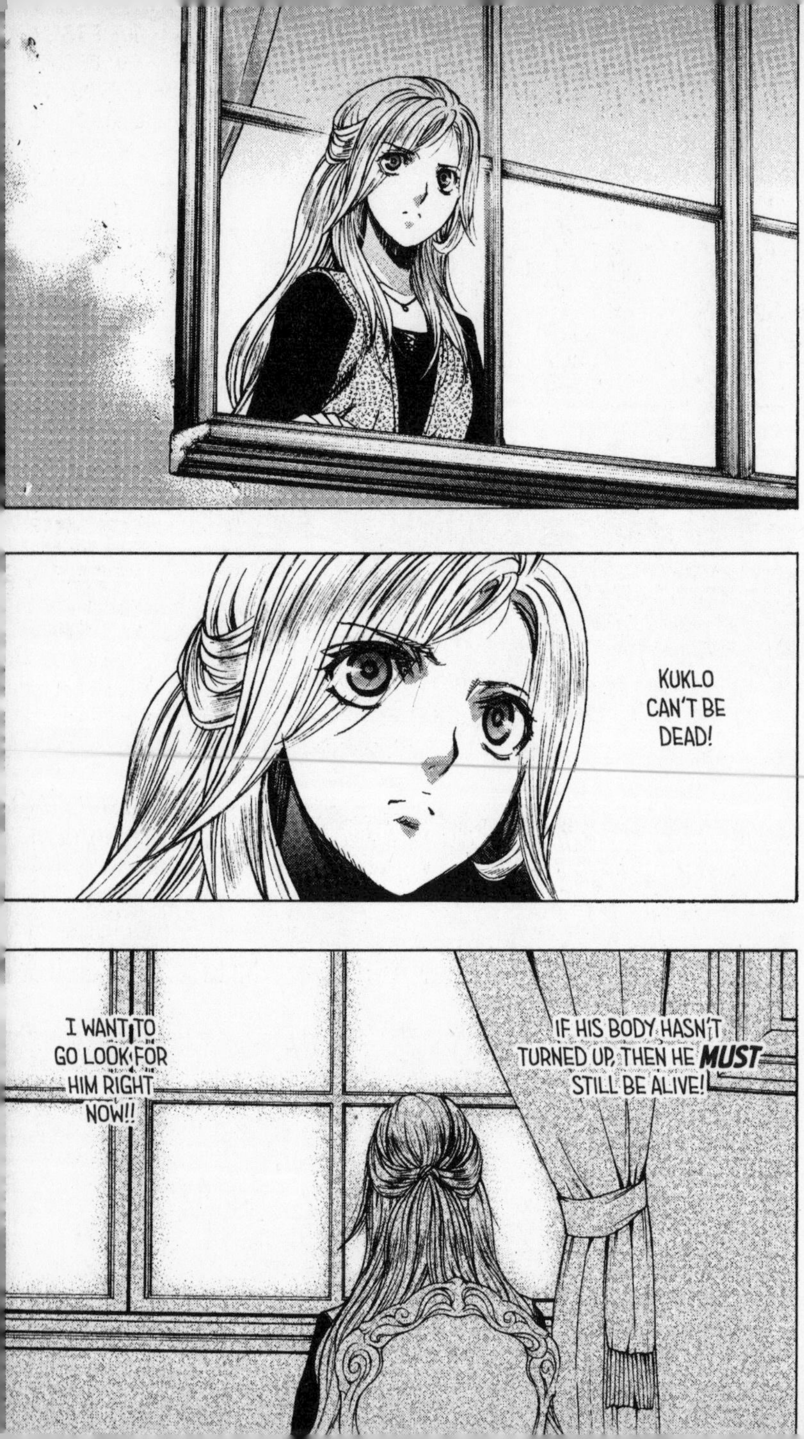
KUKLO CAN'T BE DEAD!
IF HIS BODY HASN'T TURNED UP, THEN HE **MUST** STILL BE ALIVE!
I WANT TO GO LOOK FOR HIM RIGHT NOW!!

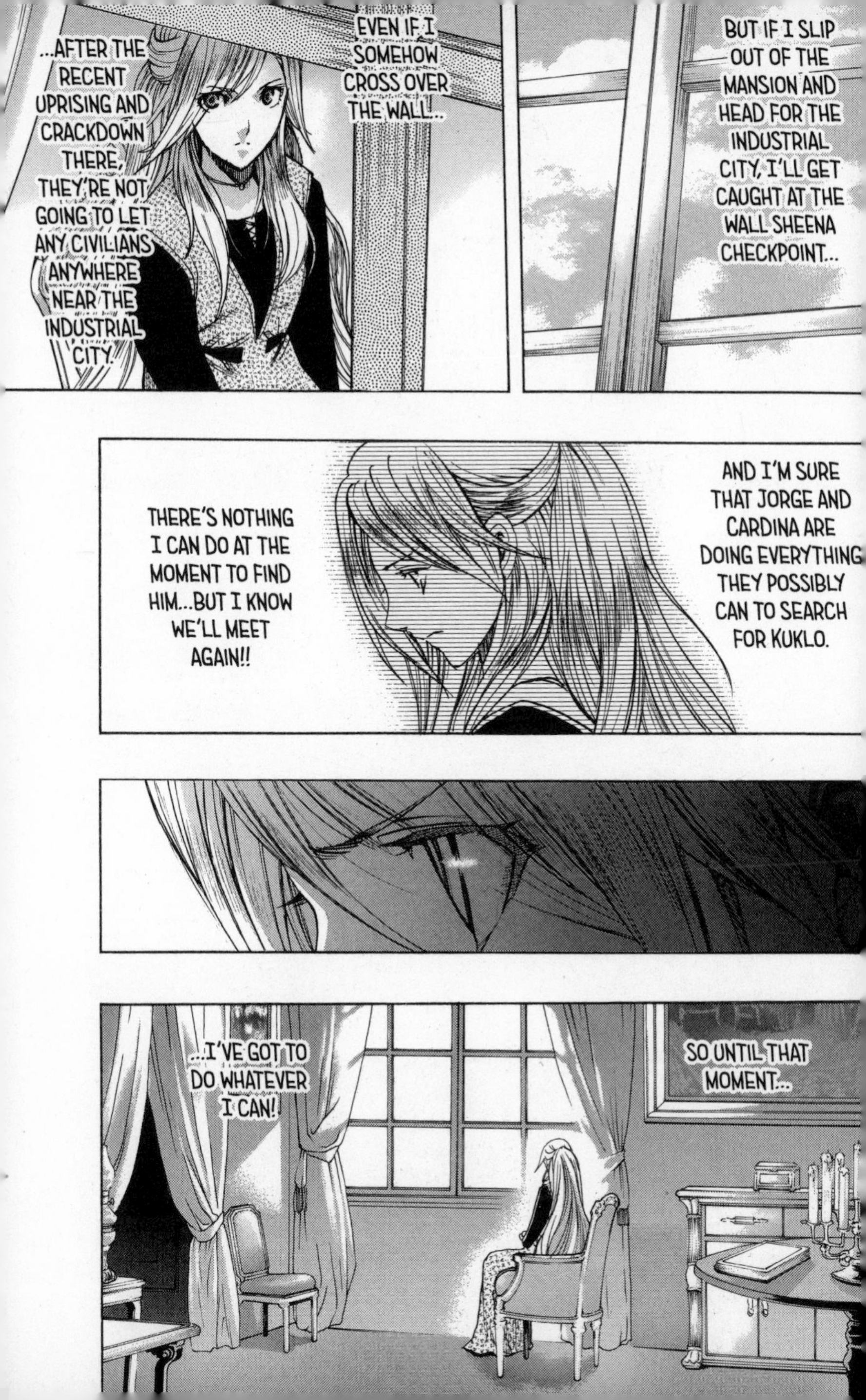
BUT IF I SLIP OUT OF THE MANSION AND HEAD FOR THE INDUSTRIAL CITY, I'LL GET CAUGHT AT THE WALL SHEENA CHECKPOINT...
EVEN IF I SOMEHOW CROSS OVER THE WALL...
...AFTER THE RECENT UPRISING AND CRACKDOWN THERE, THEY'RE NOT GOING TO LET ANY CIVILIANS ANYWHERE NEAR THE INDUSTRIAL CITY.
AND I'M SURE THAT JORGE AND CARDINA ARE DOING EVERYTHING THEY POSSIBLY CAN TO SEARCH FOR KUKLO.
THERE'S NOTHING I CAN DO AT THE MOMENT TO FIND HIM...BUT I KNOW WE'LL MEET AGAIN!!
SO UNTIL THAT MOMENT...
...I'VE GOT TO DO WHATEVER I CAN!

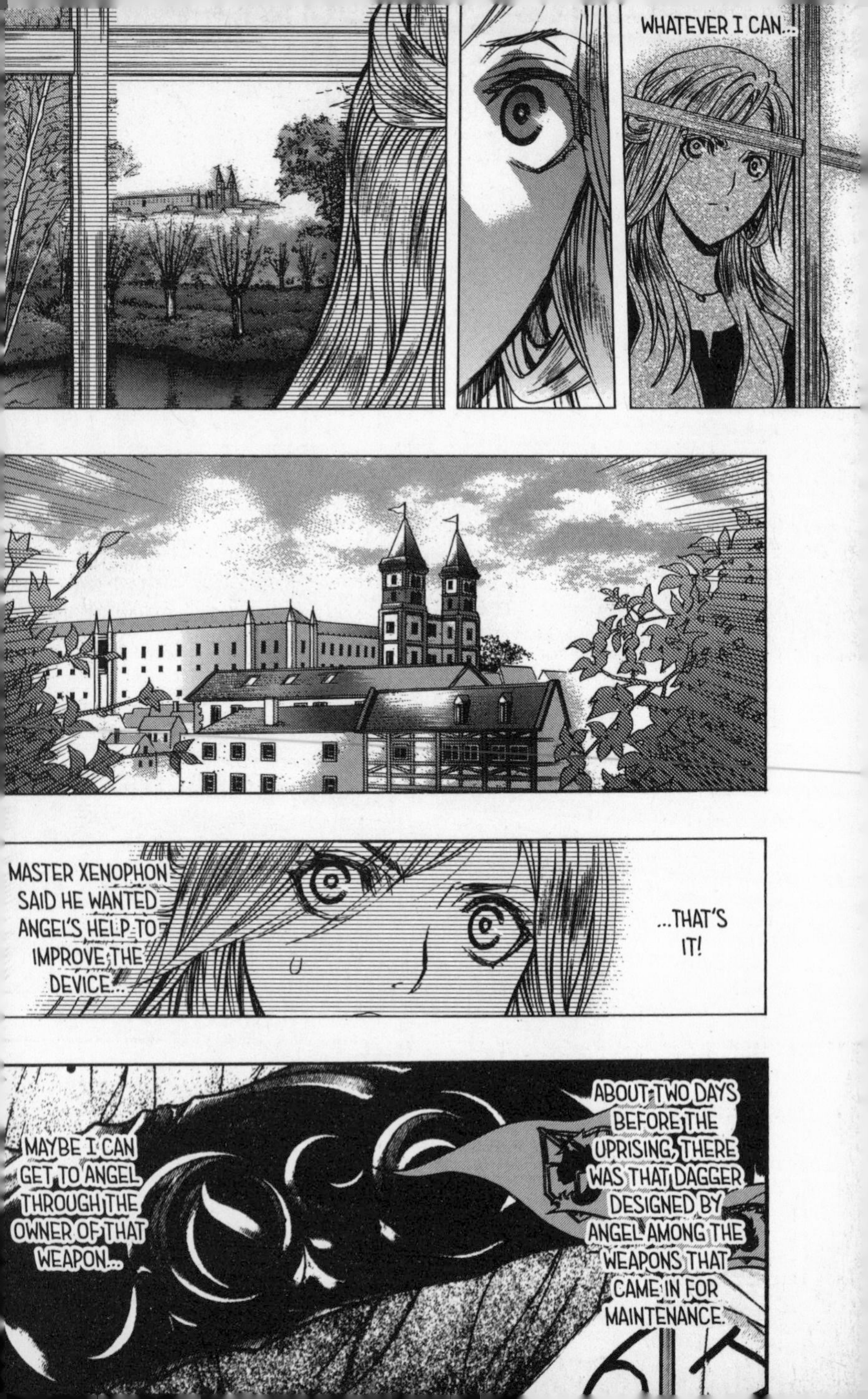
WHATEVER I CAN...
...THAT'S IT!
MASTER XENOPHON SAID HE WANTED ANGEL'S HELP TO IMPROVE THE DEVICE...
ABOUT TWO DAYS BEFORE THE UPRISING, THERE WAS THAT DAGGER DESIGNED BY ANGEL AMONG THE WEAPONS THAT CAME IN FOR MAINTENANCE.
MAYBE I CAN GET TO ANGEL THROUGH THE OWNER OF THAT WEAPON...

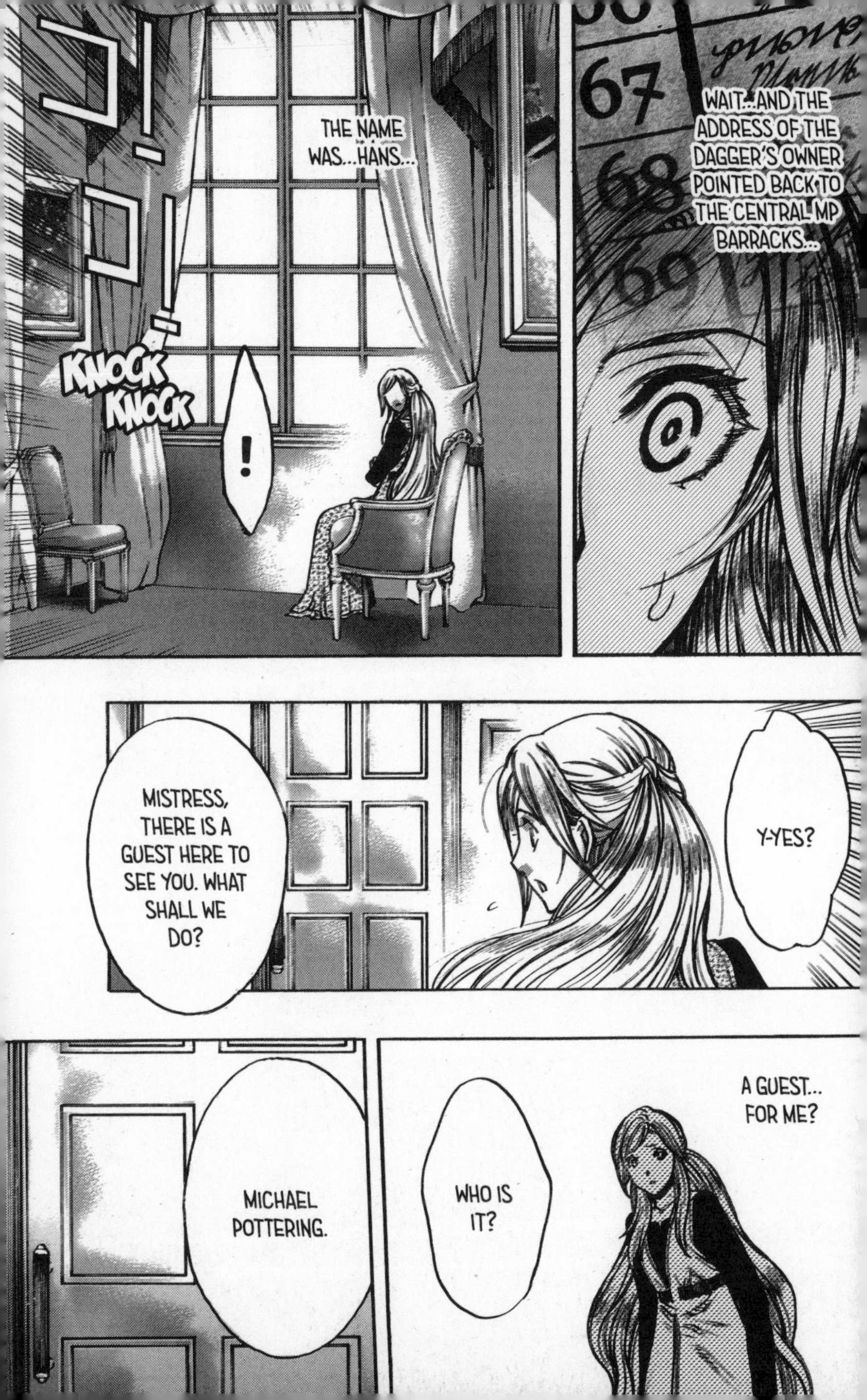
WAIT...AND THE ADDRESS OF THE DAGGER'S OWNER POINTED BACK TO THE CENTRAL MP BARRACKS...
THE NAME WAS...HANS...
KNOCK KNOCK
!
Y-YES?
MISTRESS, THERE IS A GUEST HERE TO SEE YOU. WHAT SHALL WE DO?
A GUEST... FOR ME?
WHO IS IT?
MICHAEL POTTERING.

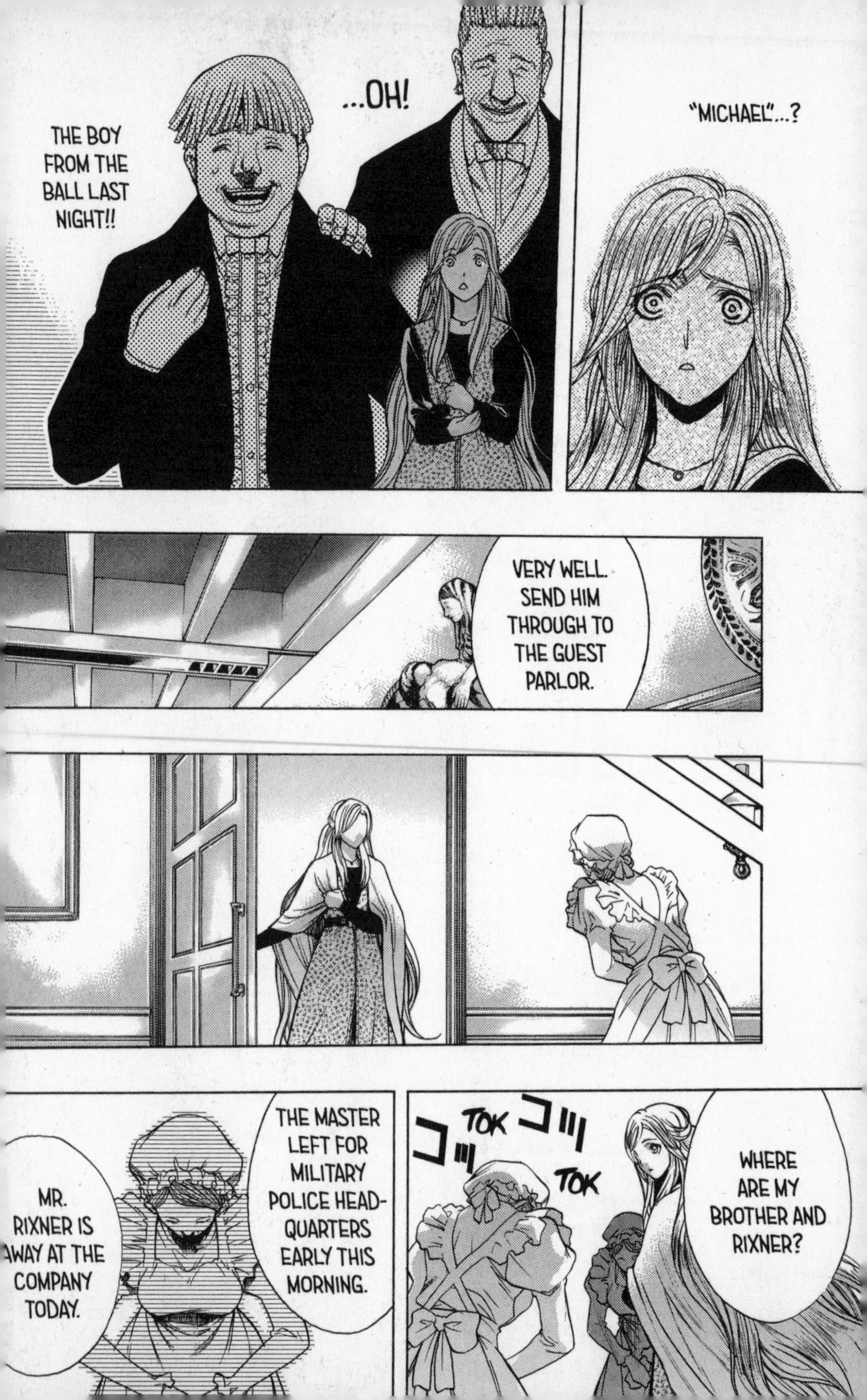
"MICHAEL"...?
...OH!
THE BOY FROM THE BALL LAST NIGHT!!
VERY WELL. SEND HIM THROUGH TO THE GUEST PARLOR.
WHERE ARE MY BROTHER AND RIXNER?
TOK
TOK
THE MASTER LEFT FOR MILITARY POLICE HEAD-QUARTERS EARLY THIS MORNING.
MR. RIXNER IS AWAY AT THE COMPANY TODAY.

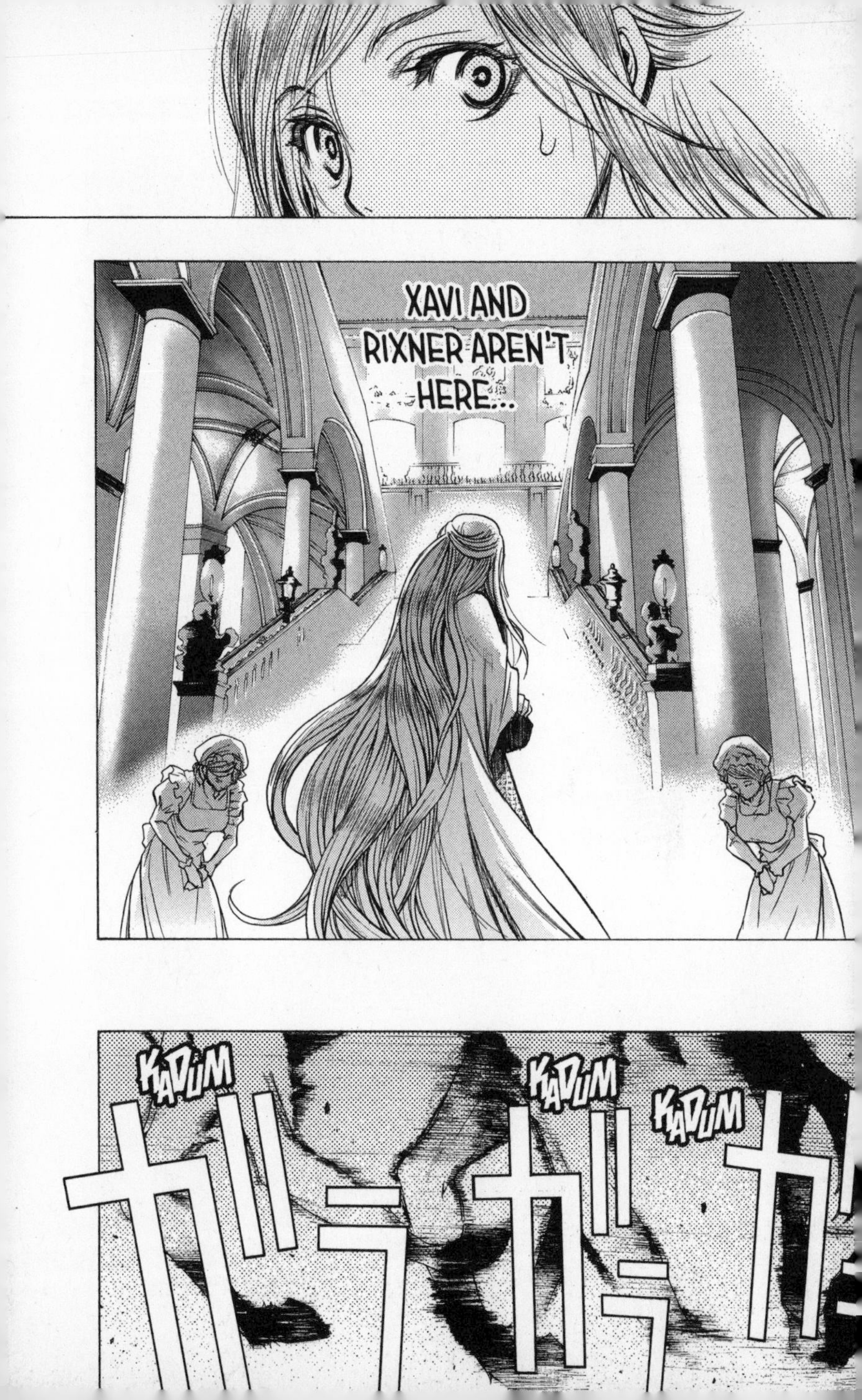
XAVI AND RIXNER AREN'T HERE...
KADUM
KADUM
KADUM

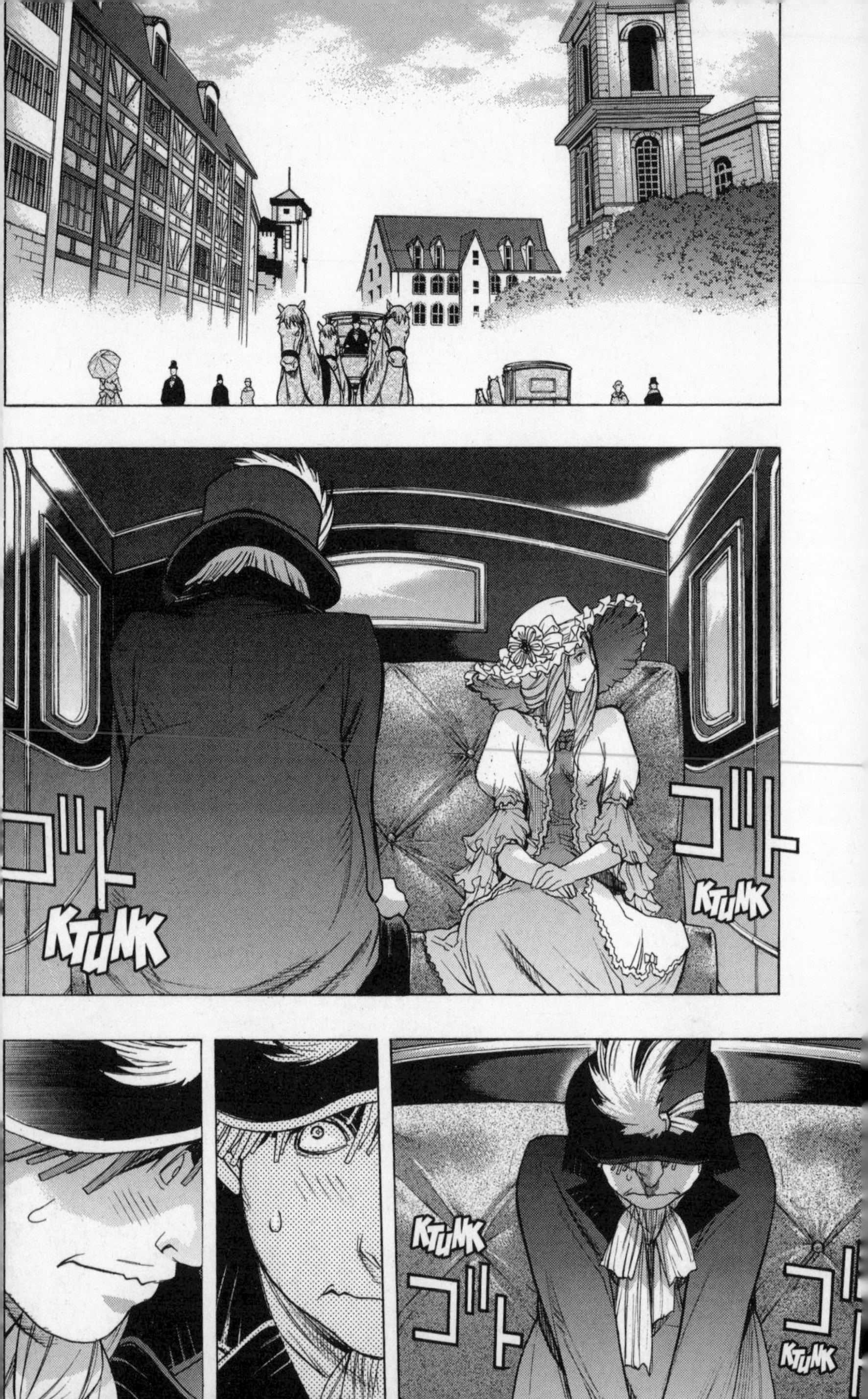
ゴト
KTUNK
ゴト
KTUNK
ゴト
KTUNK
KTUNK
ゴト

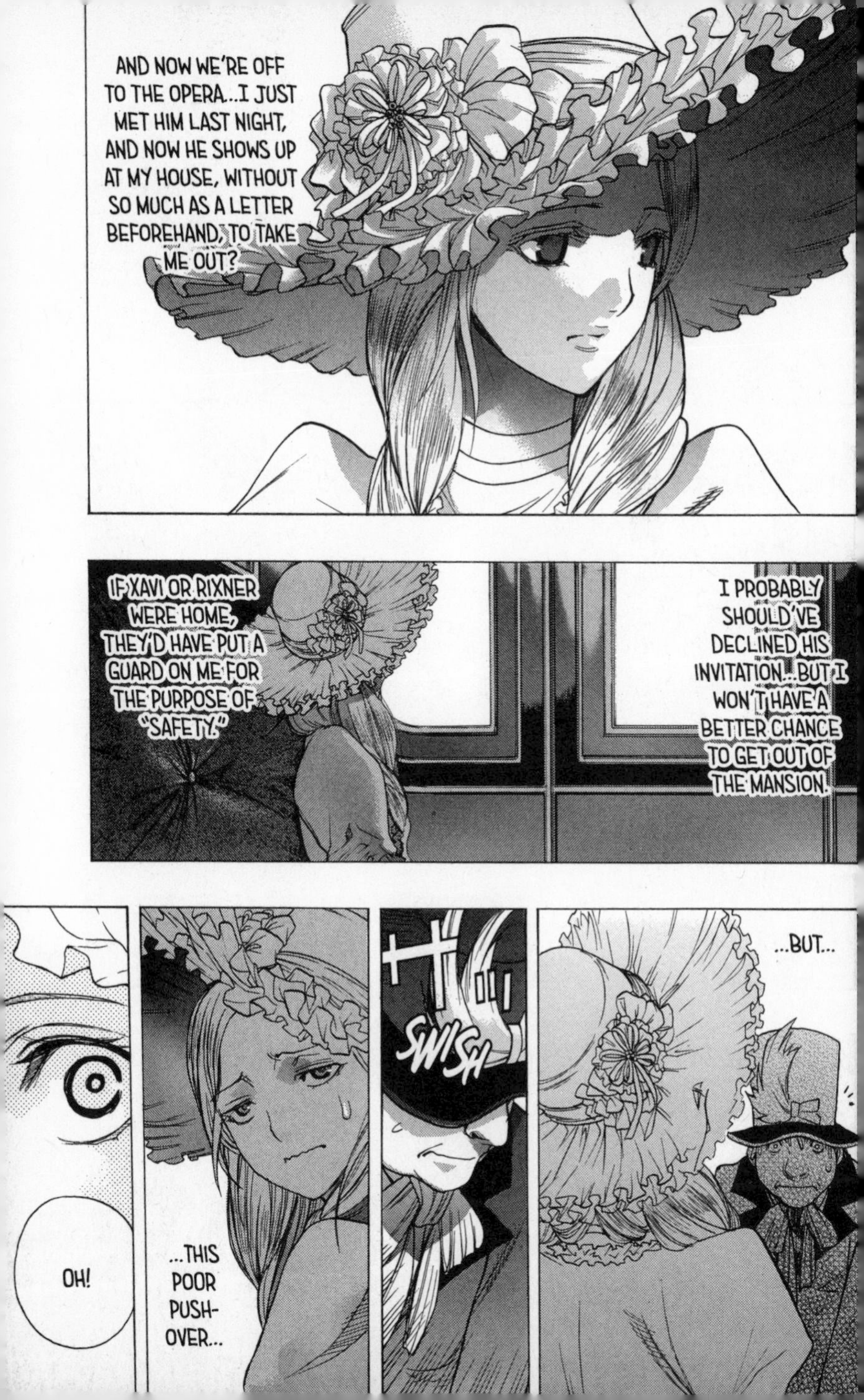
AND NOW WE'RE OFF TO THE OPERA...I JUST MET HIM LAST NIGHT, AND NOW HE SHOWS UP AT MY HOUSE, WITHOUT SO MUCH AS A LETTER BEFOREHAND, TO TAKE ME OUT?
I PROBABLY SHOULD'VE DECLINED HIS INVITATION...BUT I WON'T HAVE A BETTER CHANCE TO GET OUT OF THE MANSION.
IF XAVI OR RIXNER WERE HOME, THEY'D HAVE PUT A GUARD ON ME FOR THE PURPOSE OF "SAFETY."
...BUT...
SWISH
...THIS POOR PUSH-OVER...
OH!

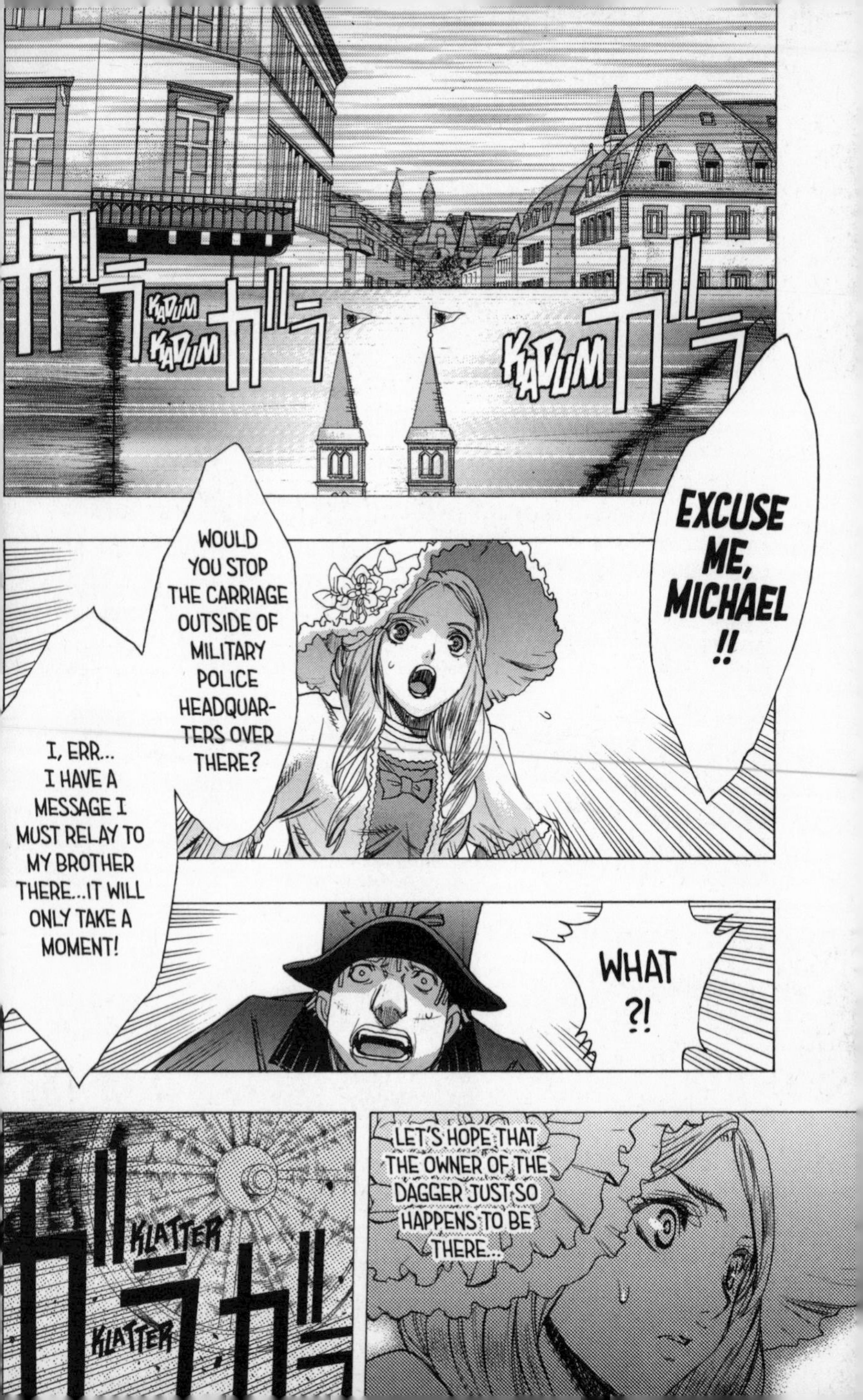

カラ
KADUM
カラ
KADUM
KADUM
カラ
EXCUSE ME, MICHAEL!!
WOULD YOU STOP THE CARRIAGE OUTSIDE OF MILITARY POLICE HEADQUARTERS OVER THERE?
WHAT?!
I, ERR... I HAVE A MESSAGE I MUST RELAY TO MY BROTHER THERE...IT WILL ONLY TAKE A MOMENT!
LET'S HOPE THAT THE OWNER OF THE DAGGER JUST SO HAPPENS TO BE THERE...
カラ
KLATTER
カラ
KLATTER

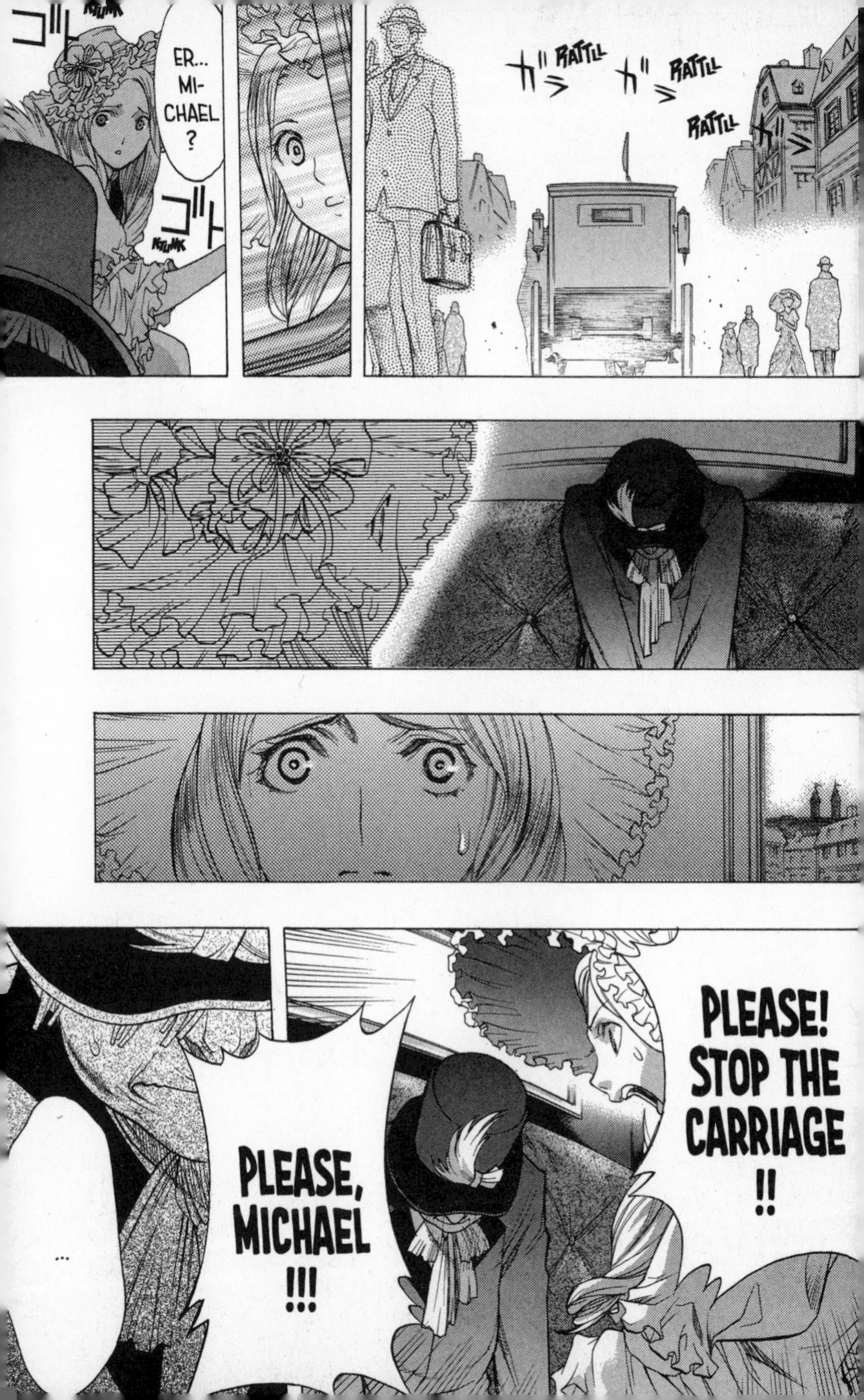

ガラ RATTLL
ガラ RATTLL
ガラ RATTLL
ER... MI-CHAEL ?
ゴト KLUNK
ゴト
PLEASE! STOP THE CARRIAGE !!
PLEASE, MICHAEL !!!
...

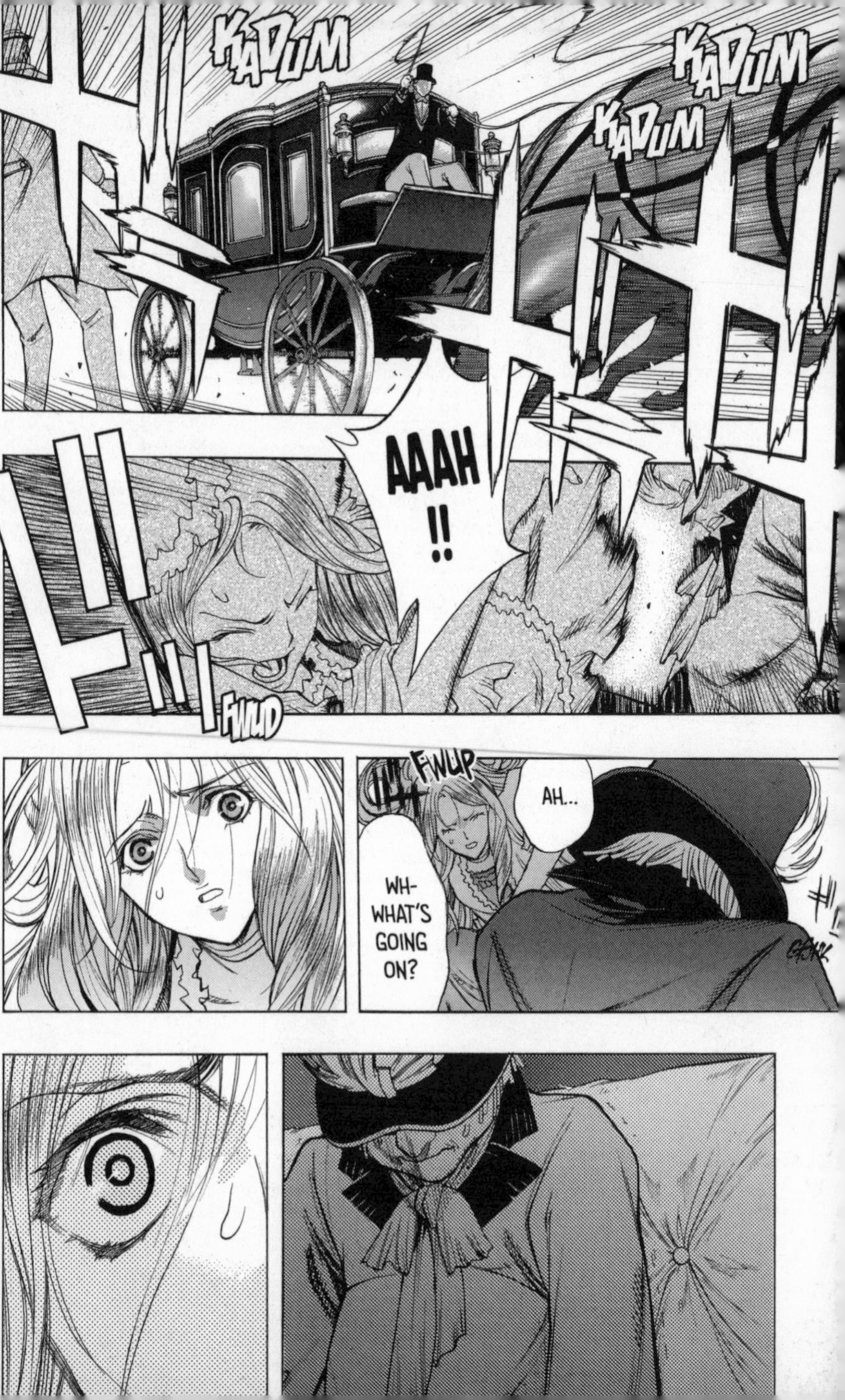
KADUM
KADUM
KADUM
AAAH!!
FWUD
FWUP
AH...
WH- WHAT'S GOING ON?

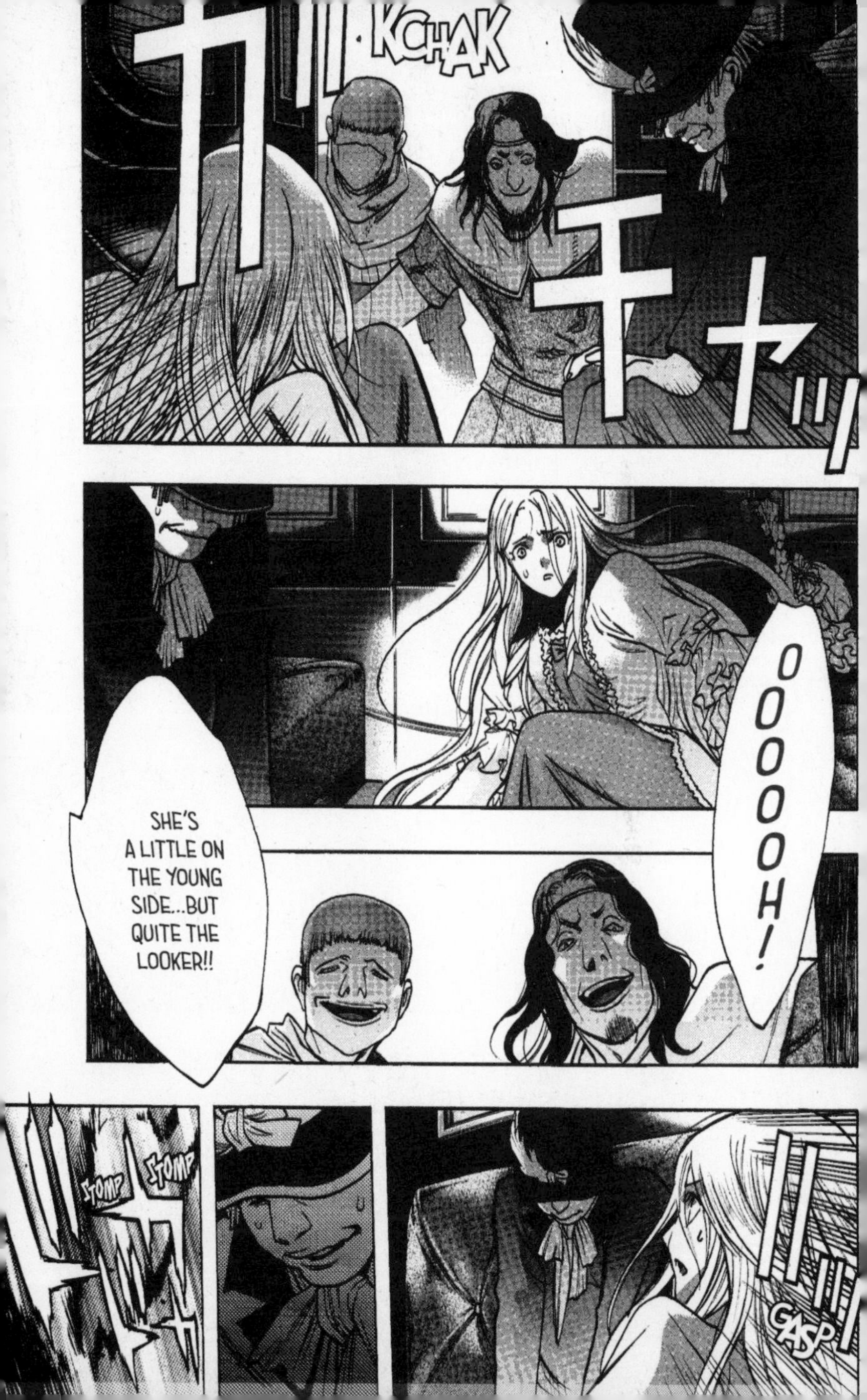

カチャッ
KCHAK
OOOOOOH!
SHE'S A LITTLE ON THE YOUNG SIDE...BUT QUITE THE LOOKER!!
GASP
STOMP STOMP

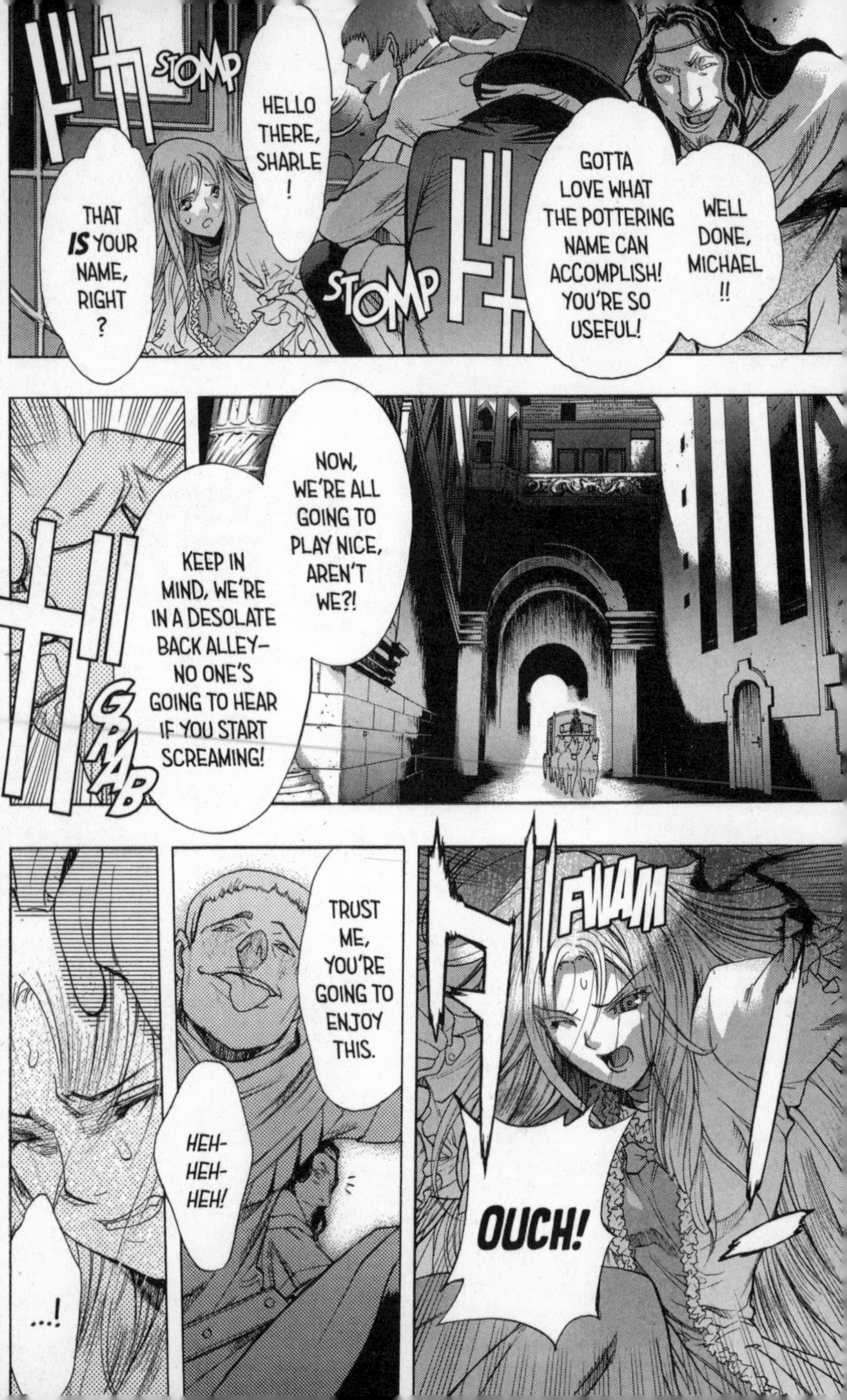
WELL DONE, MICHAEL!!
GOTTA LOVE WHAT THE POTTERING NAME CAN ACCOMPLISH! YOU'RE SO USEFUL!
STOMP
HELLO THERE, SHARLE!
STOMP
THAT **IS** YOUR NAME, RIGHT?
NOW, WE'RE ALL GOING TO PLAY NICE, AREN'T WE?!
KEEP IN MIND, WE'RE IN A DESOLATE BACK ALLEY— NO ONE'S GOING TO HEAR IF YOU START SCREAMING!
GRAB
FWAM
OUCH!
TRUST ME, YOU'RE GOING TO ENJOY THIS.
HEH-HEH-HEH!
...!

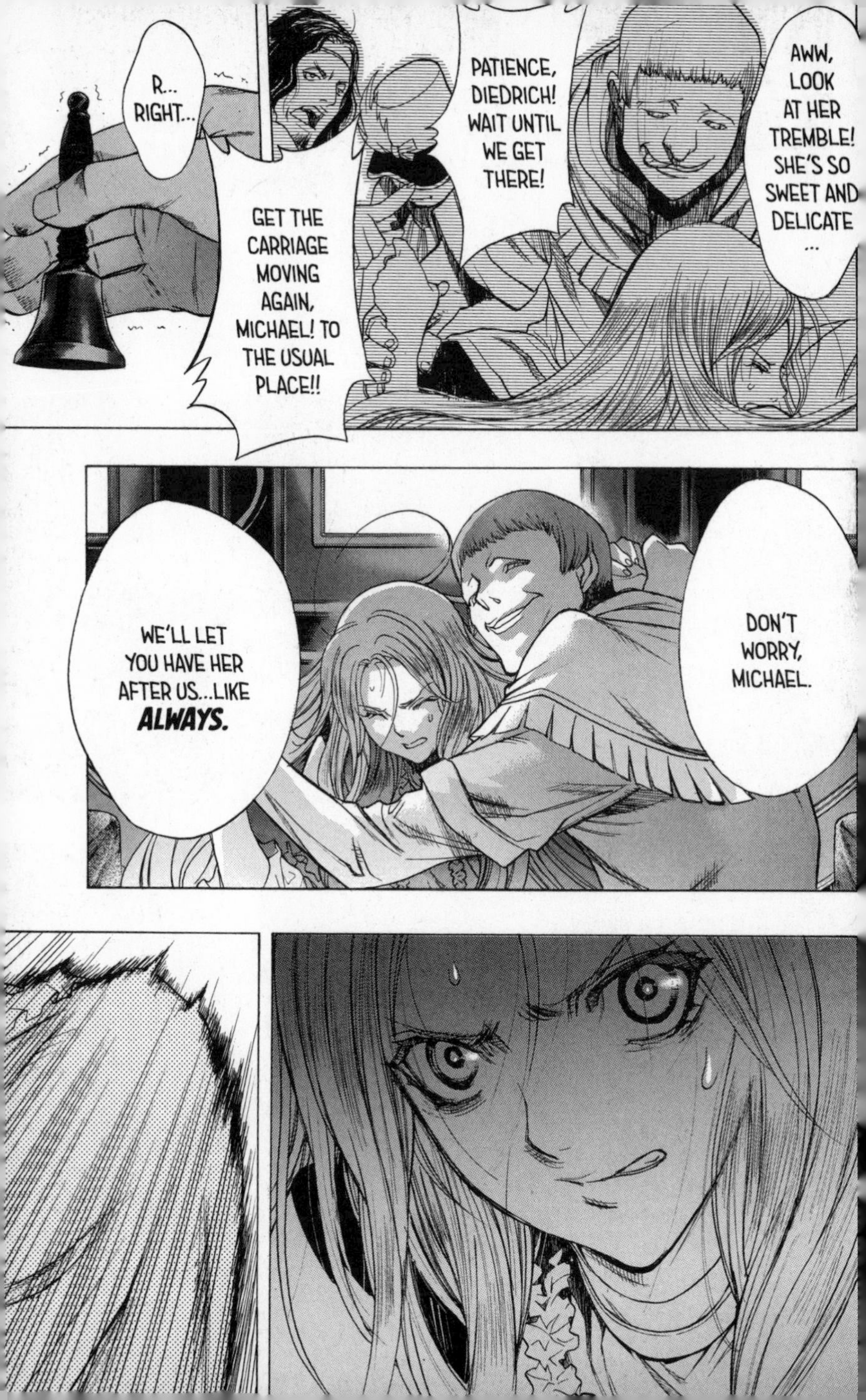
AWW, LOOK AT HER TREMBLE! SHE'S SO SWEET AND DELICATE...
PATIENCE, DIEDRICH! WAIT UNTIL WE GET THERE!
GET THE CARRIAGE MOVING AGAIN, MICHAEL! TO THE USUAL PLACE!!
R... RIGHT...
DON'T WORRY, MICHAEL.
WE'LL LET YOU HAVE HER AFTER US...LIKE **ALWAYS.**

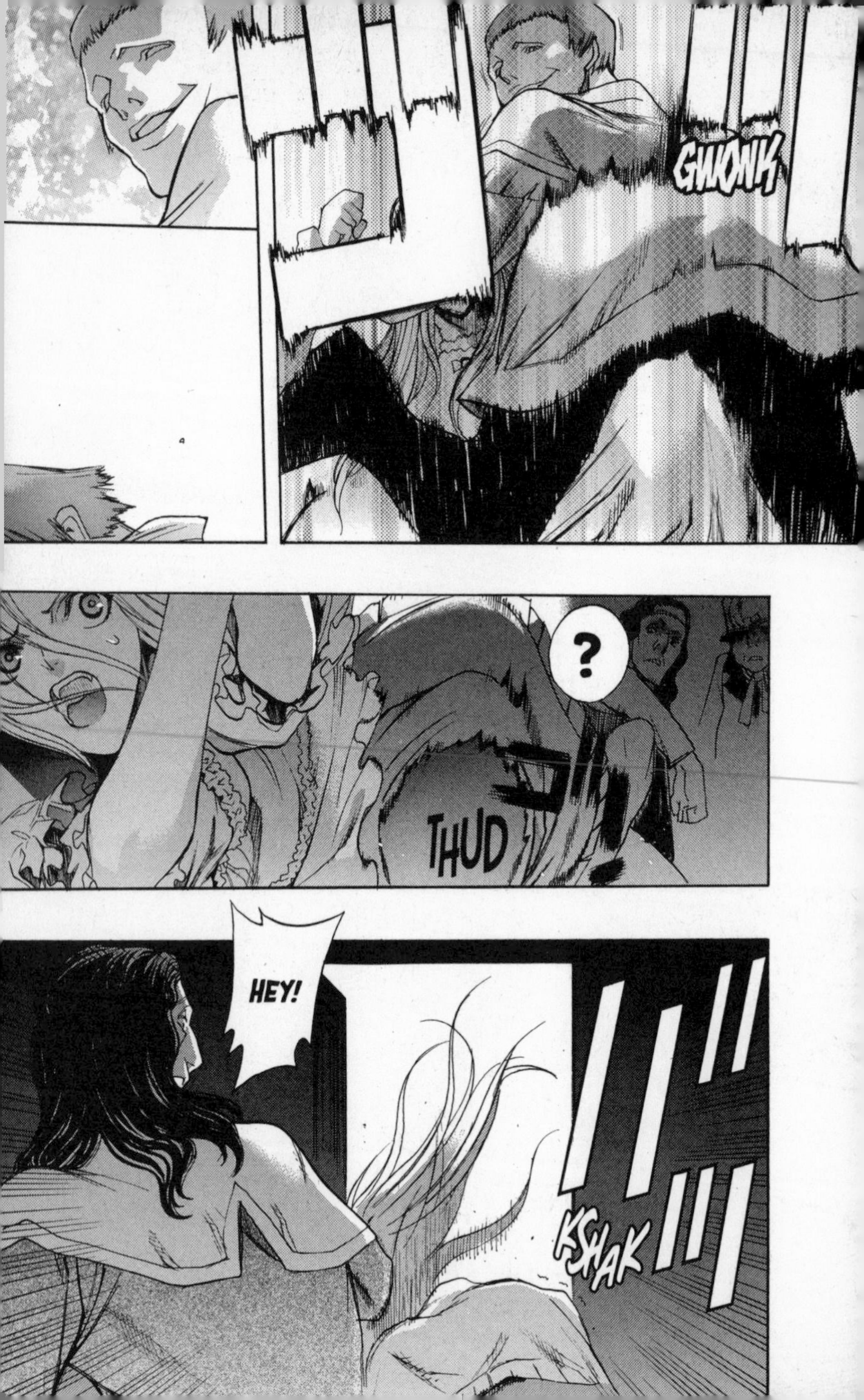
GWONK
?
THUD
HEY!
KSHAK

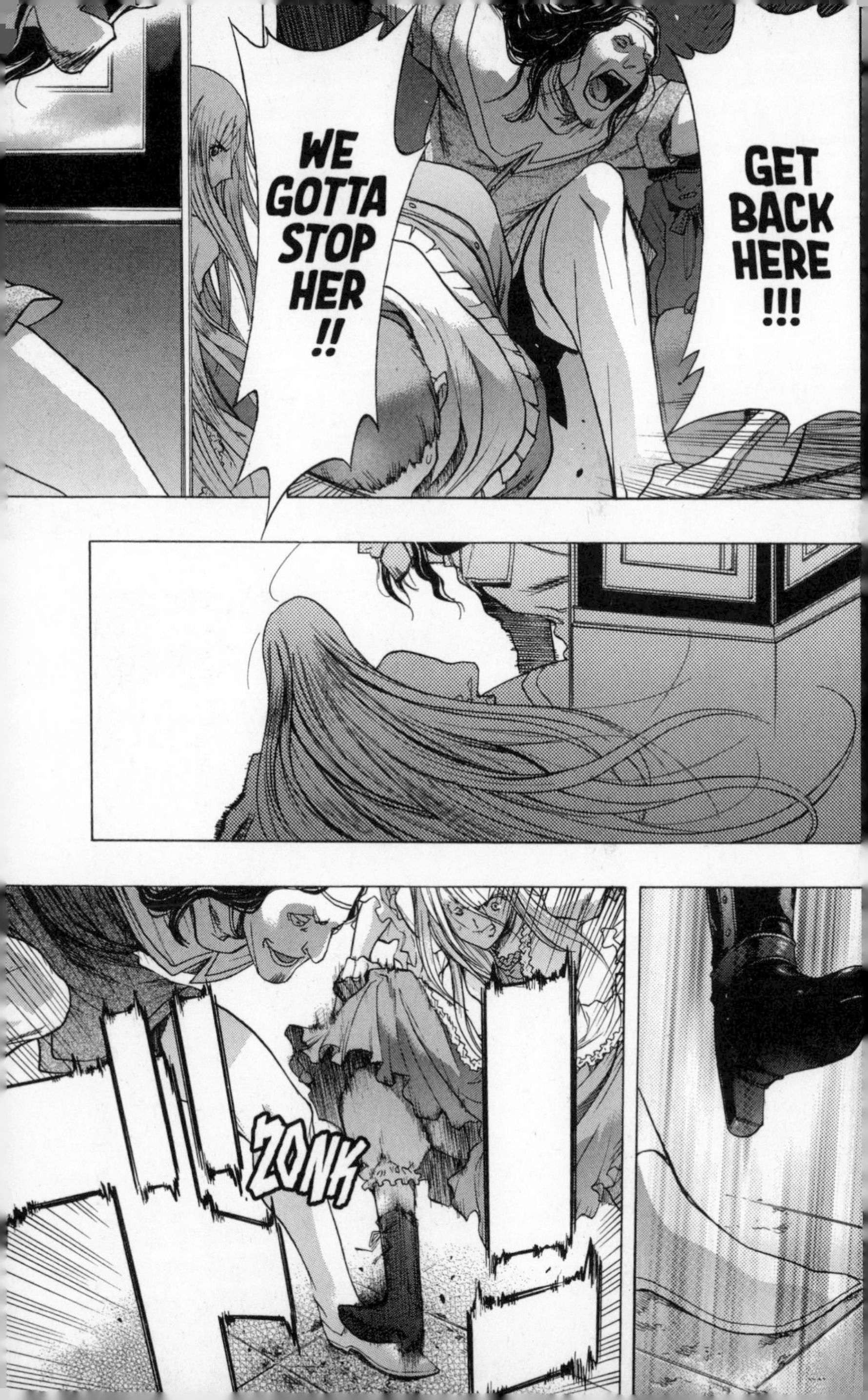
GET BACK HERE !!!
WE GOTTA STOP HER !!
ZONK

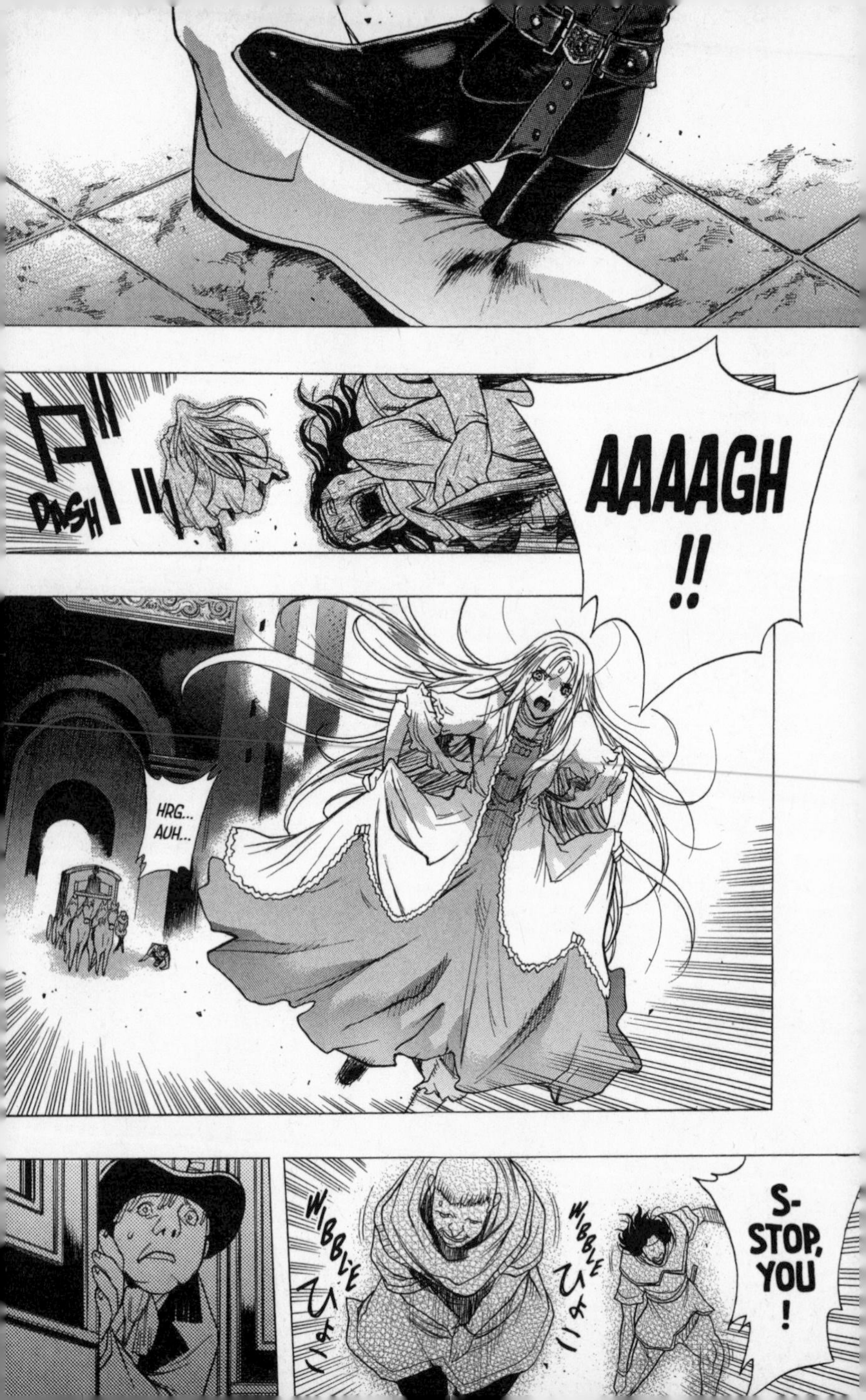

AAAAGH!!
DASH
HRG... AUH...
S-STOP, YOU!
WIBBLE ひょこ
WIBBLE ひょこ

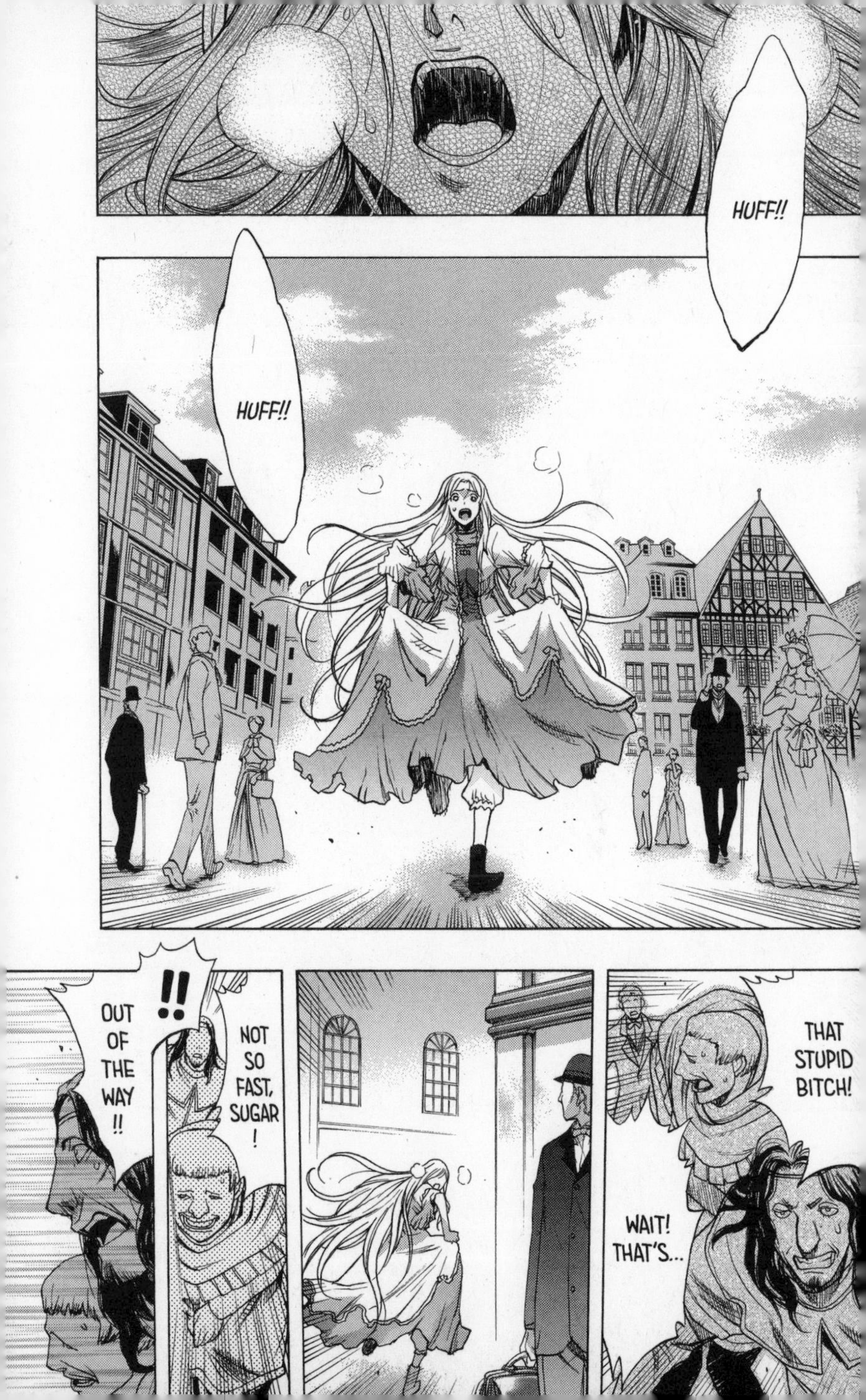
HUFF!!
HUFF!!
THAT STUPID BITCH!
WAIT! THAT'S...
NOT SO FAST, SUGAR!
!!
OUT OF THE WAY!!

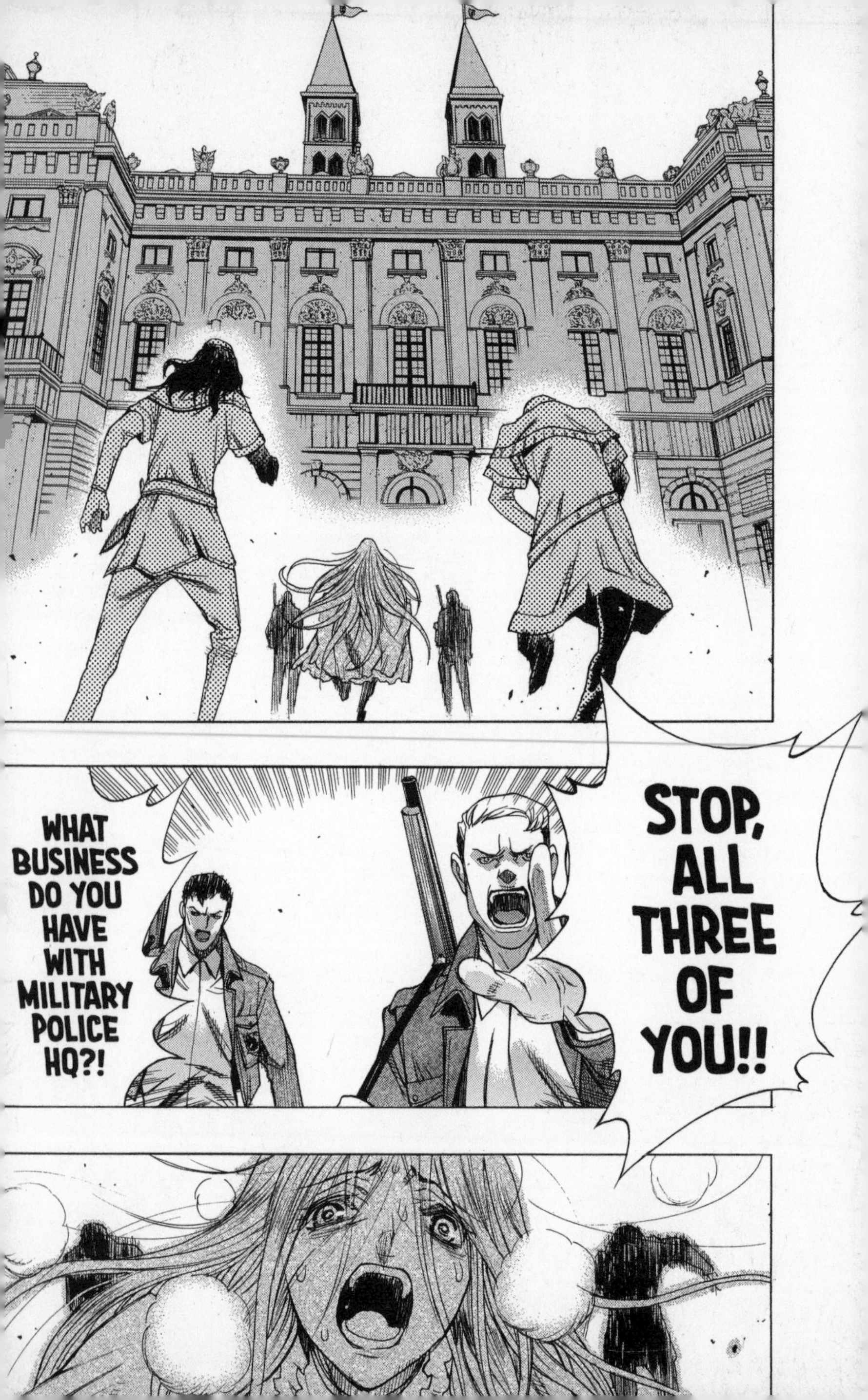
STOP, ALL THREE OF YOU!!
WHAT BUSINESS DO YOU HAVE WITH MILITARY POLICE HQ?!

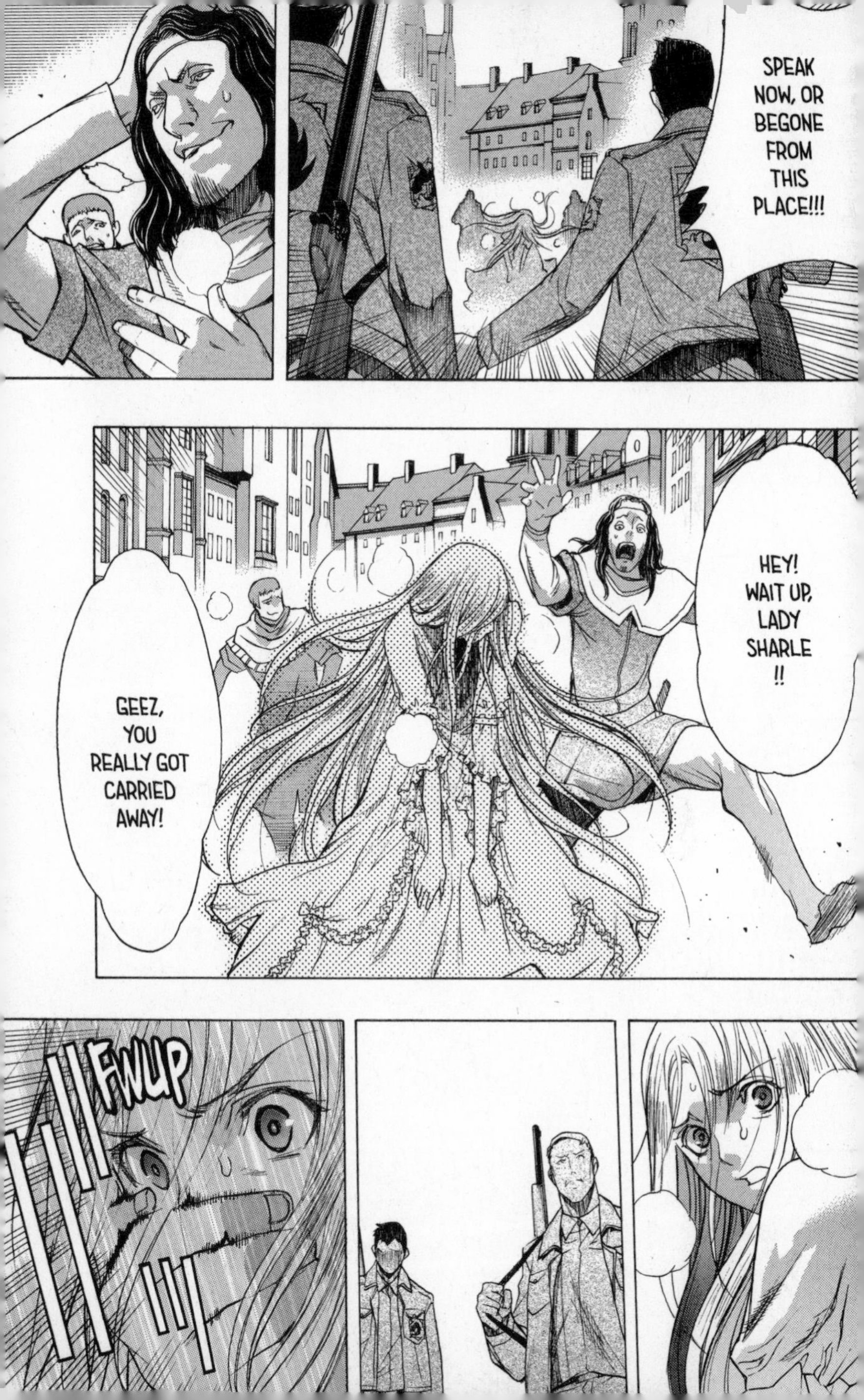
SPEAK NOW, OR BEGONE FROM THIS PLACE!!!
HEY! WAIT UP, LADY SHARLE !!
GEEZ, YOU REALLY GOT CARRIED AWAY!
FWUP

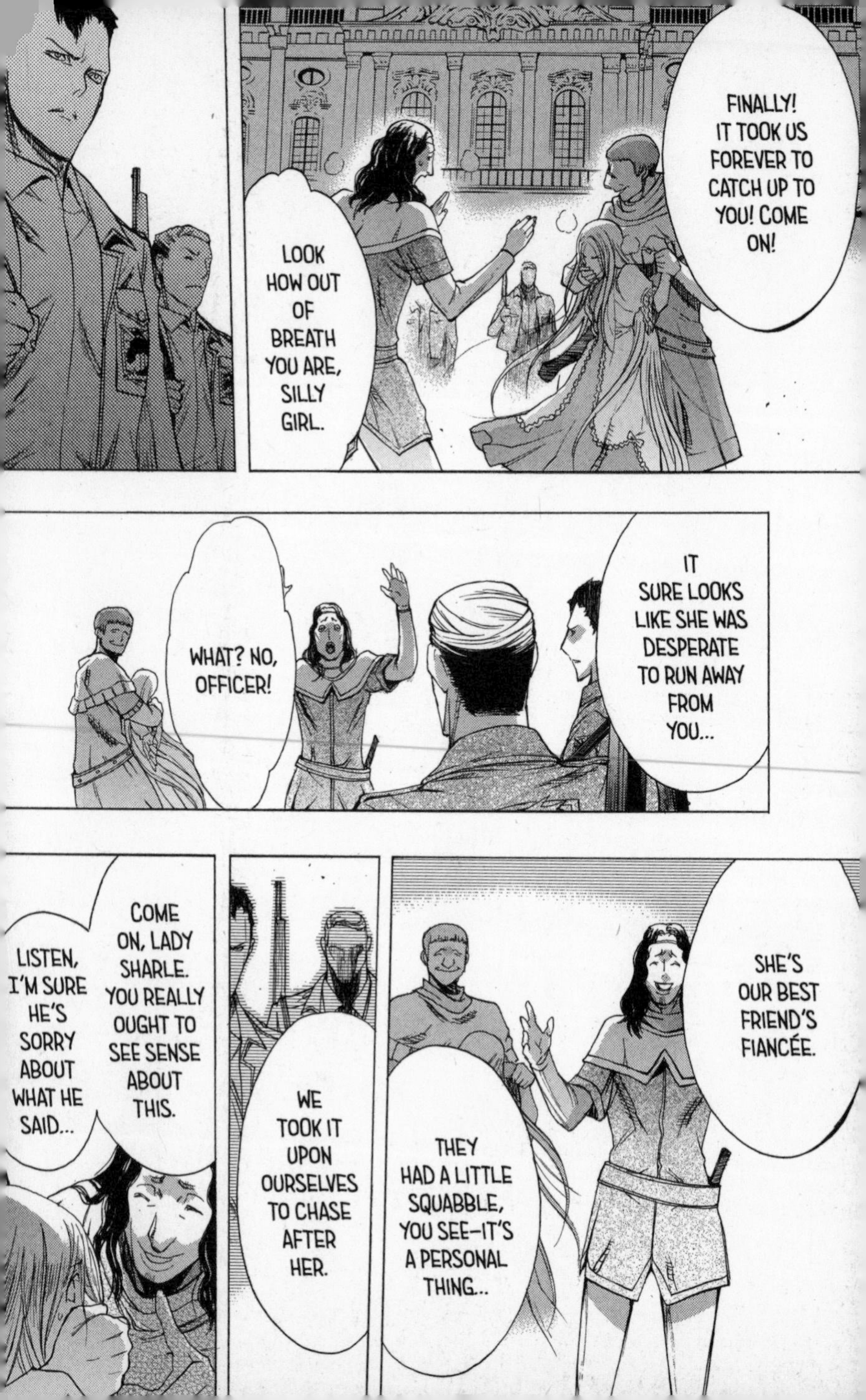
FINALLY! IT TOOK US FOREVER TO CATCH UP TO YOU! COME ON!
LOOK HOW OUT OF BREATH YOU ARE, SILLY GIRL.
IT SURE LOOKS LIKE SHE WAS DESPERATE TO RUN AWAY FROM YOU...
WHAT? NO, OFFICER!
SHE'S OUR BEST FRIEND'S FIANCÉE.
THEY HAD A LITTLE SQUABBLE, YOU SEE—IT'S A PERSONAL THING...
WE TOOK IT UPON OURSELVES TO CHASE AFTER HER.
COME ON, LADY SHARLE. YOU REALLY OUGHT TO SEE SENSE ABOUT THIS.
LISTEN, I'M SURE HE'S SORRY ABOUT WHAT HE SAID...

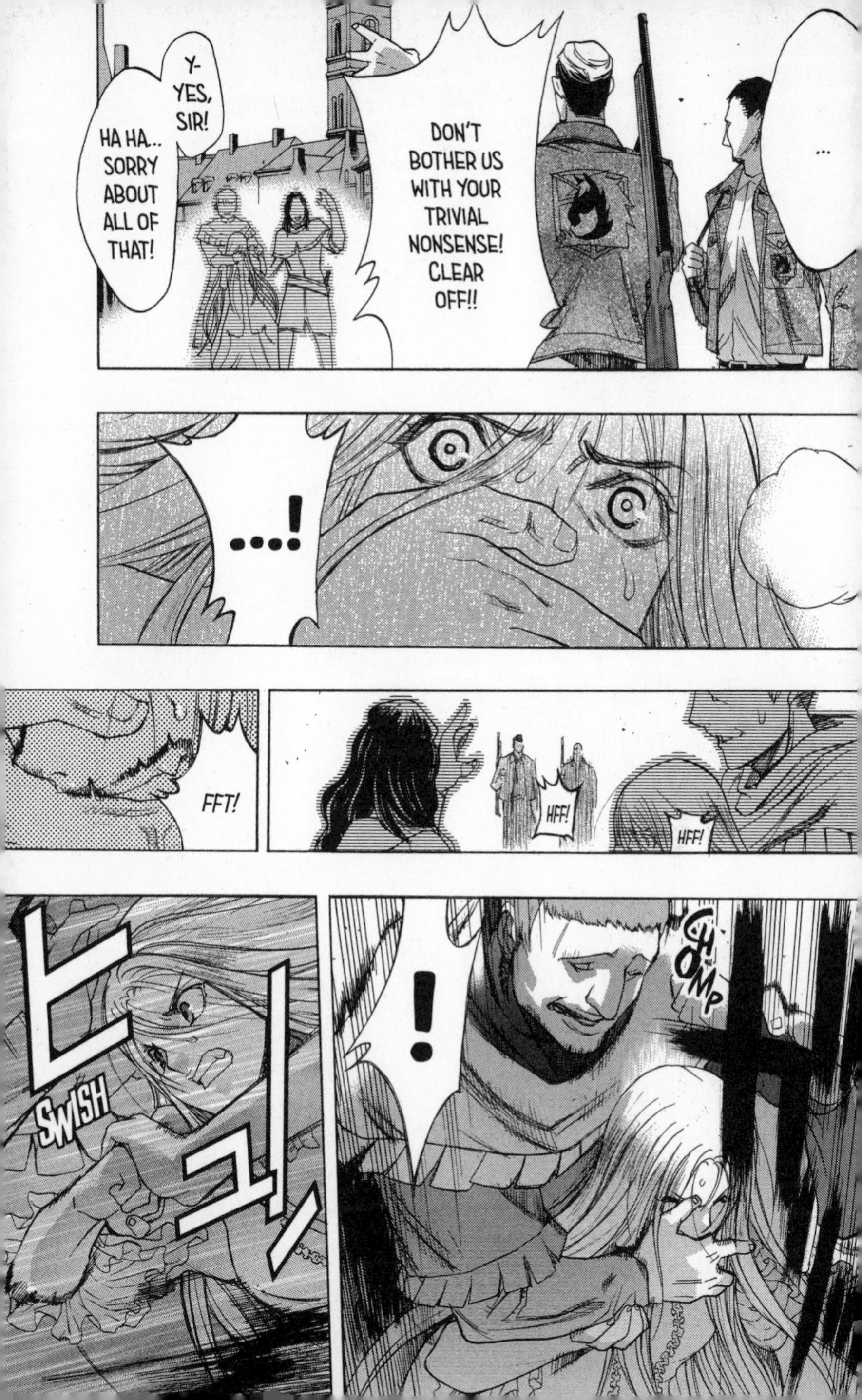
...
DON'T BOTHER US WITH YOUR TRIVIAL NONSENSE! CLEAR OFF!!
Y-YES, SIR!
HA HA... SORRY ABOUT ALL OF THAT!
...!
HFF!
HFF!
FFT!
CHOMP
!
SWISH

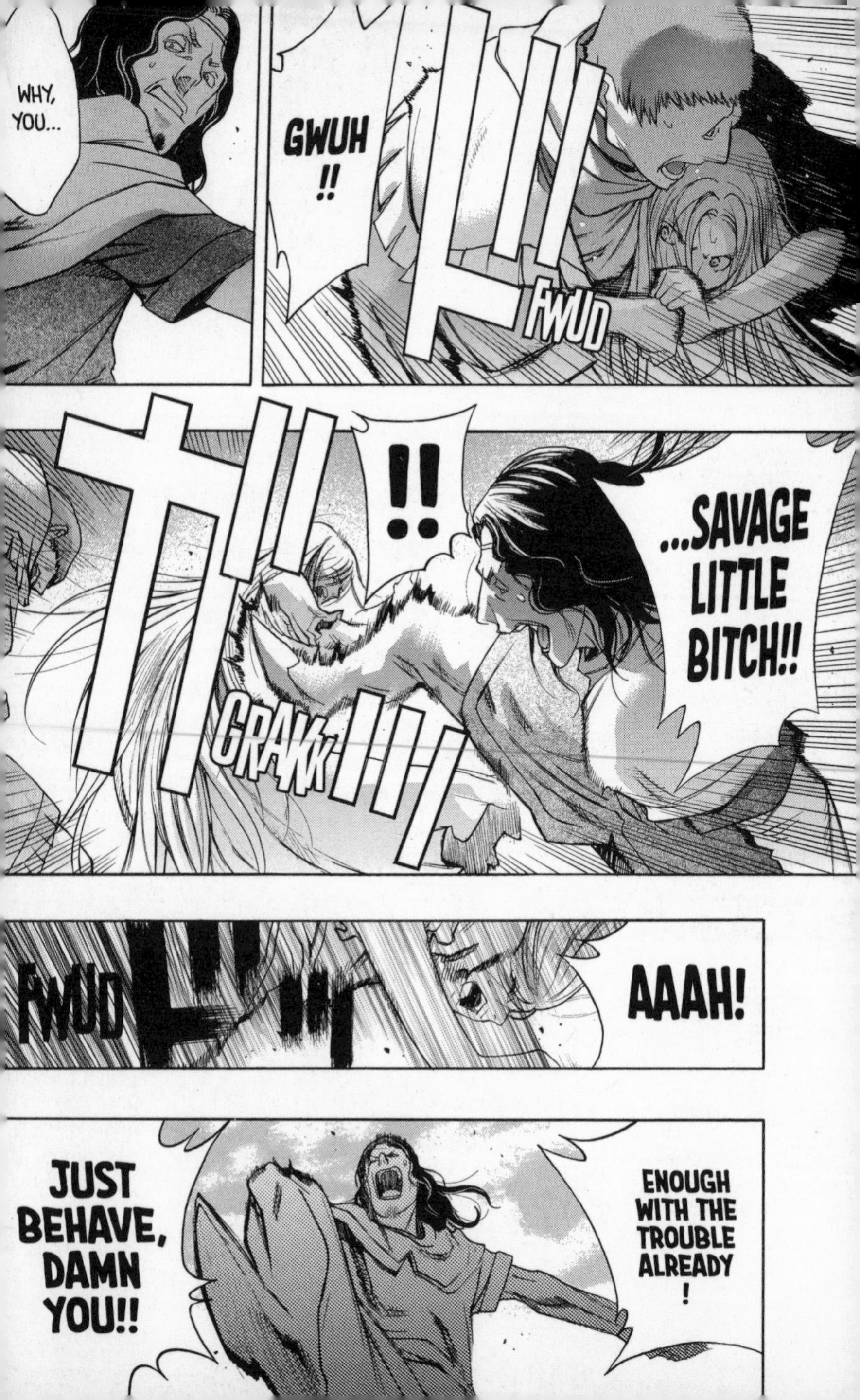
GWUH!!
FWUD
WHY, YOU...
!!
...SAVAGE LITTLE BITCH!!
CRAKK
AAAH!
FWUD
ENOUGH WITH THE TROUBLE ALREADY!
JUST BEHAVE, DAMN YOU!!

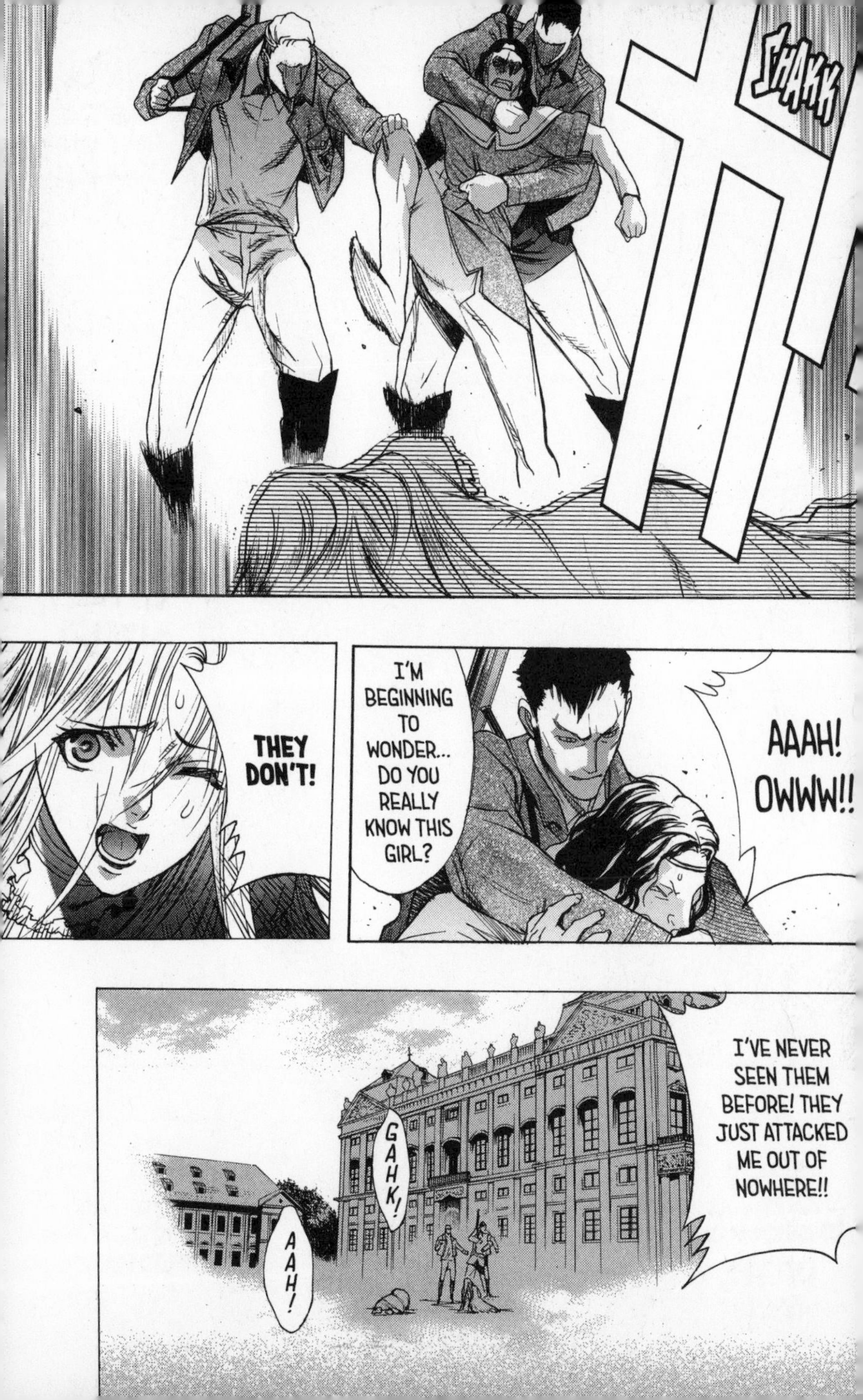
SHAKK
AAAH! OWWW!!
I'M BEGINNING TO WONDER... DO YOU REALLY KNOW THIS GIRL?
THEY DON'T!
I'VE NEVER SEEN THEM BEFORE! THEY JUST ATTACKED ME OUT OF NOWHERE!!
GAHK!
AAH!

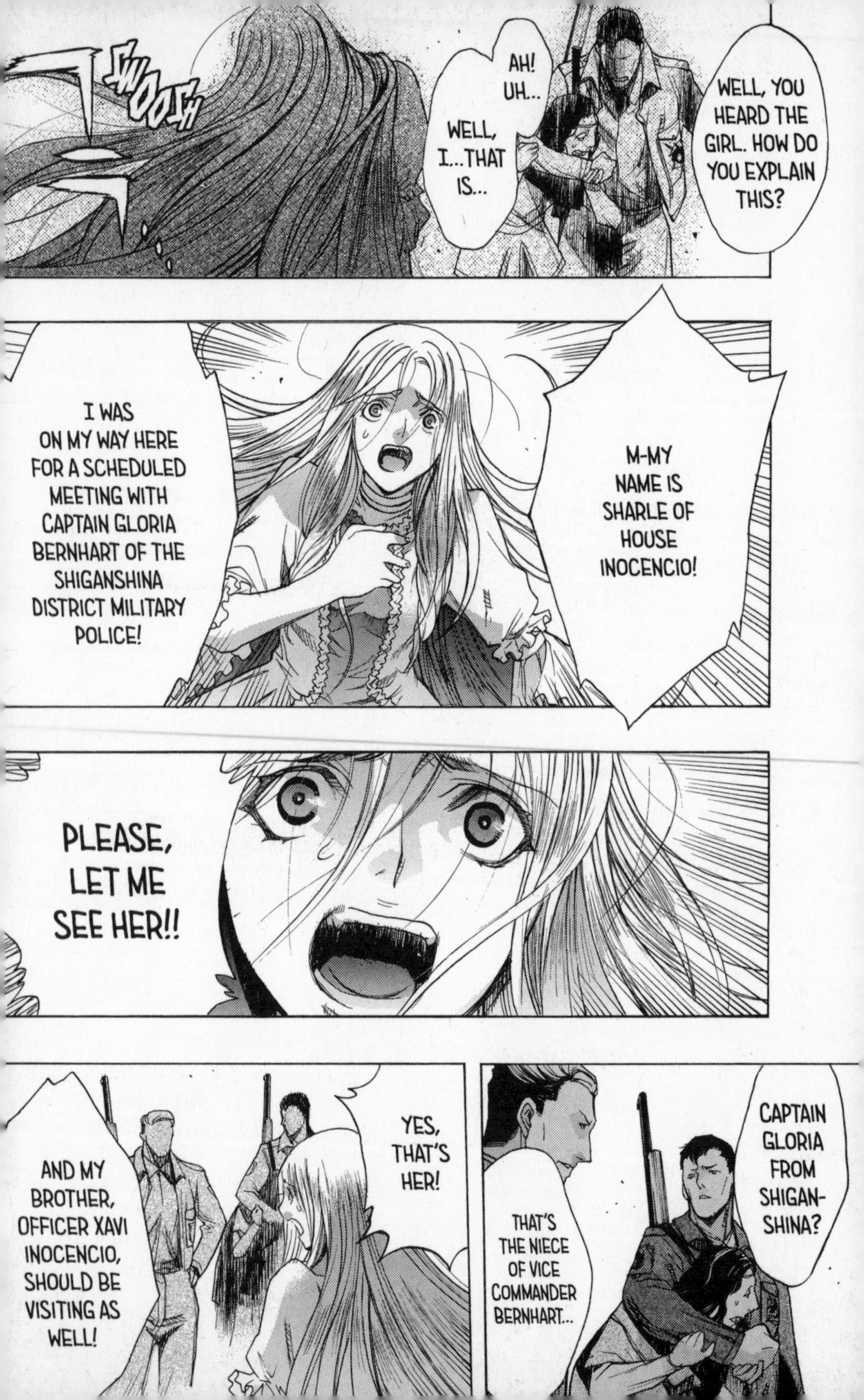
WELL, YOU HEARD THE GIRL. HOW DO YOU EXPLAIN THIS?
AH! UH...
WELL, I...THAT IS...
SWOOSH
M-MY NAME IS SHARLE OF HOUSE INOCENCIO!
I WAS ON MY WAY HERE FOR A SCHEDULED MEETING WITH CAPTAIN GLORIA BERNHART OF THE SHIGANSHINA DISTRICT MILITARY POLICE!
PLEASE, LET ME SEE HER!!
CAPTAIN GLORIA FROM SHIGAN-SHINA?
THAT'S THE NIECE OF VICE COMMANDER BERNHART...
YES, THAT'S HER!
AND MY BROTHER, OFFICER XAVI INOCENCIO, SHOULD BE VISITING AS WELL!

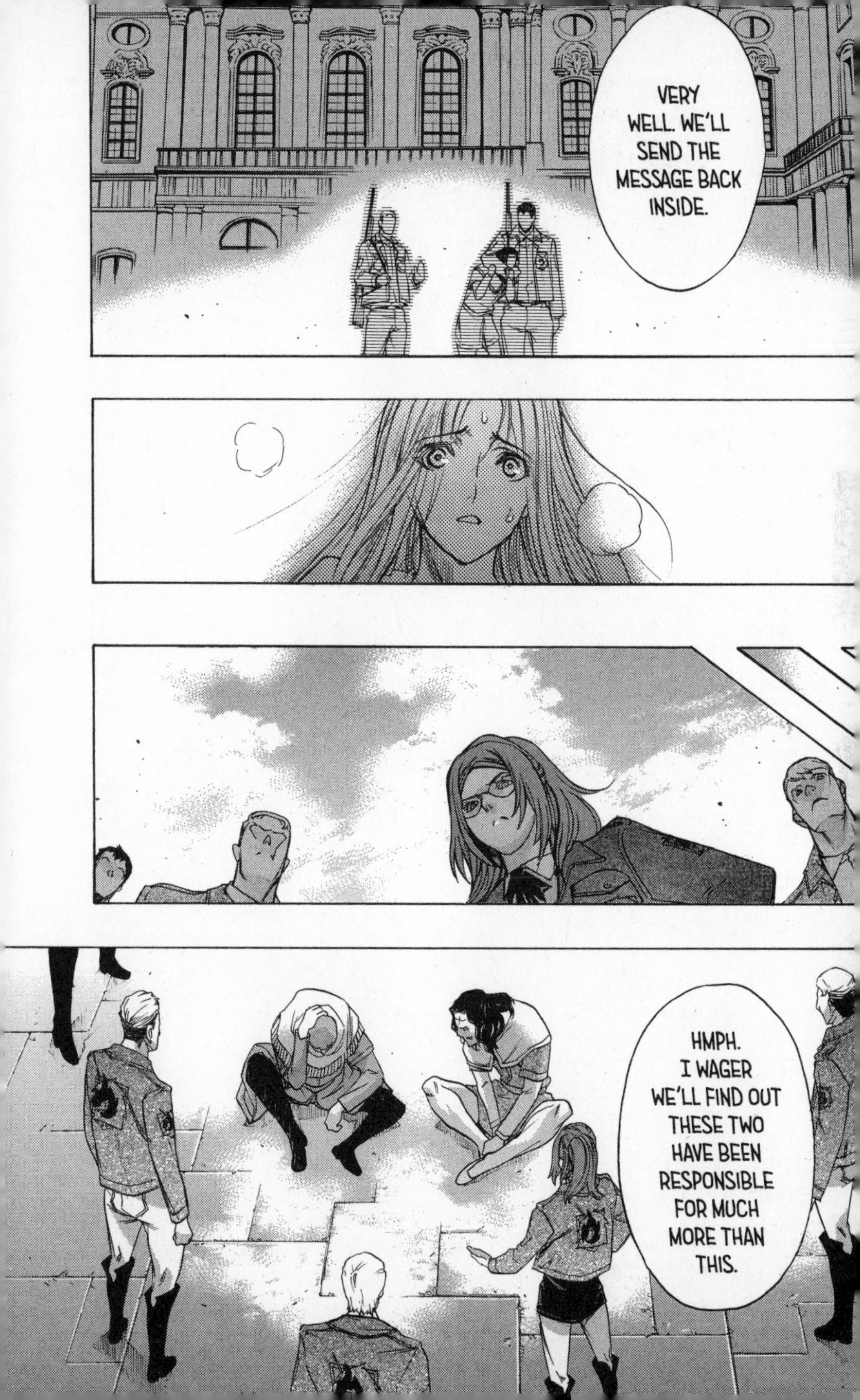
VERY WELL. WE'LL SEND THE MESSAGE BACK INSIDE.
HMPH. I WAGER WE'LL FIND OUT THESE TWO HAVE BEEN RESPONSIBLE FOR MUCH MORE THAN THIS.

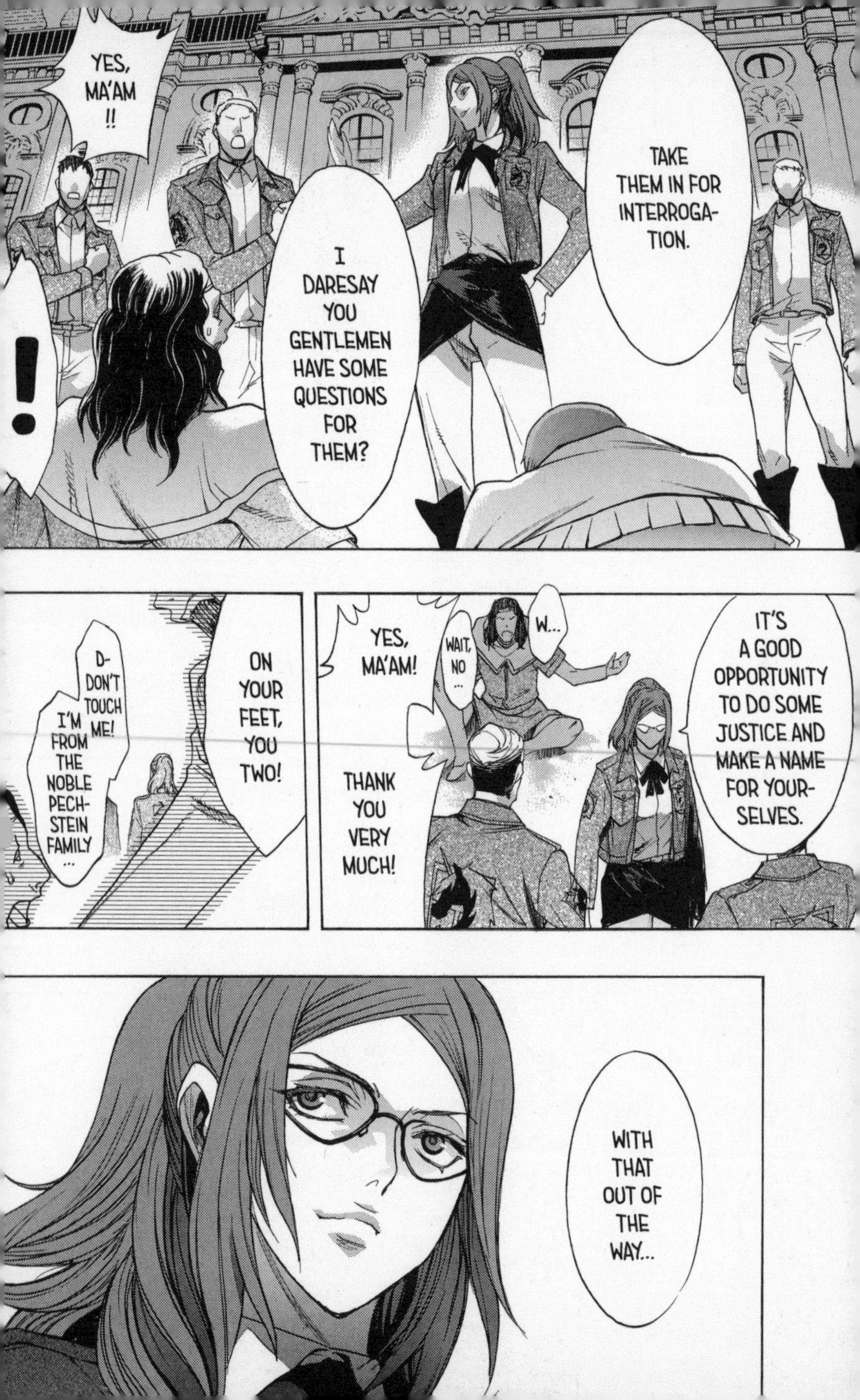
TAKE THEM IN FOR INTERROGA-TION.
I DARESAY YOU GENTLEMEN HAVE SOME QUESTIONS FOR THEM?
YES, MA'AM !!
!
IT'S A GOOD OPPORTUNITY TO DO SOME JUSTICE AND MAKE A NAME FOR YOUR-SELVES.
W...
WAIT, NO ...
YES, MA'AM!
THANK YOU VERY MUCH!
ON YOUR FEET, YOU TWO!
D-DON'T TOUCH ME! I'M FROM THE NOBLE PECH-STEIN FAMILY ...
WITH THAT OUT OF THE WAY...

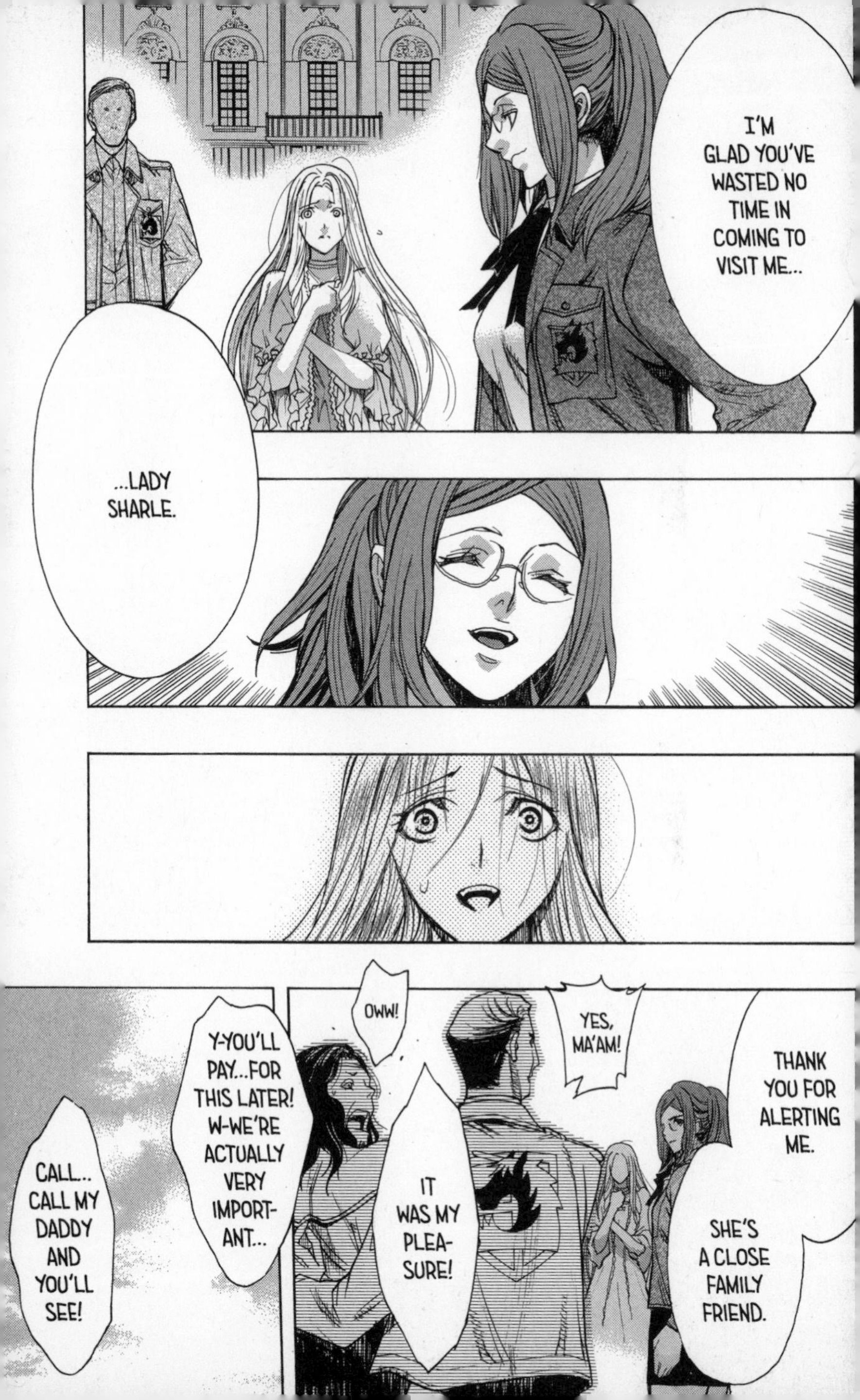
I'M GLAD YOU'VE WASTED NO TIME IN COMING TO VISIT ME...
...LADY SHARLE.
THANK YOU FOR ALERTING ME.
SHE'S A CLOSE FAMILY FRIEND.
YES, MA'AM!
OWW!
IT WAS MY PLEASURE!
Y-YOU'LL PAY...FOR THIS LATER! W-WE'RE ACTUALLY VERY IMPORTANT...
CALL... CALL MY DADDY AND YOU'LL SEE!

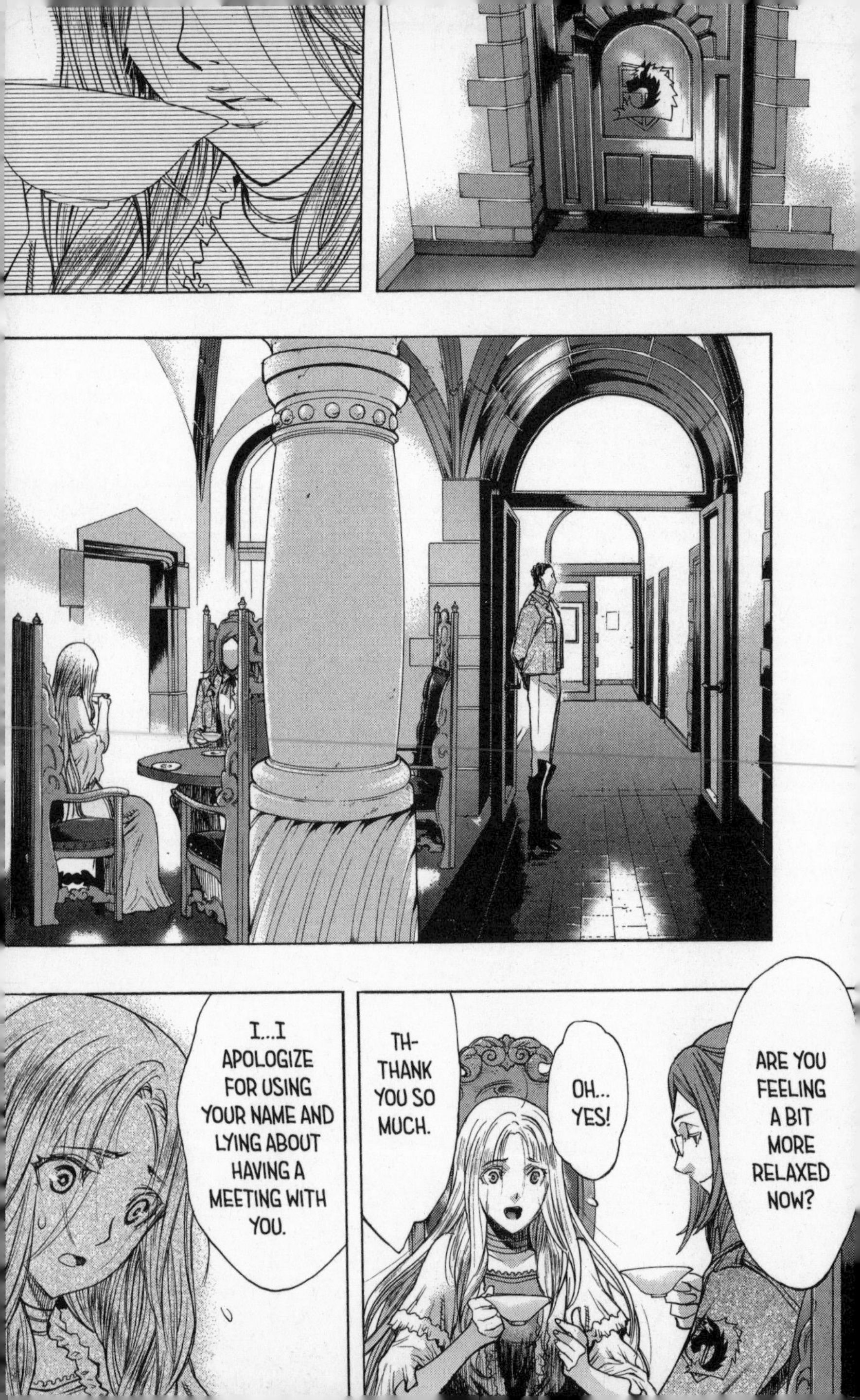
ARE YOU FEELING A BIT MORE RELAXED NOW?
OH... YES!
TH-THANK YOU SO MUCH.
I...I APOLOGIZE FOR USING YOUR NAME AND LYING ABOUT HAVING A MEETING WITH YOU.

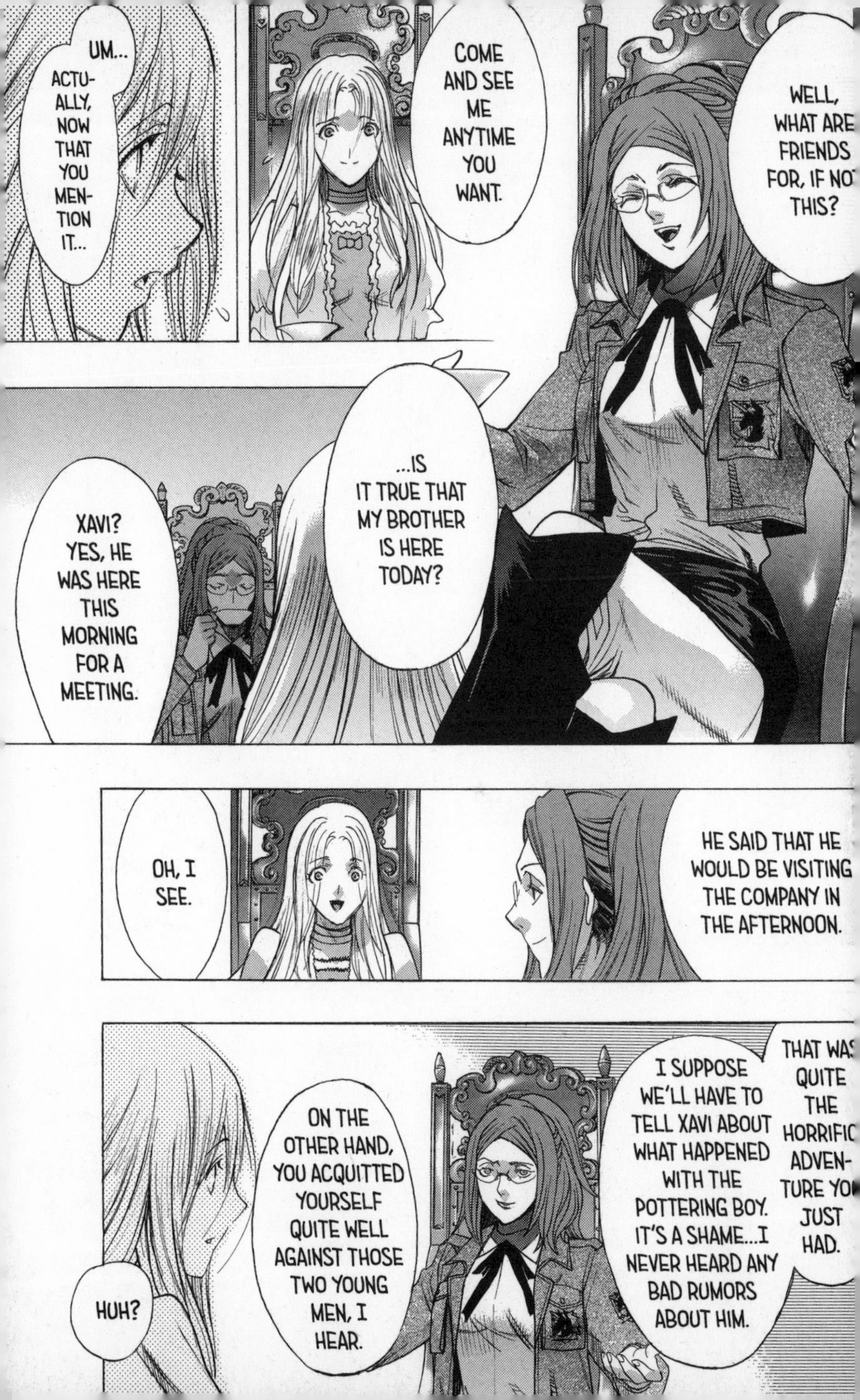
WELL, WHAT ARE FRIENDS FOR, IF NOT THIS?
COME AND SEE ME ANYTIME YOU WANT.
UM... ACTUALLY, NOW THAT YOU MENTION IT...
...IS IT TRUE THAT MY BROTHER IS HERE TODAY?
XAVI? YES, HE WAS HERE THIS MORNING FOR A MEETING.
HE SAID THAT HE WOULD BE VISITING THE COMPANY IN THE AFTERNOON.
OH, I SEE.
THAT WAS QUITE THE HORRIFIC ADVENTURE YOU JUST HAD.
I SUPPOSE WE'LL HAVE TO TELL XAVI ABOUT WHAT HAPPENED WITH THE POTTERING BOY. IT'S A SHAME...I NEVER HEARD ANY BAD RUMORS ABOUT HIM.
ON THE OTHER HAND, YOU ACQUITTED YOURSELF QUITE WELL AGAINST THOSE TWO YOUNG MEN, I HEAR.
HUH?

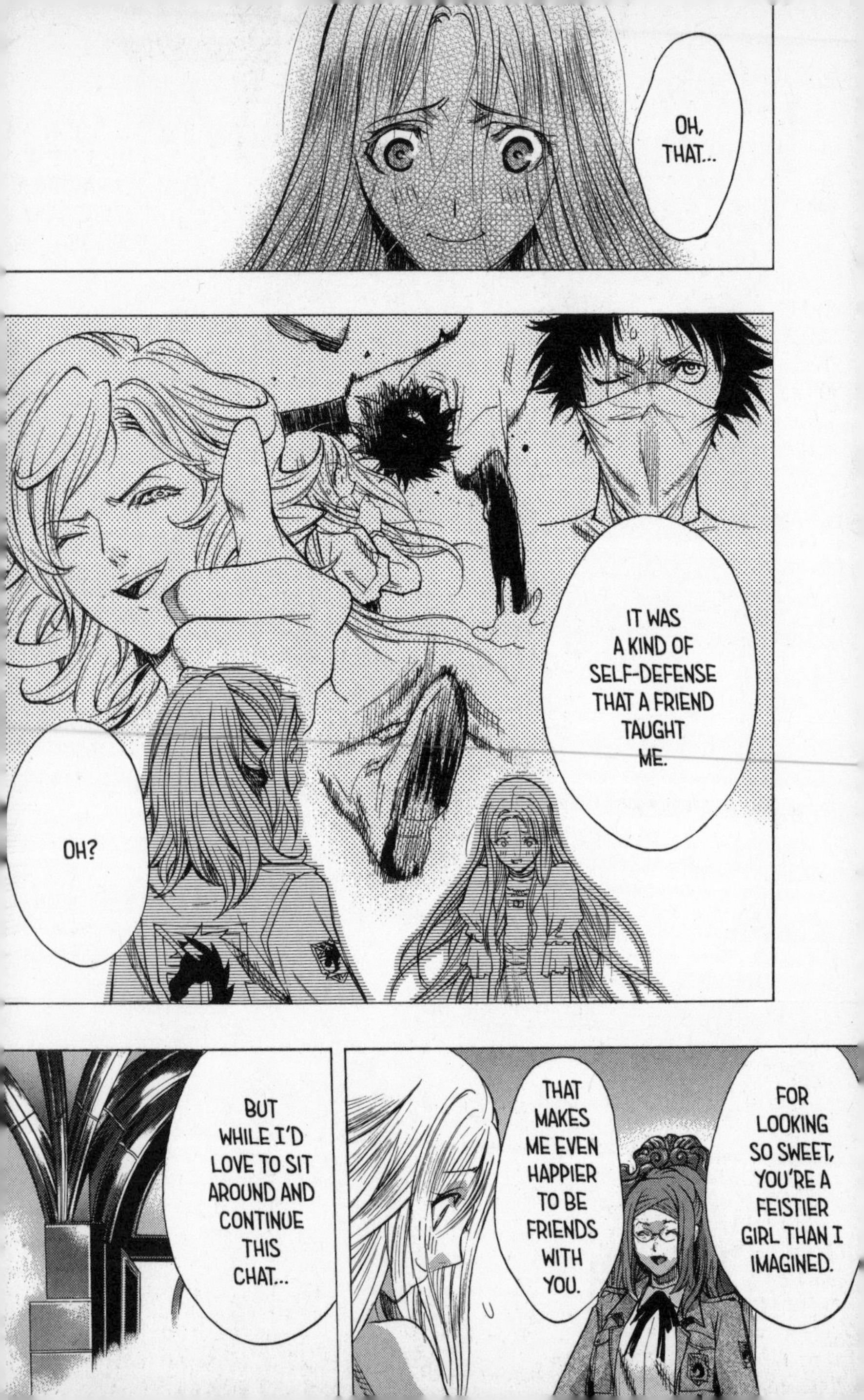
OH, THAT...
IT WAS A KIND OF SELF-DEFENSE THAT A FRIEND TAUGHT ME.
OH?
FOR LOOKING SO SWEET, YOU'RE A FEISTIER GIRL THAN I IMAGINED.
THAT MAKES ME EVEN HAPPIER TO BE FRIENDS WITH YOU.
BUT WHILE I'D LOVE TO SIT AROUND AND CONTINUE THIS CHAT...

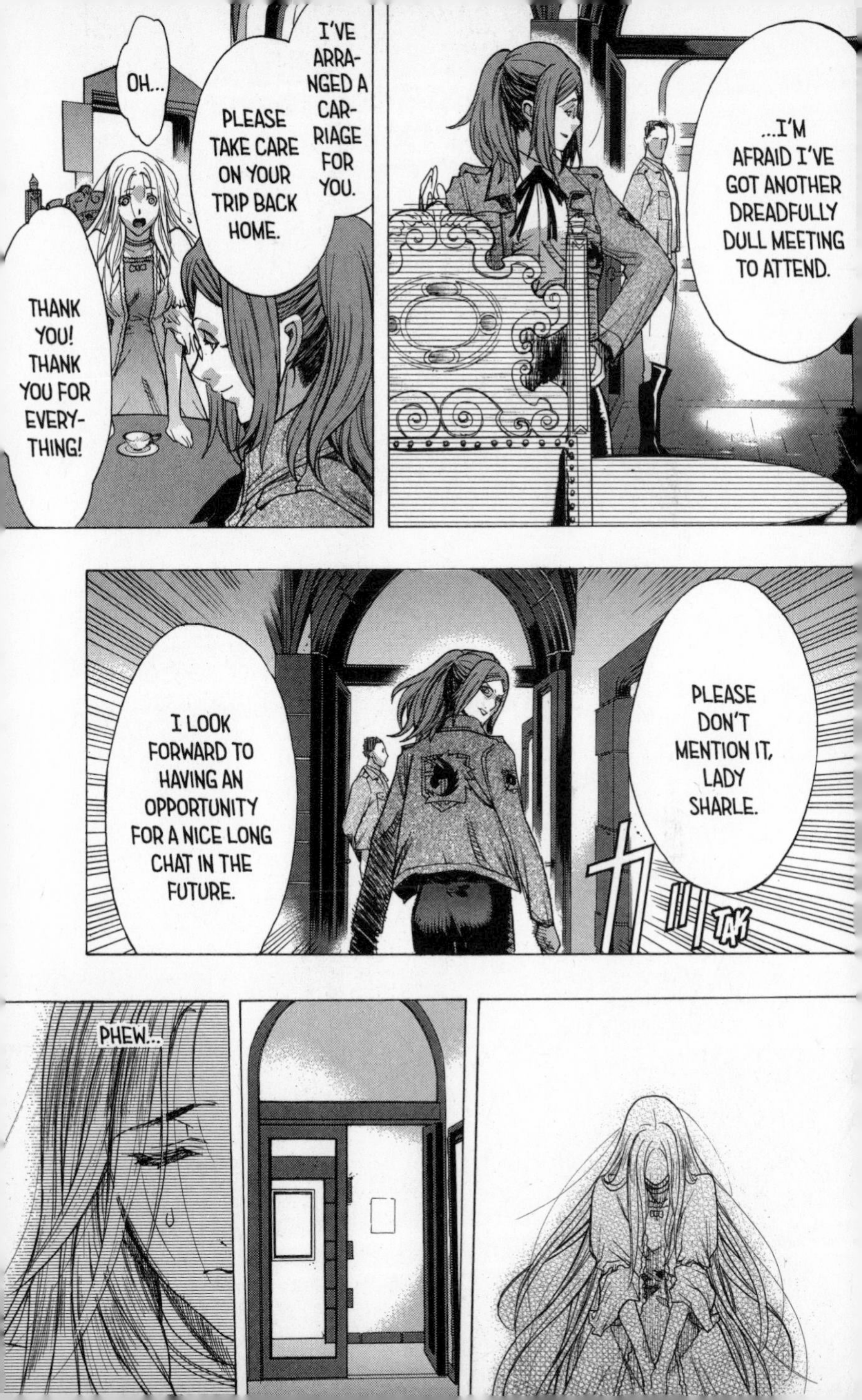
...I'M AFRAID I'VE GOT ANOTHER DREADFULLY DULL MEETING TO ATTEND.
I'VE ARRANGED A CARRIAGE FOR YOU.
PLEASE TAKE CARE ON YOUR TRIP BACK HOME.
OH...
THANK YOU! THANK YOU FOR EVERYTHING!
PLEASE DON'T MENTION IT, LADY SHARLE.
I LOOK FORWARD TO HAVING AN OPPORTUNITY FOR A NICE LONG CHAT IN THE FUTURE.
TAK
PHEW...

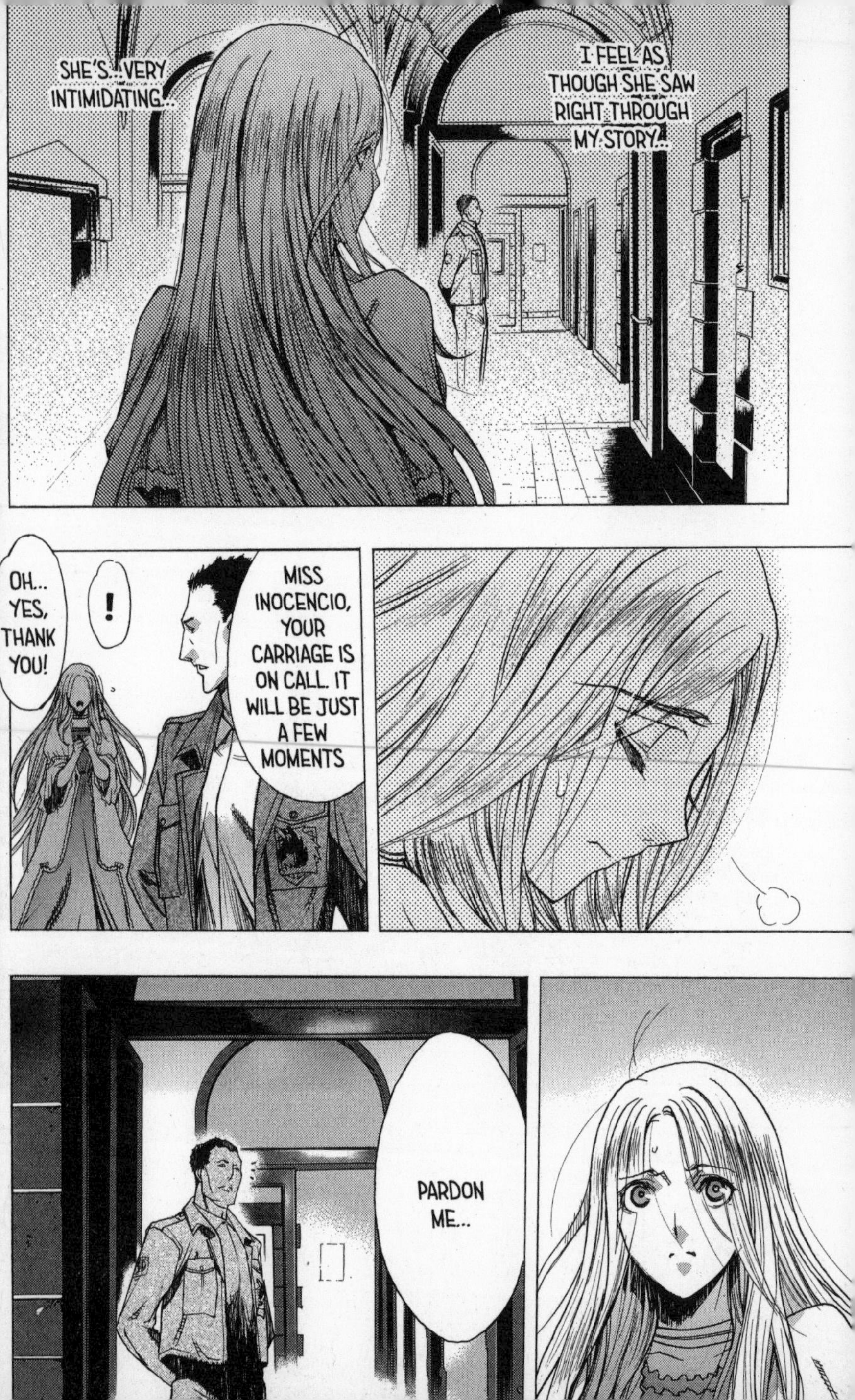
I FEEL AS THOUGH SHE SAW RIGHT THROUGH MY STORY...
SHE'S...VERY INTIMIDATING...
MISS INOCENCIO, YOUR CARRIAGE IS ON CALL. IT WILL BE JUST A FEW MOMENTS
!
OH... YES, THANK YOU!
PARDON ME...

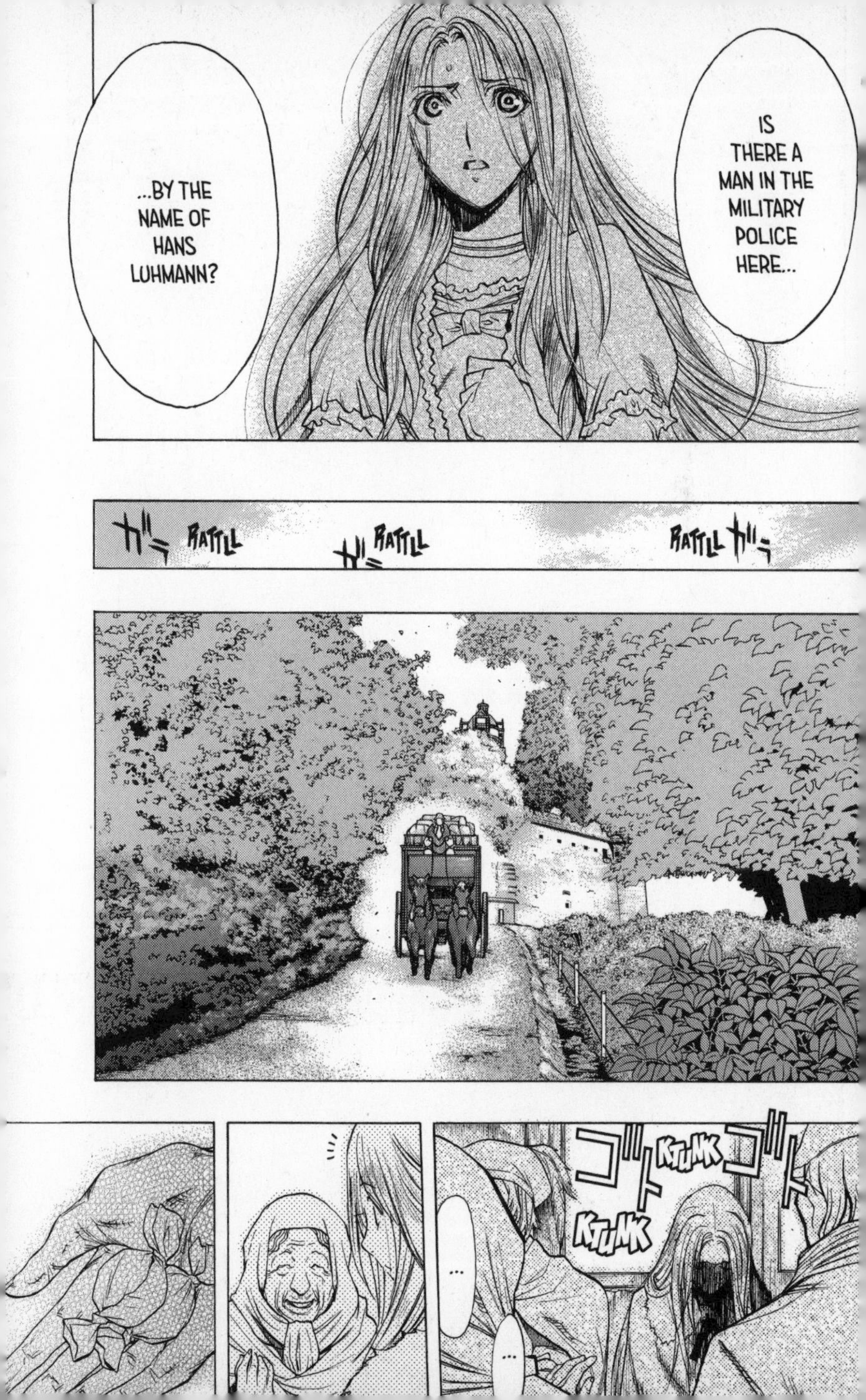
IS THERE A MAN IN THE MILITARY POLICE HERE...
...BY THE NAME OF HANS LUHMANN?
RATTLL
RATTLL
RATTLL
KTUNK
KTUNK
...
...

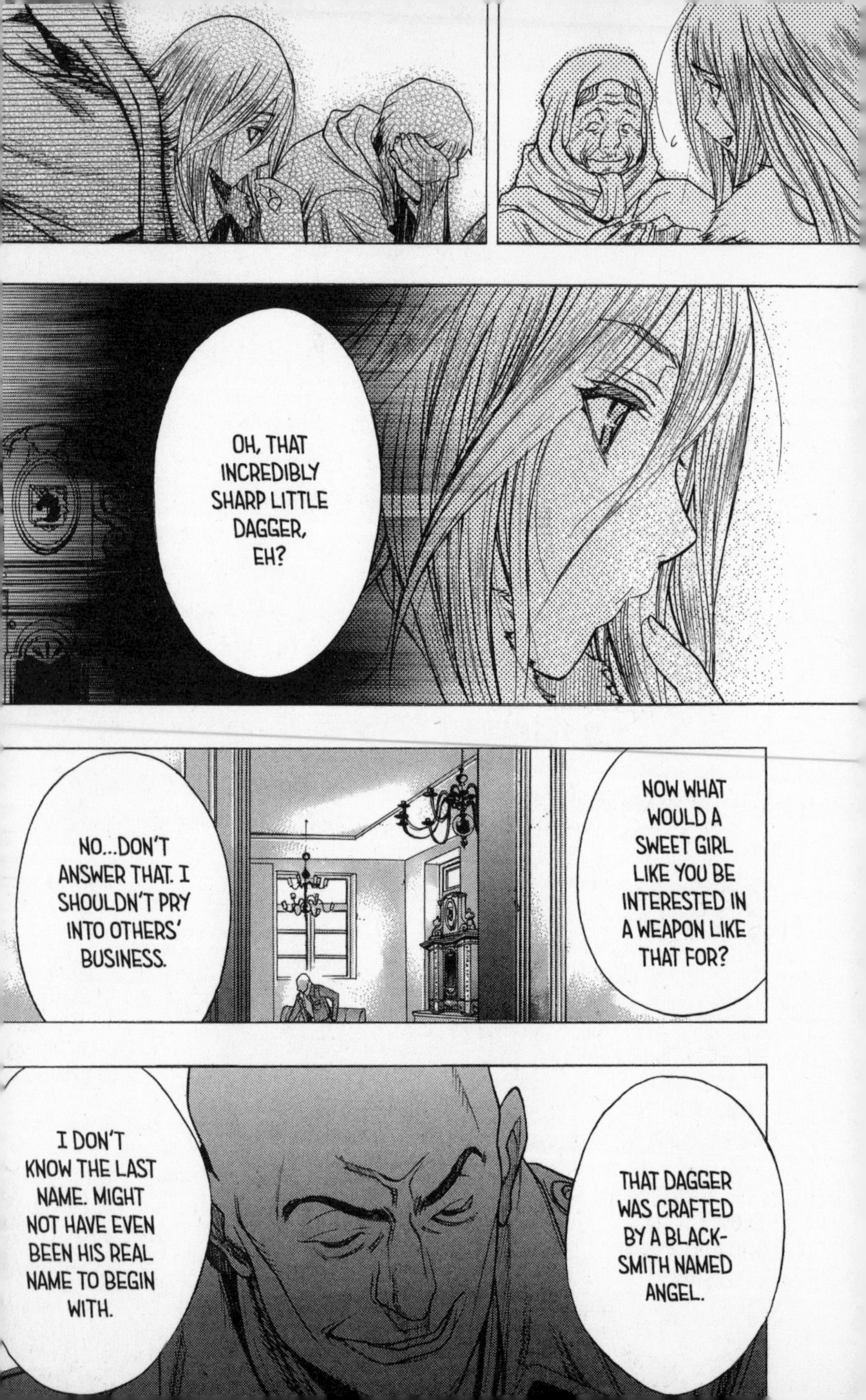
OH, THAT INCREDIBLY SHARP LITTLE DAGGER, EH?
NOW WHAT WOULD A SWEET GIRL LIKE YOU BE INTERESTED IN A WEAPON LIKE THAT FOR?
NO...DON'T ANSWER THAT. I SHOULDN'T PRY INTO OTHERS' BUSINESS.
THAT DAGGER WAS CRAFTED BY A BLACK-SMITH NAMED ANGEL.
I DON'T KNOW THE LAST NAME. MIGHT NOT HAVE EVEN BEEN HIS REAL NAME TO BEGIN WITH.

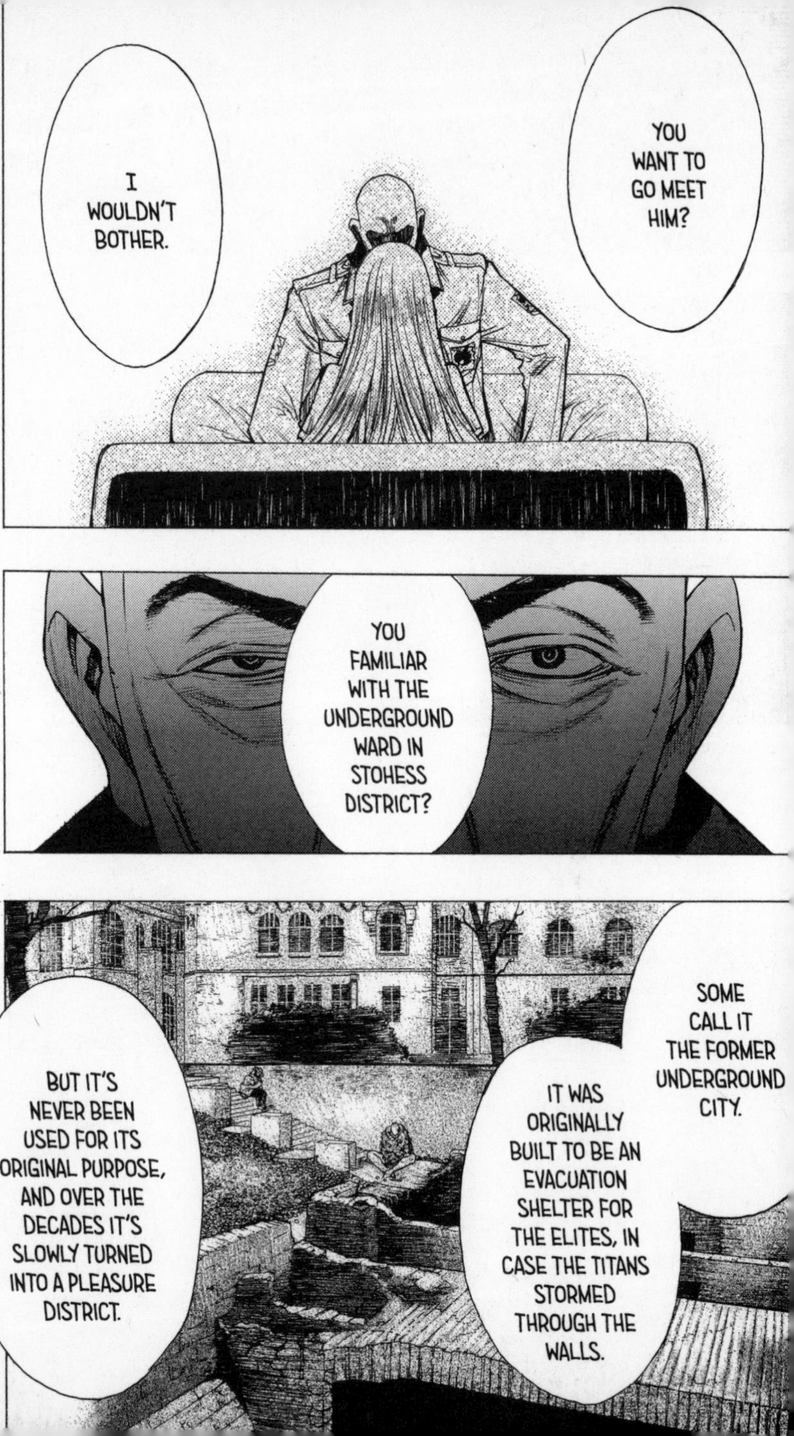
YOU WANT TO GO MEET HIM?
I WOULDN'T BOTHER.
YOU FAMILIAR WITH THE UNDERGROUND WARD IN STOHESS DISTRICT?
SOME CALL IT THE FORMER UNDERGROUND CITY.
IT WAS ORIGINALLY BUILT TO BE AN EVACUATION SHELTER FOR THE ELITES, IN CASE THE TITANS STORMED THROUGH THE WALLS.
BUT IT'S NEVER BEEN USED FOR ITS ORIGINAL PURPOSE, AND OVER THE DECADES IT'S SLOWLY TURNED INTO A PLEASURE DISTRICT.

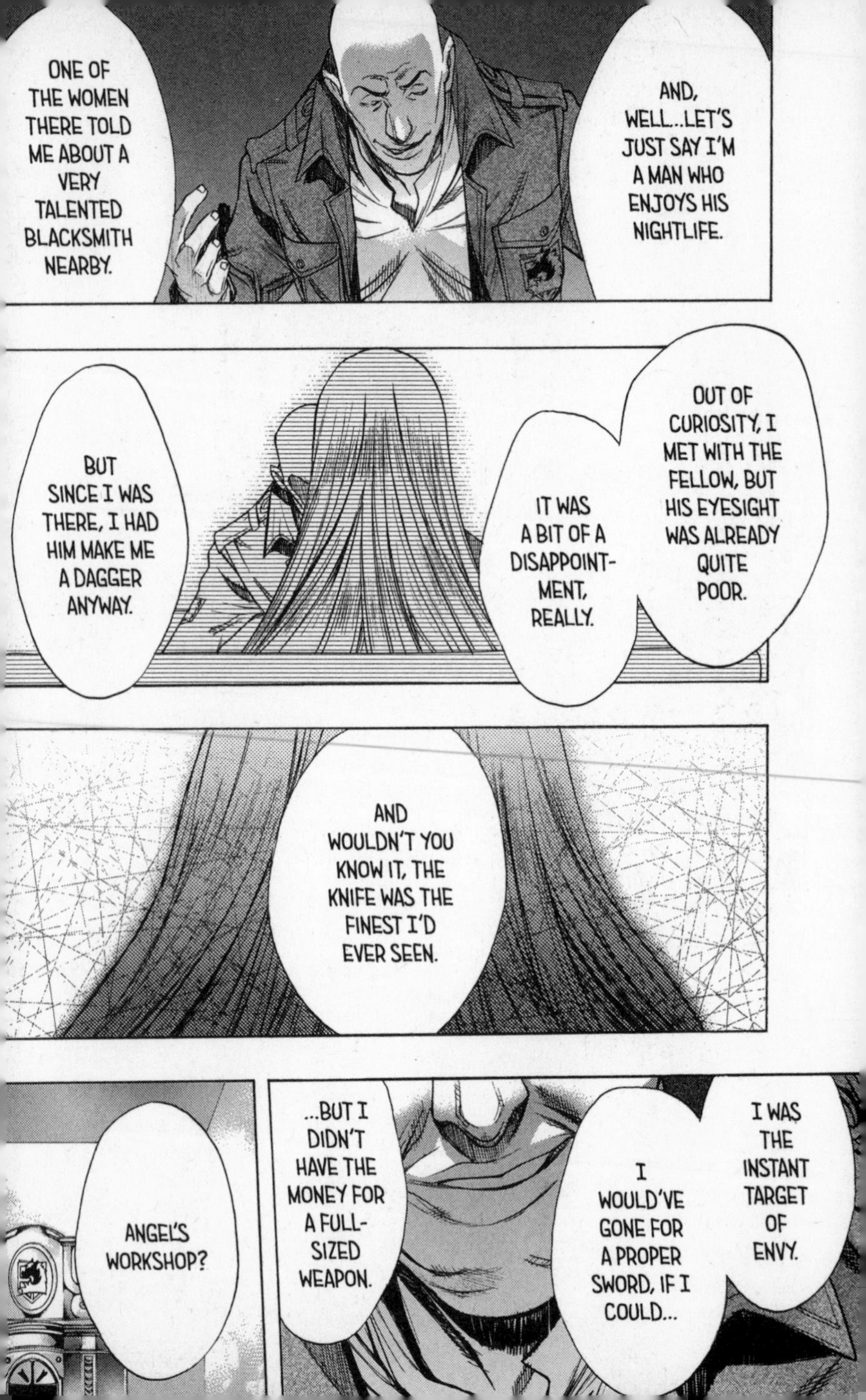
AND, WELL...LET'S JUST SAY I'M A MAN WHO ENJOYS HIS NIGHTLIFE.
ONE OF THE WOMEN THERE TOLD ME ABOUT A VERY TALENTED BLACKSMITH NEARBY.
OUT OF CURIOSITY, I MET WITH THE FELLOW, BUT HIS EYESIGHT WAS ALREADY QUITE POOR.
IT WAS A BIT OF A DISAPPOINT-MENT, REALLY.
BUT SINCE I WAS THERE, I HAD HIM MAKE ME A DAGGER ANYWAY.
AND WOULDN'T YOU KNOW IT, THE KNIFE WAS THE FINEST I'D EVER SEEN.
I WAS THE INSTANT TARGET OF ENVY.
I WOULD'VE GONE FOR A PROPER SWORD, IF I COULD...
...BUT I DIDN'T HAVE THE MONEY FOR A FULL-SIZED WEAPON.
ANGEL'S WORKSHOP?

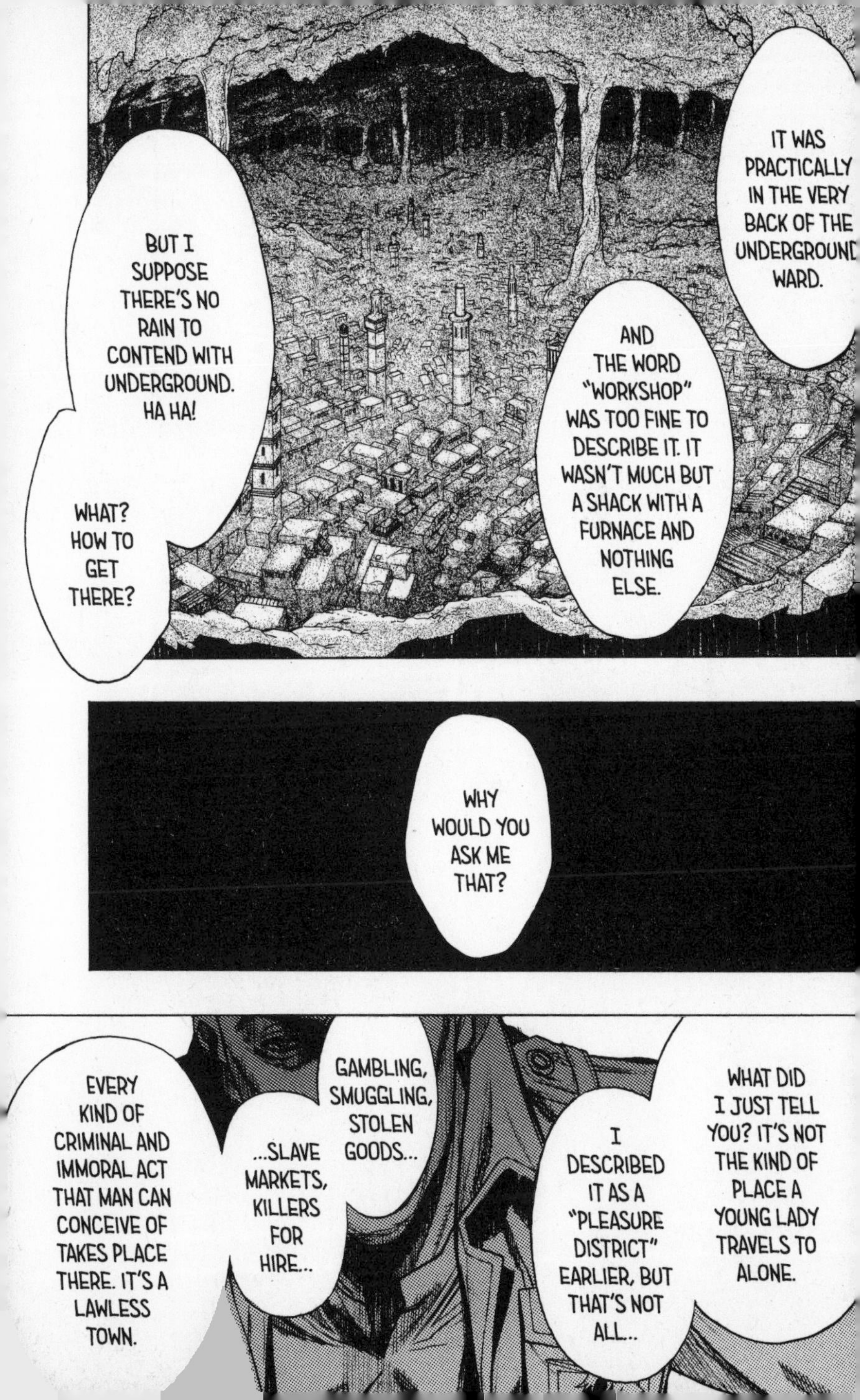
IT WAS PRACTICALLY IN THE VERY BACK OF THE UNDERGROUND WARD.
AND THE WORD "WORKSHOP" WAS TOO FINE TO DESCRIBE IT. IT WASN'T MUCH BUT A SHACK WITH A FURNACE AND NOTHING ELSE.
BUT I SUPPOSE THERE'S NO RAIN TO CONTEND WITH UNDERGROUND. HA HA!
WHAT? HOW TO GET THERE?
WHY WOULD YOU ASK ME THAT?
WHAT DID I JUST TELL YOU? IT'S NOT THE KIND OF PLACE A YOUNG LADY TRAVELS TO ALONE.
I DESCRIBED IT AS A "PLEASURE DISTRICT" EARLIER, BUT THAT'S NOT ALL...
GAMBLING, SMUGGLING, STOLEN GOODS...
...SLAVE MARKETS, KILLERS FOR HIRE...
EVERY KIND OF CRIMINAL AND IMMORAL ACT THAT MAN CAN CONCEIVE OF TAKES PLACE THERE. IT'S A LAWLESS TOWN.

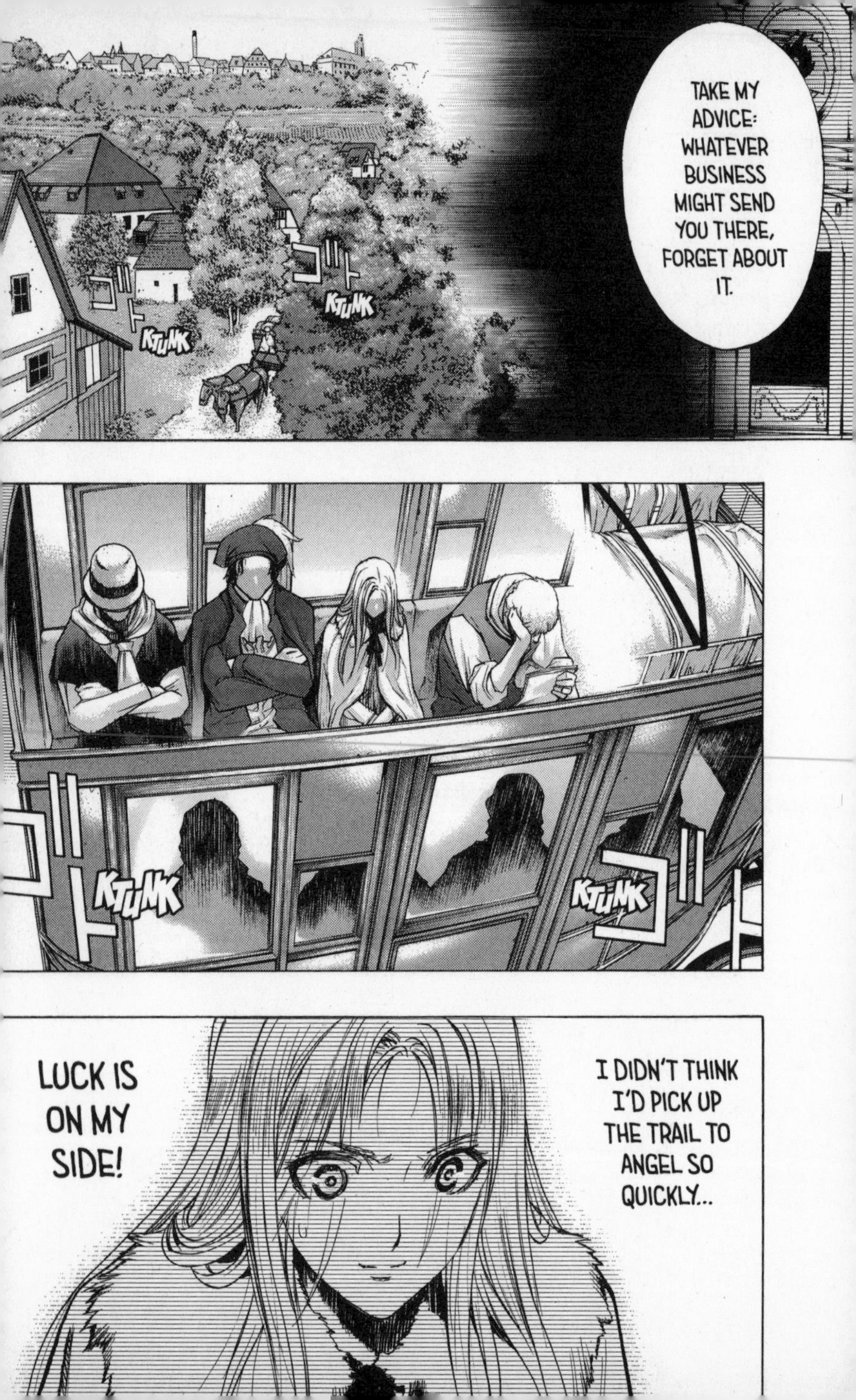
TAKE MY ADVICE: WHATEVER BUSINESS MIGHT SEND YOU THERE, FORGET ABOUT IT.
KTUNK
KTUNK
KTUNK
KTUNK
I DIDN'T THINK I'D PICK UP THE TRAIL TO ANGEL SO QUICKLY...
LUCK IS ON MY SIDE!

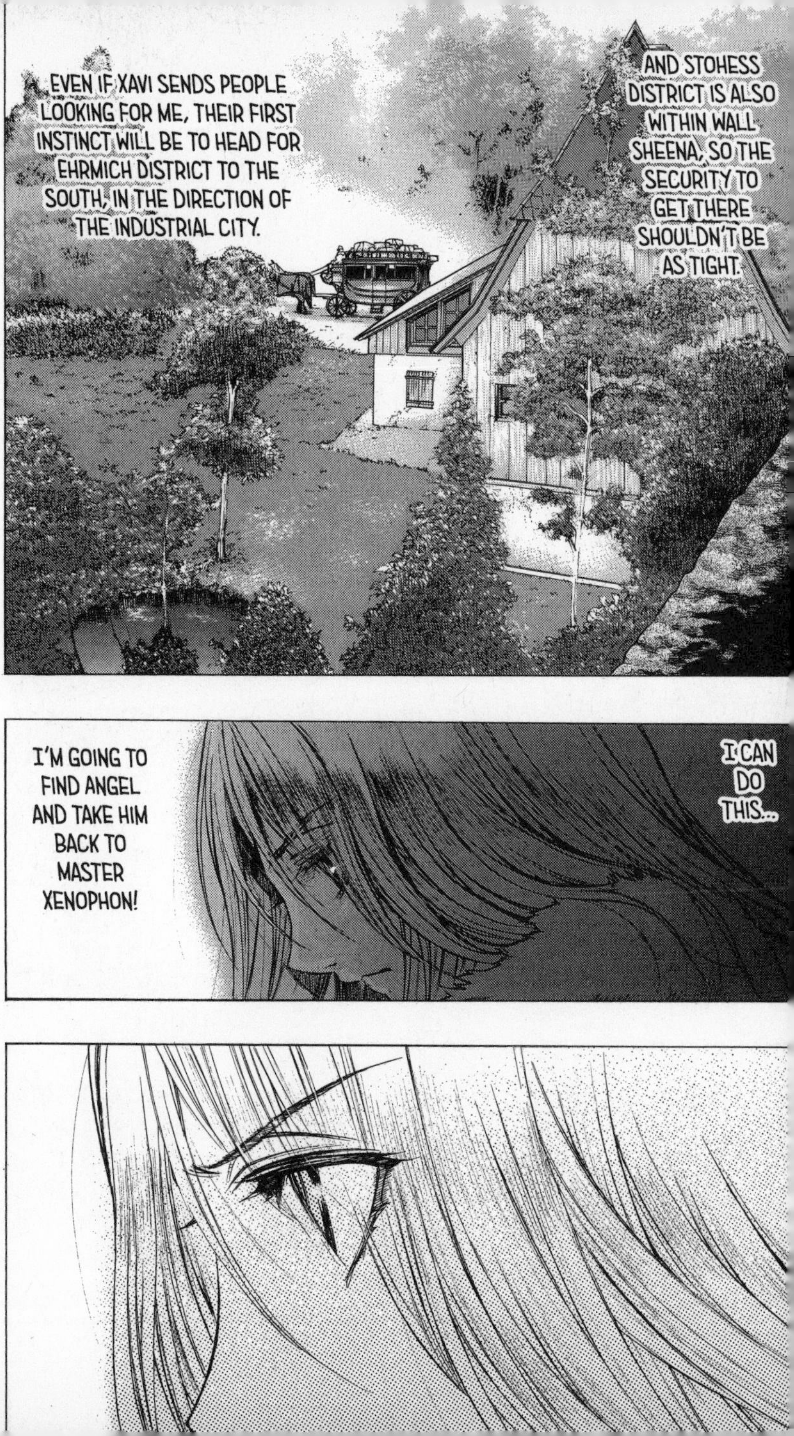
EVEN IF XAVI SENDS PEOPLE LOOKING FOR ME, THEIR FIRST INSTINCT WILL BE TO HEAD FOR EHRMICH DISTRICT TO THE SOUTH, IN THE DIRECTION OF THE INDUSTRIAL CITY.
AND STOHESS DISTRICT IS ALSO WITHIN WALL SHEENA, SO THE SECURITY TO GET THERE SHOULDN'T BE AS TIGHT.
I'M GOING TO FIND ANGEL AND TAKE HIM BACK TO MASTER XENOPHON!
I CAN DO THIS...

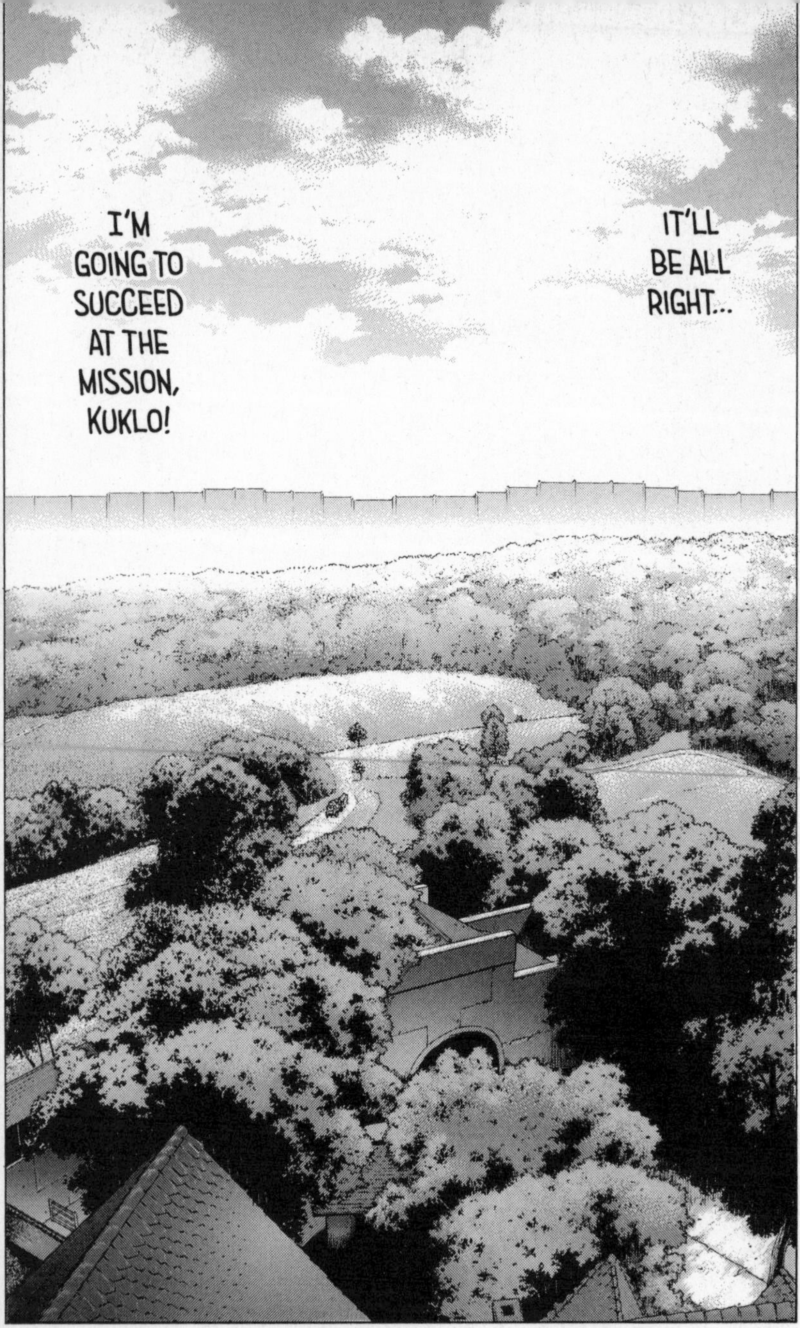
IT'LL BE ALL RIGHT...
I'M GOING TO SUCCEED AT THE MISSION, KUKLO!

Chapter 33: The Imprisoned Princess Flees · End

ATTACK on TITAN

BEFORE THE FALL

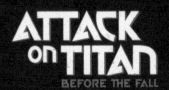

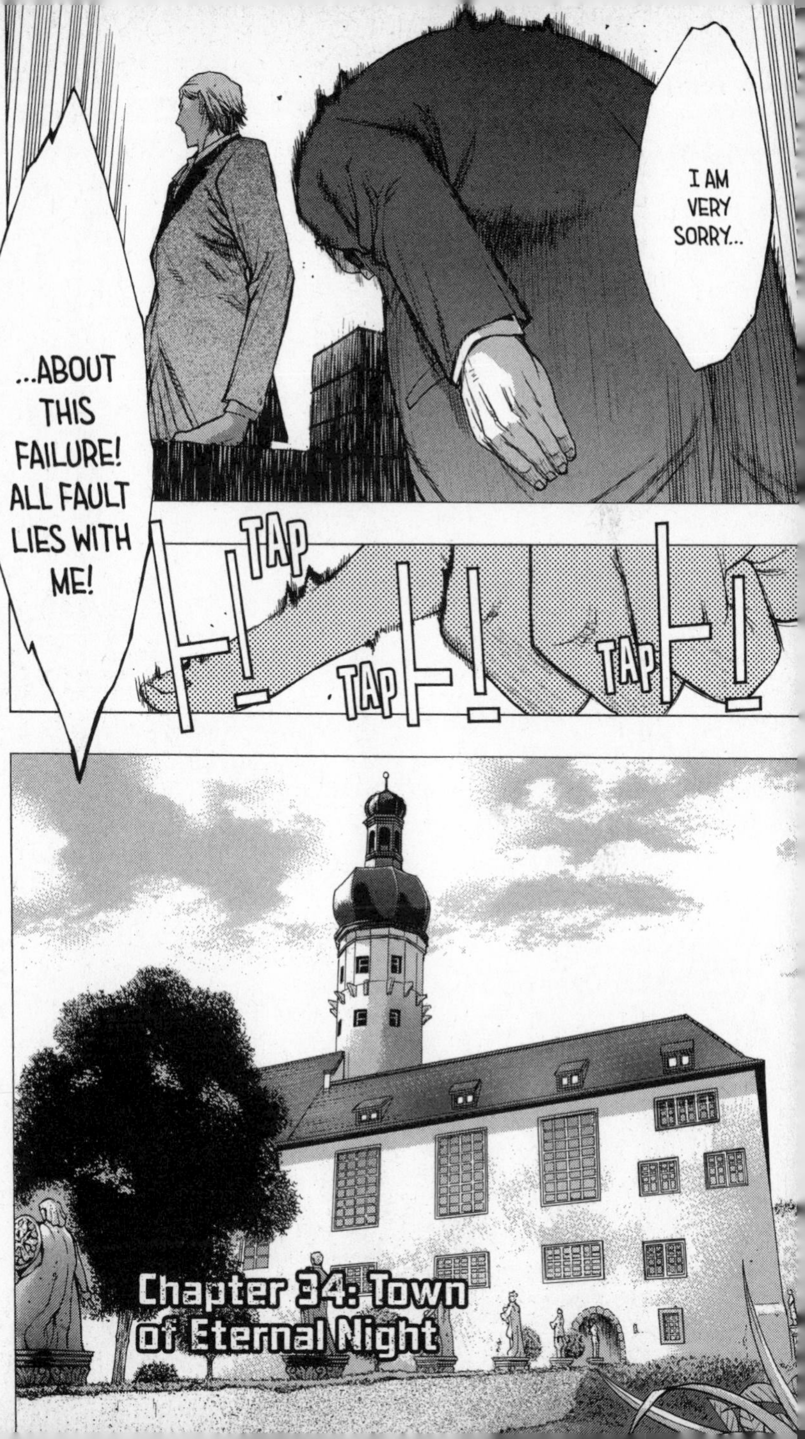
I AM VERY SORRY...
...ABOUT THIS FAILURE! ALL FAULT LIES WITH ME!
TAP
TAP
TAP
Chapter 34: Town of Eternal Night

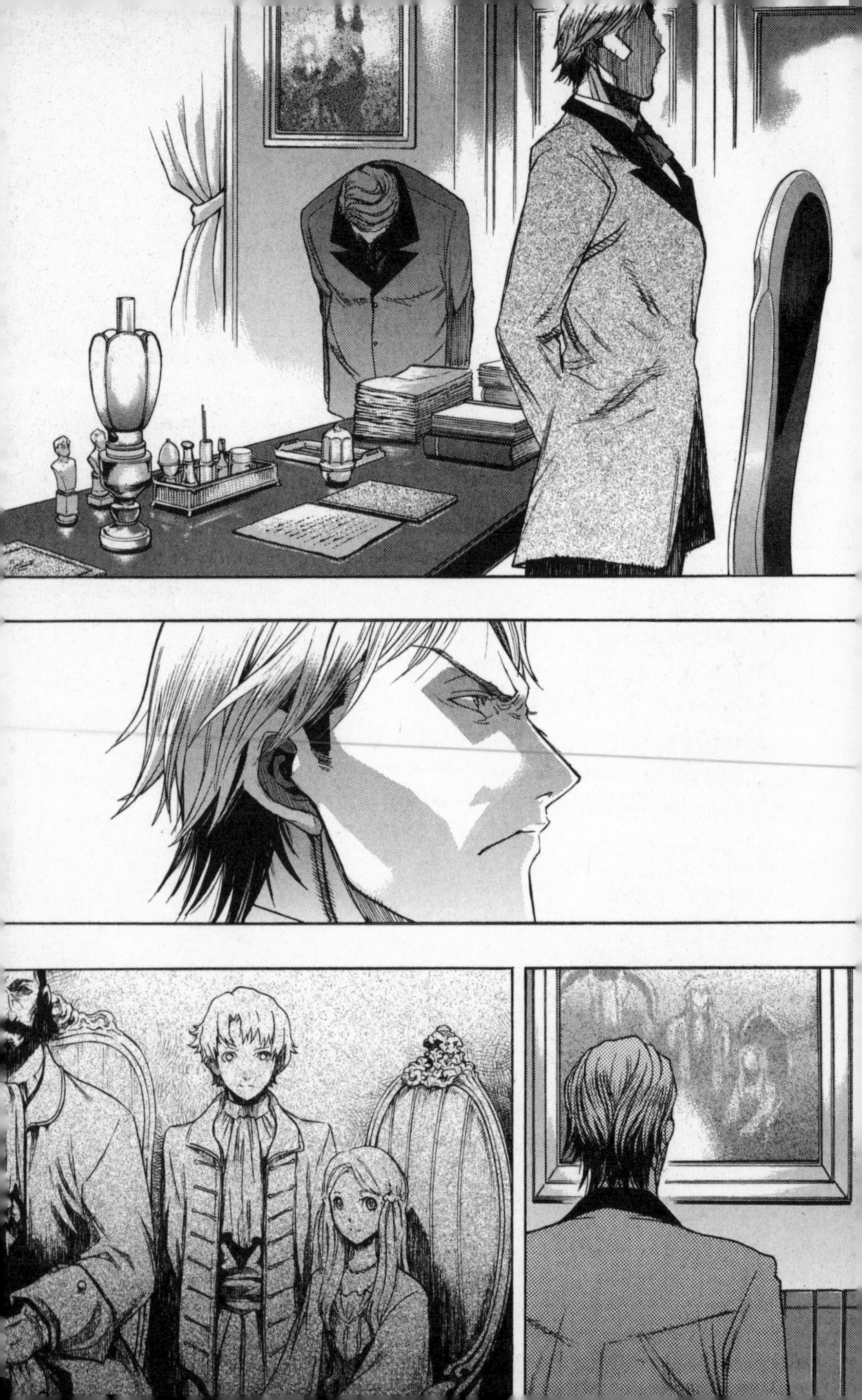

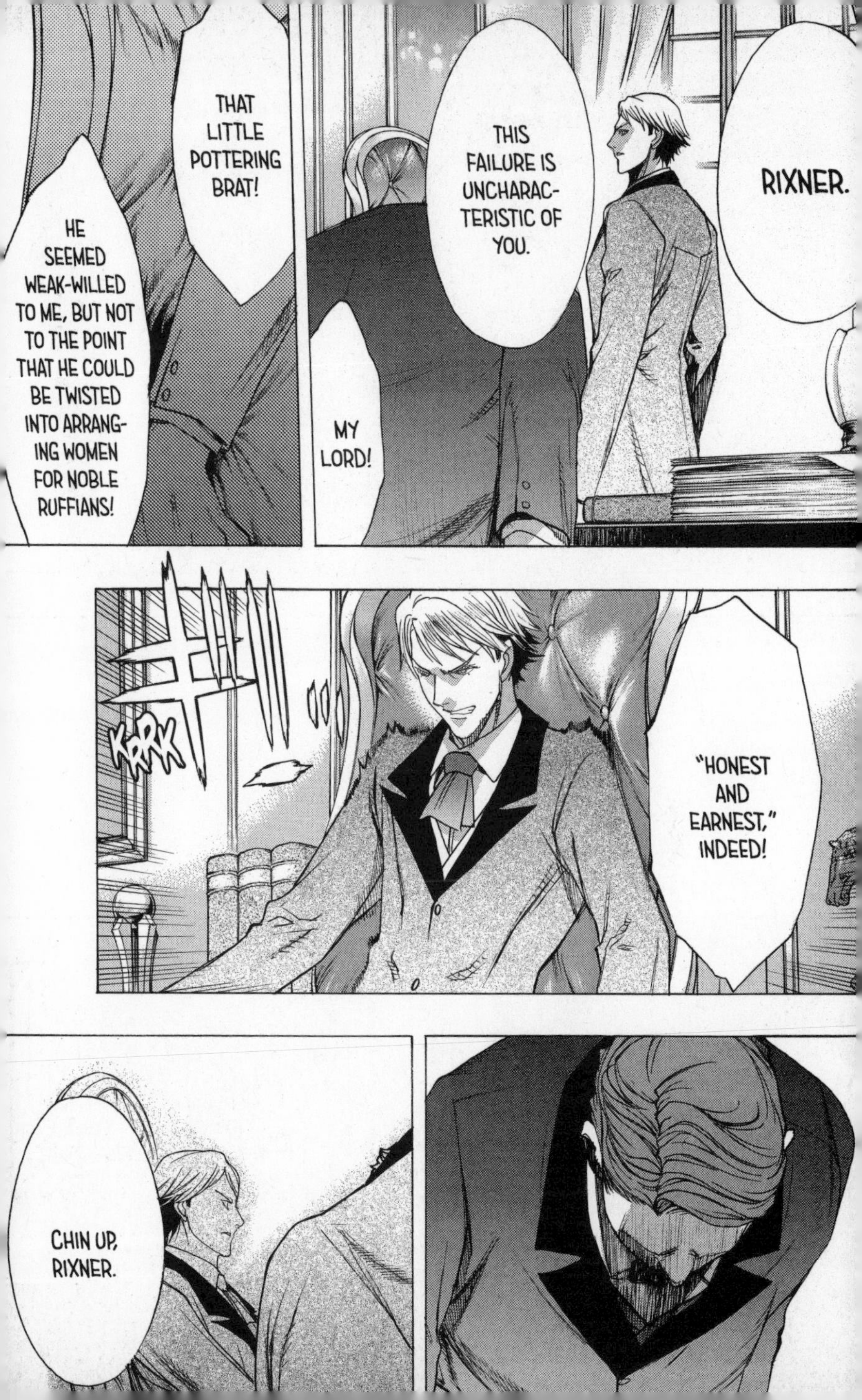
RIXNER.
THIS FAILURE IS UNCHARAC-TERISTIC OF YOU.
MY LORD!
THAT LITTLE POTTERING BRAT!
HE SEEMED WEAK-WILLED TO ME, BUT NOT TO THE POINT THAT HE COULD BE TWISTED INTO ARRANG-ING WOMEN FOR NOBLE RUFFIANS!
"HONEST AND EARNEST," INDEED!
KRRK
CHIN UP, RIXNER.

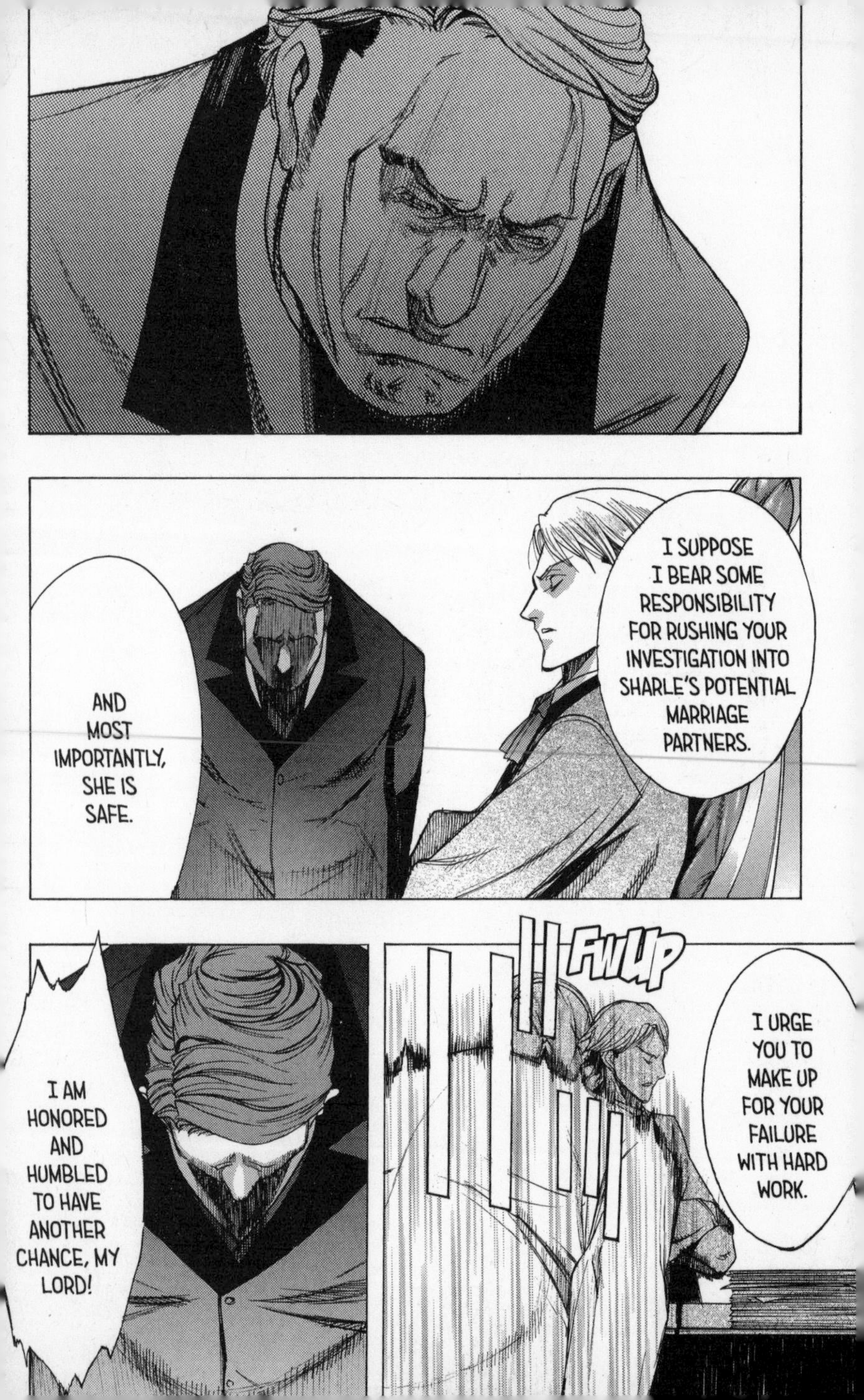
I SUPPOSE I BEAR SOME RESPONSIBILITY FOR RUSHING YOUR INVESTIGATION INTO SHARLE'S POTENTIAL MARRIAGE PARTNERS.
AND MOST IMPORTANTLY, SHE IS SAFE.
FWUP
I URGE YOU TO MAKE UP FOR YOUR FAILURE WITH HARD WORK.
I AM HONORED AND HUMBLED TO HAVE ANOTHER CHANCE, MY LORD!

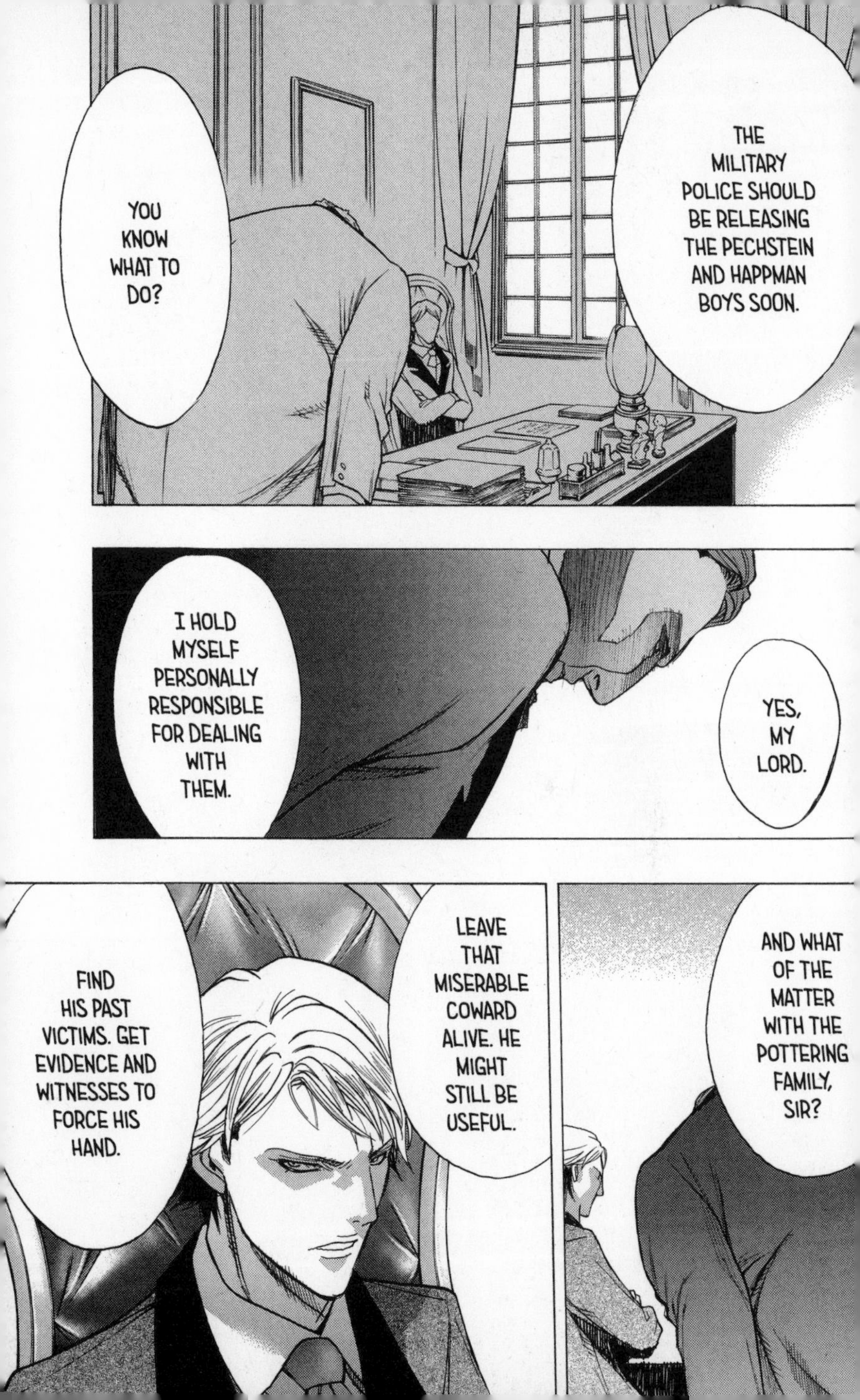
THE MILITARY POLICE SHOULD BE RELEASING THE PECHSTEIN AND HAPPMAN BOYS SOON.
YOU KNOW WHAT TO DO?
YES, MY LORD.
I HOLD MYSELF PERSONALLY RESPONSIBLE FOR DEALING WITH THEM.
AND WHAT OF THE MATTER WITH THE POTTERING FAMILY, SIR?
LEAVE THAT MISERABLE COWARD ALIVE. HE MIGHT STILL BE USEFUL.
FIND HIS PAST VICTIMS. GET EVIDENCE AND WITNESSES TO FORCE HIS HAND.

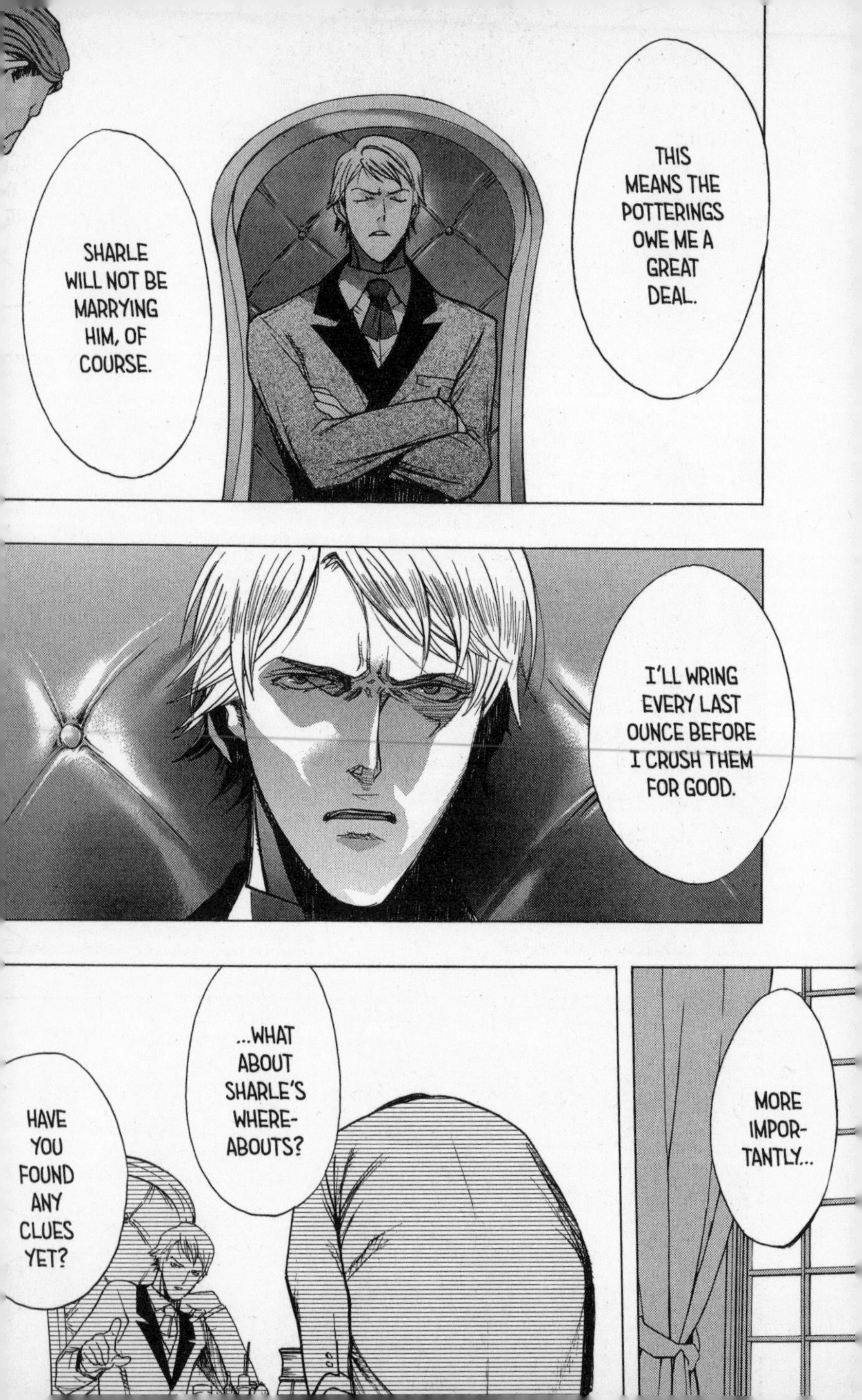
THIS MEANS THE POTTERINGS OWE ME A GREAT DEAL.
SHARLE WILL NOT BE MARRYING HIM, OF COURSE.
I'LL WRING EVERY LAST OUNCE BEFORE I CRUSH THEM FOR GOOD.
MORE IMPOR-TANTLY...
...WHAT ABOUT SHARLE'S WHERE-ABOUTS?
HAVE YOU FOUND ANY CLUES YET?

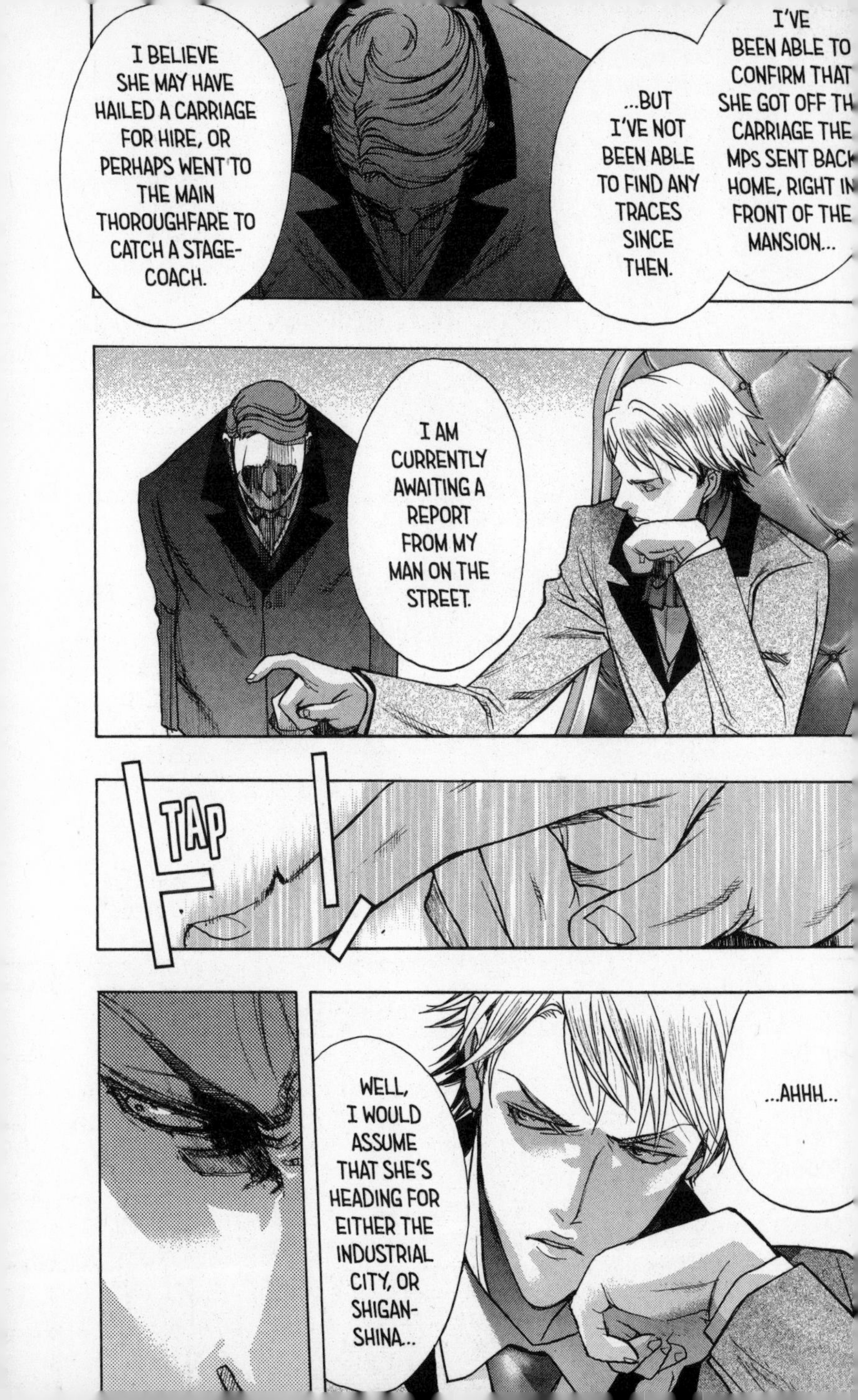
I'VE BEEN ABLE TO CONFIRM THAT SHE GOT OFF TH CARRIAGE THE MPS SENT BACK HOME, RIGHT IN FRONT OF THE MANSION...
...BUT I'VE NOT BEEN ABLE TO FIND ANY TRACES SINCE THEN.
I BELIEVE SHE MAY HAVE HAILED A CARRIAGE FOR HIRE, OR PERHAPS WENT TO THE MAIN THOROUGHFARE TO CATCH A STAGE-COACH.
I AM CURRENTLY AWAITING A REPORT FROM MY MAN ON THE STREET.
TAP
...AHHH...
WELL, I WOULD ASSUME THAT SHE'S HEADING FOR EITHER THE INDUSTRIAL CITY, OR SHIGAN-SHINA...

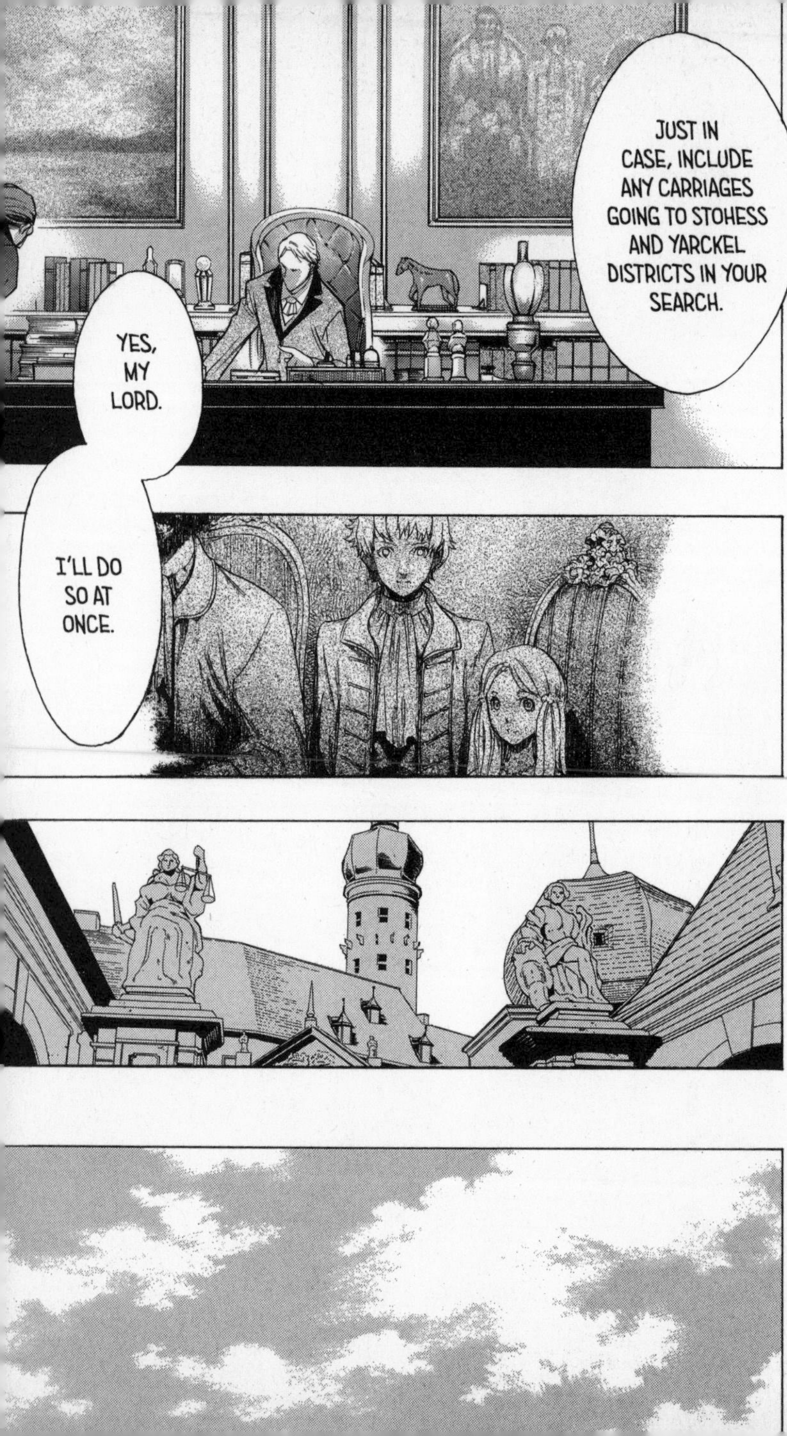
JUST IN CASE, INCLUDE ANY CARRIAGES GOING TO STOHESS AND YARCKEL DISTRICTS IN YOUR SEARCH.
YES, MY LORD.
I'LL DO SO AT ONCE.

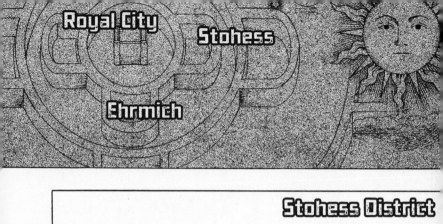

Royal City

Stohess

Ehrmich

Stohess District

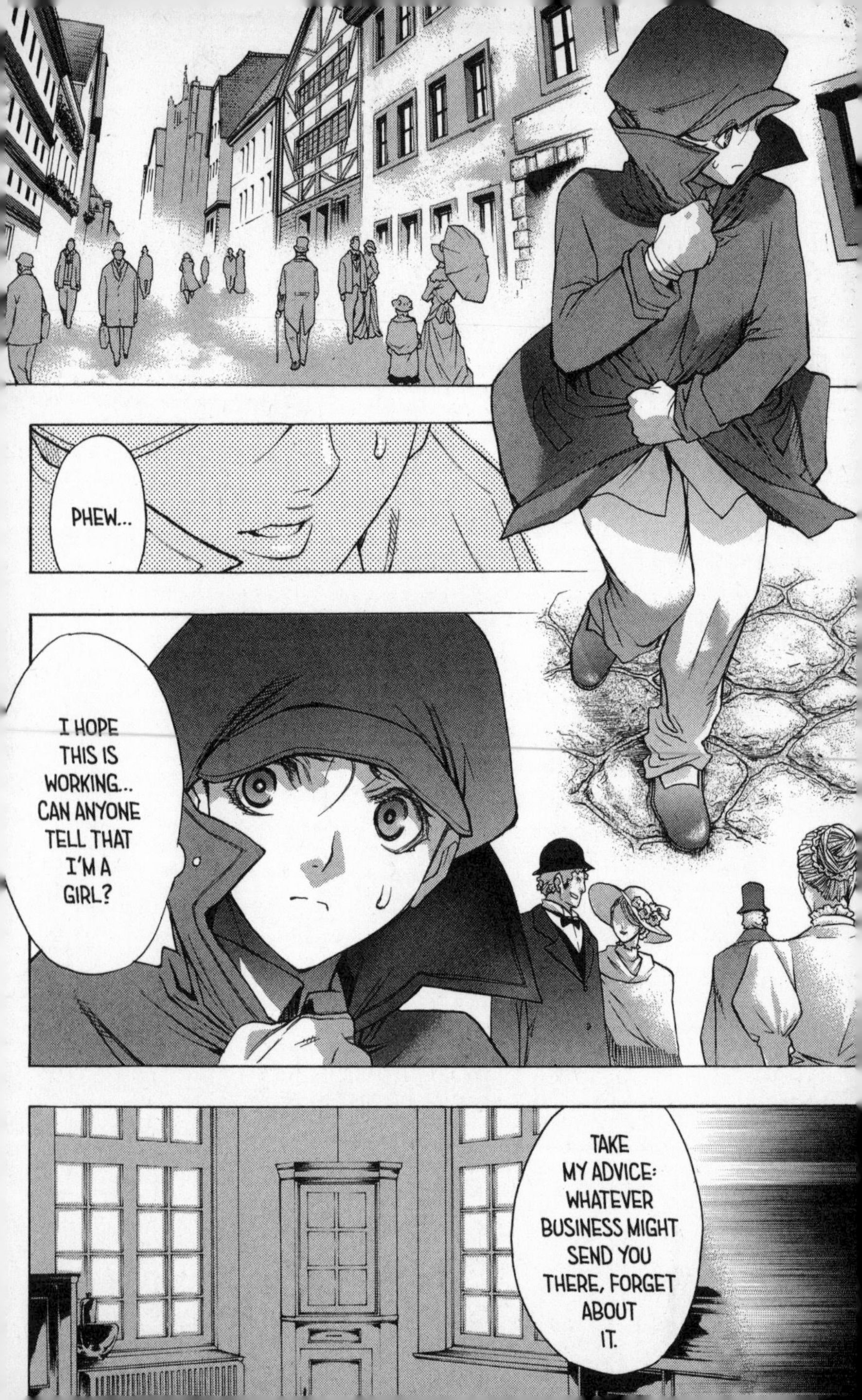
PHEW...
I HOPE THIS IS WORKING... CAN ANYONE TELL THAT I'M A GIRL?
TAKE MY ADVICE: WHATEVER BUSINESS MIGHT SEND YOU THERE, FORGET ABOUT IT.

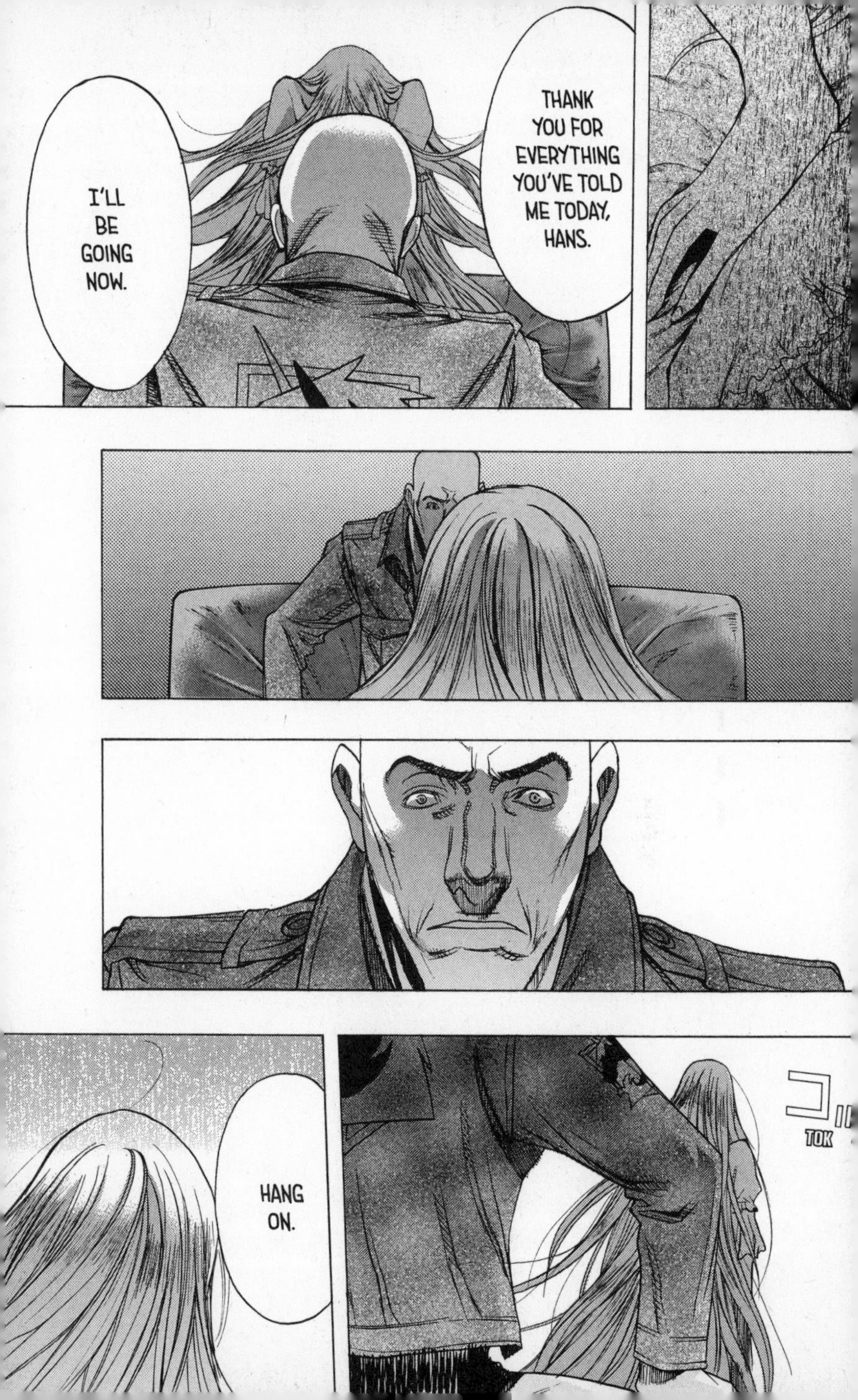
THANK YOU FOR EVERYTHING YOU'VE TOLD ME TODAY, HANS.
I'LL BE GOING NOW.
TOK
HANG ON.

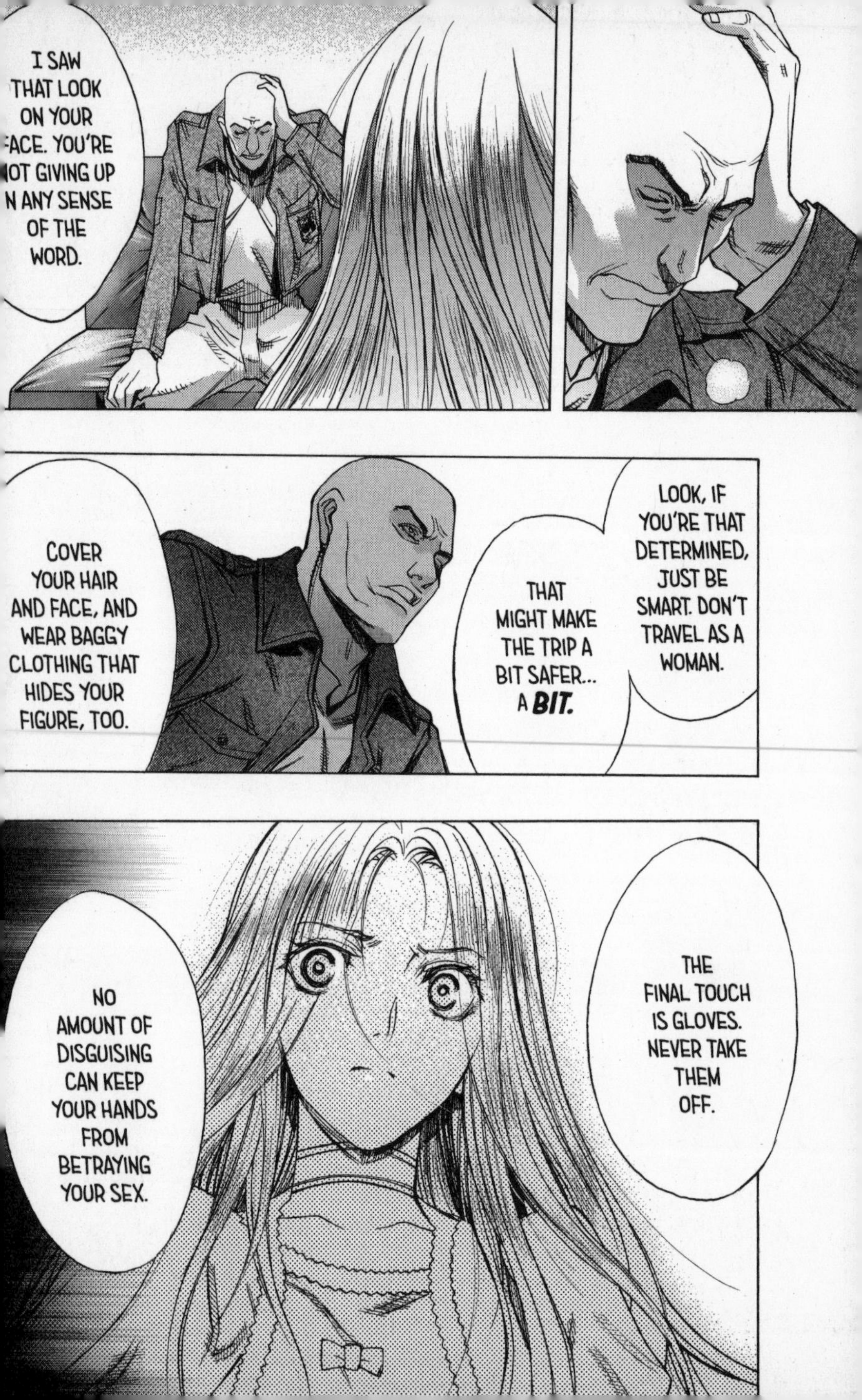
I SAW THAT LOOK ON YOUR ACE. YOU'RE OT GIVING UP N ANY SENSE OF THE WORD.
LOOK, IF YOU'RE THAT DETERMINED, JUST BE SMART. DON'T TRAVEL AS A WOMAN.
THAT MIGHT MAKE THE TRIP A BIT SAFER... A ***BIT.***
COVER YOUR HAIR AND FACE, AND WEAR BAGGY CLOTHING THAT HIDES YOUR FIGURE, TOO.
THE FINAL TOUCH IS GLOVES. NEVER TAKE THEM OFF.
NO AMOUNT OF DISGUISING CAN KEEP YOUR HANDS FROM BETRAYING YOUR SEX.

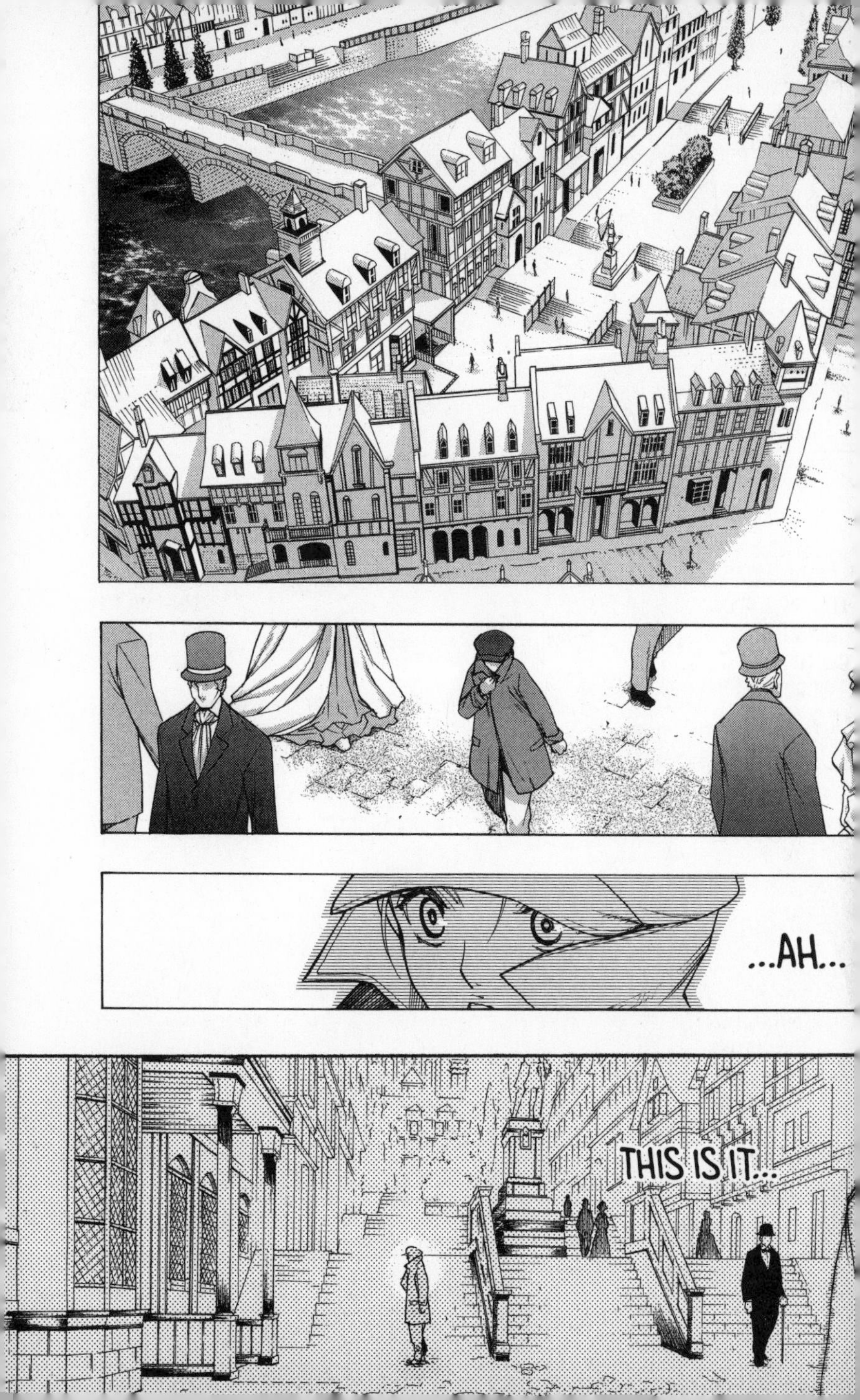
...AH...
THIS IS IT...

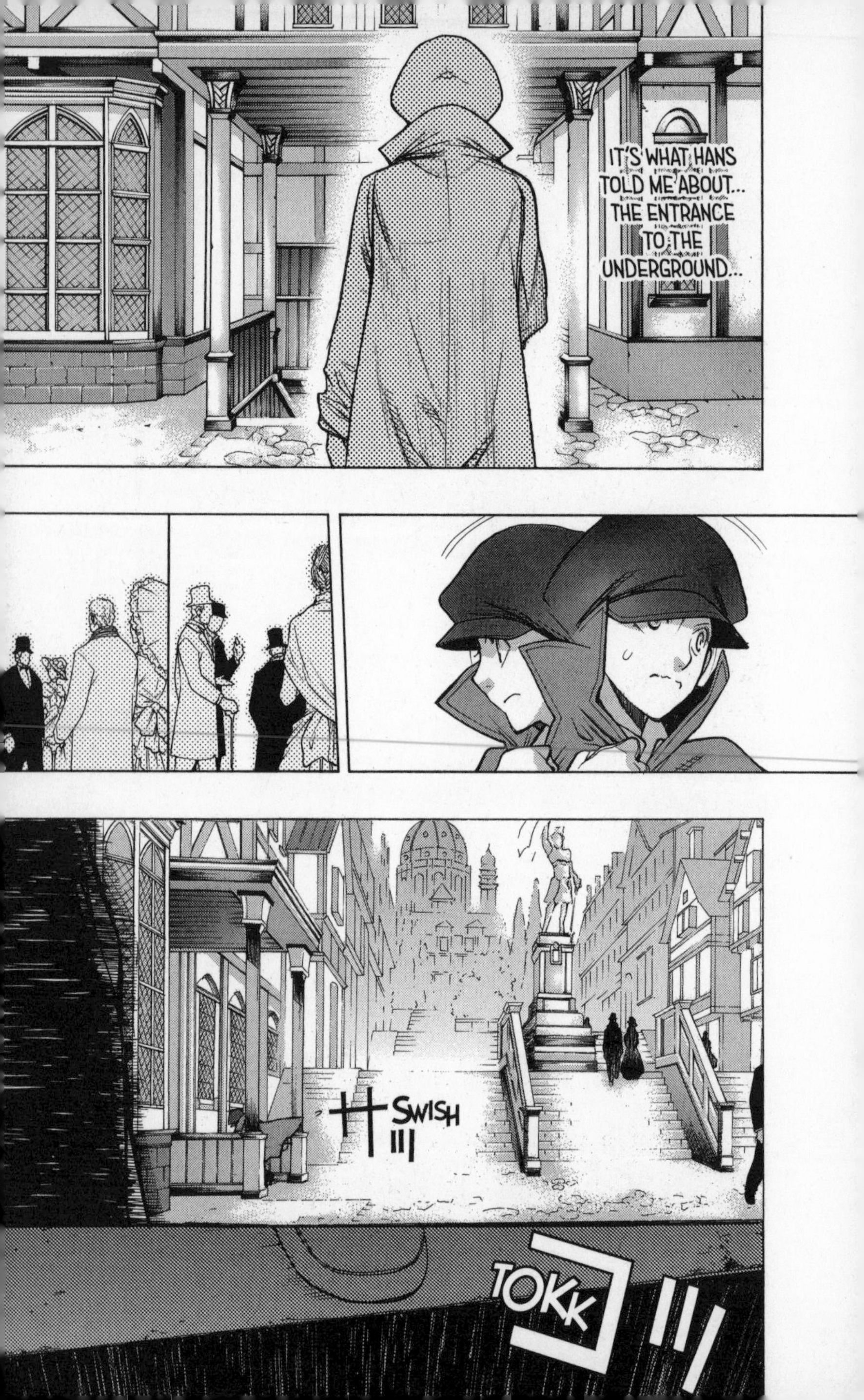
IT'S WHAT HANS TOLD ME ABOUT... THE ENTRANCE TO THE UNDERGROUND...
SWISH
TOKK

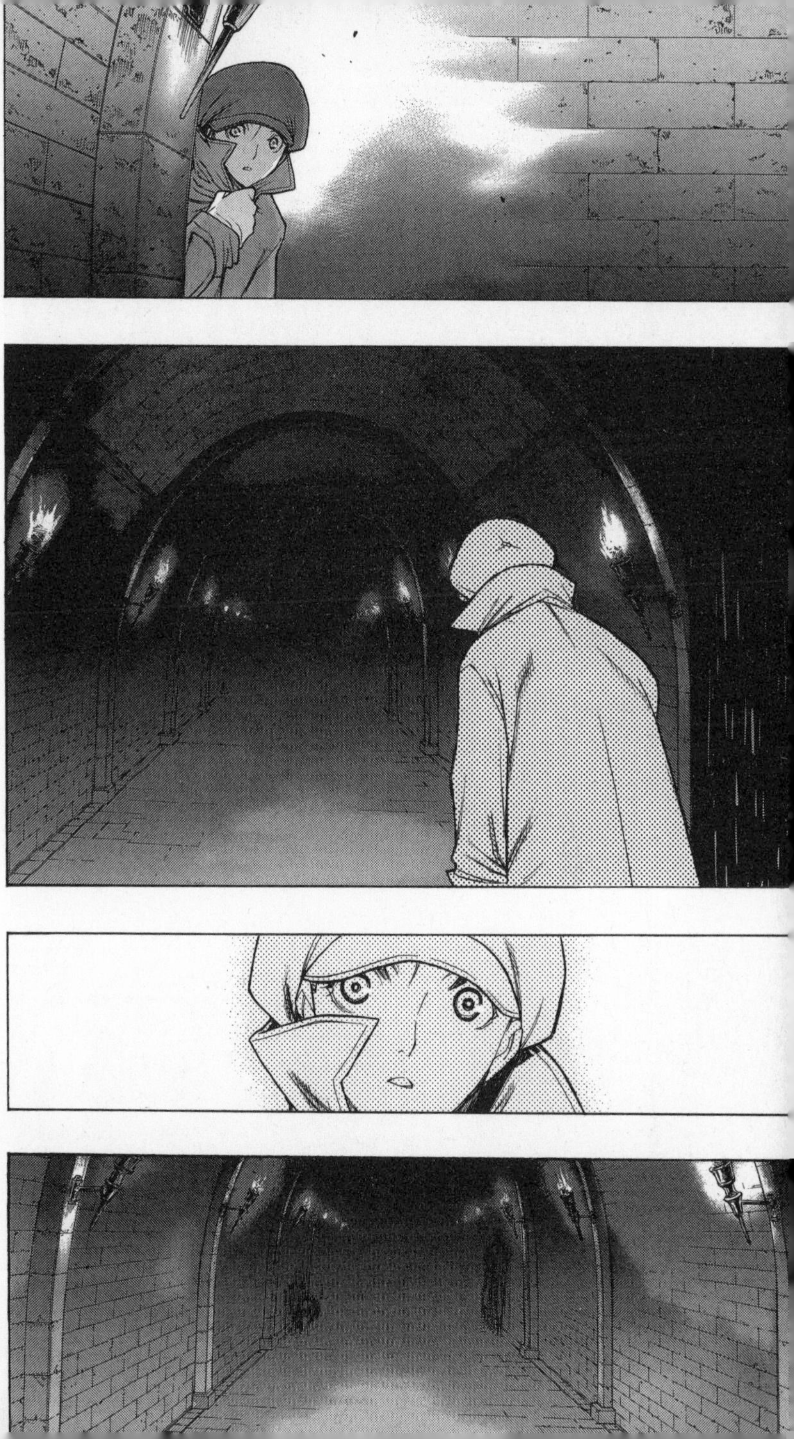

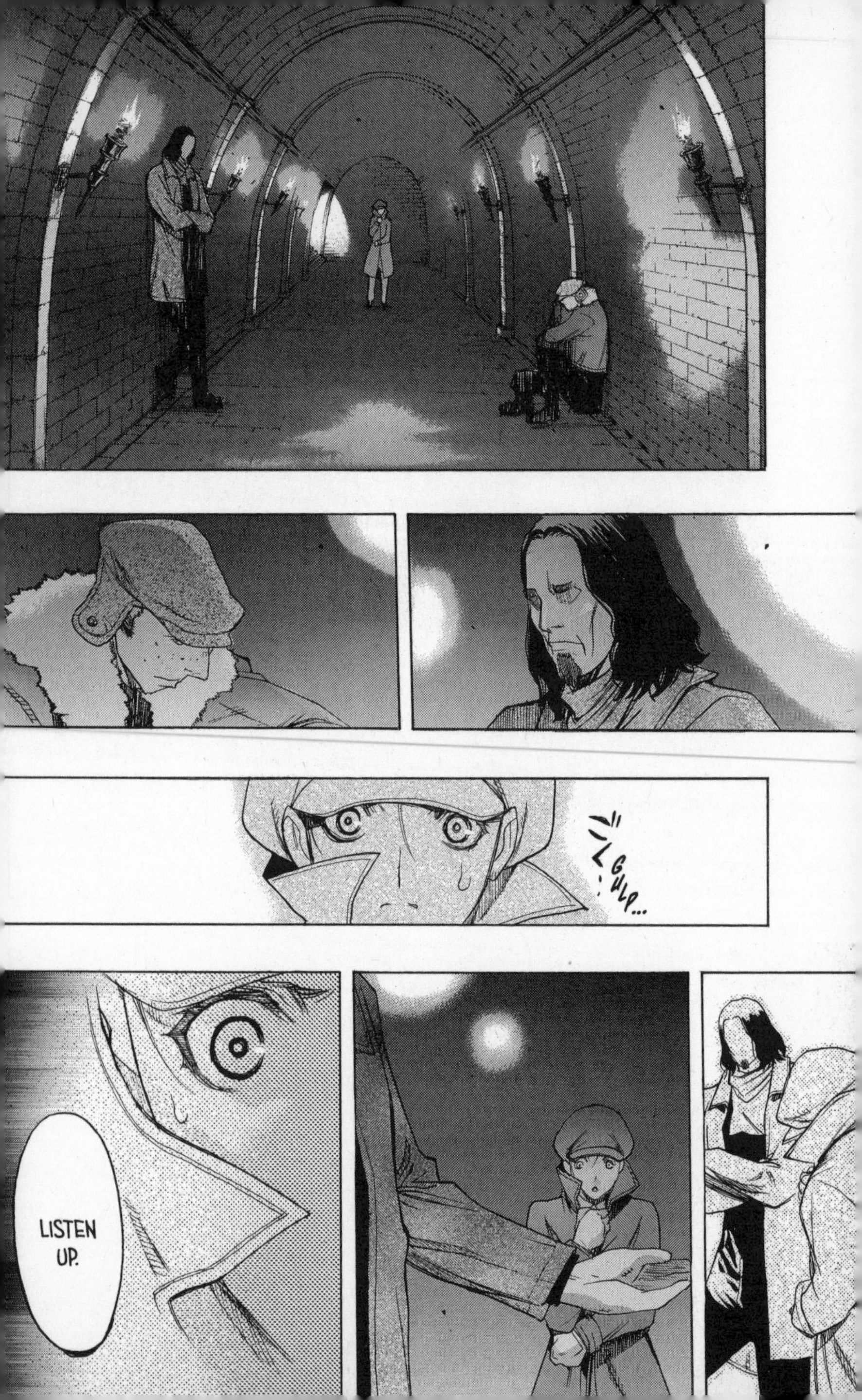
GULP...
LISTEN UP.

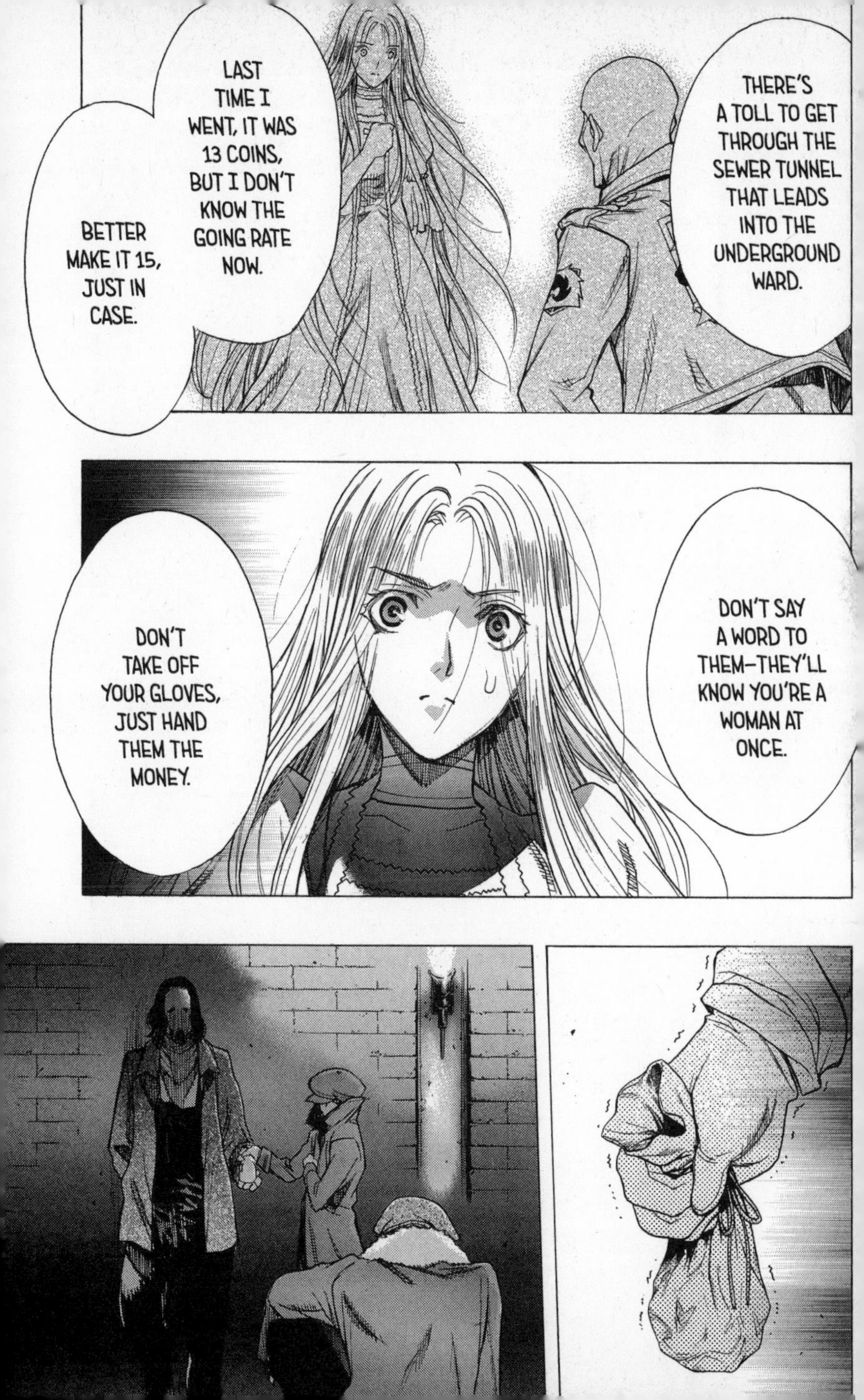
THERE'S A TOLL TO GET THROUGH THE SEWER TUNNEL THAT LEADS INTO THE UNDERGROUND WARD.
LAST TIME I WENT, IT WAS 13 COINS, BUT I DON'T KNOW THE GOING RATE NOW.
BETTER MAKE IT 15, JUST IN CASE.
DON'T SAY A WORD TO THEM—THEY'LL KNOW YOU'RE A WOMAN AT ONCE.
DON'T TAKE OFF YOUR GLOVES, JUST HAND THEM THE MONEY.

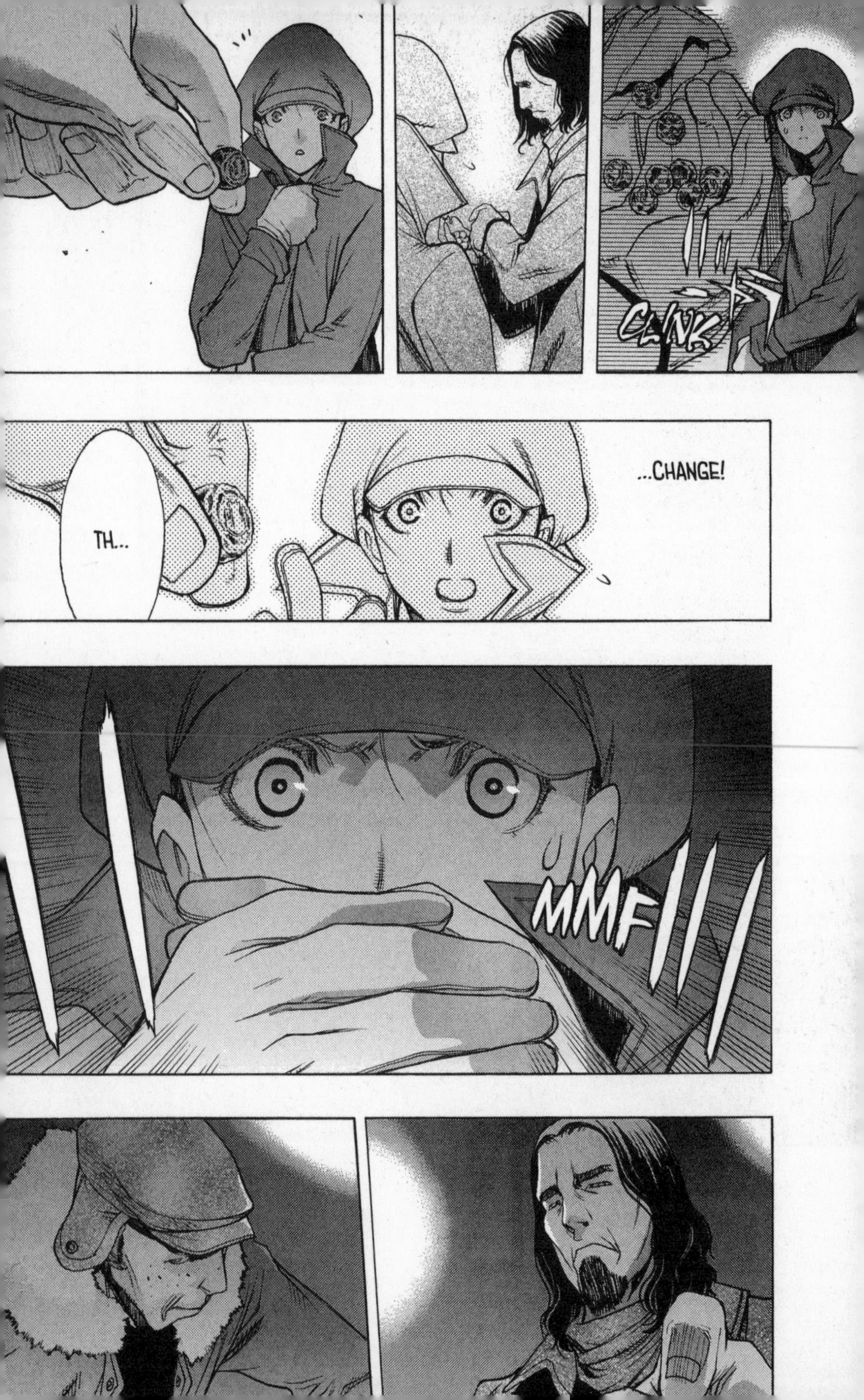
CLINK
...CHANGE!
TH...
MMF

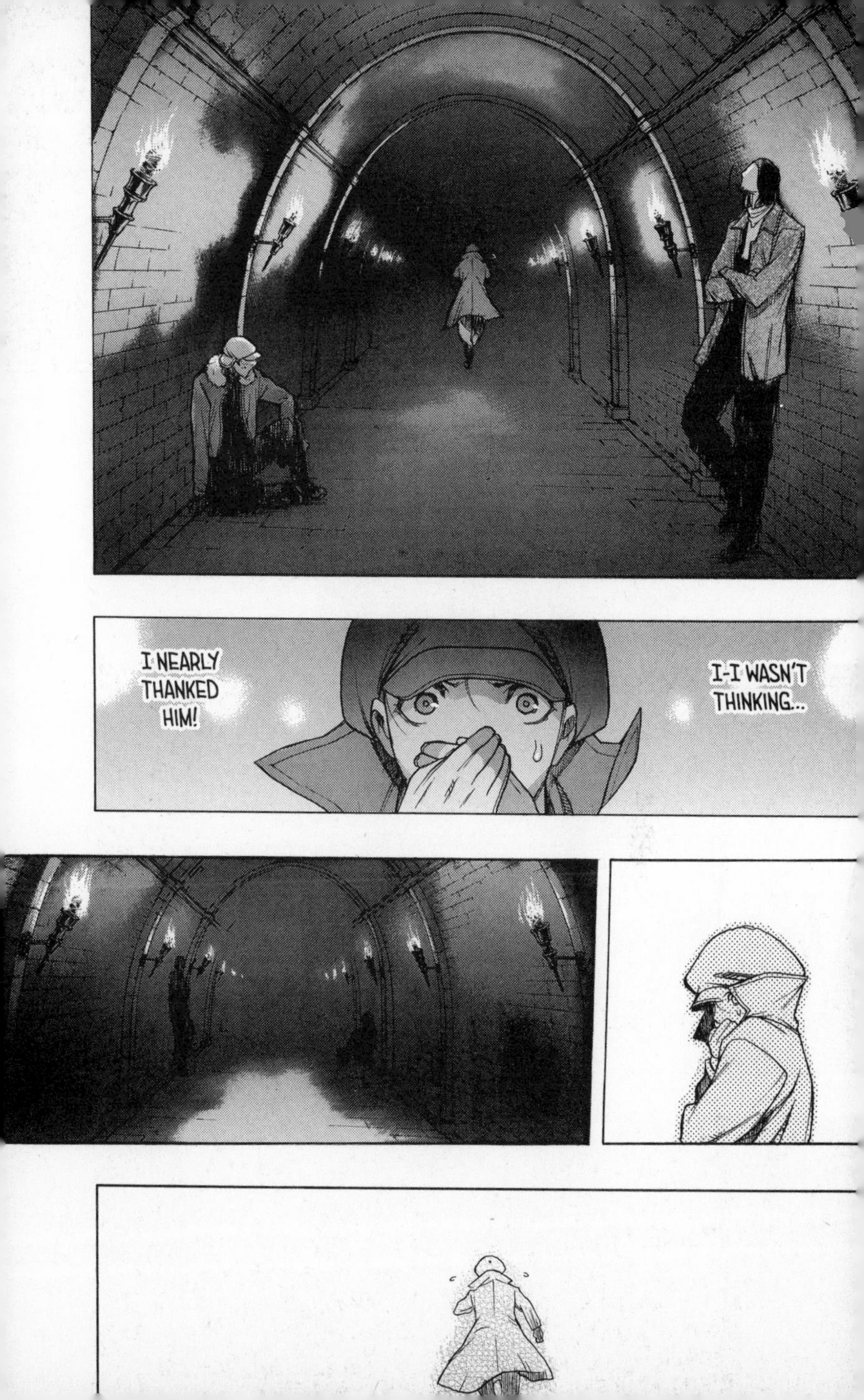
I-I WASN'T THINKING...
I NEARLY THANKED HIM!

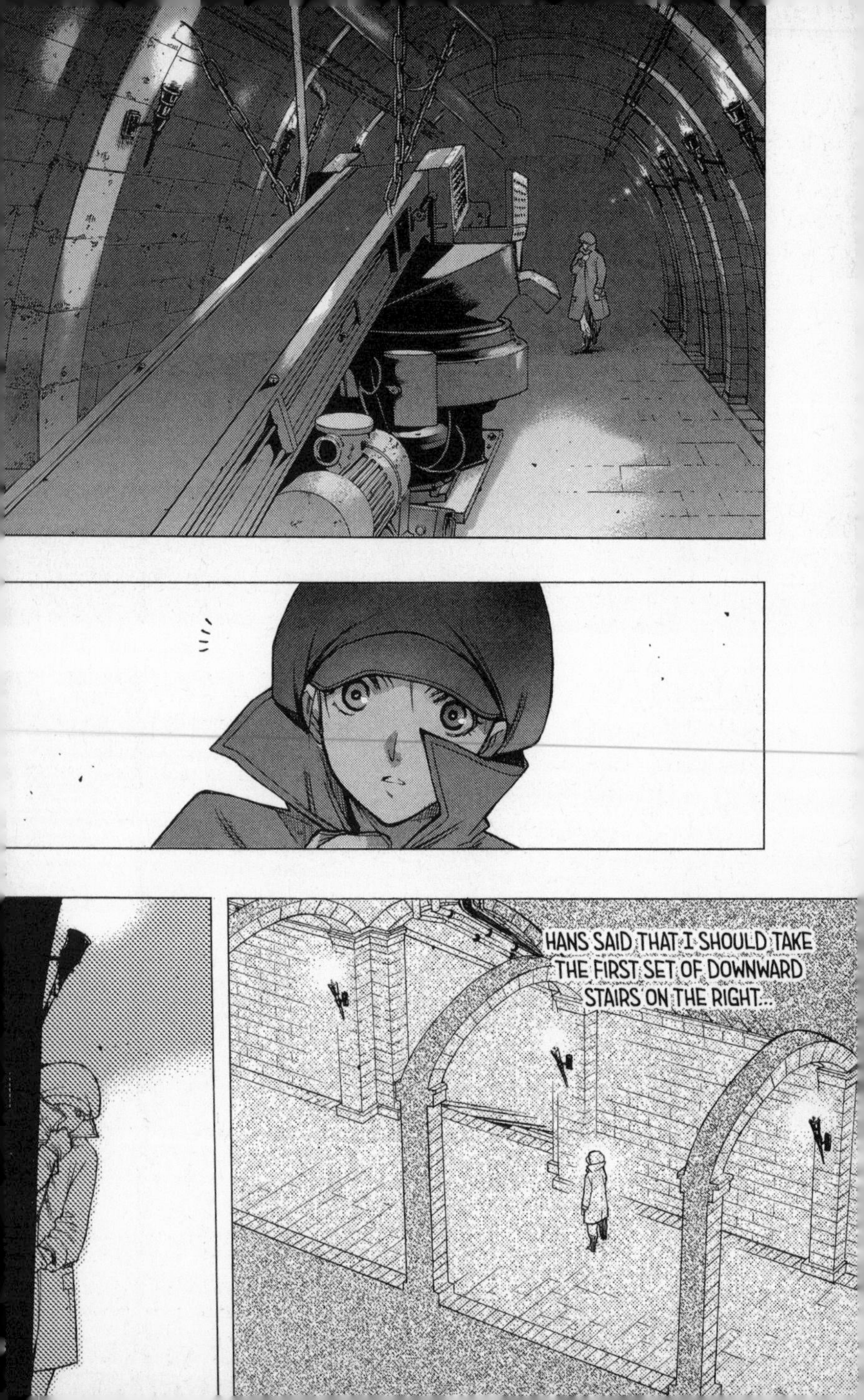
HANS SAID THAT I SHOULD TAKE THE FIRST SET OF DOWNWARD STAIRS ON THE RIGHT...

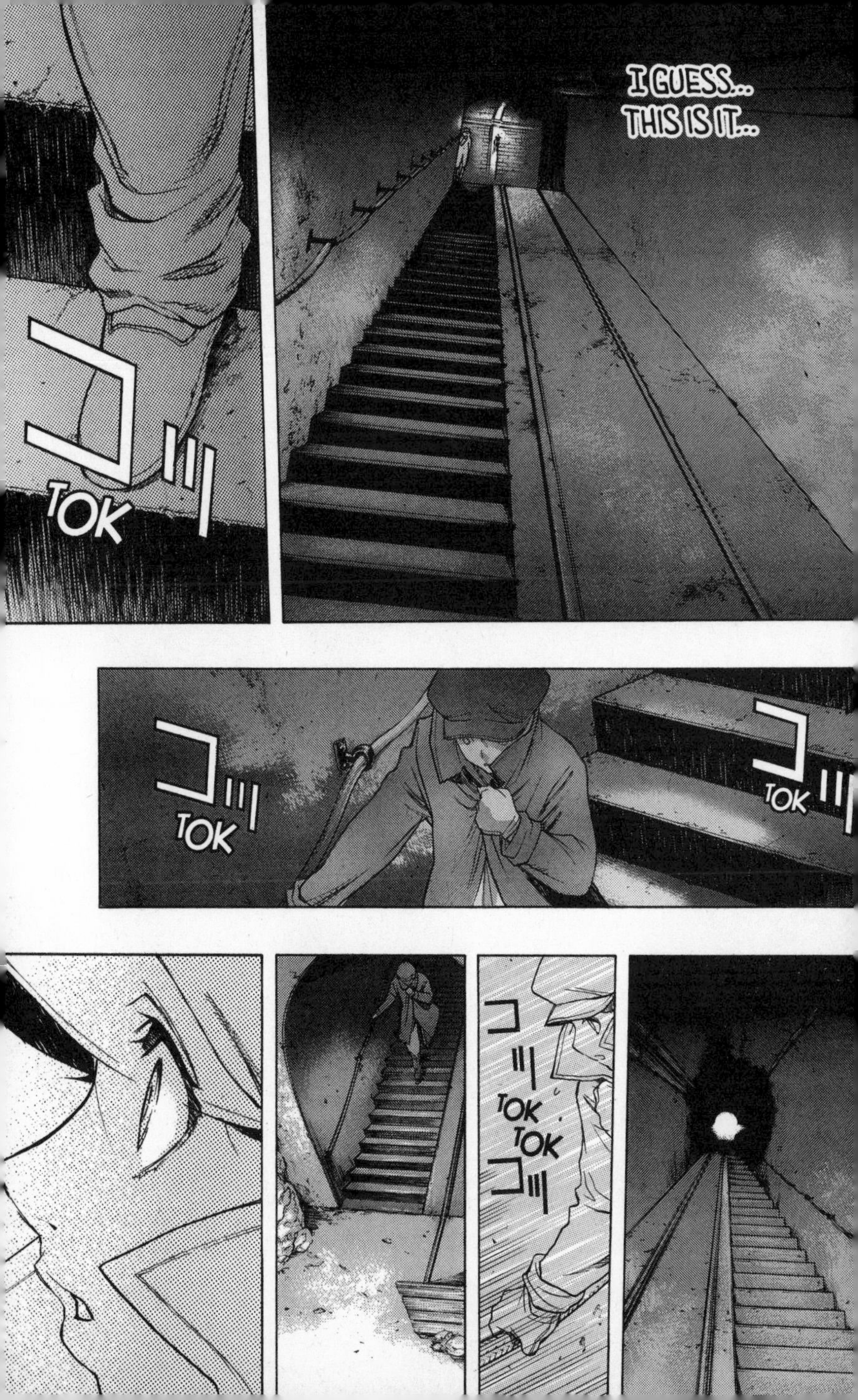
I GUESS...
THIS IS IT...
TOK
TOK
TOK
TOK
TOK

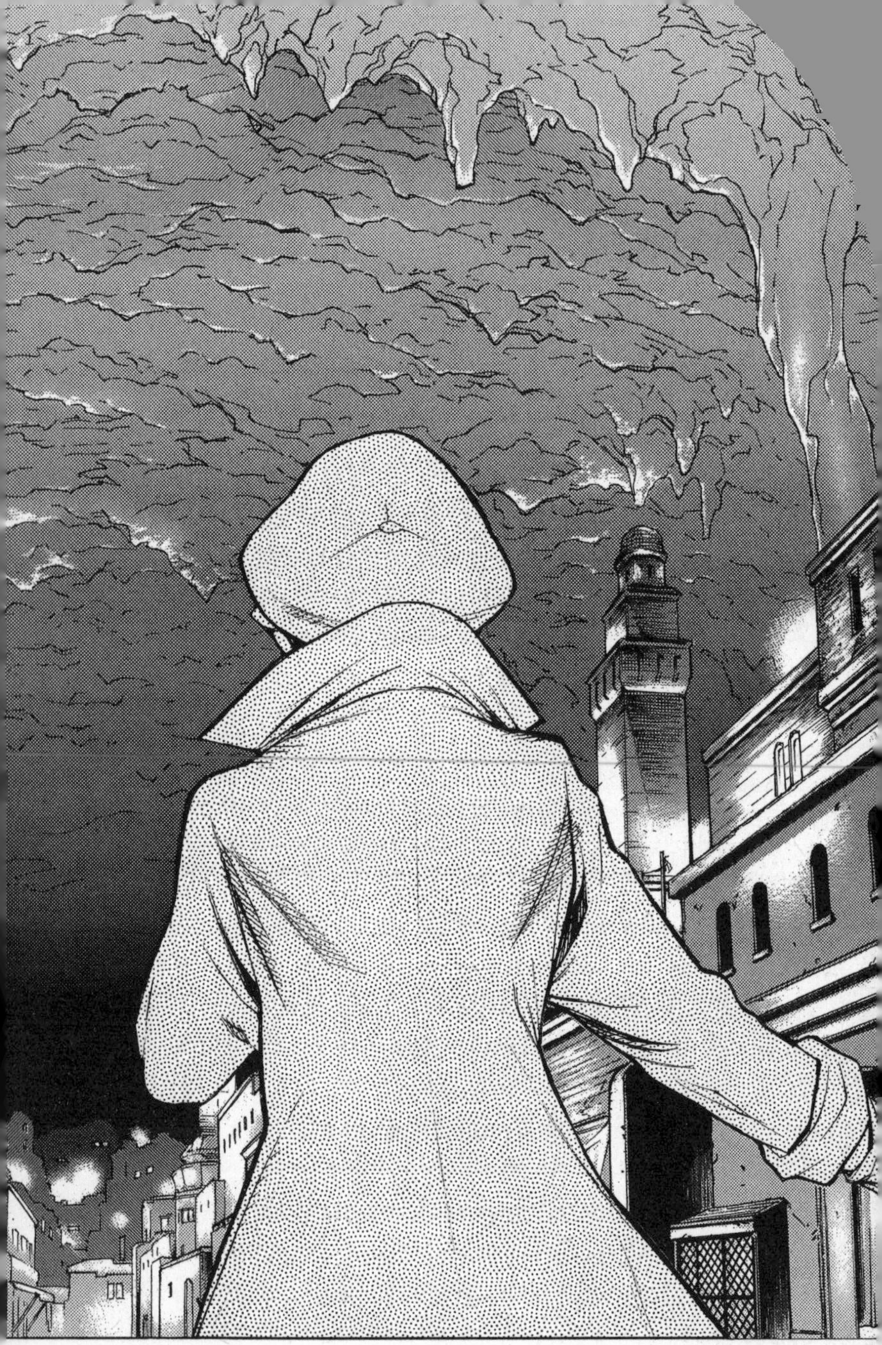

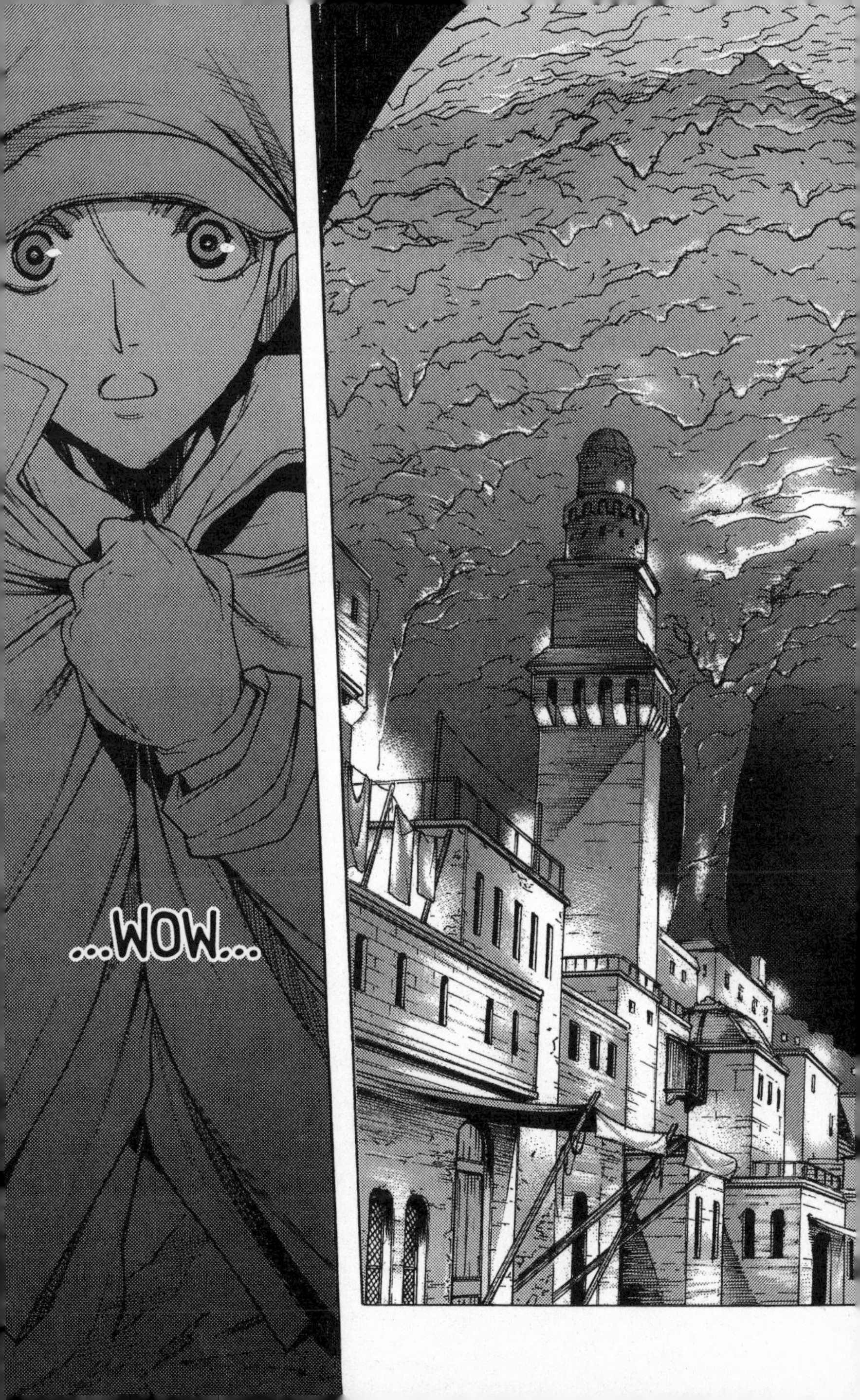
...WOW...

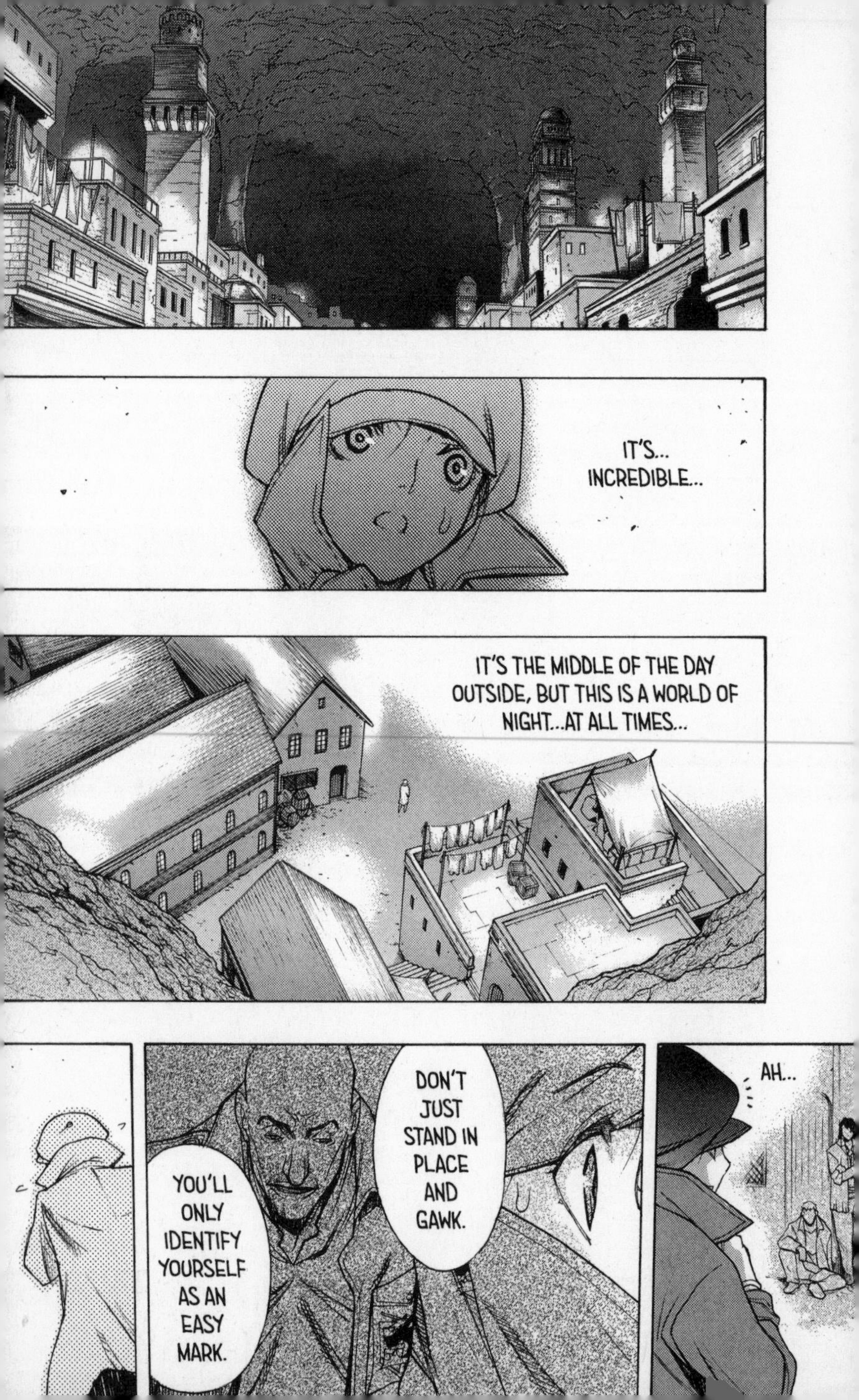
IT'S... INCREDIBLE...
IT'S THE MIDDLE OF THE DAY OUTSIDE, BUT THIS IS A WORLD OF NIGHT...AT ALL TIMES...
AH...
DON'T JUST STAND IN PLACE AND GAWK.
YOU'LL ONLY IDENTIFY YOURSELF AS AN EASY MARK.

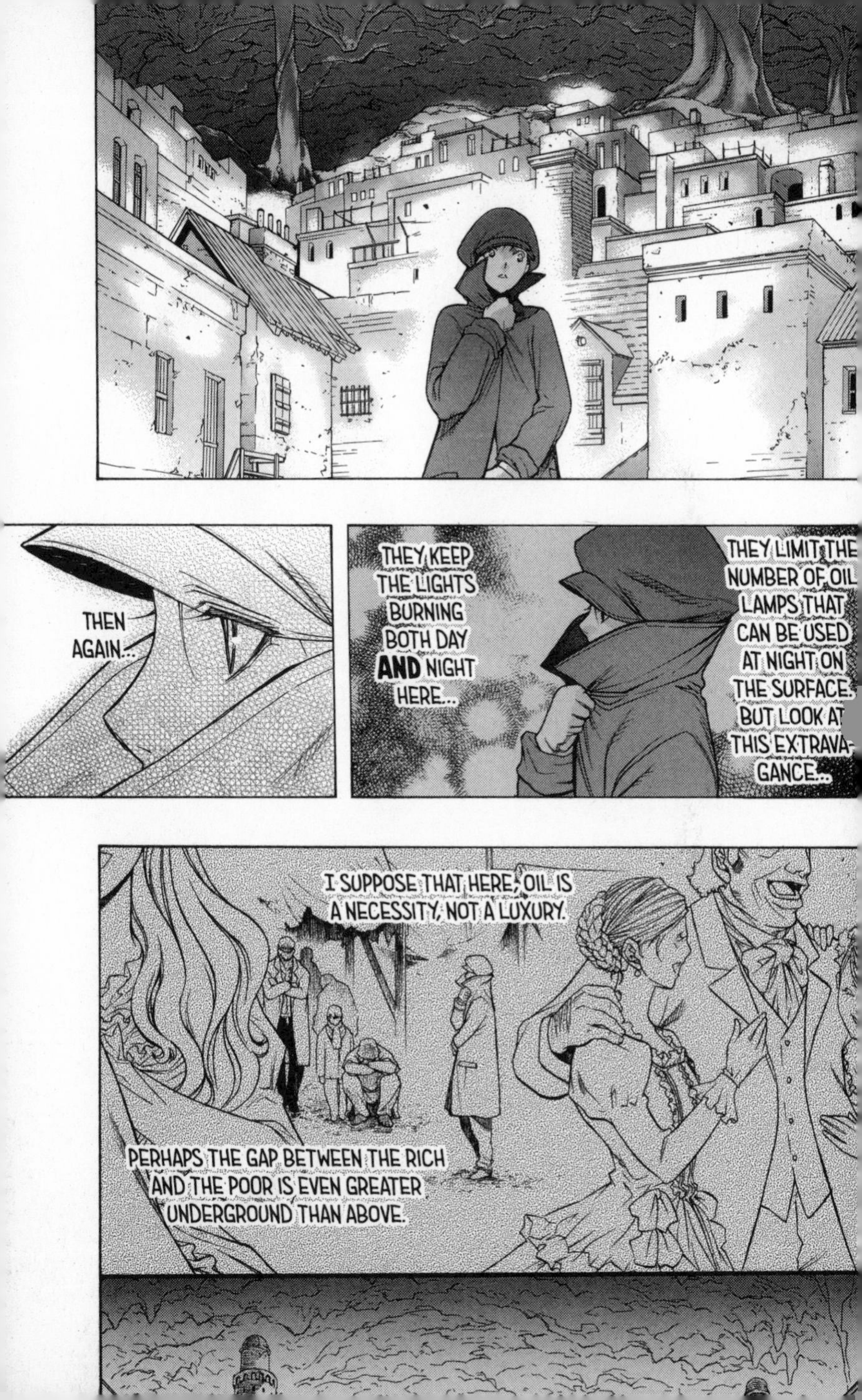
THEY LIMIT THE NUMBER OF OIL LAMPS THAT CAN BE USED AT NIGHT ON THE SURFACE.
BUT LOOK AT THIS EXTRAVA-GANCE...
THEY KEEP THE LIGHTS BURNING BOTH DAY AND NIGHT HERE...
THEN AGAIN...
I SUPPOSE THAT HERE, OIL IS A NECESSITY, NOT A LUXURY.
PERHAPS THE GAP BETWEEN THE RICH AND THE POOR IS EVEN GREATER UNDERGROUND THAN ABOVE.

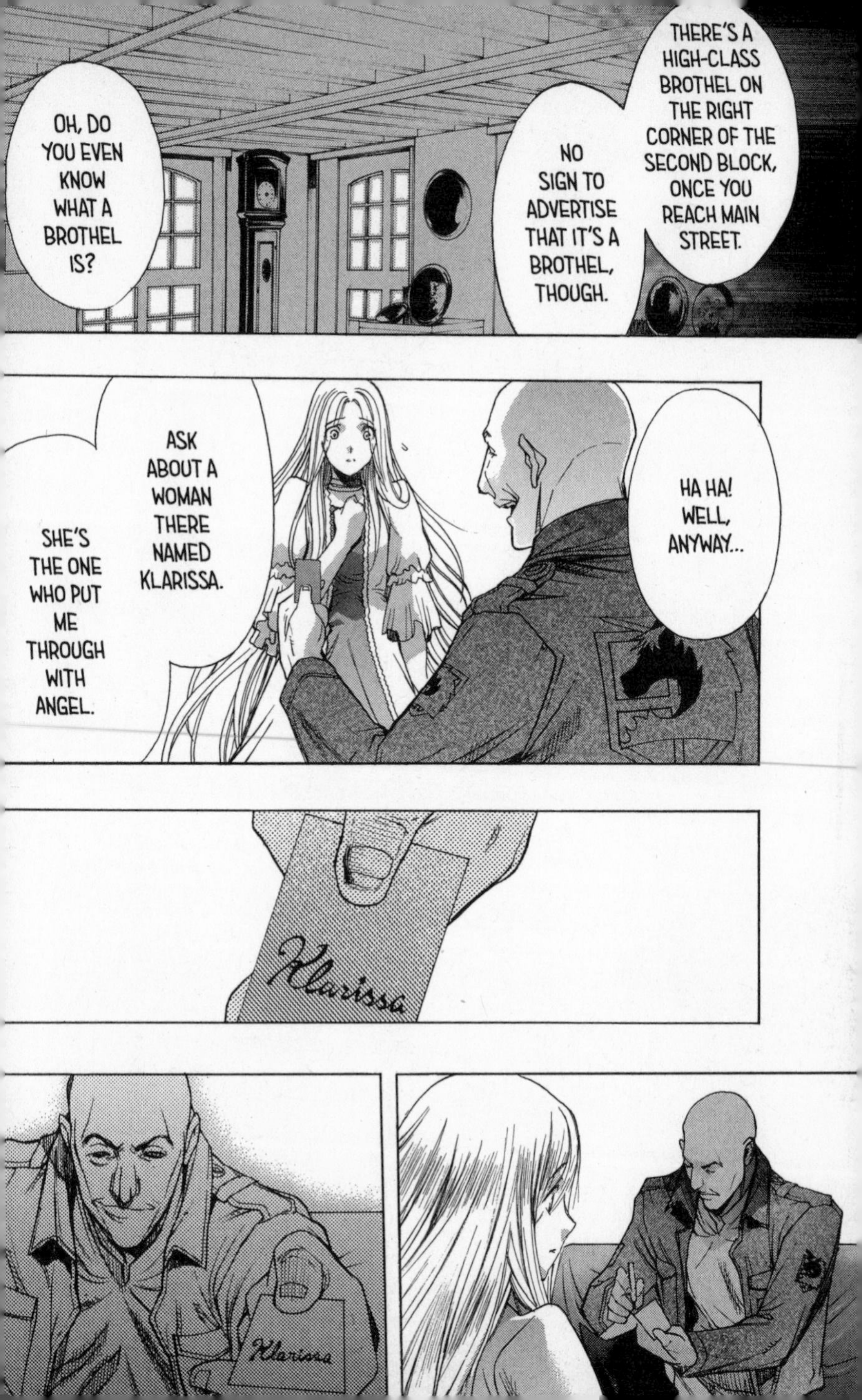
THERE'S A HIGH-CLASS BROTHEL ON THE RIGHT CORNER OF THE SECOND BLOCK, ONCE YOU REACH MAIN STREET.
NO SIGN TO ADVERTISE THAT IT'S A BROTHEL, THOUGH.
OH, DO YOU EVEN KNOW WHAT A BROTHEL IS?
HA HA! WELL, ANYWAY...
ASK ABOUT A WOMAN THERE NAMED KLARISSA.
SHE'S THE ONE WHO PUT ME THROUGH WITH ANGEL.
Klarissa
Klarissa

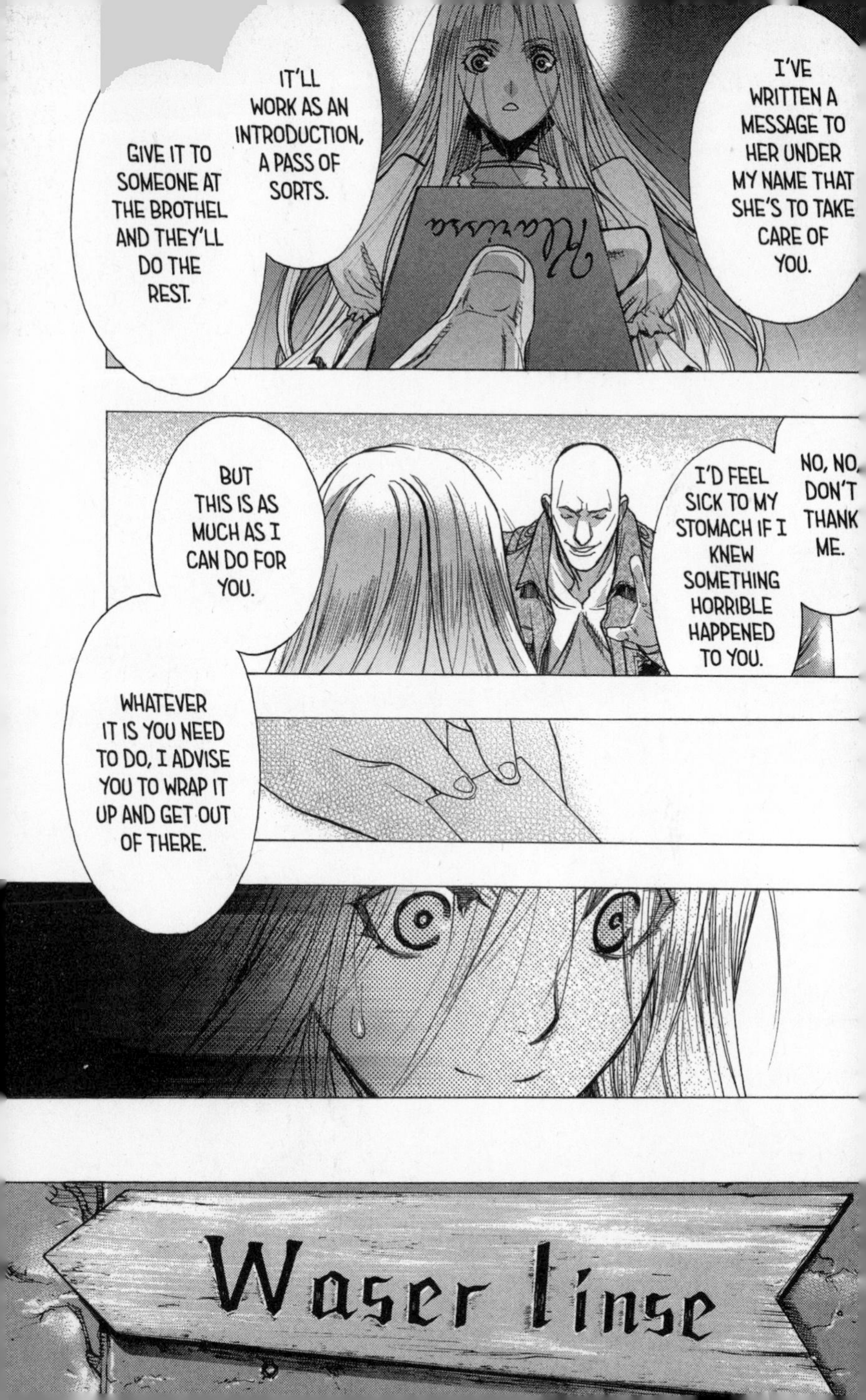
I'VE WRITTEN A MESSAGE TO HER UNDER MY NAME THAT SHE'S TO TAKE CARE OF YOU.
IT'LL WORK AS AN INTRODUCTION, A PASS OF SORTS.
GIVE IT TO SOMEONE AT THE BROTHEL AND THEY'LL DO THE REST.
NO, NO, DON'T THANK ME.
I'D FEEL SICK TO MY STOMACH IF I KNEW SOMETHING HORRIBLE HAPPENED TO YOU.
BUT THIS IS AS MUCH AS I CAN DO FOR YOU.
WHATEVER IT IS YOU NEED TO DO, I ADVISE YOU TO WRAP IT UP AND GET OUT OF THERE.
Waser linse

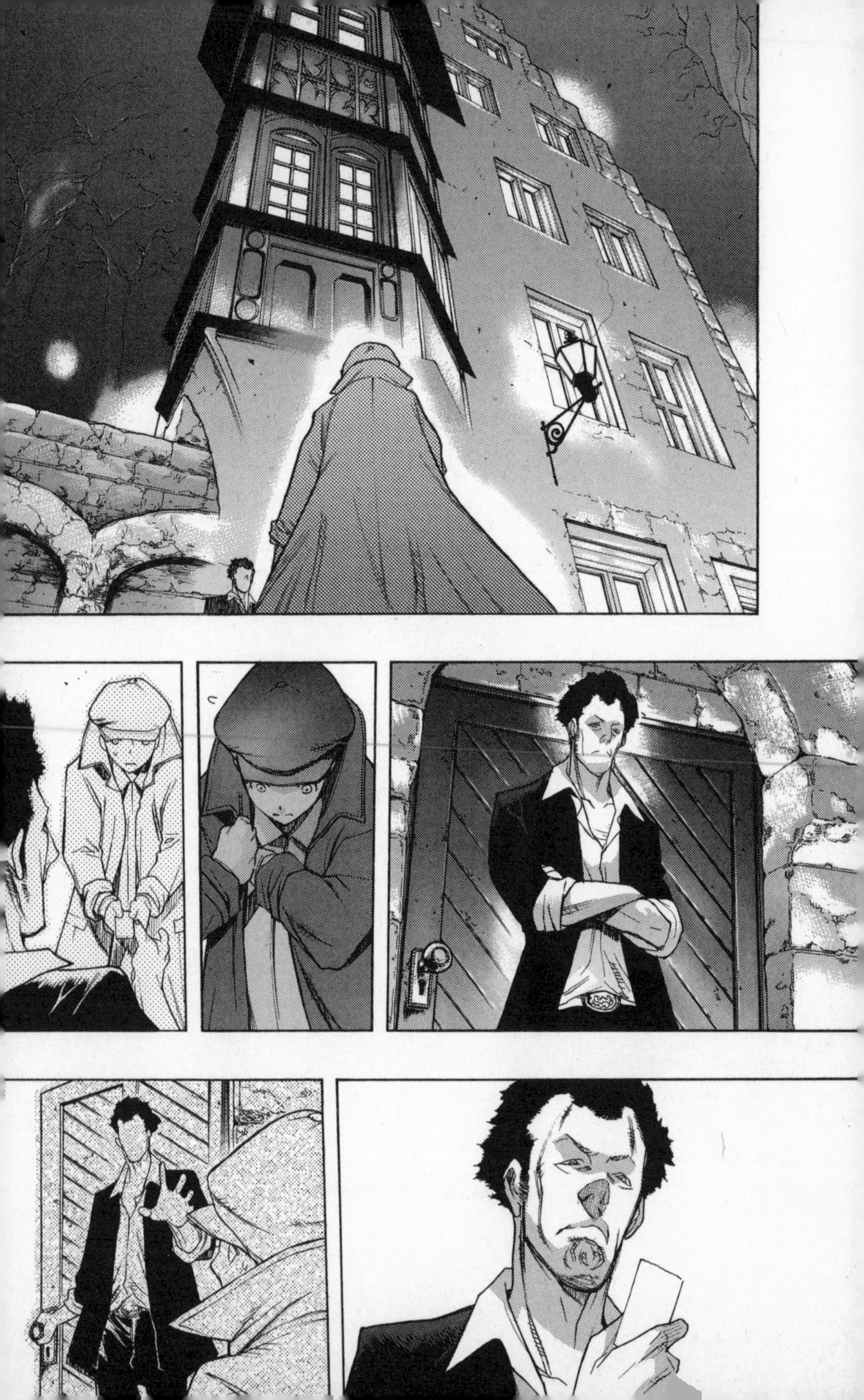

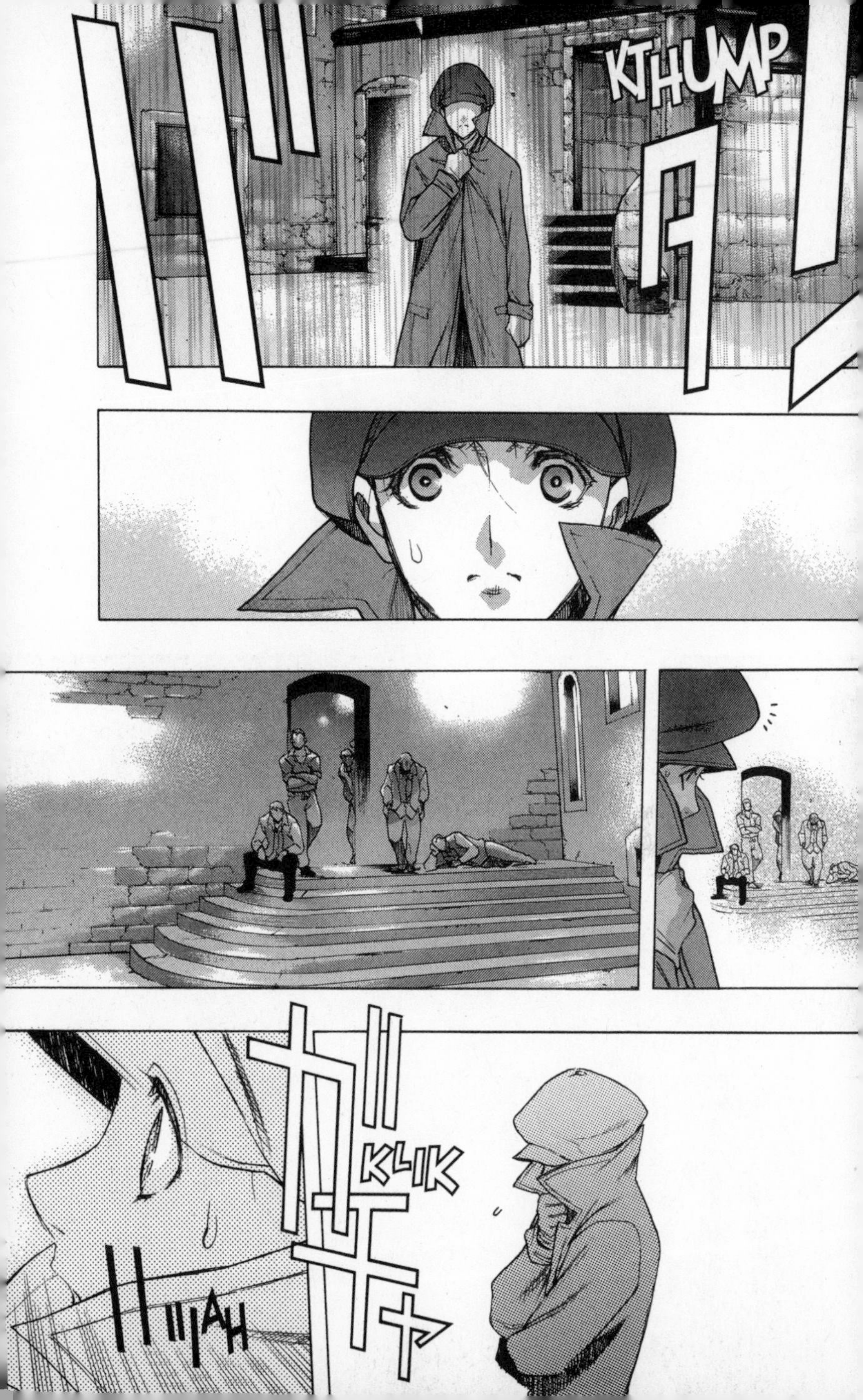
KTHUMP
KLIK
HIIIIAH

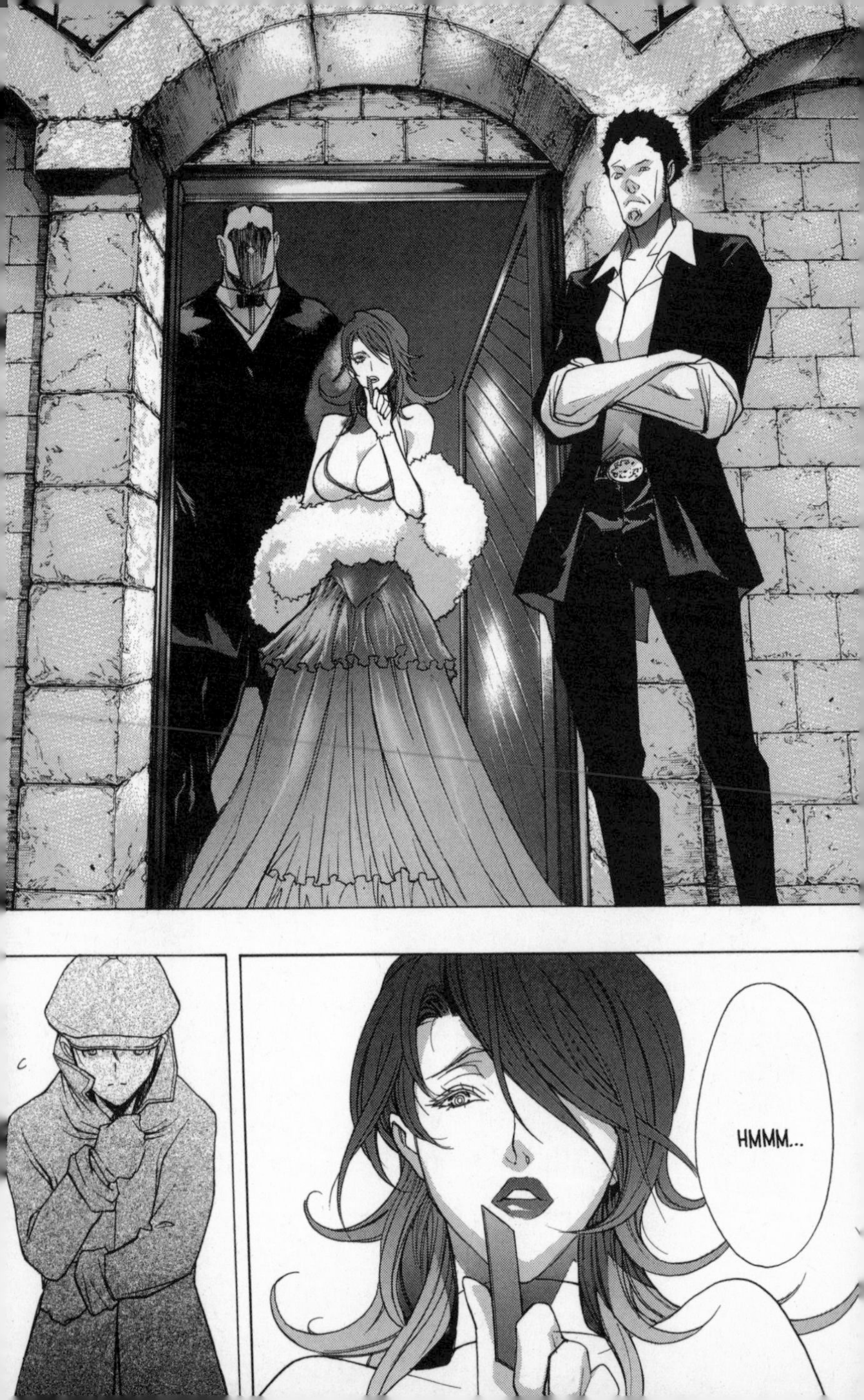
HMMM...

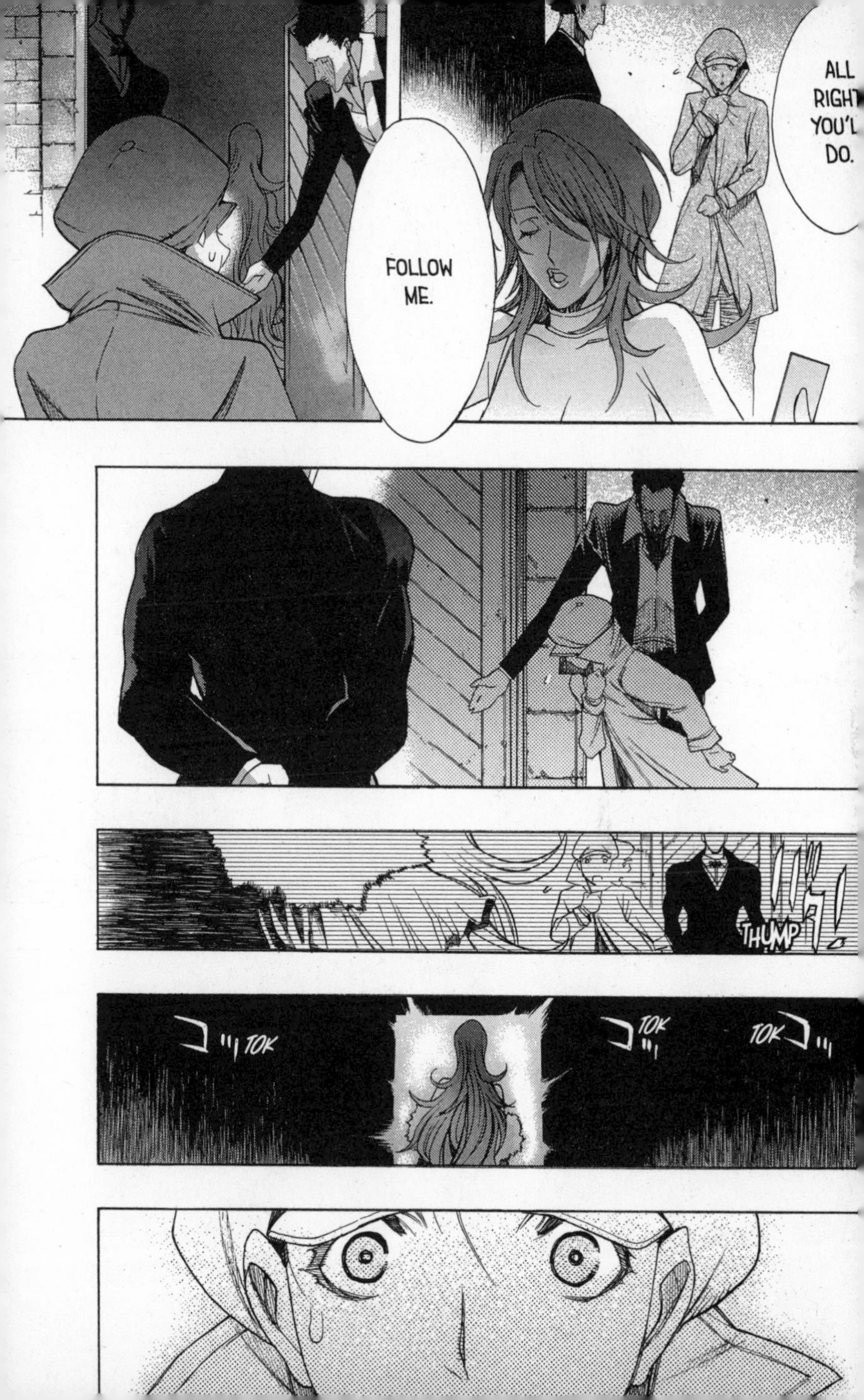
ALL RIGHT YOU'L DO.
FOLLOW ME.
THUMP
TOK
TOK
TOK

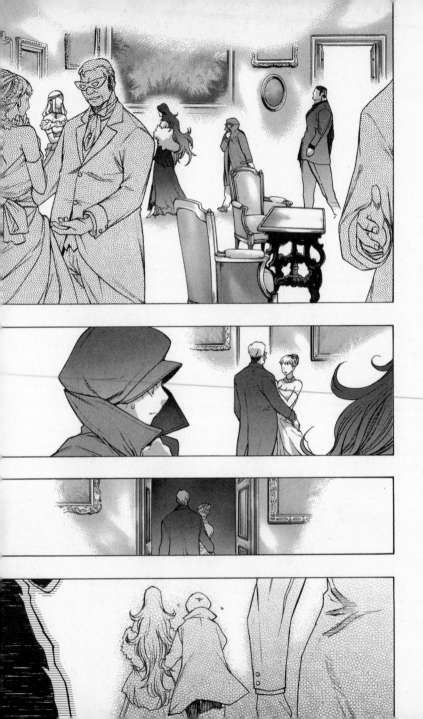

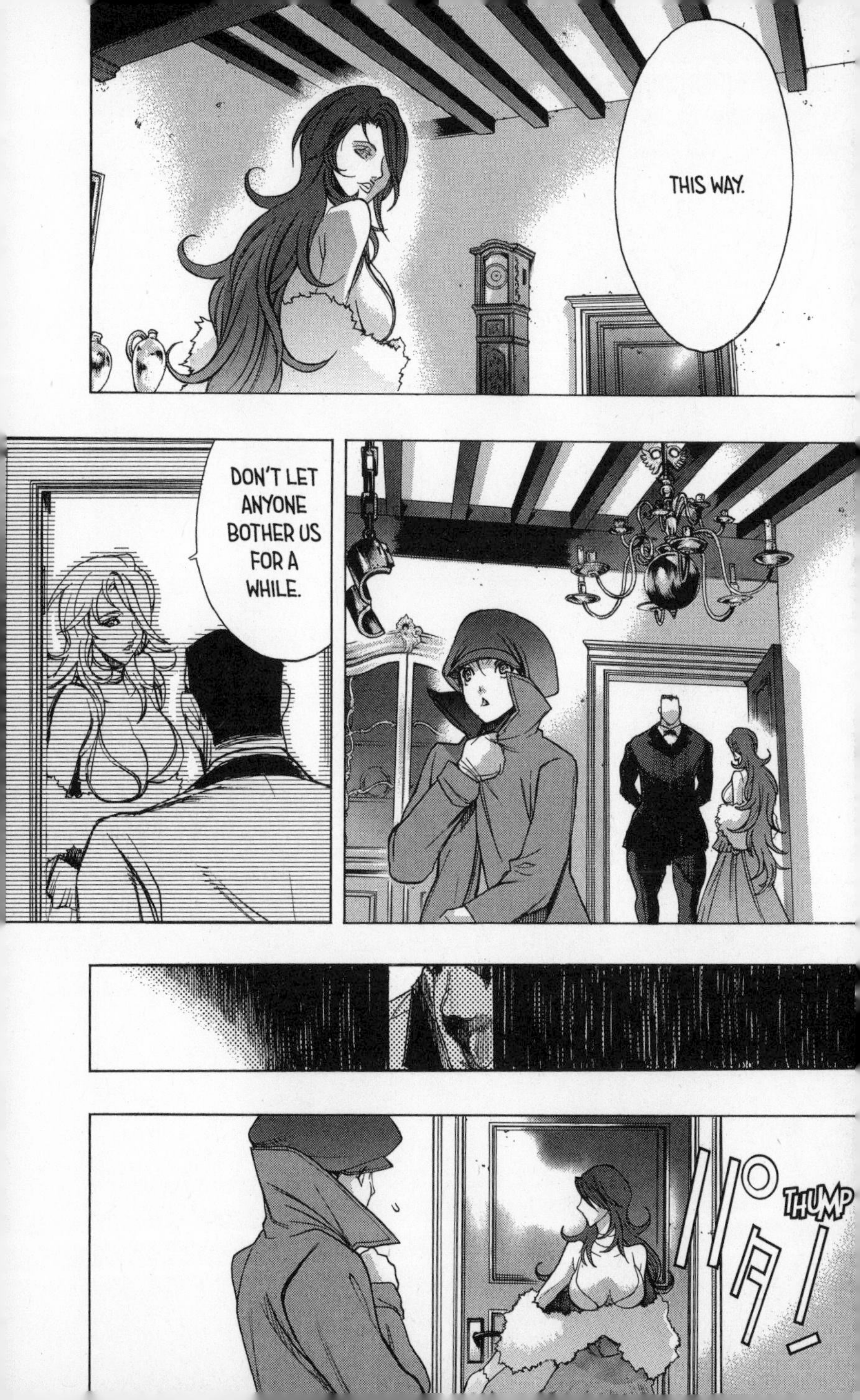
THIS WAY.
DON'T LET ANYONE BOTHER US FOR A WHILE.
パタ!
THUMP

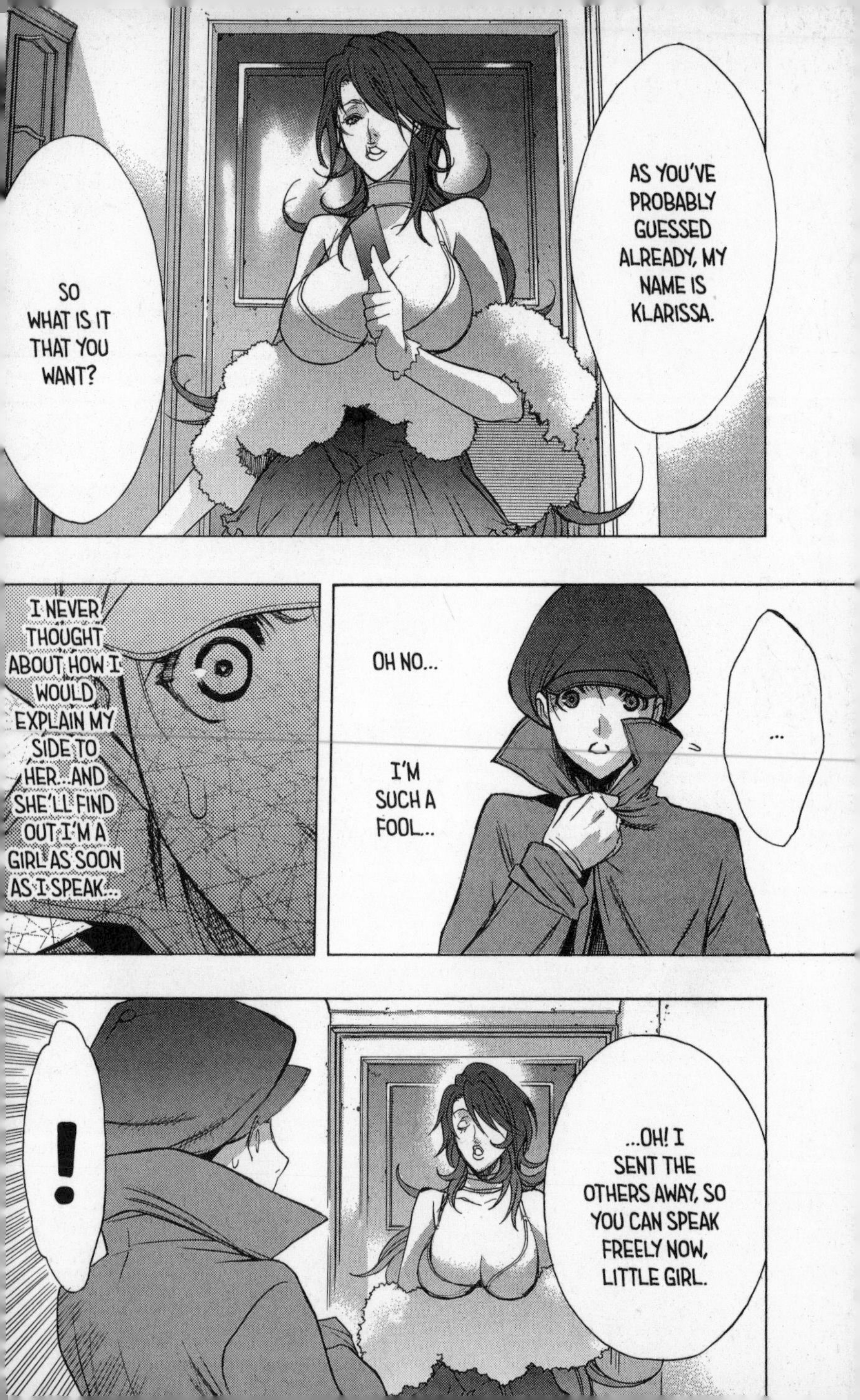
AS YOU'VE PROBABLY GUESSED ALREADY, MY NAME IS KLARISSA.
SO WHAT IS IT THAT YOU WANT?
...
OH NO...
I'M SUCH A FOOL...
I NEVER THOUGHT ABOUT HOW I WOULD EXPLAIN MY SIDE TO HER...AND SHE'LL FIND OUT I'M A GIRL AS SOON AS I SPEAK...
...OH! I SENT THE OTHERS AWAY, SO YOU CAN SPEAK FREELY NOW, LITTLE GIRL.
!

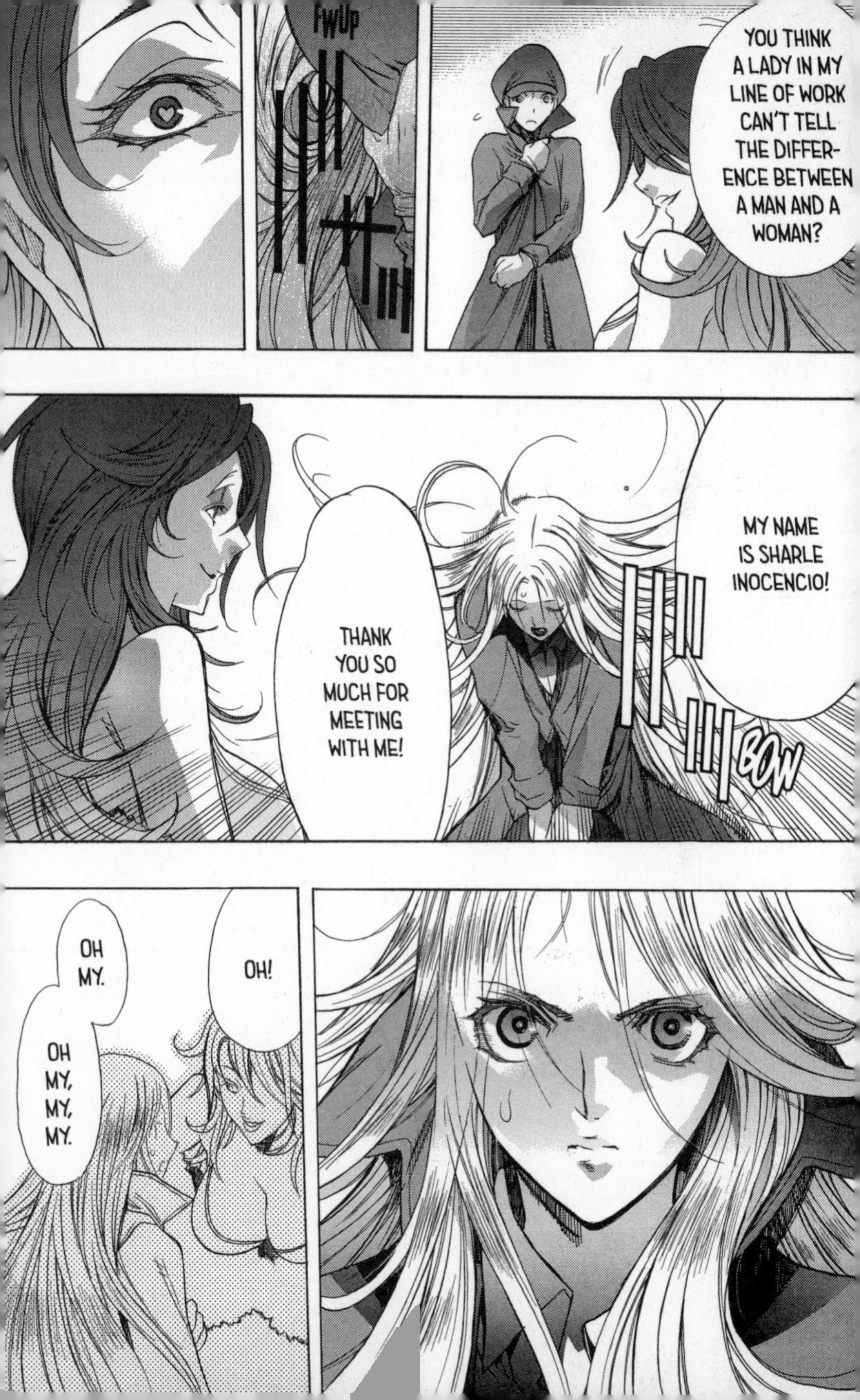
YOU THINK A LADY IN MY LINE OF WORK CAN'T TELL THE DIFFERENCE BETWEEN A MAN AND A WOMAN?
FWUP
MY NAME IS SHARLE INOCENCIO!
BOW
THANK YOU SO MUCH FOR MEETING WITH ME!
OH!
OH MY.
OH MY, MY, MY.

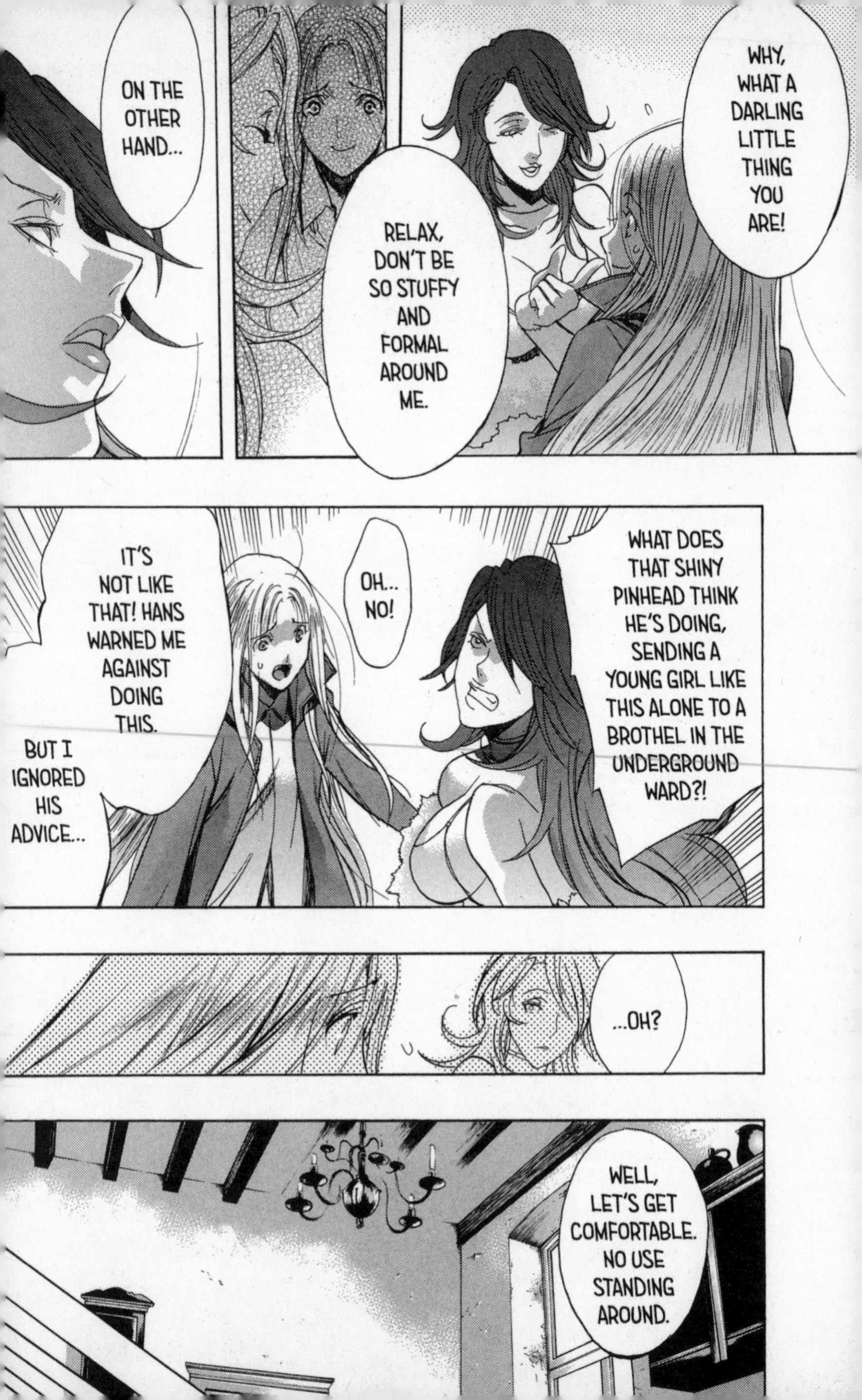
WHY, WHAT A DARLING LITTLE THING YOU ARE!
RELAX, DON'T BE SO STUFFY AND FORMAL AROUND ME.
ON THE OTHER HAND...
WHAT DOES THAT SHINY PINHEAD THINK HE'S DOING, SENDING A YOUNG GIRL LIKE THIS ALONE TO A BROTHEL IN THE UNDERGROUND WARD?!
OH... NO!
IT'S NOT LIKE THAT! HANS WARNED ME AGAINST DOING THIS.
BUT I IGNORED HIS ADVICE...
...OH?
WELL, LET'S GET COMFORTABLE. NO USE STANDING AROUND.

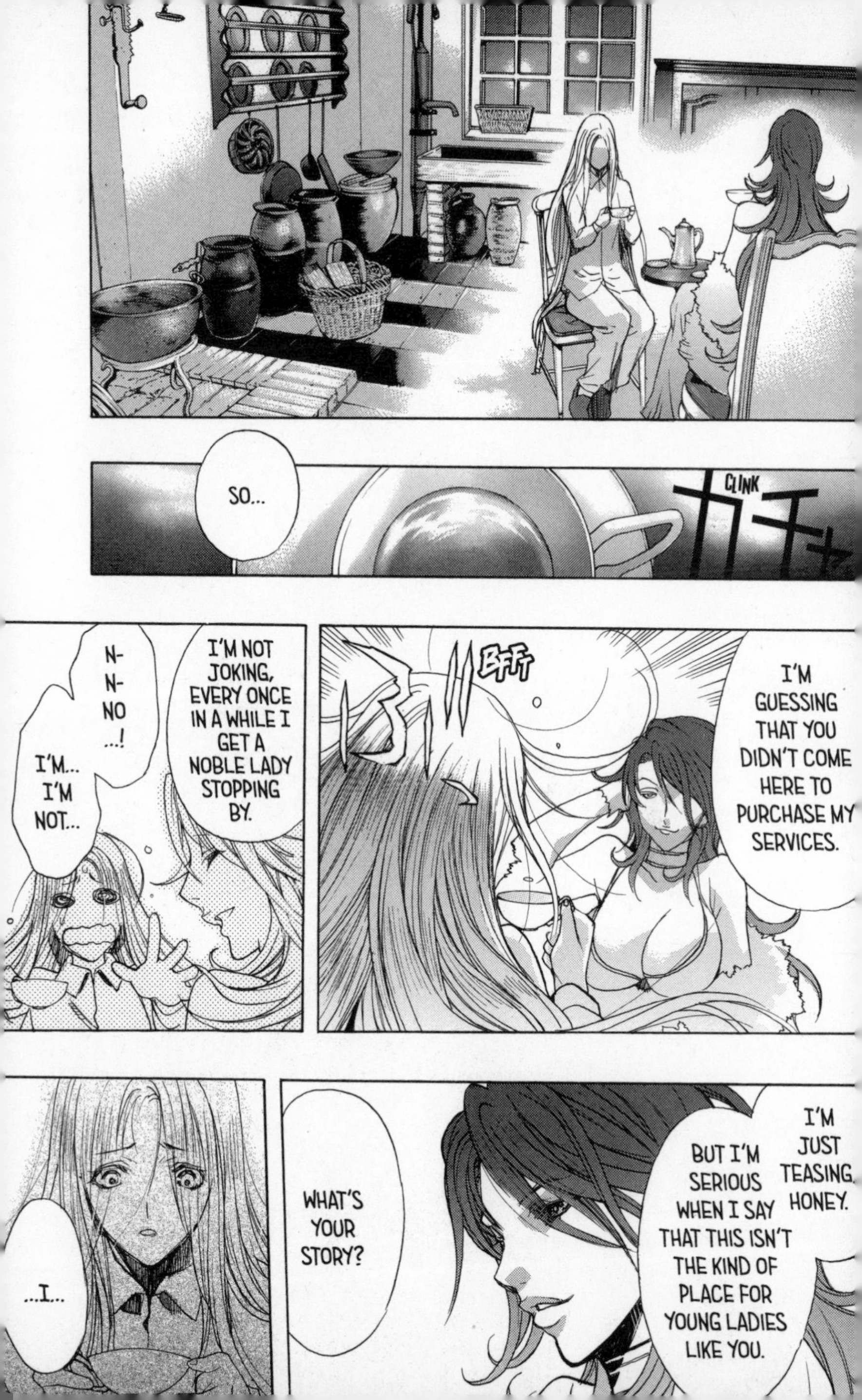
CLINK
カチャ
SO...
I'M GUESSING THAT YOU DIDN'T COME HERE TO PURCHASE MY SERVICES.
BFFT
I'M NOT JOKING, EVERY ONCE IN A WHILE I GET A NOBLE LADY STOPPING BY.
N-N-NO...! I'M... I'M NOT...
I'M JUST TEASING, HONEY.
BUT I'M SERIOUS WHEN I SAY THAT THIS ISN'T THE KIND OF PLACE FOR YOUNG LADIES LIKE YOU.
WHAT'S YOUR STORY?
...I...

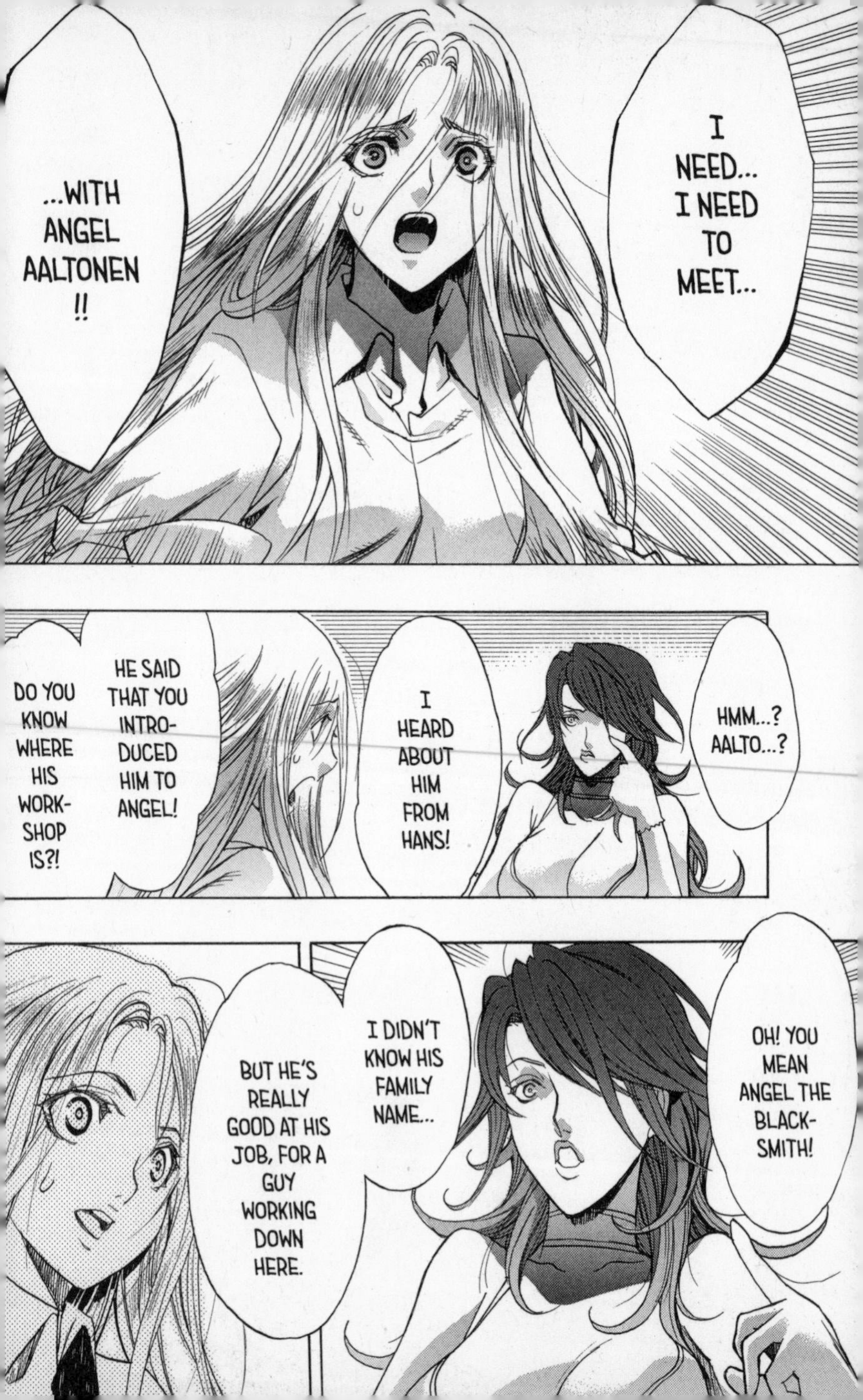
I NEED... I NEED TO MEET...
...WITH ANGEL AALTONEN!!
HMM...? AALTO...?
I HEARD ABOUT HIM FROM HANS!
HE SAID THAT YOU INTRO-DUCED HIM TO ANGEL!
DO YOU KNOW WHERE HIS WORK-SHOP IS?!
OH! YOU MEAN ANGEL THE BLACK-SMITH!
I DIDN'T KNOW HIS FAMILY NAME...
BUT HE'S REALLY GOOD AT HIS JOB, FOR A GUY WORKING DOWN HERE.

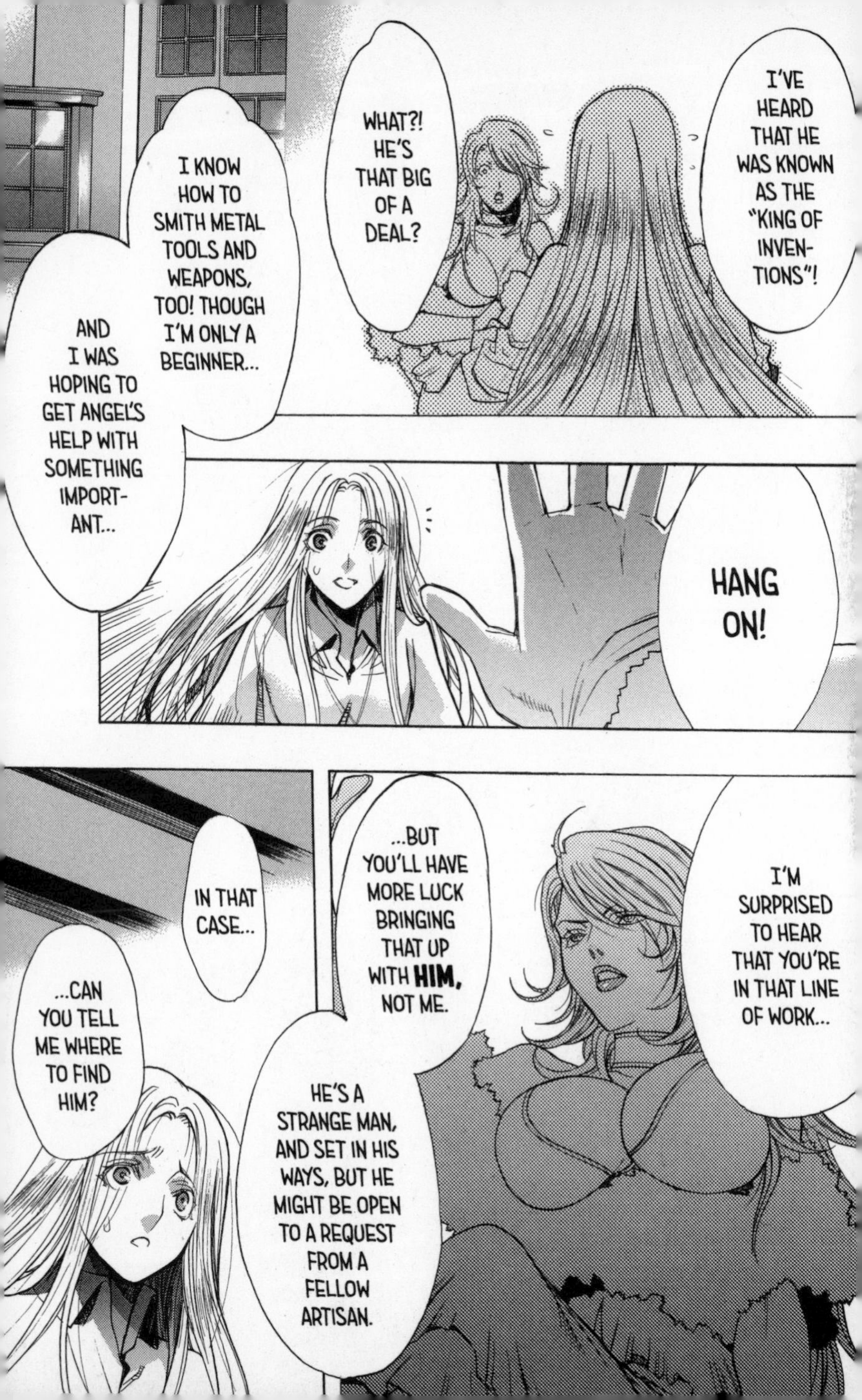
I'VE HEARD THAT HE WAS KNOWN AS THE "KING OF INVEN- TIONS"!
WHAT?! HE'S THAT BIG OF A DEAL?
I KNOW HOW TO SMITH METAL TOOLS AND WEAPONS, TOO! THOUGH I'M ONLY A BEGINNER...
AND I WAS HOPING TO GET ANGEL'S HELP WITH SOMETHING IMPORT- ANT...
HANG ON!
I'M SURPRISED TO HEAR THAT YOU'RE IN THAT LINE OF WORK...
...BUT YOU'LL HAVE MORE LUCK BRINGING THAT UP WITH **HIM,** NOT ME.
HE'S A STRANGE MAN, AND SET IN HIS WAYS, BUT HE MIGHT BE OPEN TO A REQUEST FROM A FELLOW ARTISAN.
IN THAT CASE...
...CAN YOU TELL ME WHERE TO FIND HIM?

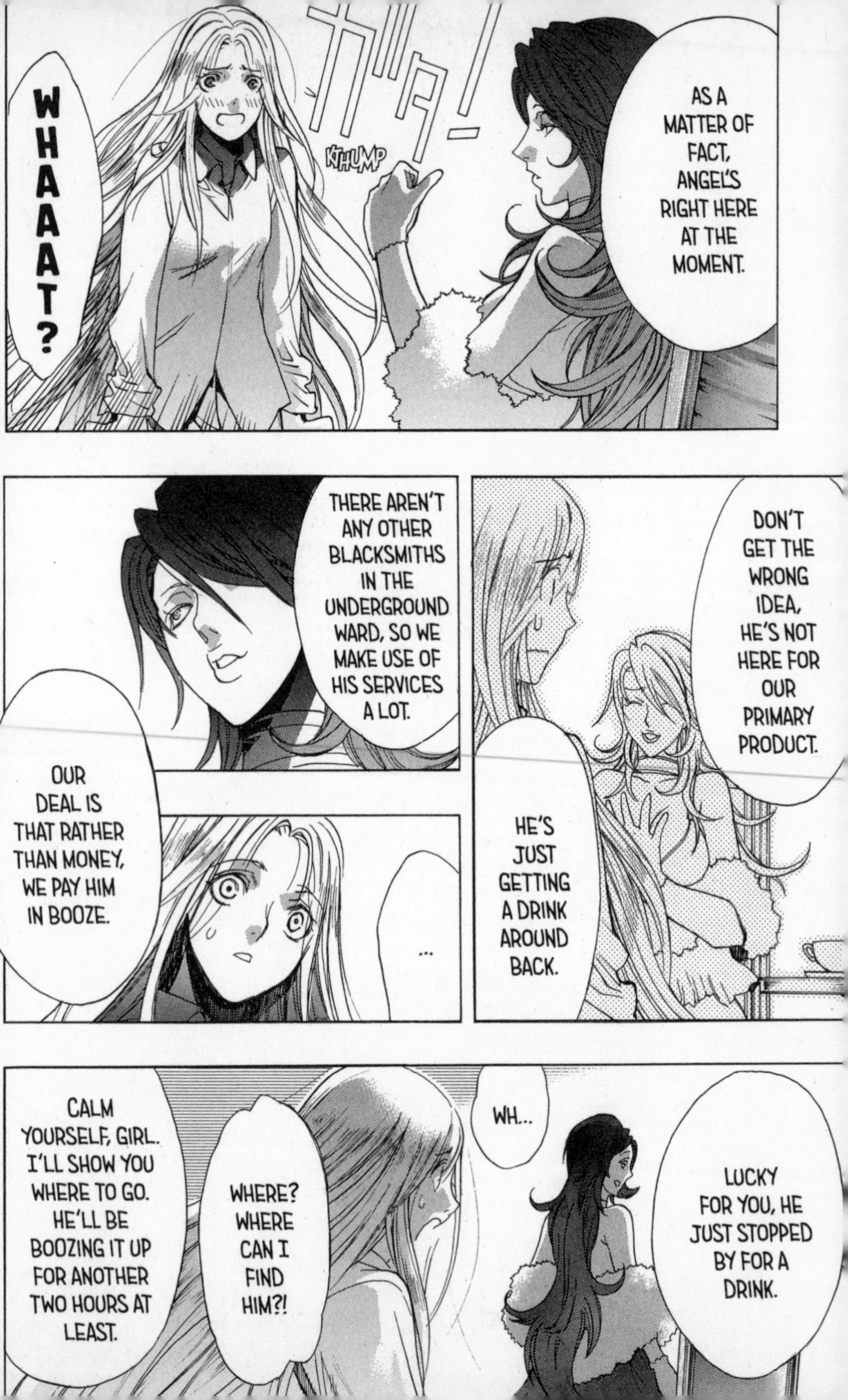
AS A MATTER OF FACT, ANGEL'S RIGHT HERE AT THE MOMENT.
KTHUMP
WHAAAAT?
DON'T GET THE WRONG IDEA, HE'S NOT HERE FOR OUR PRIMARY PRODUCT.
HE'S JUST GETTING A DRINK AROUND BACK.
THERE AREN'T ANY OTHER BLACKSMITHS IN THE UNDERGROUND WARD, SO WE MAKE USE OF HIS SERVICES A LOT.
OUR DEAL IS THAT RATHER THAN MONEY, WE PAY HIM IN BOOZE.
...
LUCKY FOR YOU, HE JUST STOPPED BY FOR A DRINK.
WH...
WHERE? WHERE CAN I FIND HIM?!
CALM YOURSELF, GIRL. I'LL SHOW YOU WHERE TO GO. HE'LL BE BOOZING IT UP FOR ANOTHER TWO HOURS AT LEAST.

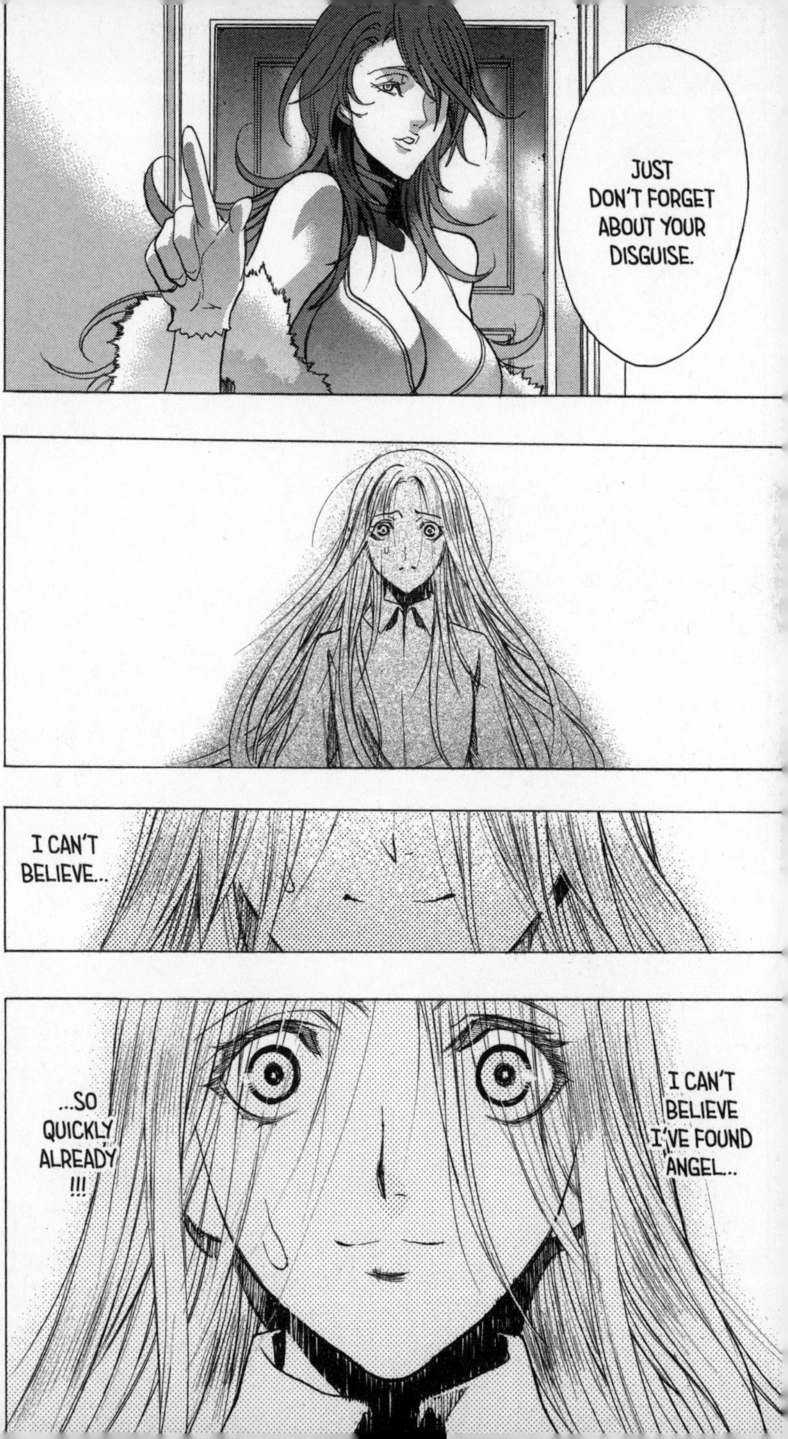
JUST DON'T FORGET ABOUT YOUR DISGUISE.
I CAN'T BELIEVE...
I CAN'T BELIEVE I'VE FOUND ANGEL...
...SO QUICKLY ALREADY !!!

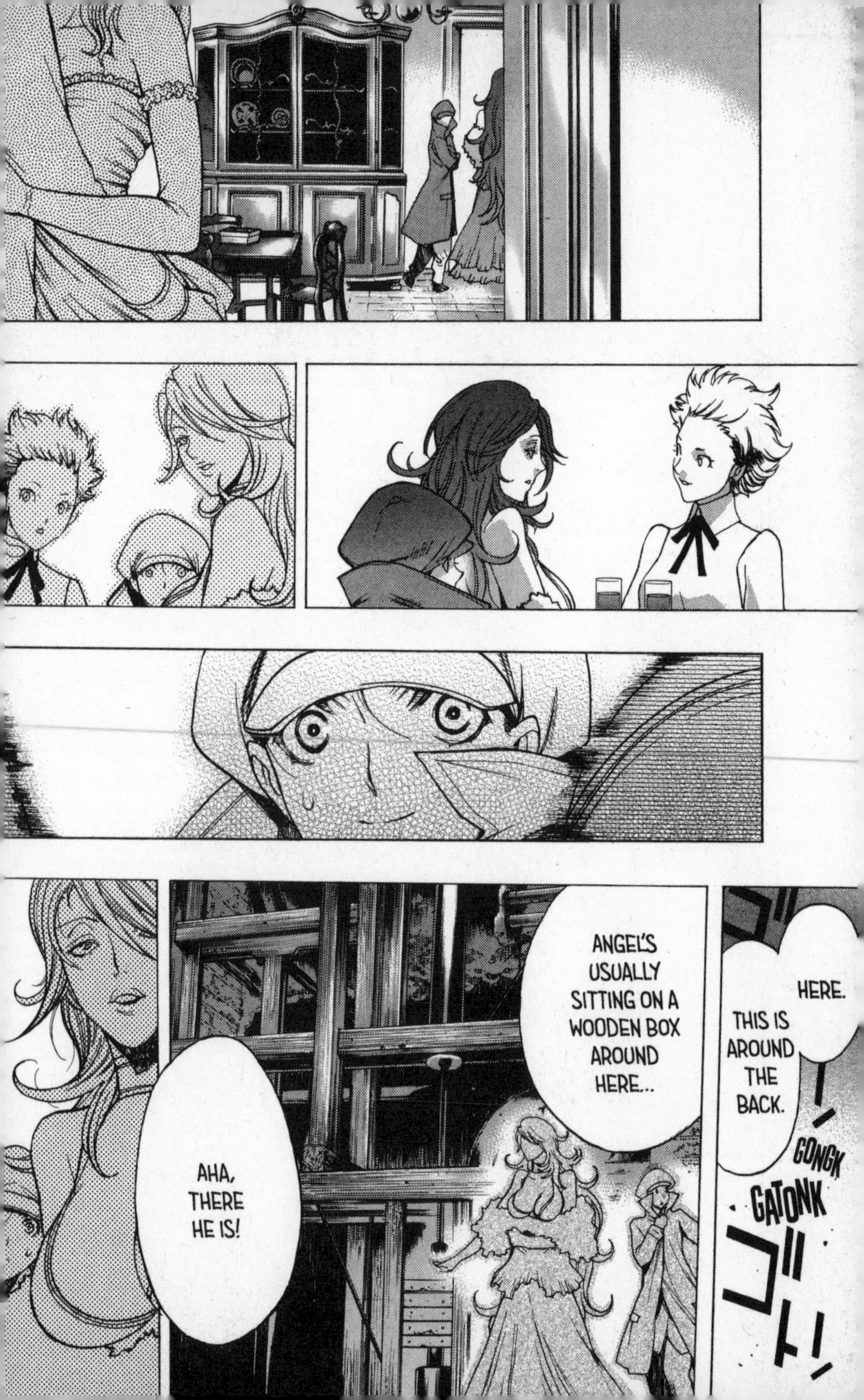

HERE.
THIS IS AROUND THE BACK.
GONGK
GATONK
ANGEL'S USUALLY SITTING ON A WOODEN BOX AROUND HERE...
AHA, THERE HE IS!

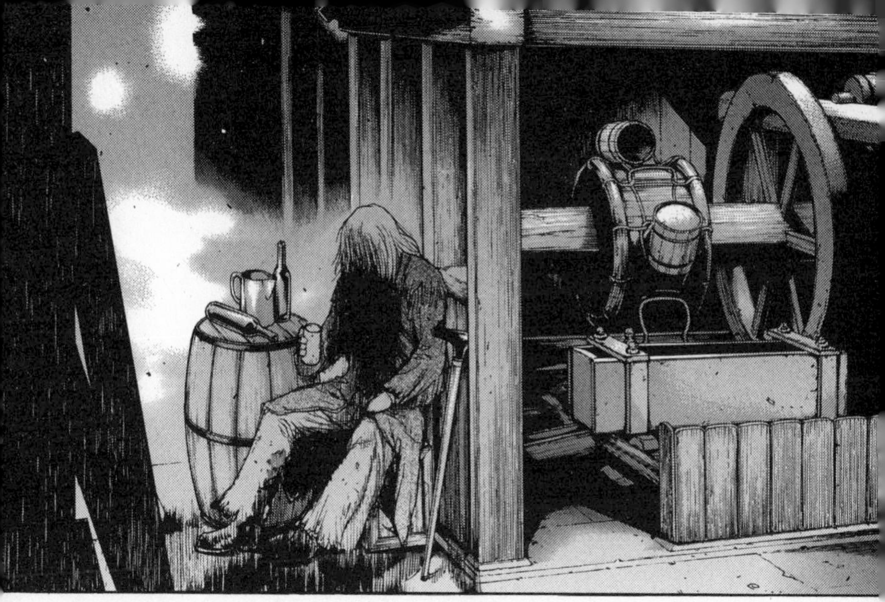
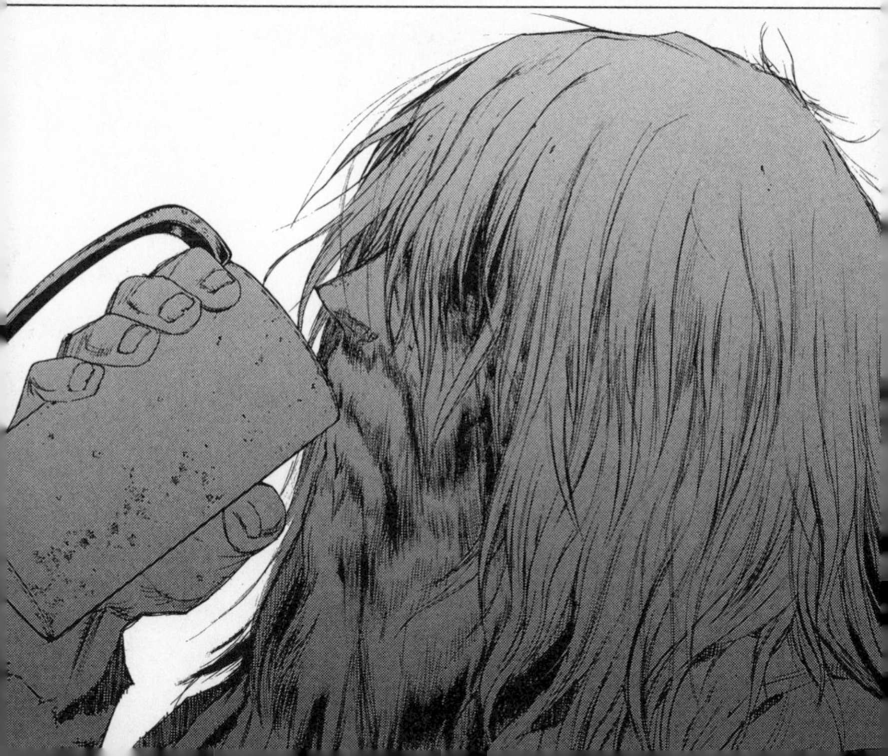

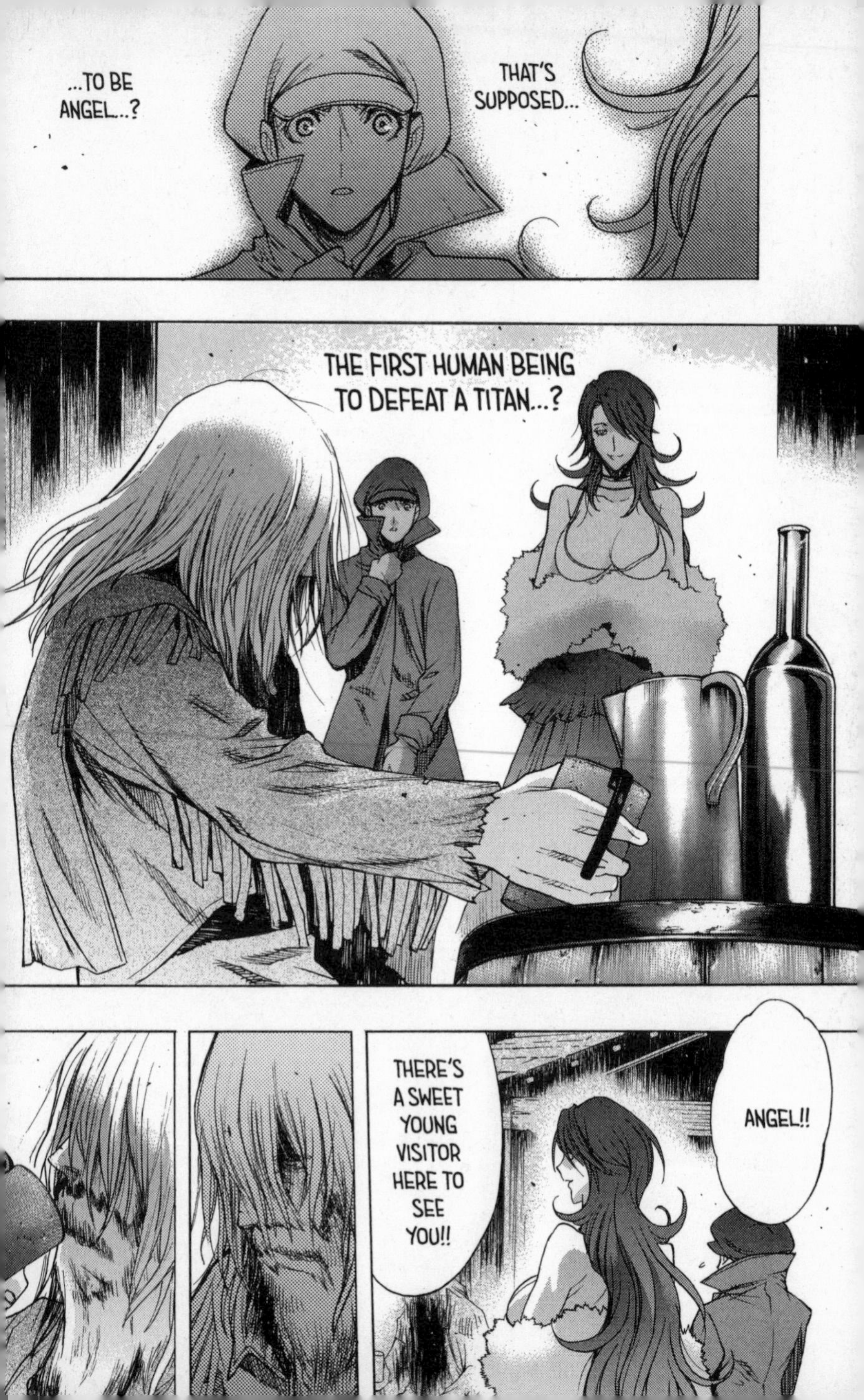
THAT'S SUPPOSED...
...TO BE ANGEL...?
THE FIRST HUMAN BEING TO DEFEAT A TITAN...?
ANGEL!!
THERE'S A SWEET YOUNG VISITOR HERE TO SEE YOU!!

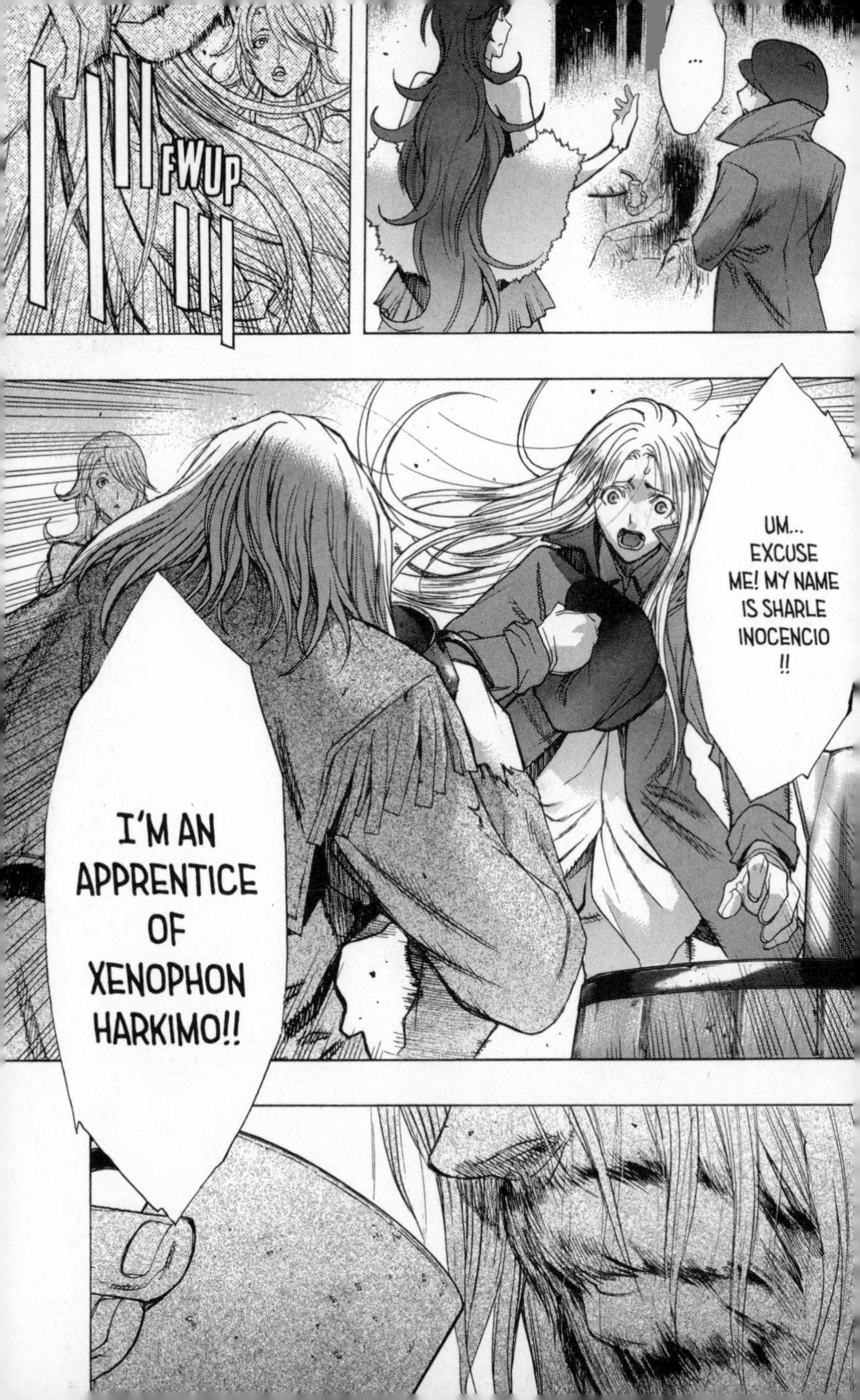
...
FWUP
UM... EXCUSE ME! MY NAME IS SHARLE INOCENCIO !!
I'M AN APPRENTICE OF XENOPHON HARKIMO!!

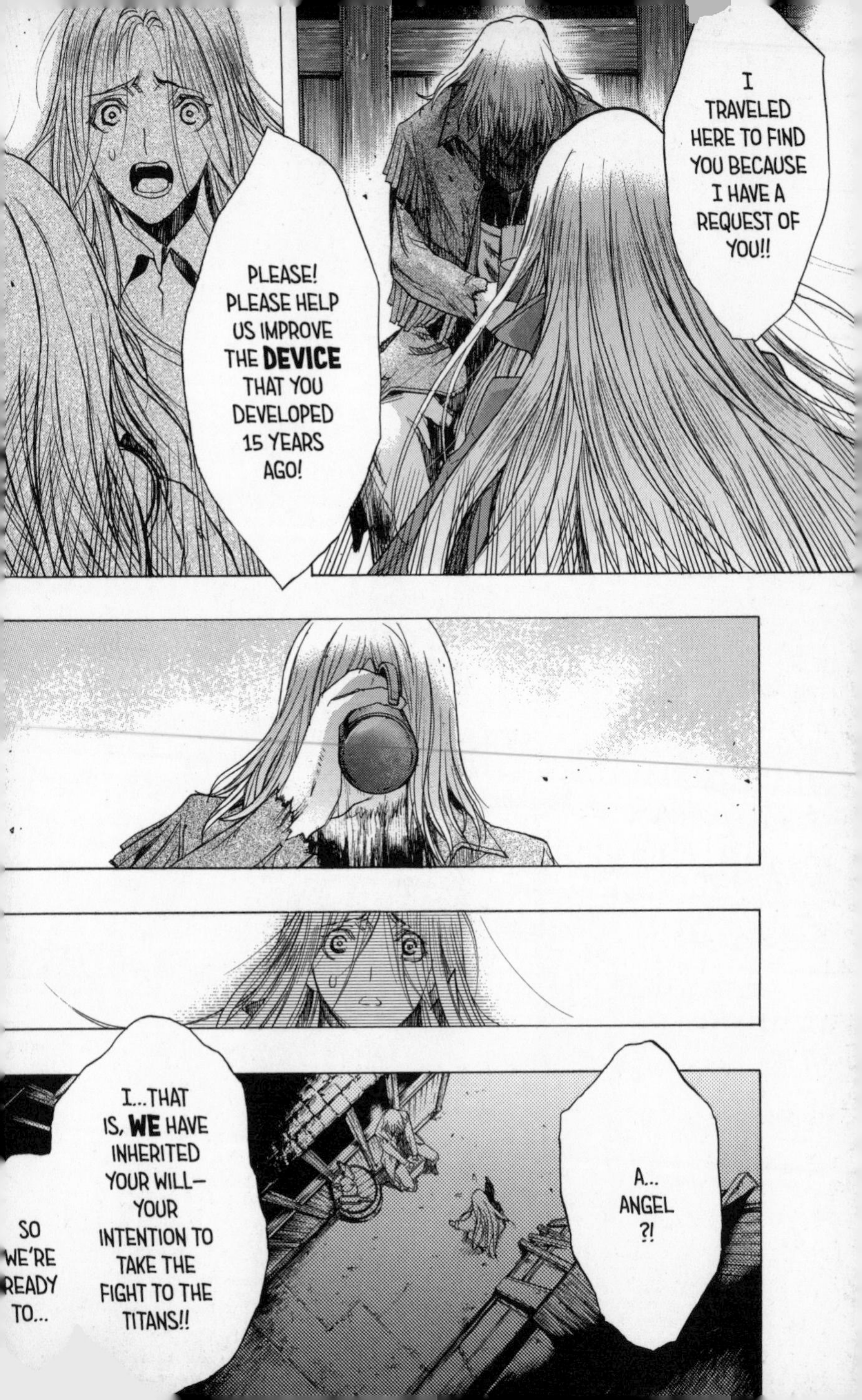
I TRAVELED HERE TO FIND YOU BECAUSE I HAVE A REQUEST OF YOU!!
PLEASE! PLEASE HELP US IMPROVE THE **DEVICE** THAT YOU DEVELOPED 15 YEARS AGO!
A... ANGEL ?!
I...THAT IS, **WE** HAVE INHERITED YOUR WILL—YOUR INTENTION TO TAKE THE FIGHT TO THE TITANS!!
SO WE'RE READY TO...

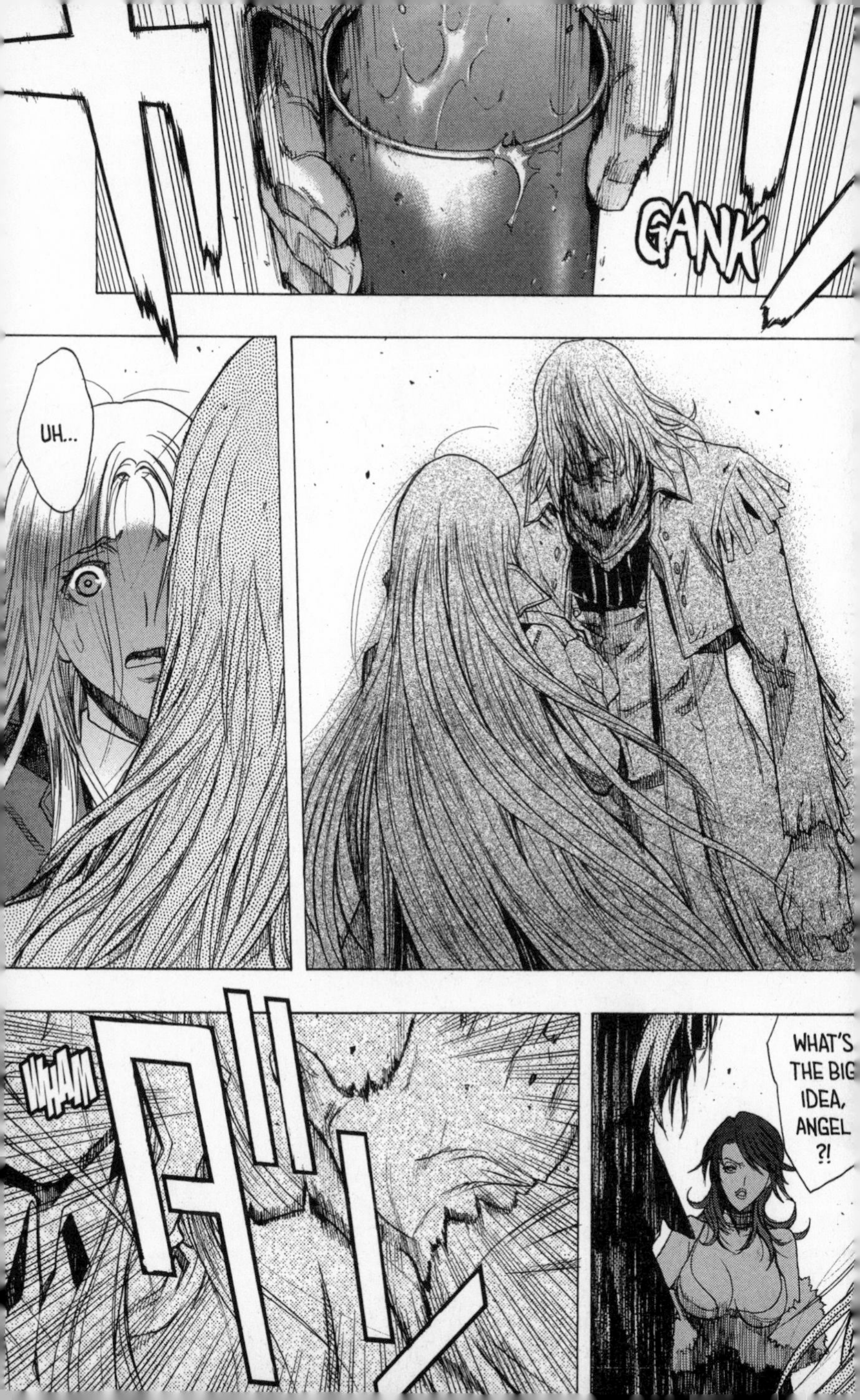
GANK
UH...
WHAT'S THE BIG IDEA, ANGEL?!
WHAM

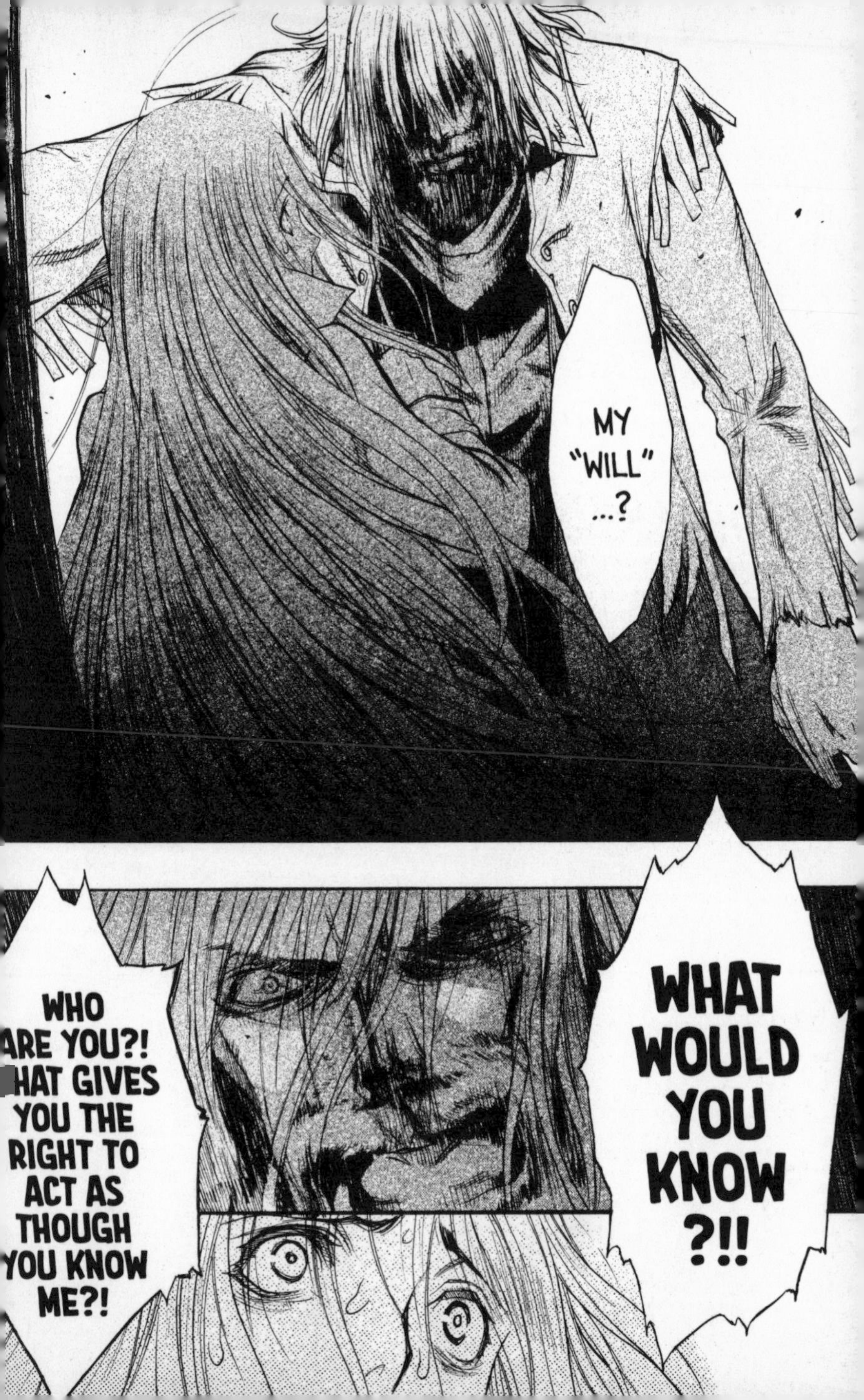
MY "WILL" ...?
WHAT WOULD YOU KNOW ?!!
WHO ARE YOU?! HAT GIVES YOU THE RIGHT TO ACT AS THOUGH YOU KNOW ME?!

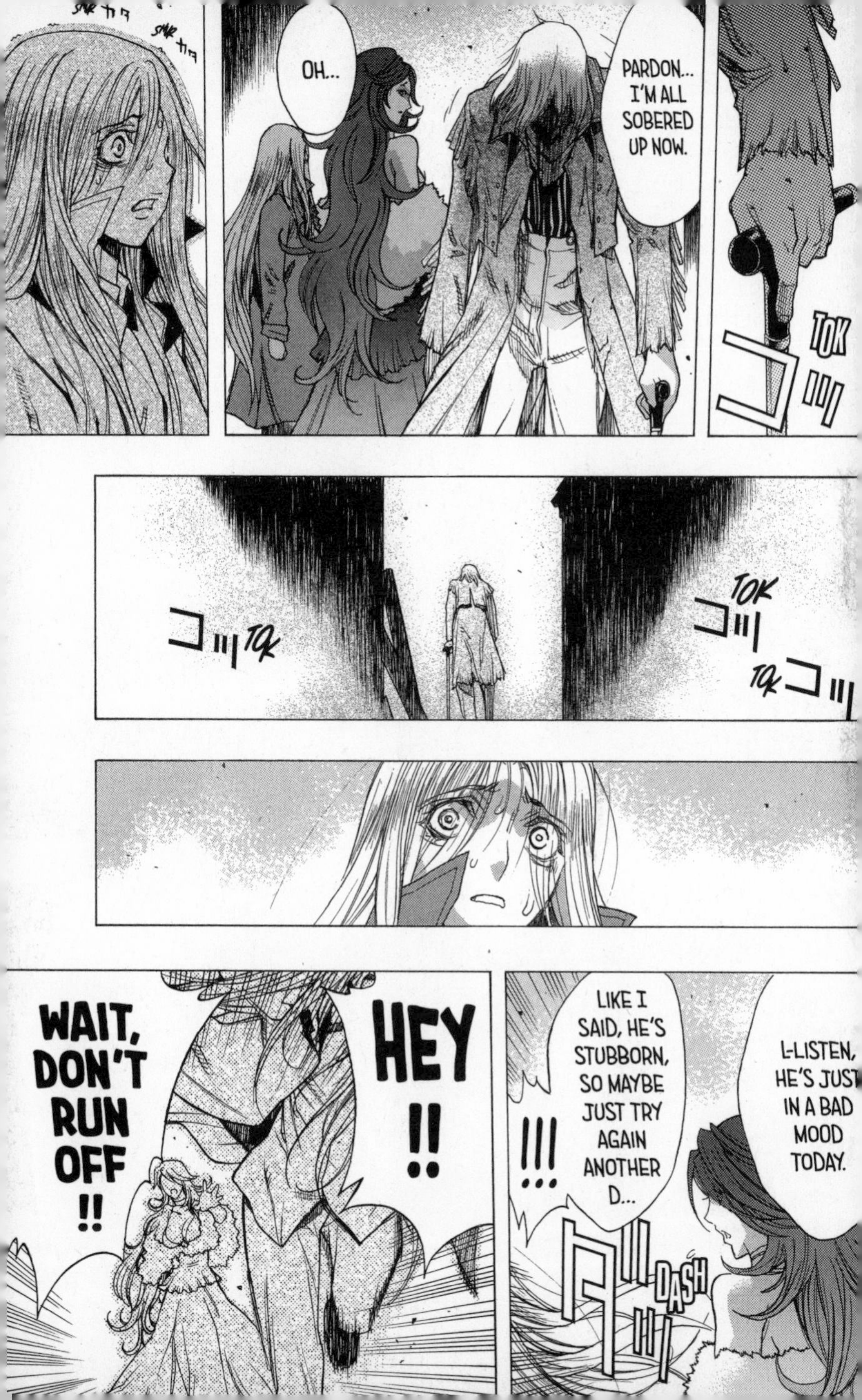
TOK
PARDON... I'M ALL SOBERED UP NOW.
OH...
TOK
TOK
TOK
L-LISTEN, HE'S JUST IN A BAD MOOD TODAY.
LIKE I SAID, HE'S STUBBORN, SO MAYBE JUST TRY AGAIN ANOTHER D...
!!!
DASH
HEY!!
WAIT, DON'T RUN OFF!!

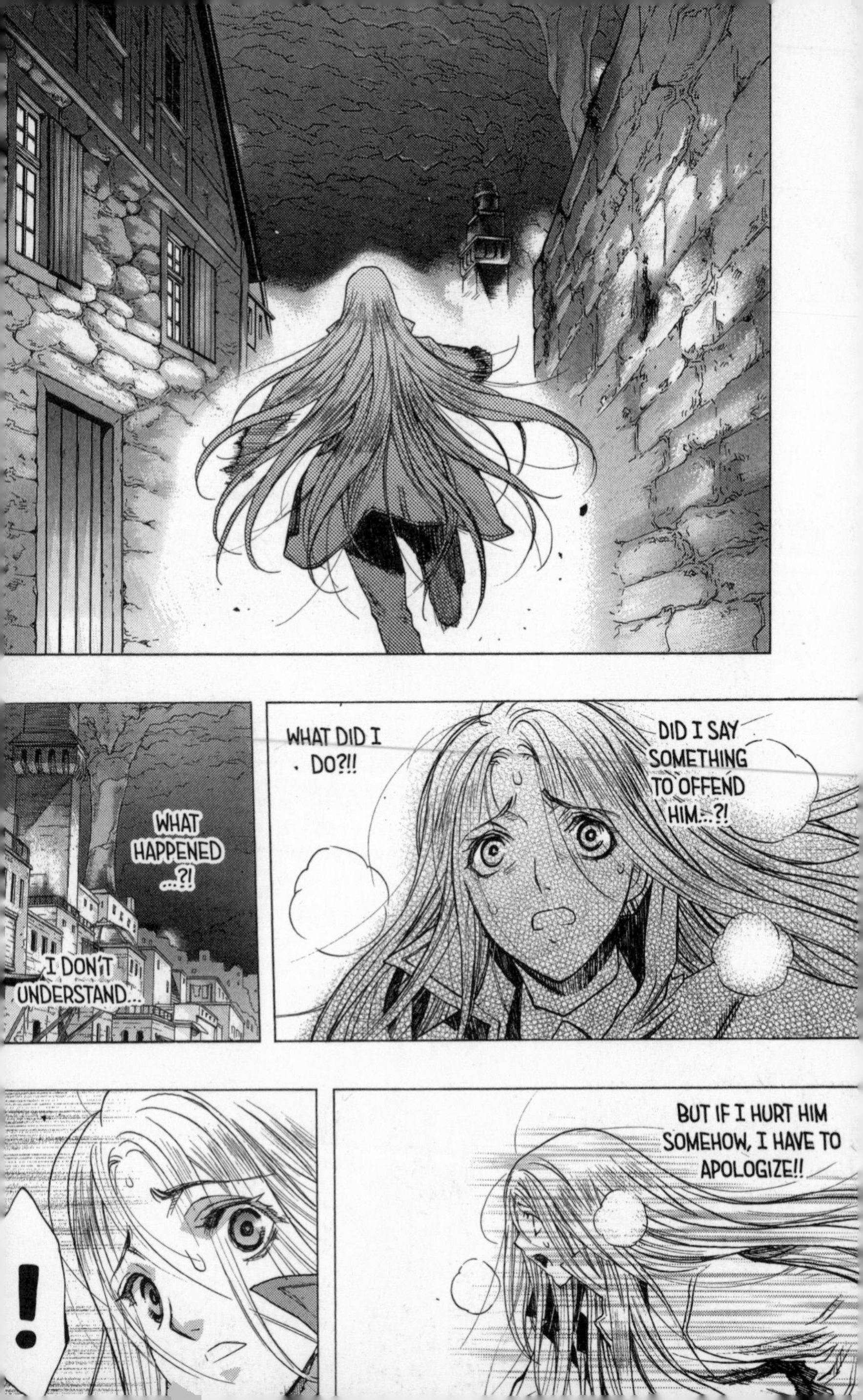
DID I SAY SOMETHING TO OFFEND HIM...?!
WHAT DID I DO?!!
WHAT HAPPENED ...?!
I DON'T UNDERSTAND...
BUT IF I HURT HIM SOMEHOW, I HAVE TO APOLOGIZE!!
!

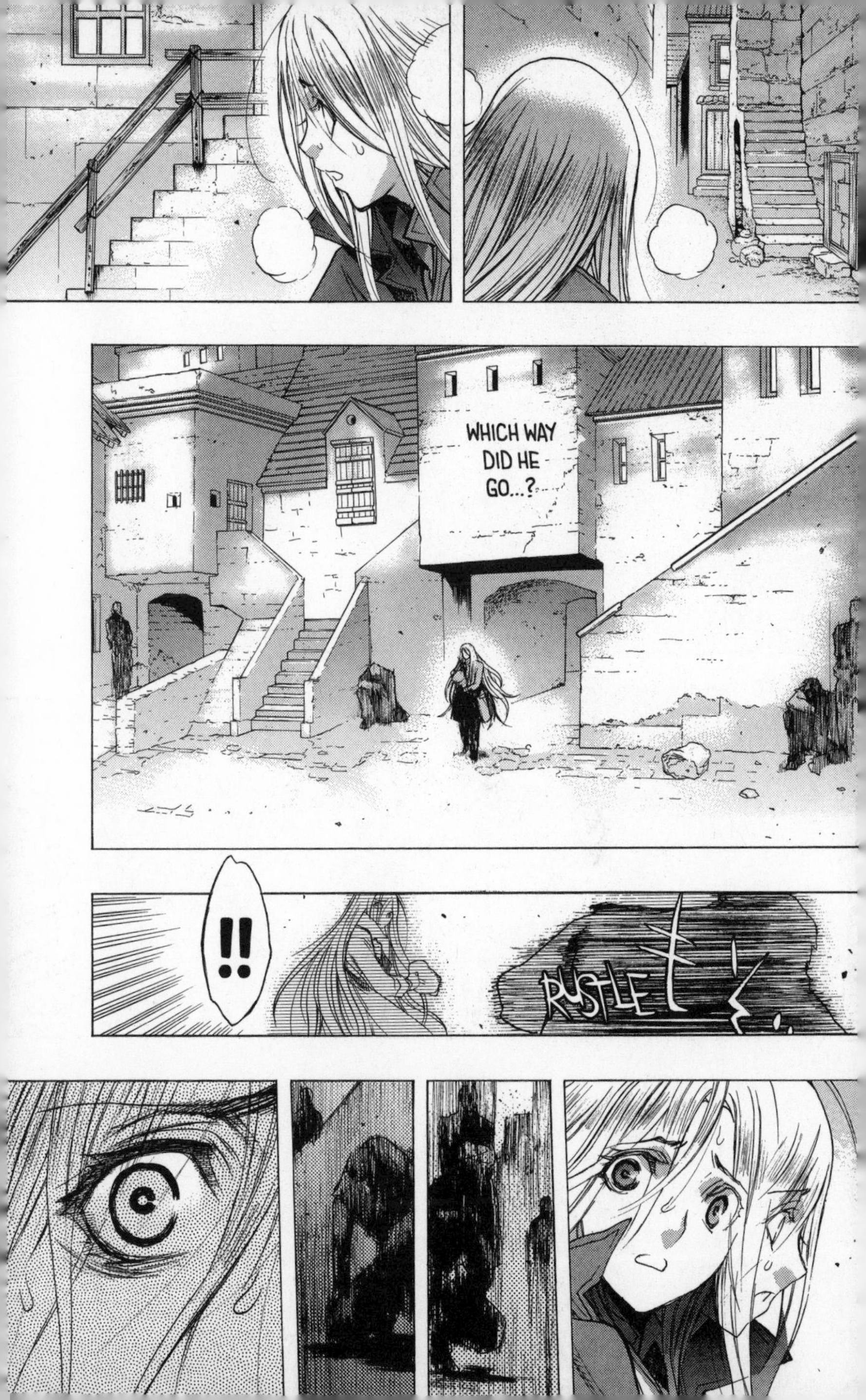
WHICH WAY DID HE GO...?
!!
RUSTLE

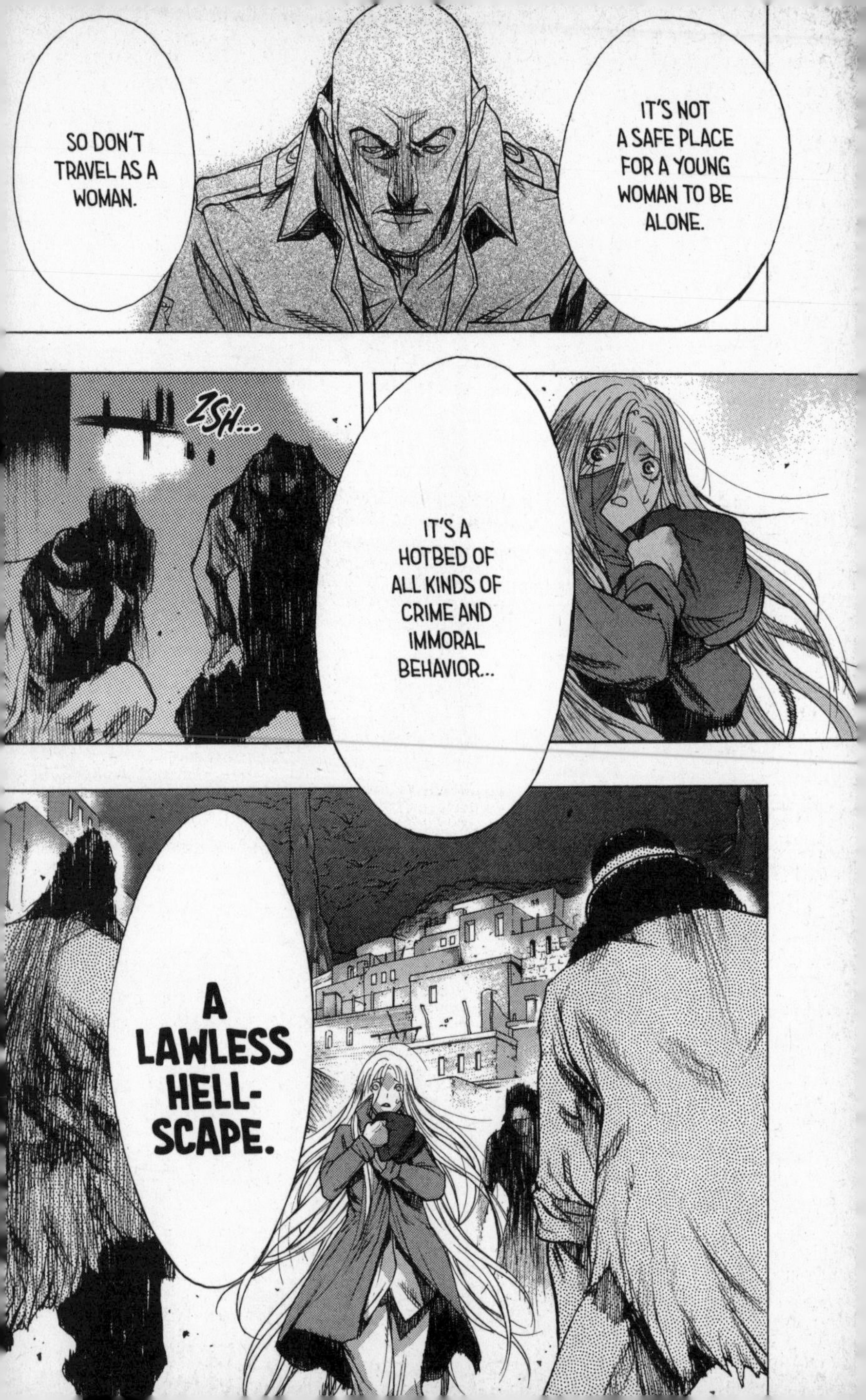
IT'S NOT A SAFE PLACE FOR A YOUNG WOMAN TO BE ALONE.
SO DON'T TRAVEL AS A WOMAN.
IT'S A HOTBED OF ALL KINDS OF CRIME AND IMMORAL BEHAVIOR...
ZSH...
A LAWLESS HELL-SCAPE.

Chapter 34: Town of Eternal Night · End

ATTACK on TITAN
BEFORE THE FALL

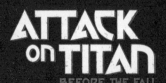

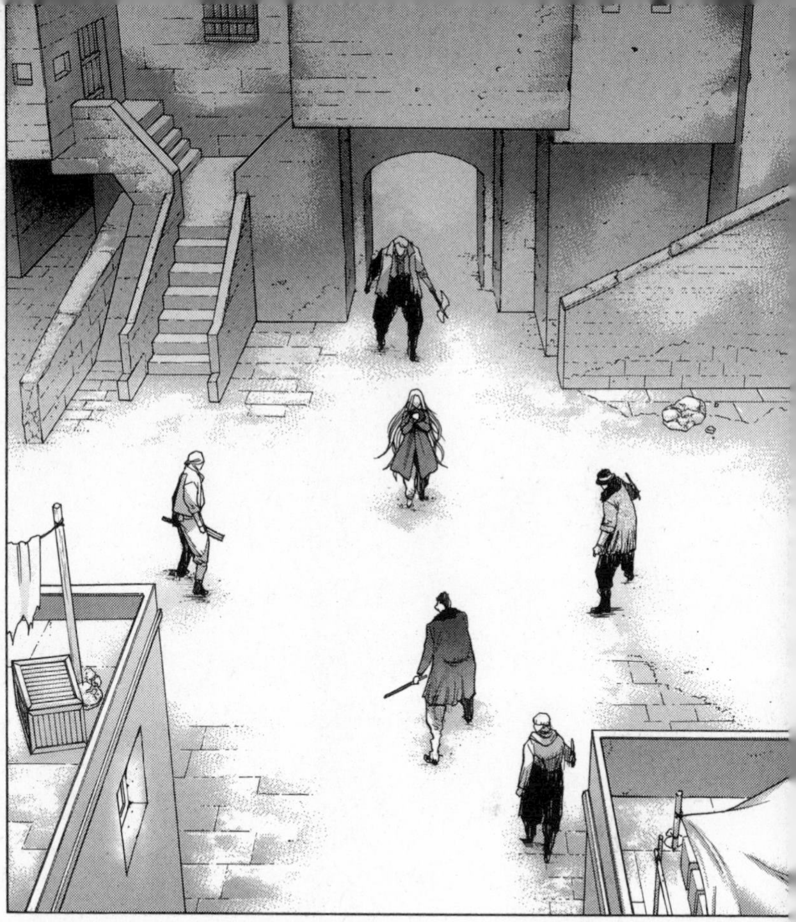
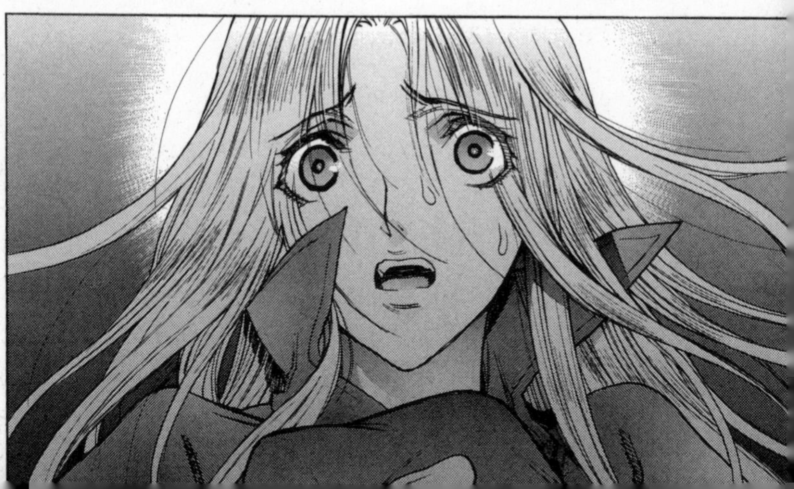

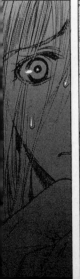

...AH...

Chapter 35: Lone Shadow in the Town That Never Sleeps

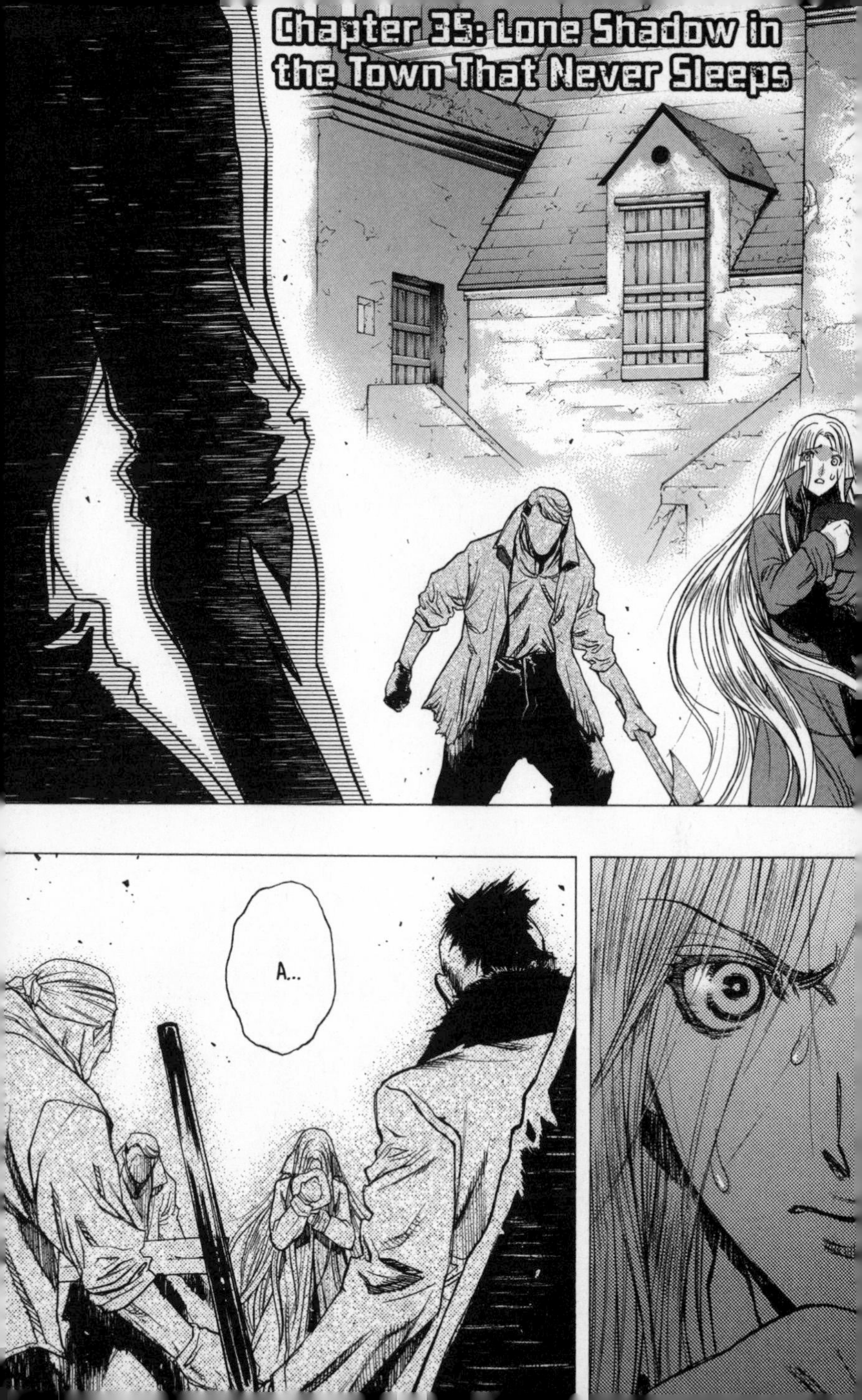
A...

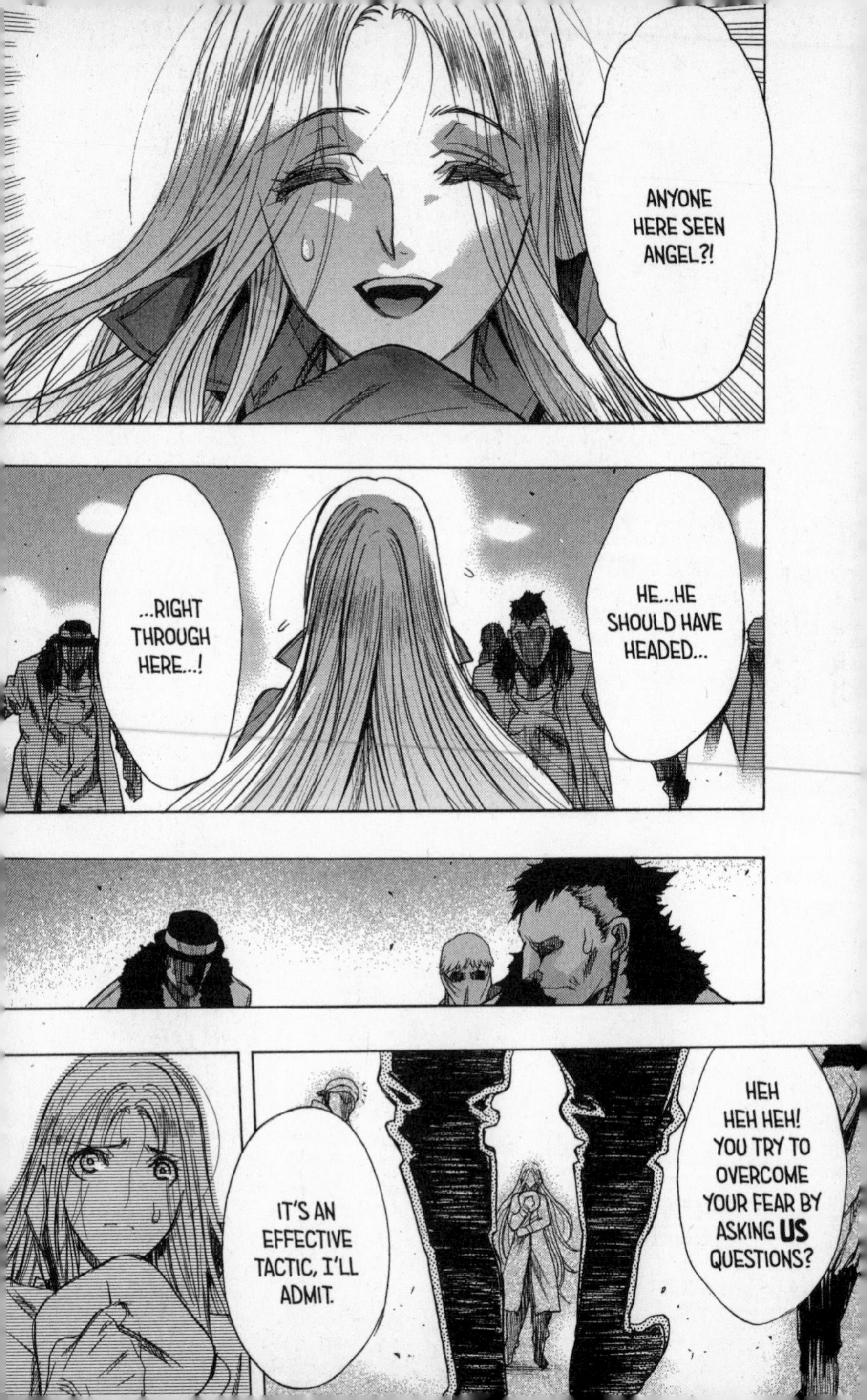
ANYONE HERE SEEN ANGEL?!
HE...HE SHOULD HAVE HEADED...
...RIGHT THROUGH HERE...!
HEH HEH HEH! YOU TRY TO OVERCOME YOUR FEAR BY ASKING US QUESTIONS?
IT'S AN EFFECTIVE TACTIC, I'LL ADMIT.

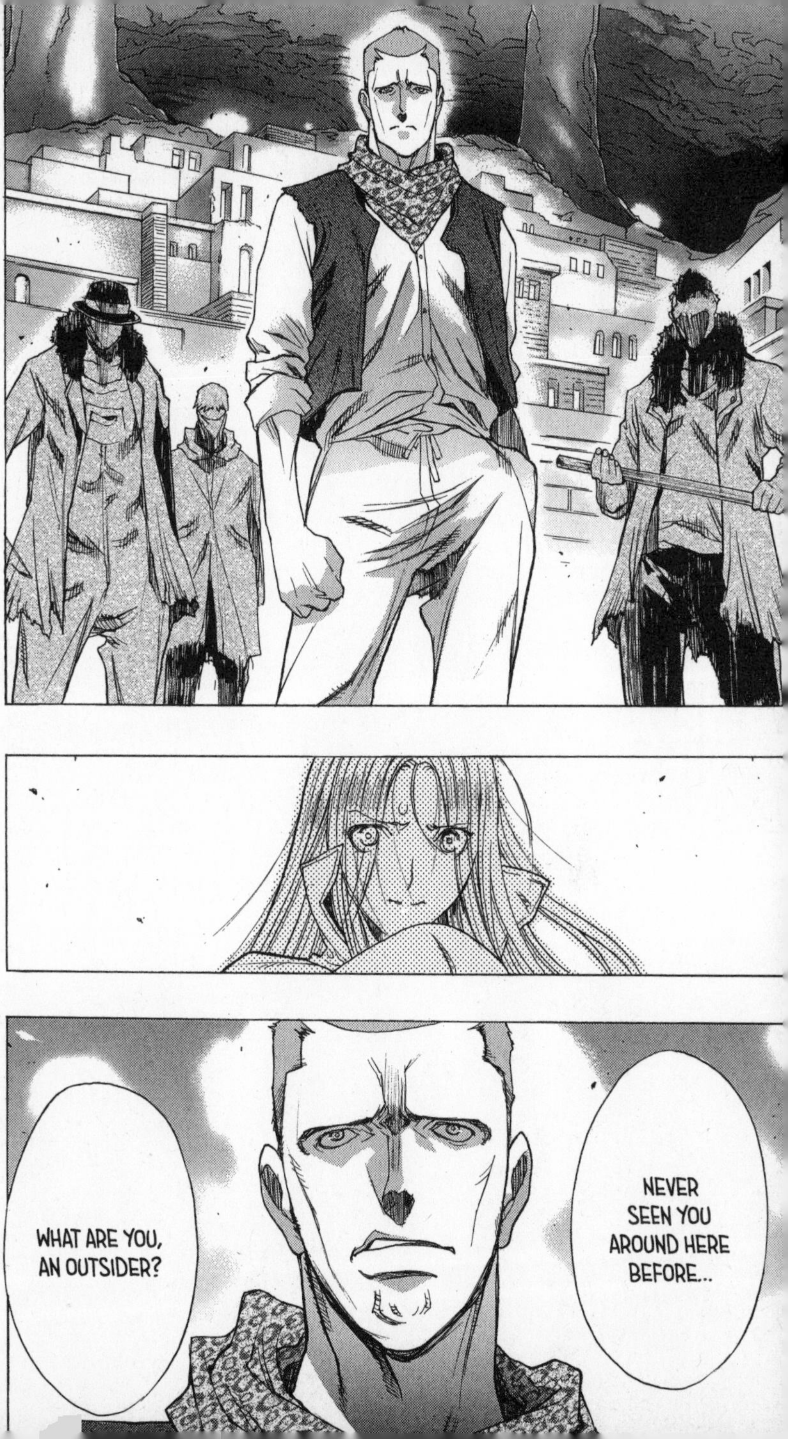
NEVER SEEN YOU AROUND HERE BEFORE...
WHAT ARE YOU, AN OUTSIDER?

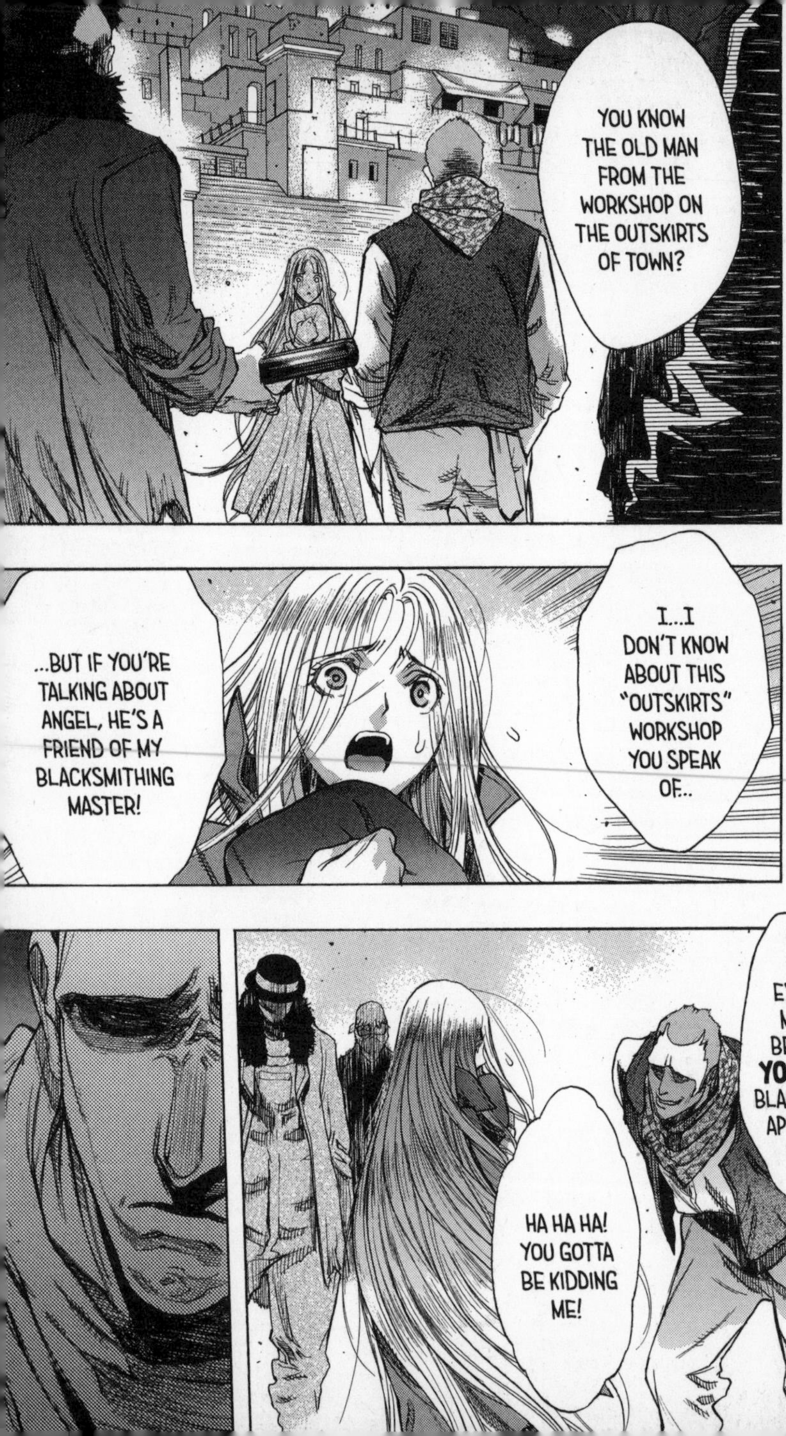
YOU KNOW THE OLD MAN FROM THE WORKSHOP ON THE OUTSKIRTS OF TOWN?
I...I DON'T KNOW ABOUT THIS "OUTSKIRTS" WORKSHOP YOU SPEAK OF...
...BUT IF YOU'RE TALKING ABOUT ANGEL, HE'S A FRIEND OF MY BLACKSMITHING MASTER!
HAH! YOU EXPECT ME TO BELIEVE **YOU'RE** A BLACKSMITH APPRENT-ICE?
HA HA HA! YOU GOTTA BE KIDDING ME!

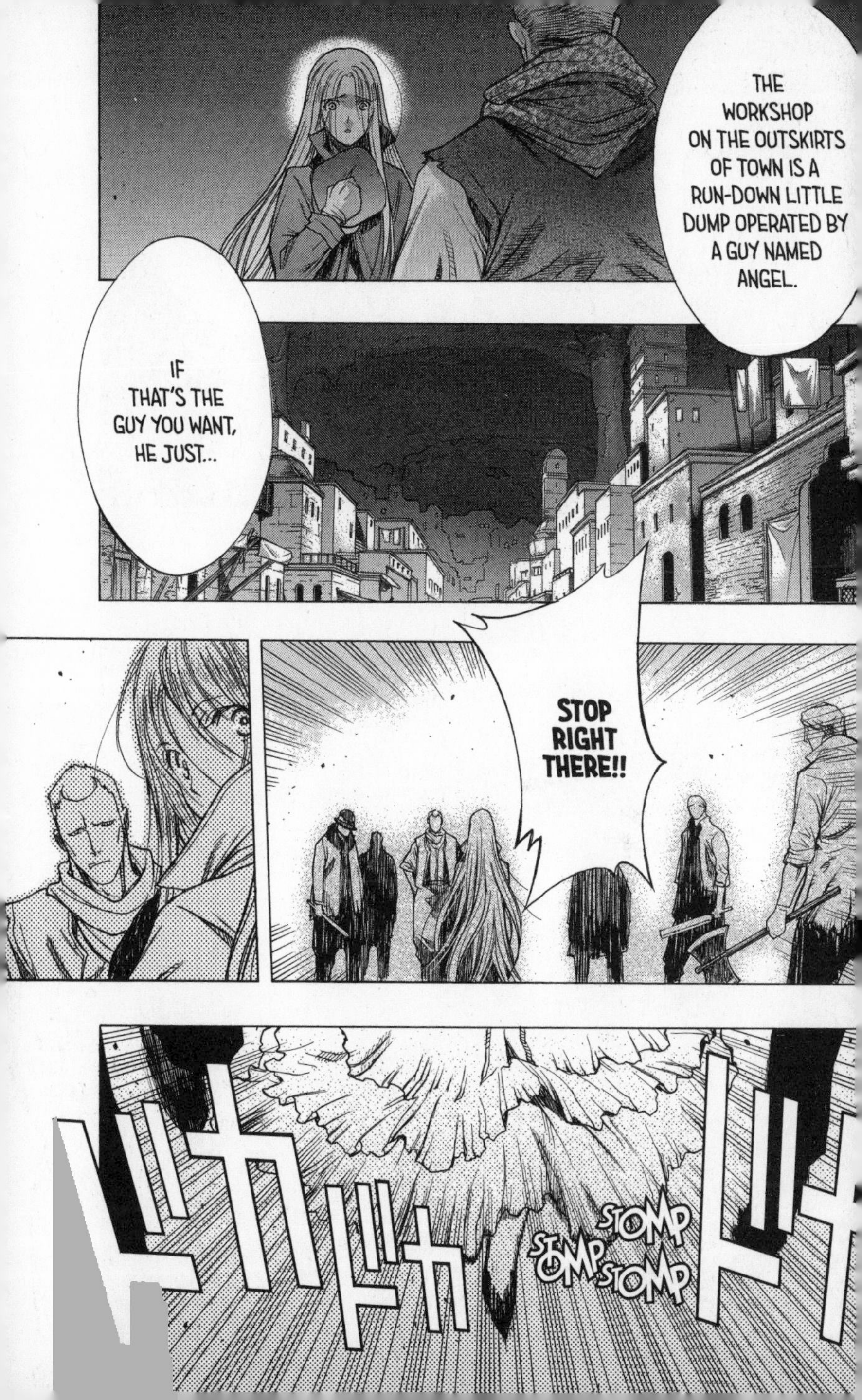
THE WORKSHOP ON THE OUTSKIRTS OF TOWN IS A RUN-DOWN LITTLE DUMP OPERATED BY A GUY NAMED ANGEL.
IF THAT'S THE GUY YOU WANT, HE JUST...
STOP RIGHT THERE!!
STOMP STOMP STOMP

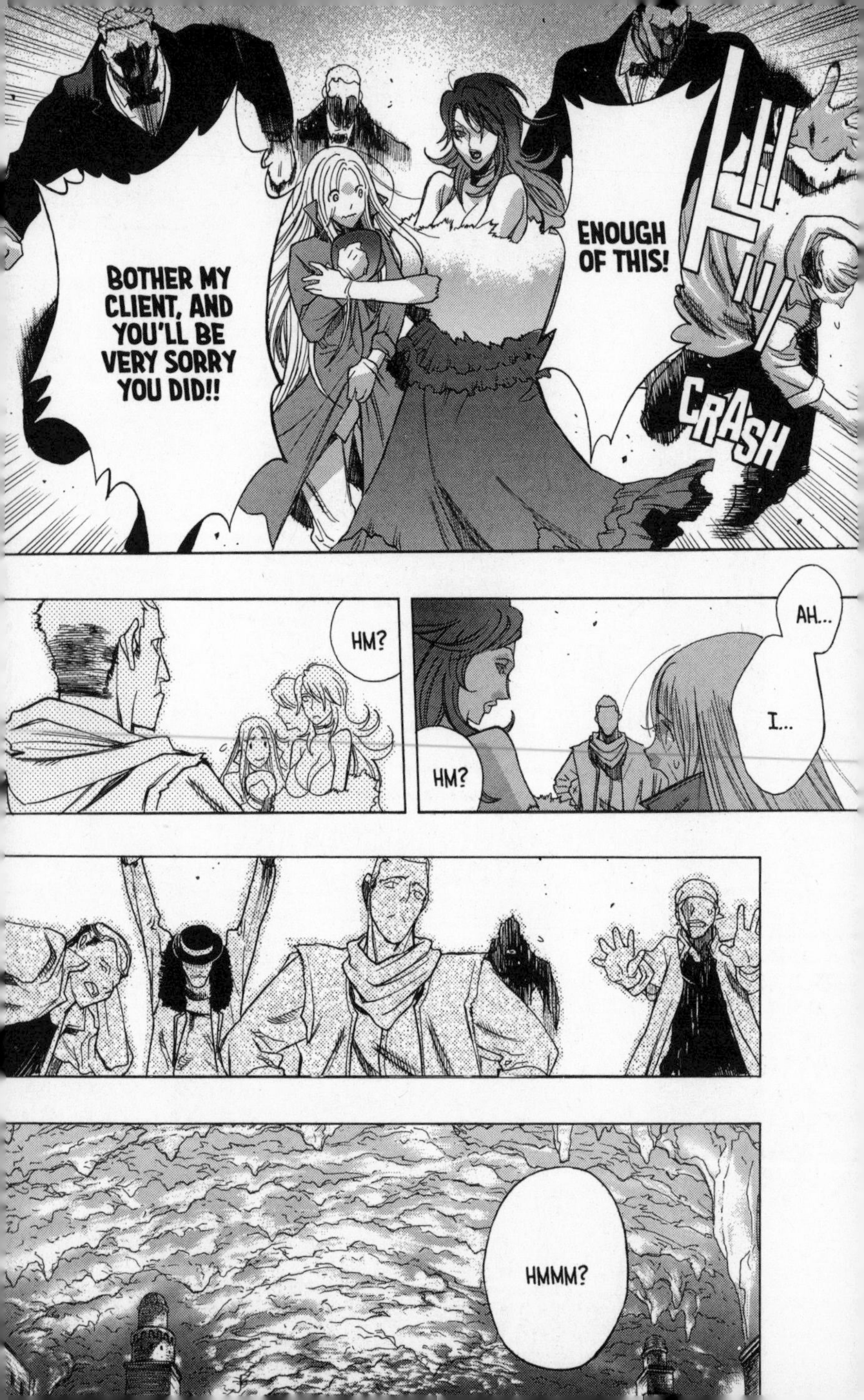
ENOUGH OF THIS!
CRASH
BOTHER MY CLIENT, AND YOU'LL BE VERY SORRY YOU DID!!
AH...
I...
HM?
HM?
HMMM?

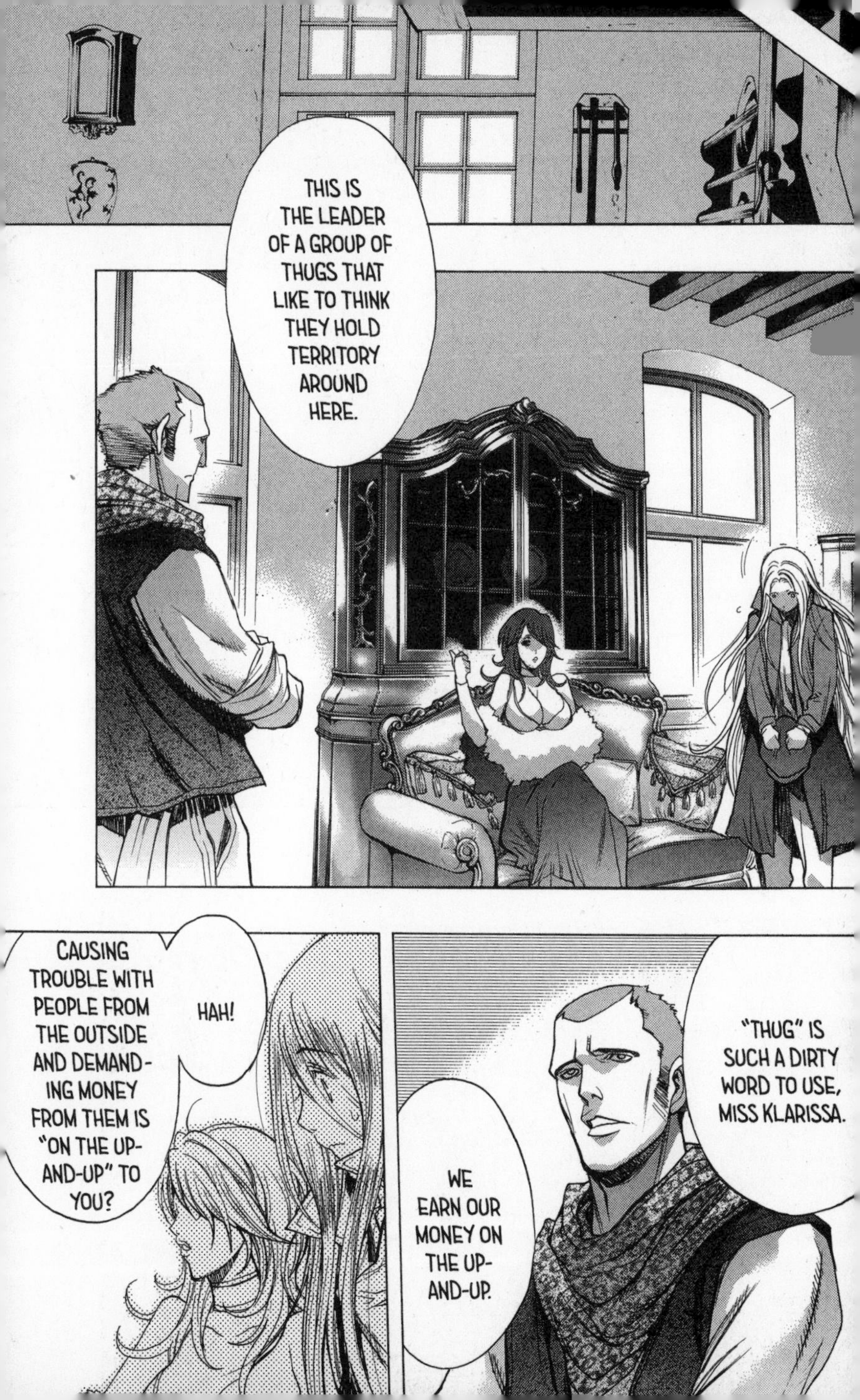

THIS IS THE LEADER OF A GROUP OF THUGS THAT LIKE TO THINK THEY HOLD TERRITORY AROUND HERE.
"THUG" IS SUCH A DIRTY WORD TO USE, MISS KLARISSA.
WE EARN OUR MONEY ON THE UP-AND-UP.
HAH!
CAUSING TROUBLE WITH PEOPLE FROM THE OUTSIDE AND DEMAND-ING MONEY FROM THEM IS "ON THE UP-AND-UP" TO YOU?

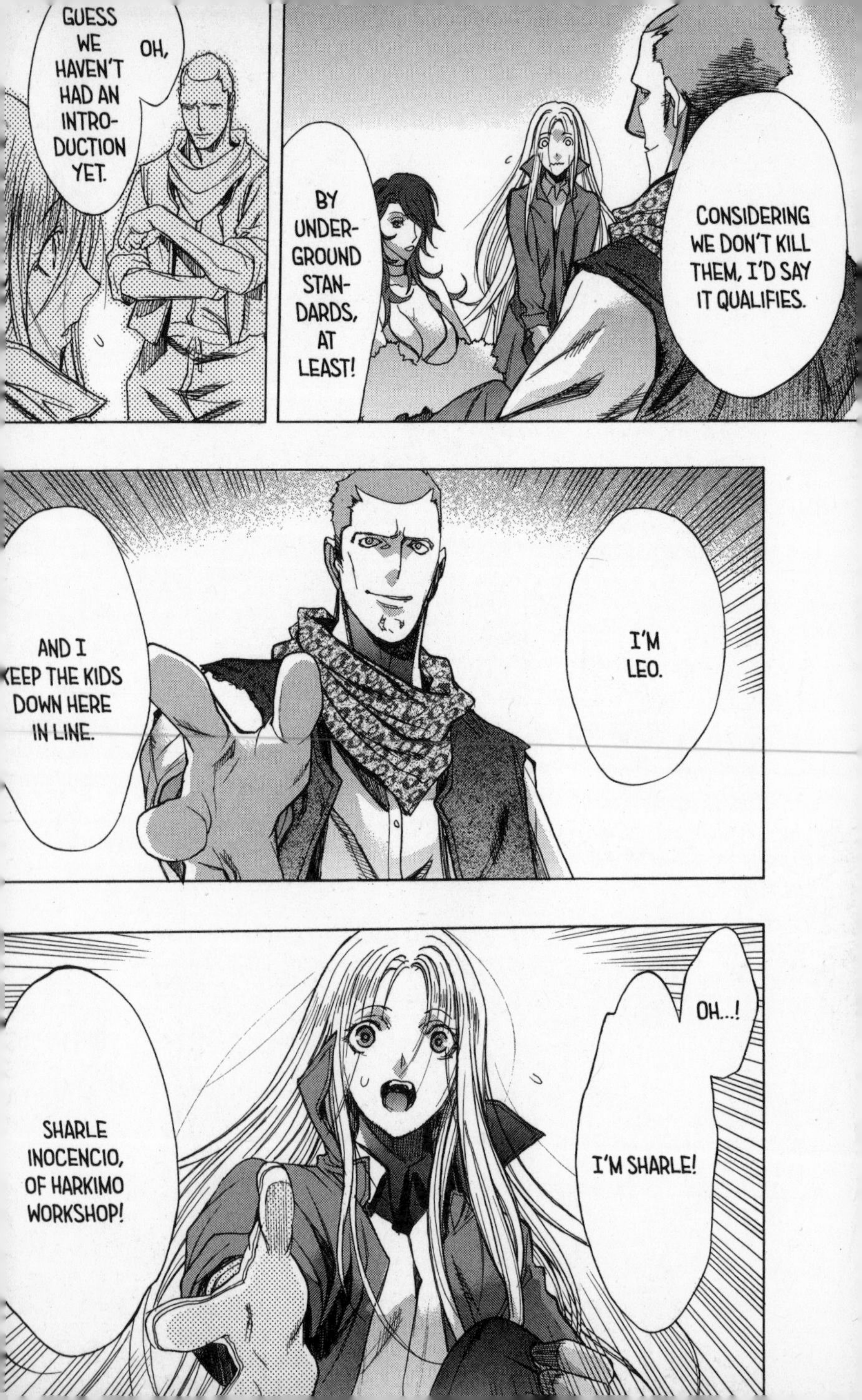
CONSIDERING WE DON'T KILL THEM, I'D SAY IT QUALIFIES.
BY UNDERGROUND STANDARDS, AT LEAST!
OH, GUESS WE HAVEN'T HAD AN INTRODUCTION YET.
I'M LEO.
AND I KEEP THE KIDS DOWN HERE IN LINE.
OH...!
I'M SHARLE!
SHARLE INOCENCIO, OF HARKIMO WORKSHOP!

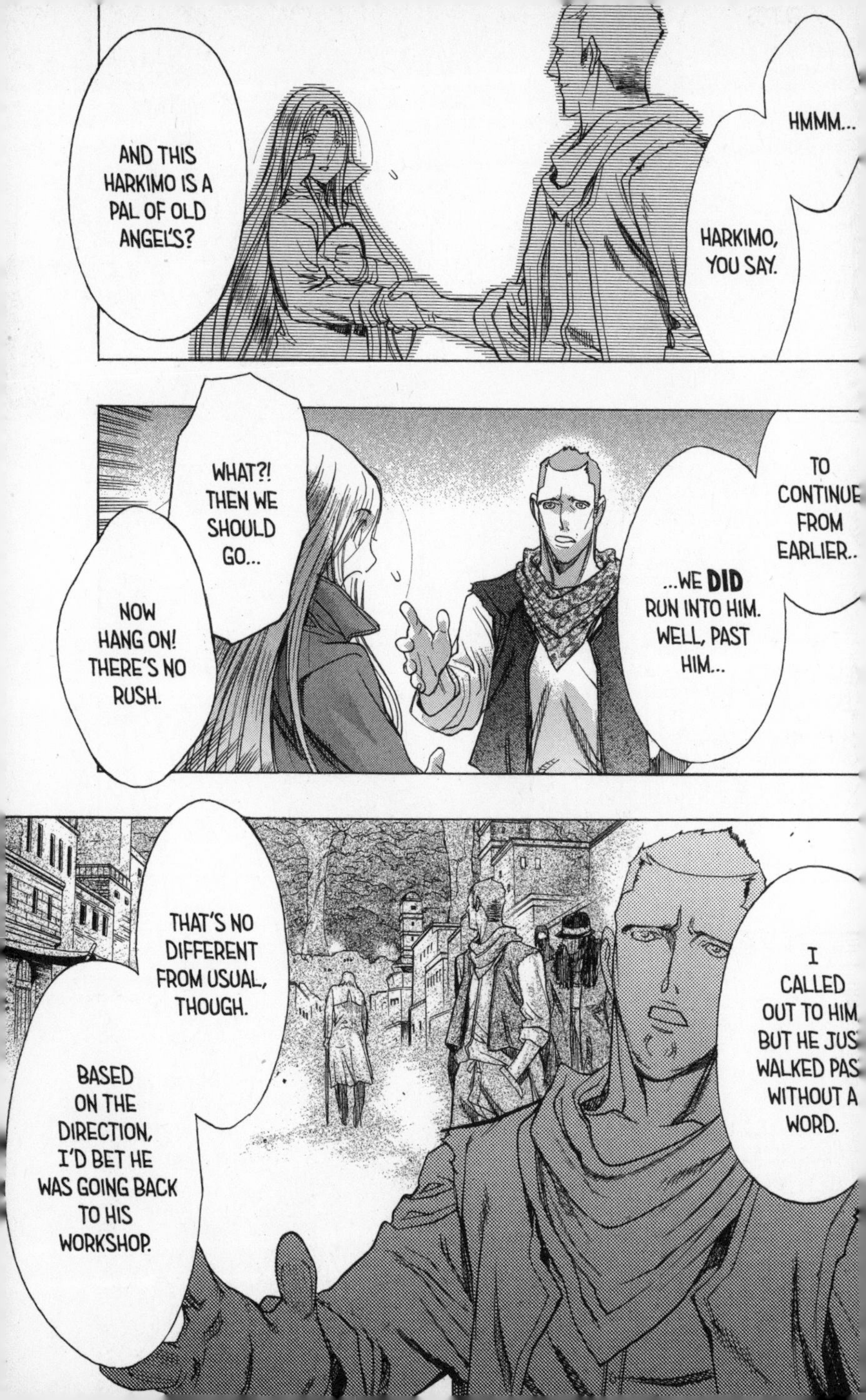
HMMM...
HARKIMO, YOU SAY.
AND THIS HARKIMO IS A PAL OF OLD ANGEL'S?
TO CONTINUE FROM EARLIER..
...WE **DID** RUN INTO HIM. WELL, PAST HIM...
WHAT?! THEN WE SHOULD GO...
NOW HANG ON! THERE'S NO RUSH.
I CALLED OUT TO HIM BUT HE JUS WALKED PAS WITHOUT A WORD.
THAT'S NO DIFFERENT FROM USUAL, THOUGH.
BASED ON THE DIRECTION, I'D BET HE WAS GOING BACK TO HIS WORKSHOP.

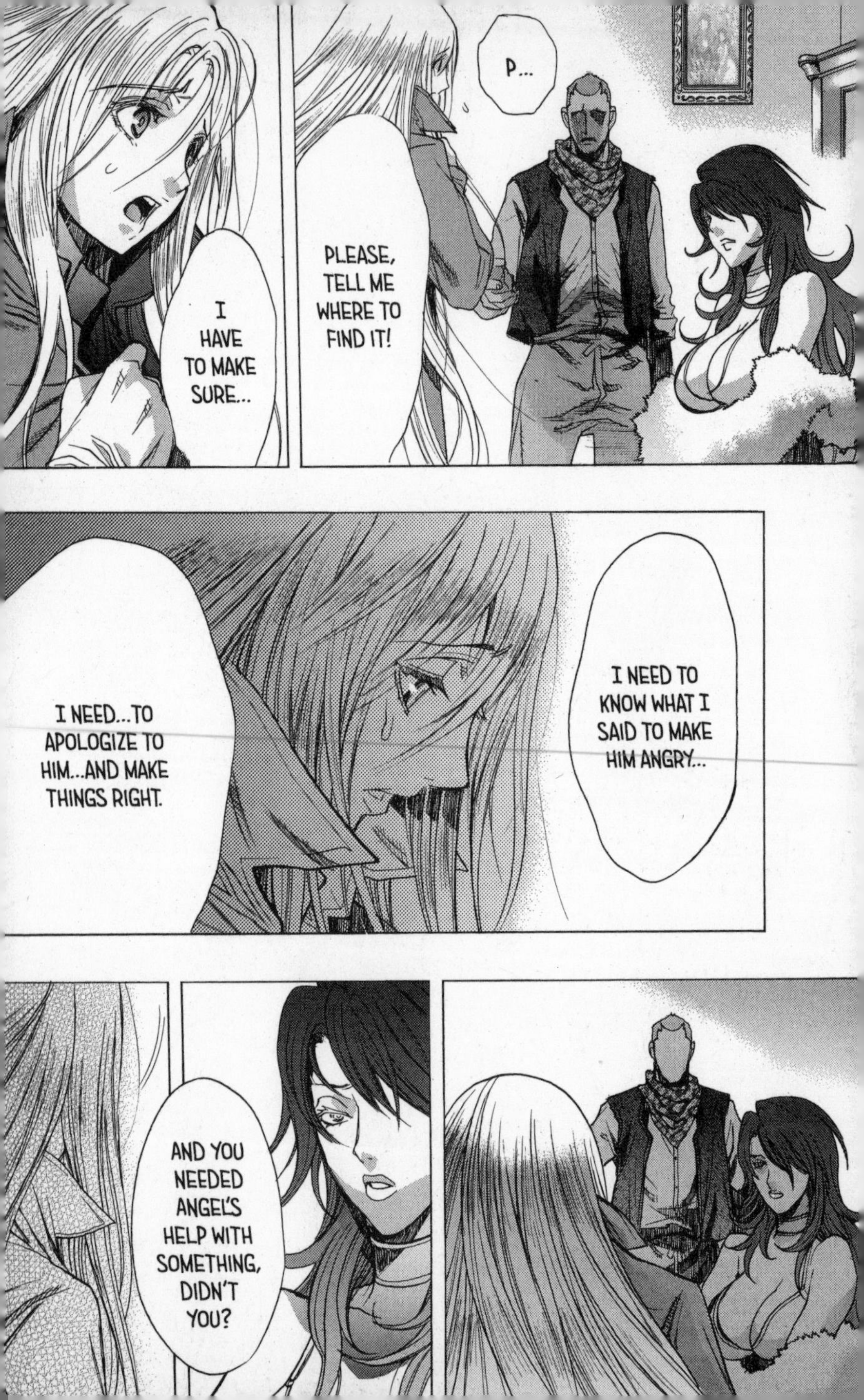
P...
PLEASE, TELL ME WHERE TO FIND IT!
I HAVE TO MAKE SURE...
I NEED TO KNOW WHAT I SAID TO MAKE HIM ANGRY...
I NEED...TO APOLOGIZE TO HIM...AND MAKE THINGS RIGHT.
AND YOU NEEDED ANGEL'S HELP WITH SOMETHING, DIDN'T YOU?

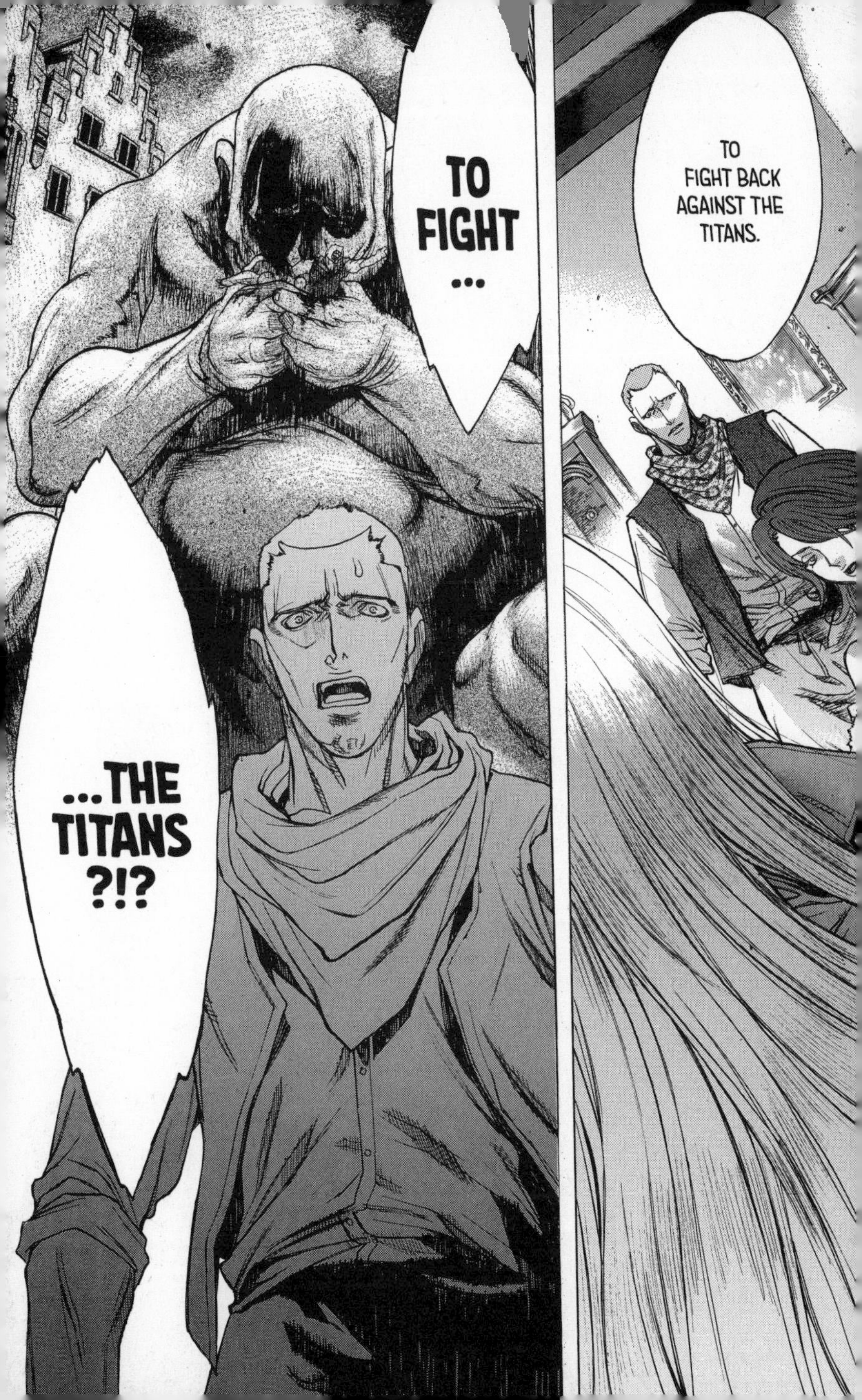
TO FIGHT BACK AGAINST THE TITANS.
TO FIGHT...
...THE TITANS?!?

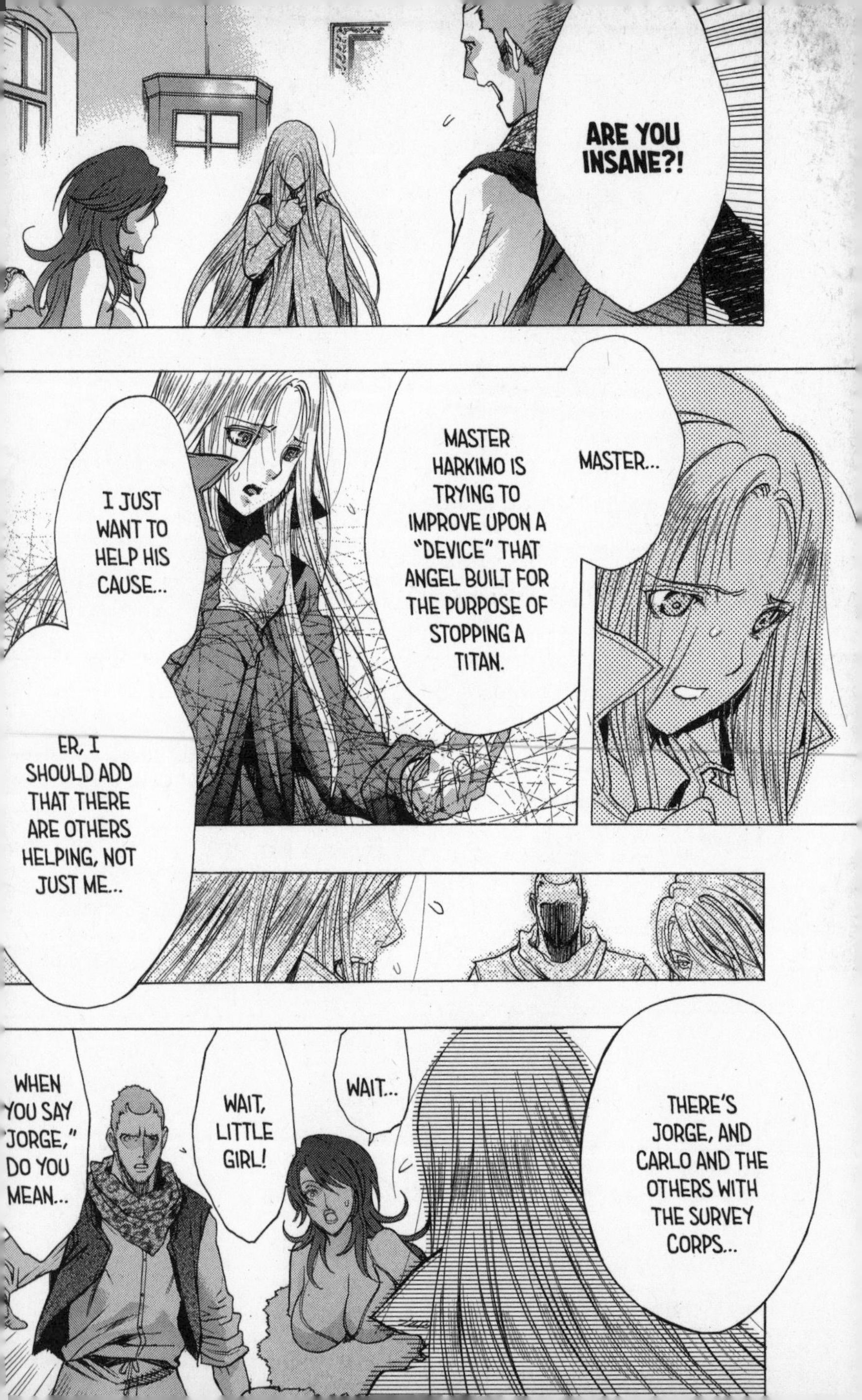
ARE YOU INSANE?!
MASTER...
MASTER HARKIMO IS TRYING TO IMPROVE UPON A "DEVICE" THAT ANGEL BUILT FOR THE PURPOSE OF STOPPING A TITAN.
I JUST WANT TO HELP HIS CAUSE...
ER, I SHOULD ADD THAT THERE ARE OTHERS HELPING, NOT JUST ME...
THERE'S JORGE, AND CARLO AND THE OTHERS WITH THE SURVEY CORPS...
WAIT...
WAIT, LITTLE GIRL!
WHEN YOU SAY "JORGE," DO YOU MEAN...

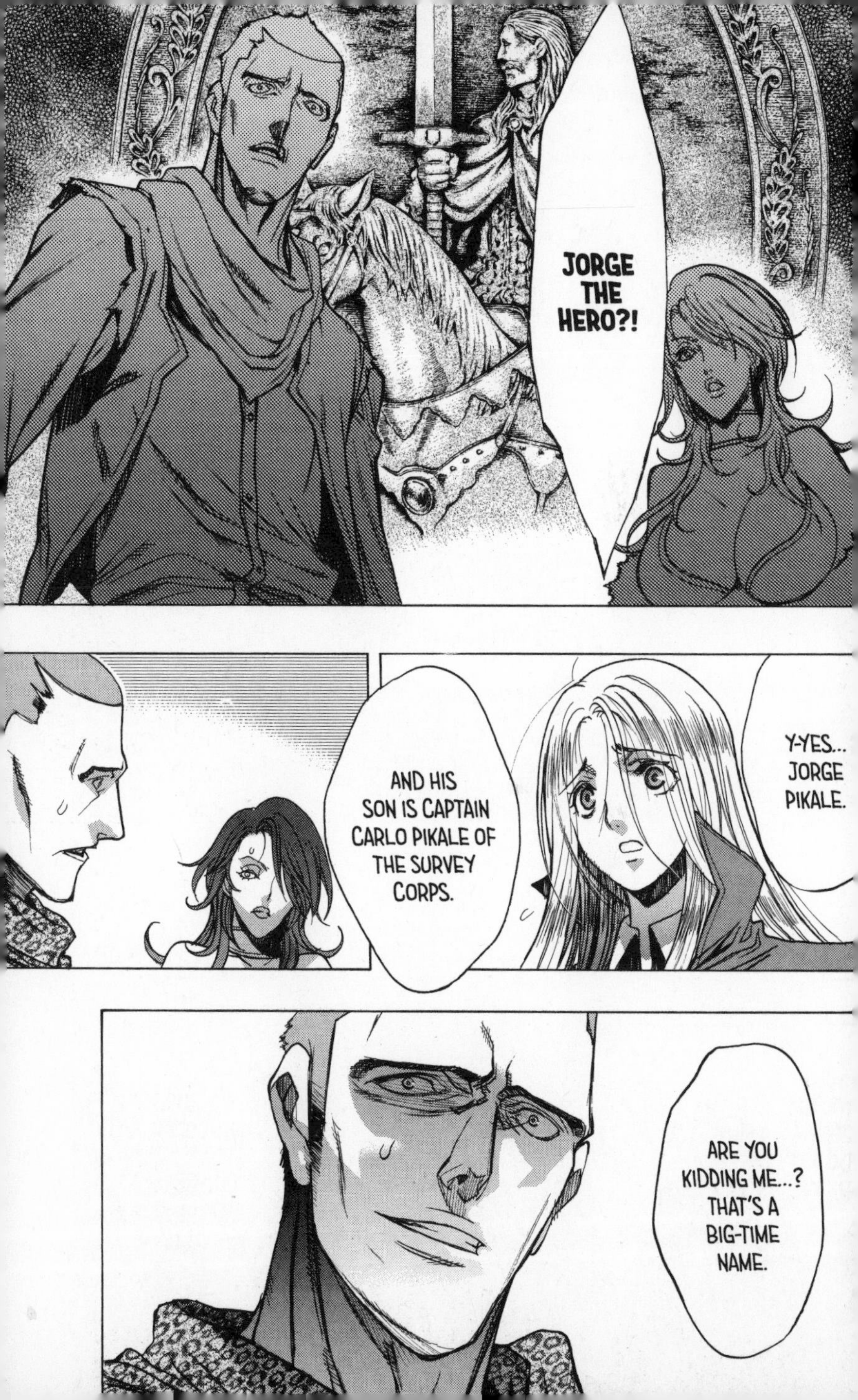
JORGE THE HERO?!
Y-YES... JORGE PIKALE.
AND HIS SON IS CAPTAIN CARLO PIKALE OF THE SURVEY CORPS.
ARE YOU KIDDING ME...? THAT'S A BIG-TIME NAME.

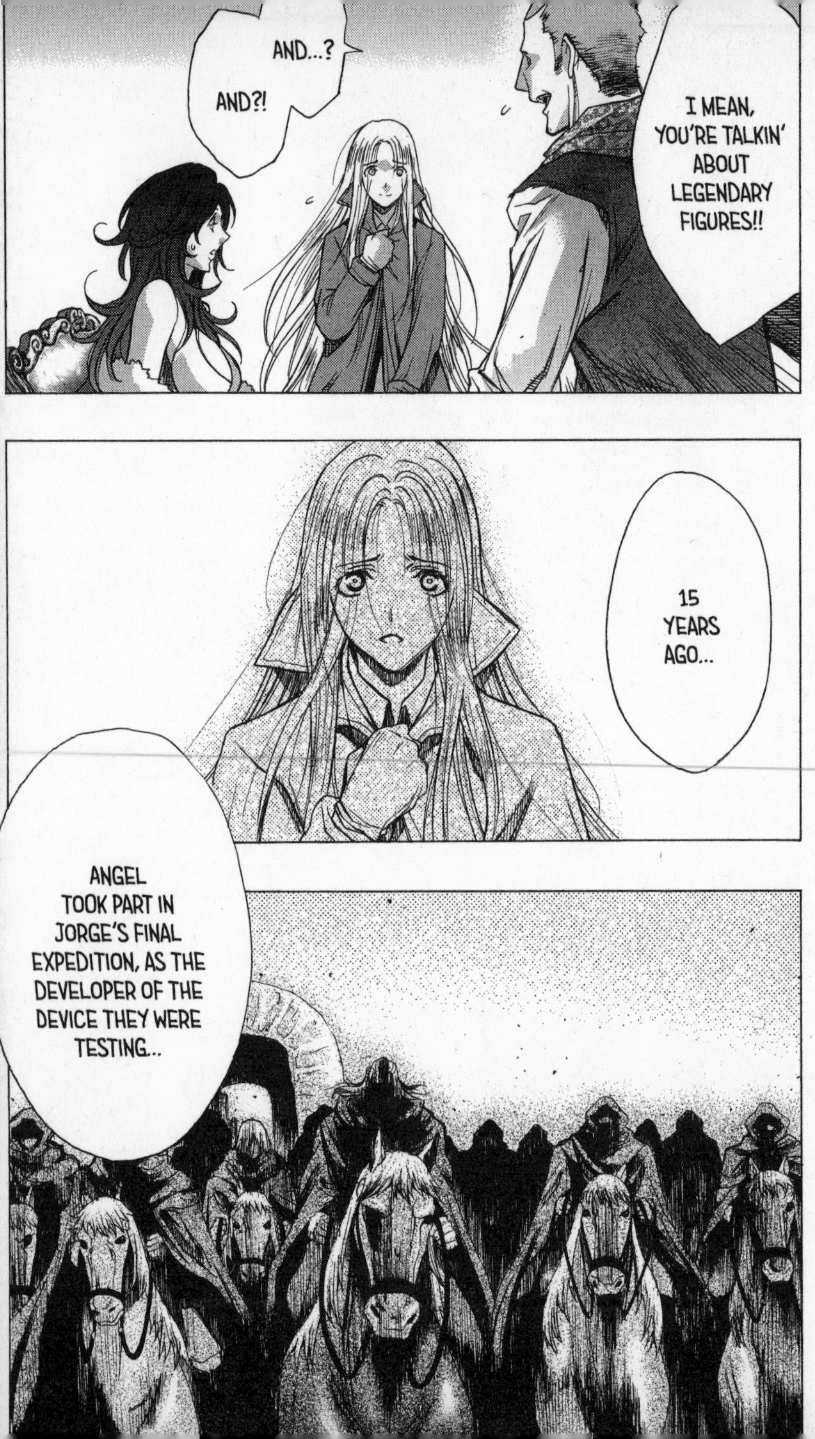
I MEAN, YOU'RE TALKIN' ABOUT LEGENDARY FIGURES!!
AND...?
AND?!
15 YEARS AGO...
ANGEL TOOK PART IN JORGE'S FINAL EXPEDITION, AS THE DEVELOPER OF THE DEVICE THEY WERE TESTING...

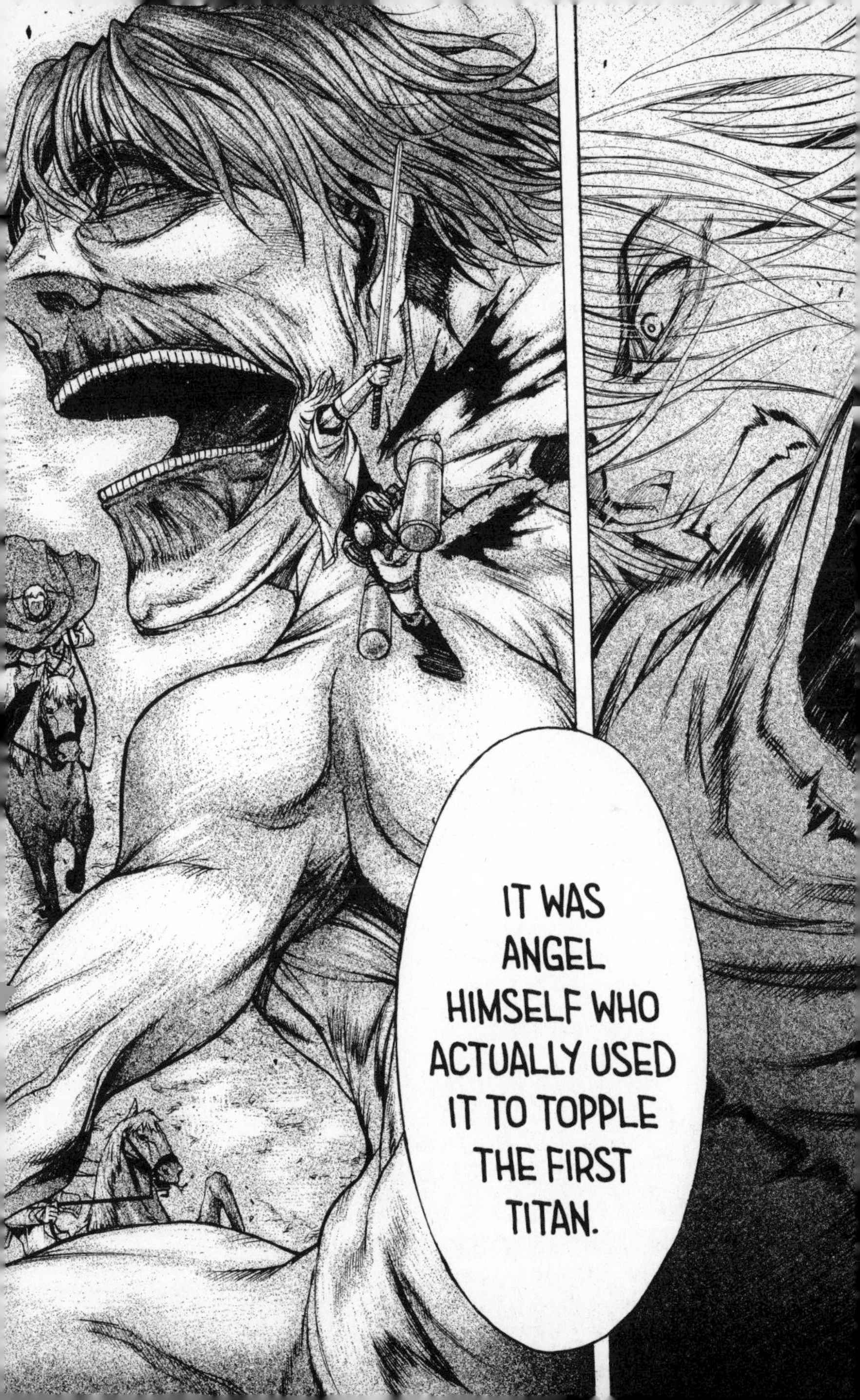
IT WAS ANGEL HIMSELF WHO ACTUALLY USED IT TO TOPPLE THE FIRST TITAN.

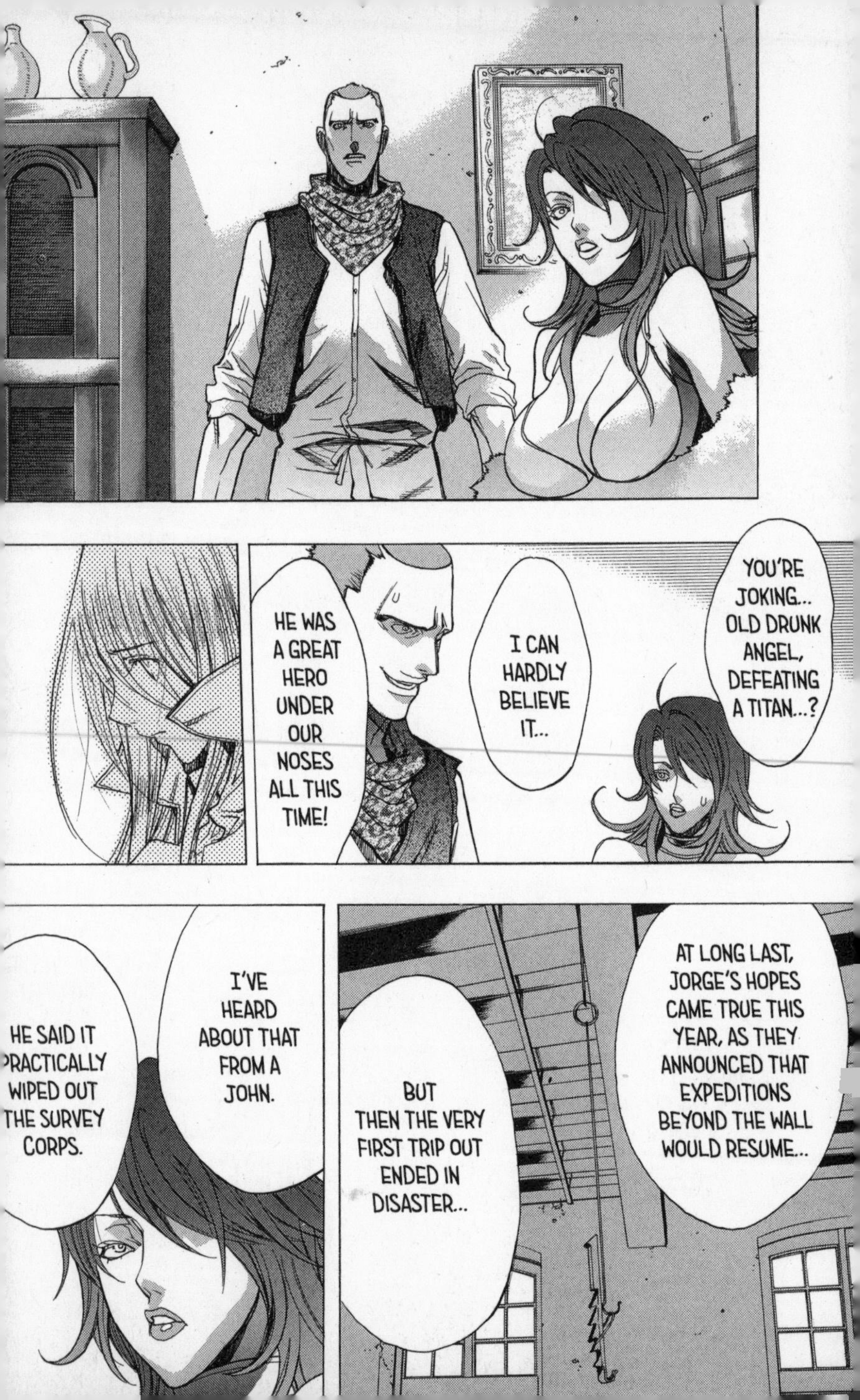
YOU'RE JOKING... OLD DRUNK ANGEL, DEFEATING A TITAN...?
I CAN HARDLY BELIEVE IT...
HE WAS A GREAT HERO UNDER OUR NOSES ALL THIS TIME!
AT LONG LAST, JORGE'S HOPES CAME TRUE THIS YEAR, AS THEY ANNOUNCED THAT EXPEDITIONS BEYOND THE WALL WOULD RESUME...
BUT THEN THE VERY FIRST TRIP OUT ENDED IN DISASTER...
I'VE HEARD ABOUT THAT FROM A JOHN.
HE SAID IT PRACTICALLY WIPED OUT THE SURVEY CORPS.

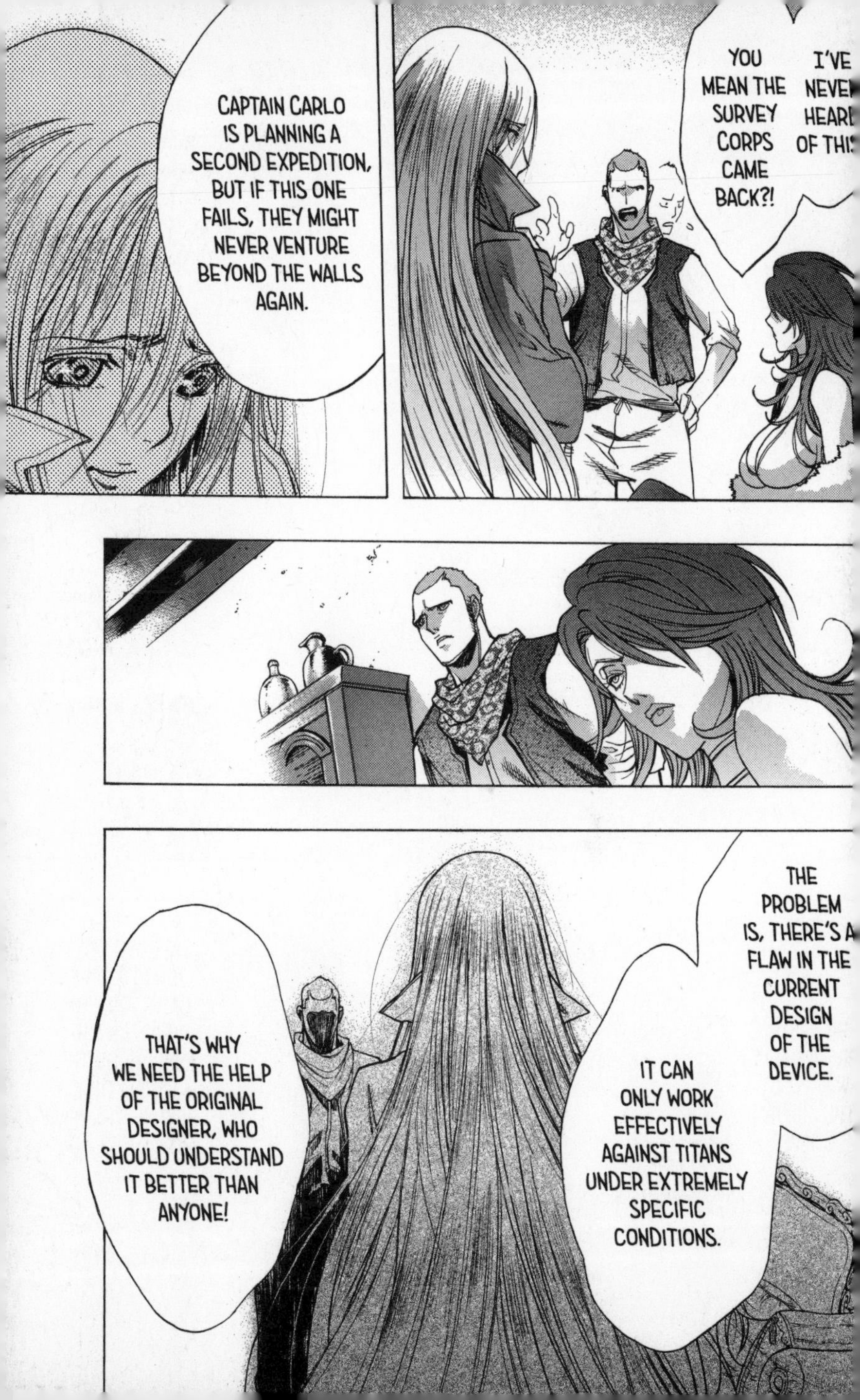

I'VE NEVE HEAR OF THI
YOU MEAN THE SURVEY CORPS CAME BACK?!
CAPTAIN CARLO IS PLANNING A SECOND EXPEDITION, BUT IF THIS ONE FAILS, THEY MIGHT NEVER VENTURE BEYOND THE WALLS AGAIN.
THE PROBLEM IS, THERE'S A FLAW IN THE CURRENT DESIGN OF THE DEVICE.
IT CAN ONLY WORK EFFECTIVELY AGAINST TITANS UNDER EXTREMELY SPECIFIC CONDITIONS.
THAT'S WHY WE NEED THE HELP OF THE ORIGINAL DESIGNER, WHO SHOULD UNDERSTAND IT BETTER THAN ANYONE!

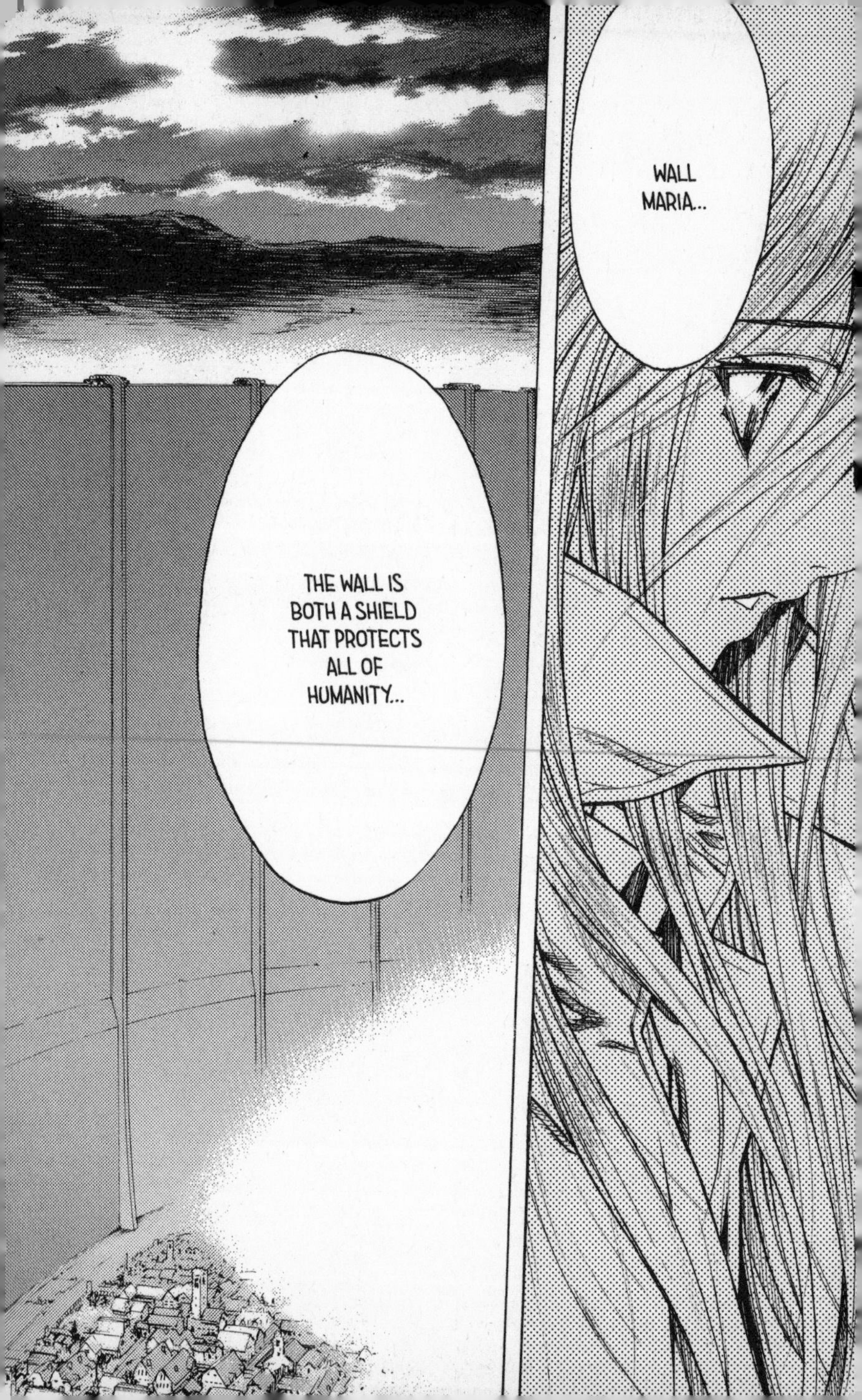
WALL MARIA...
THE WALL IS BOTH A SHIELD THAT PROTECTS ALL OF HUMANITY...

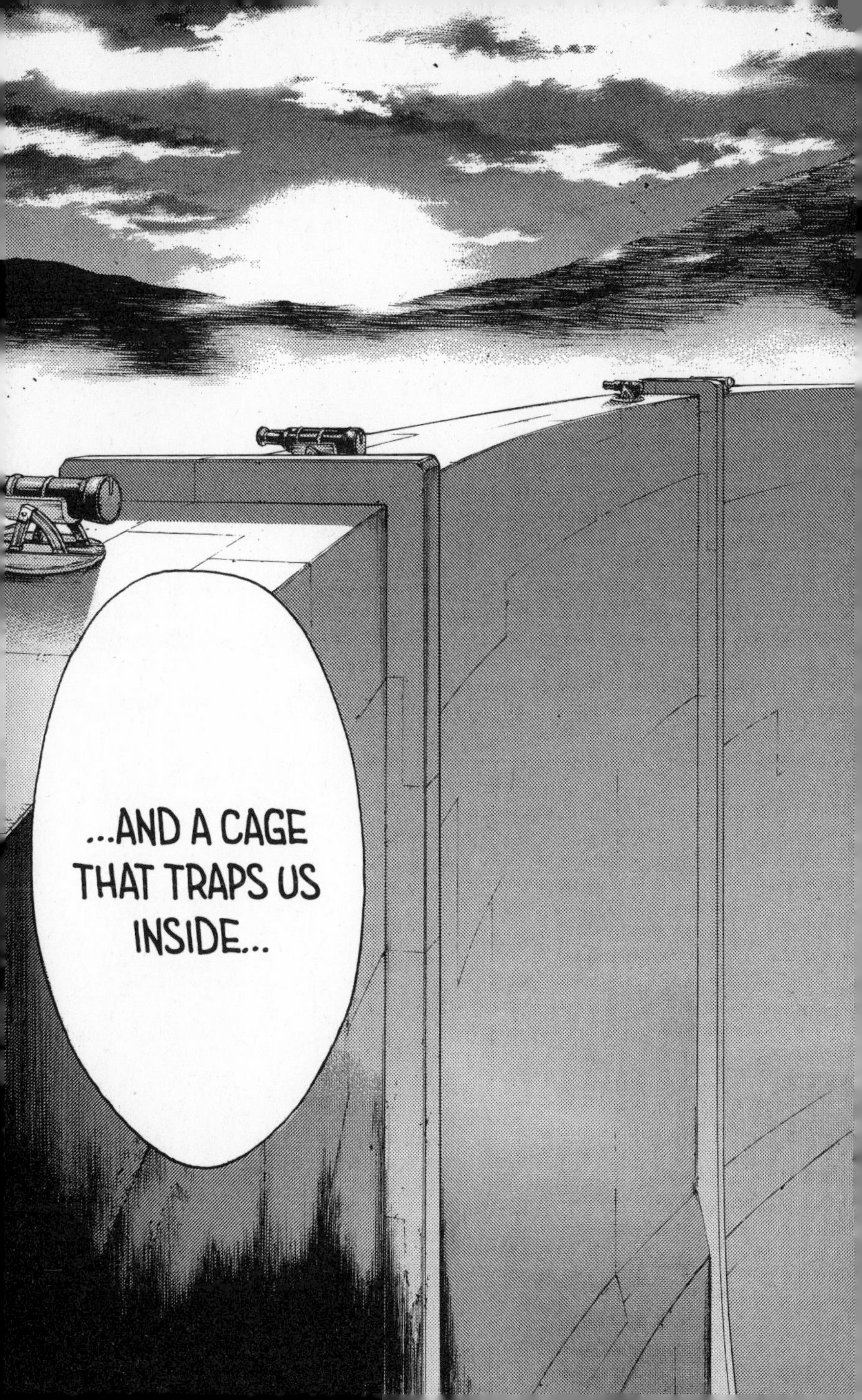
...AND A CAGE THAT TRAPS US INSIDE...

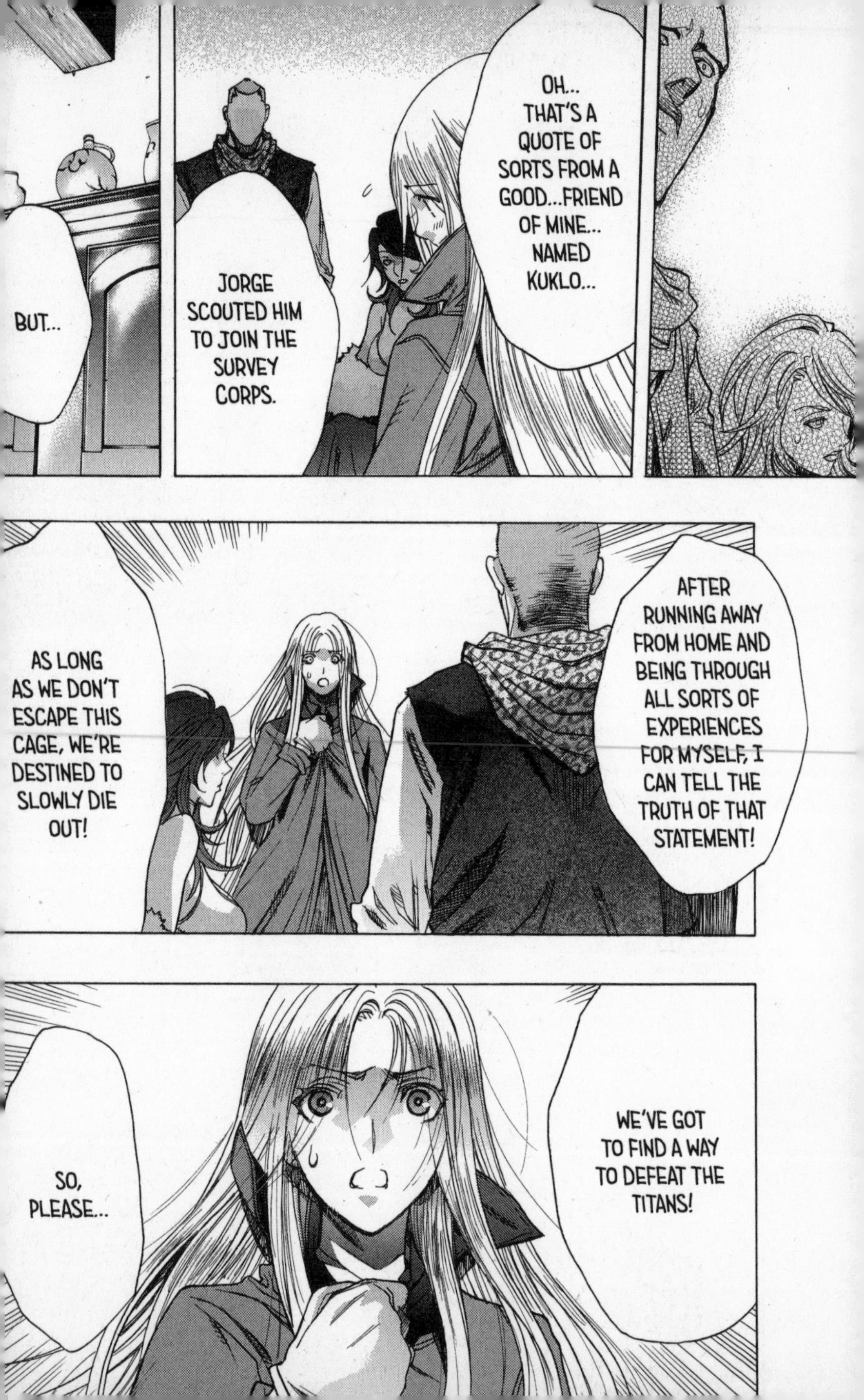
OH... THAT'S A QUOTE OF SORTS FROM A GOOD...FRIEND OF MINE... NAMED KUKLO...
JORGE SCOUTED HIM TO JOIN THE SURVEY CORPS.
BUT...
AFTER RUNNING AWAY FROM HOME AND BEING THROUGH ALL SORTS OF EXPERIENCES FOR MYSELF, I CAN TELL THE TRUTH OF THAT STATEMENT!
AS LONG AS WE DON'T ESCAPE THIS CAGE, WE'RE DESTINED TO SLOWLY DIE OUT!
WE'VE GOT TO FIND A WAY TO DEFEAT THE TITANS!
SO, PLEASE...

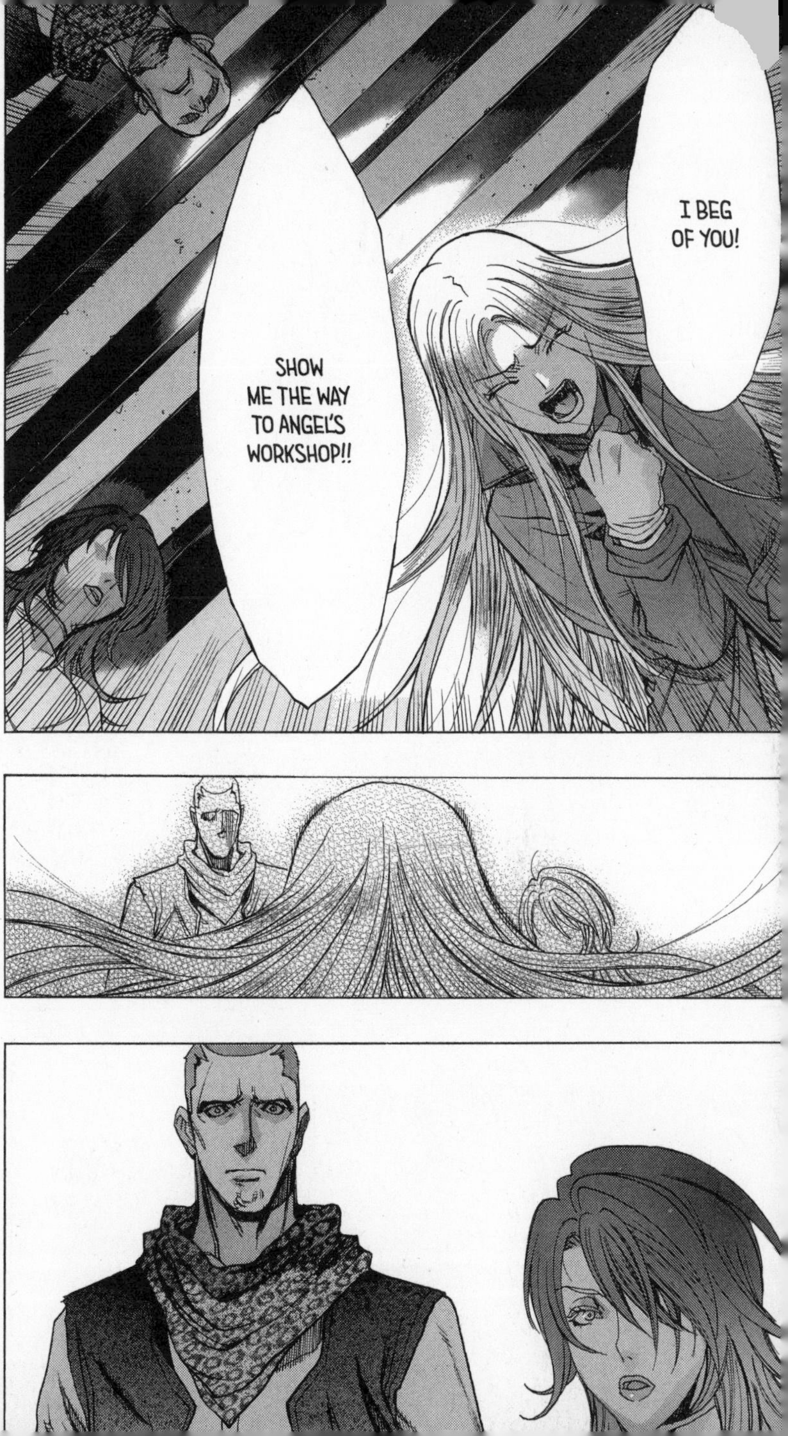
I BEG OF YOU!
SHOW ME THE WAY TO ANGEL'S WORKSHOP!!

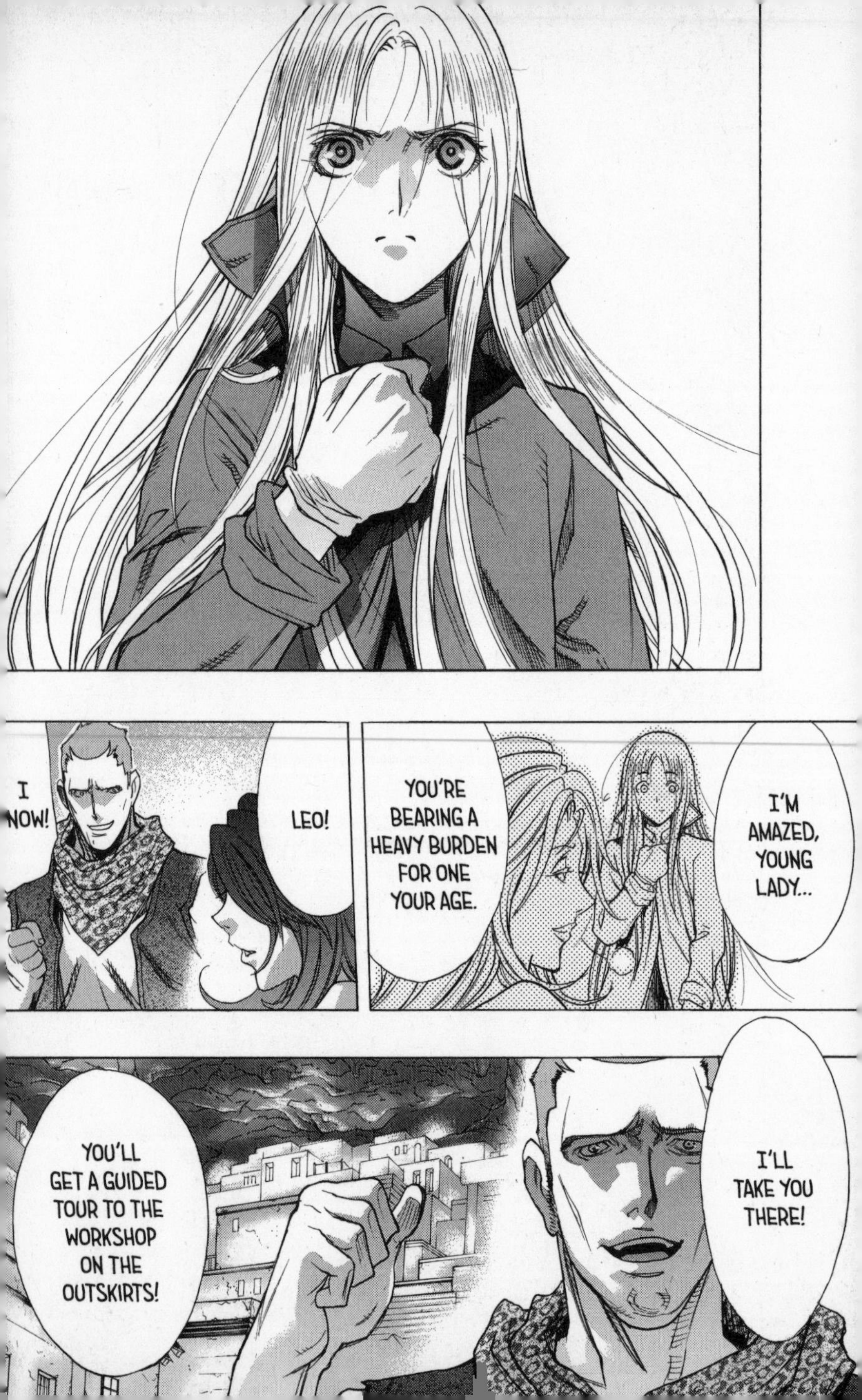
I'M AMAZED, YOUNG LADY...
YOU'RE BEARING A HEAVY BURDEN FOR ONE YOUR AGE.
LEO!
I
NOW!
I'LL TAKE YOU THERE!
YOU'LL GET A GUIDED TOUR TO THE WORKSHOP ON THE OUTSKIRTS!

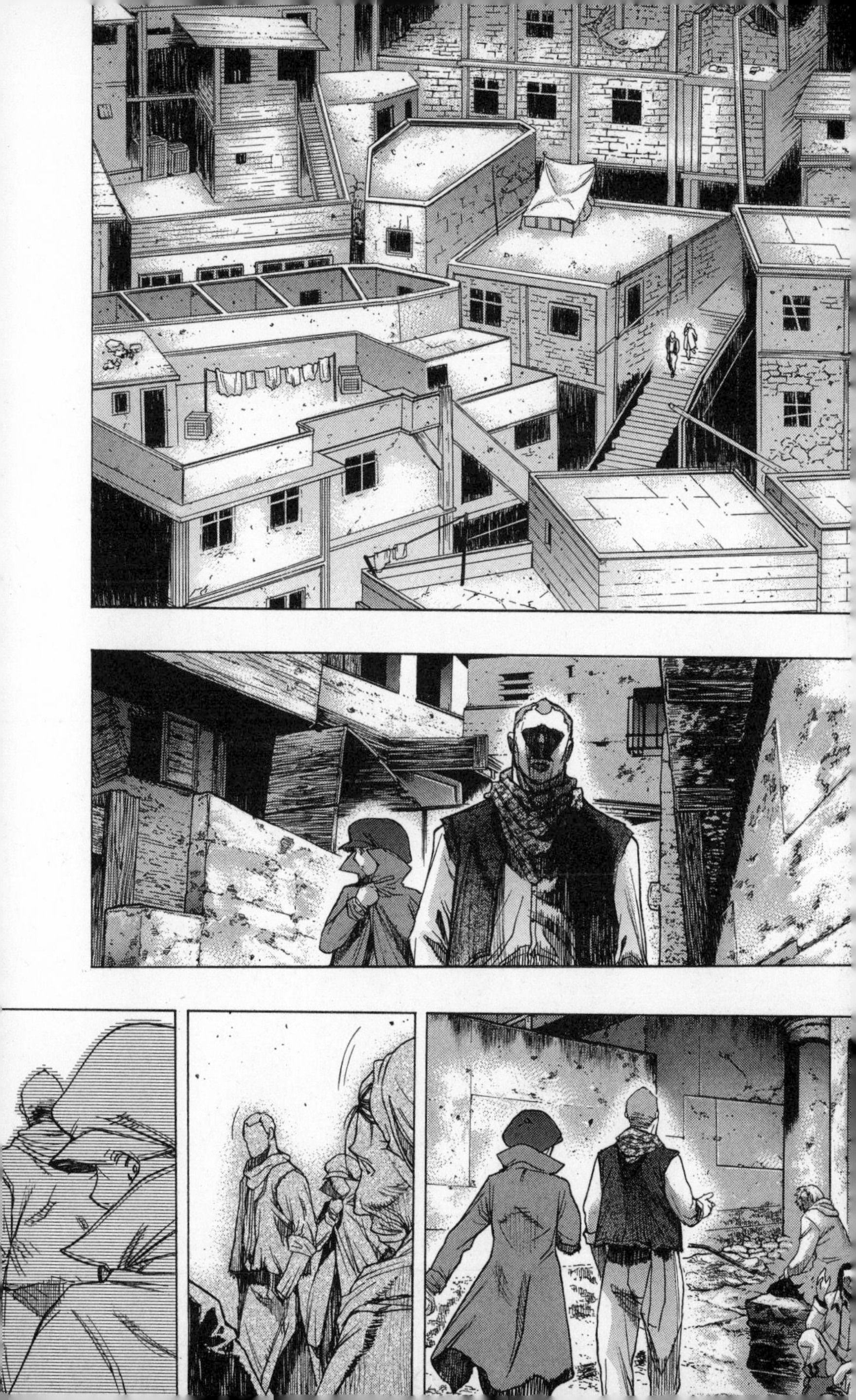

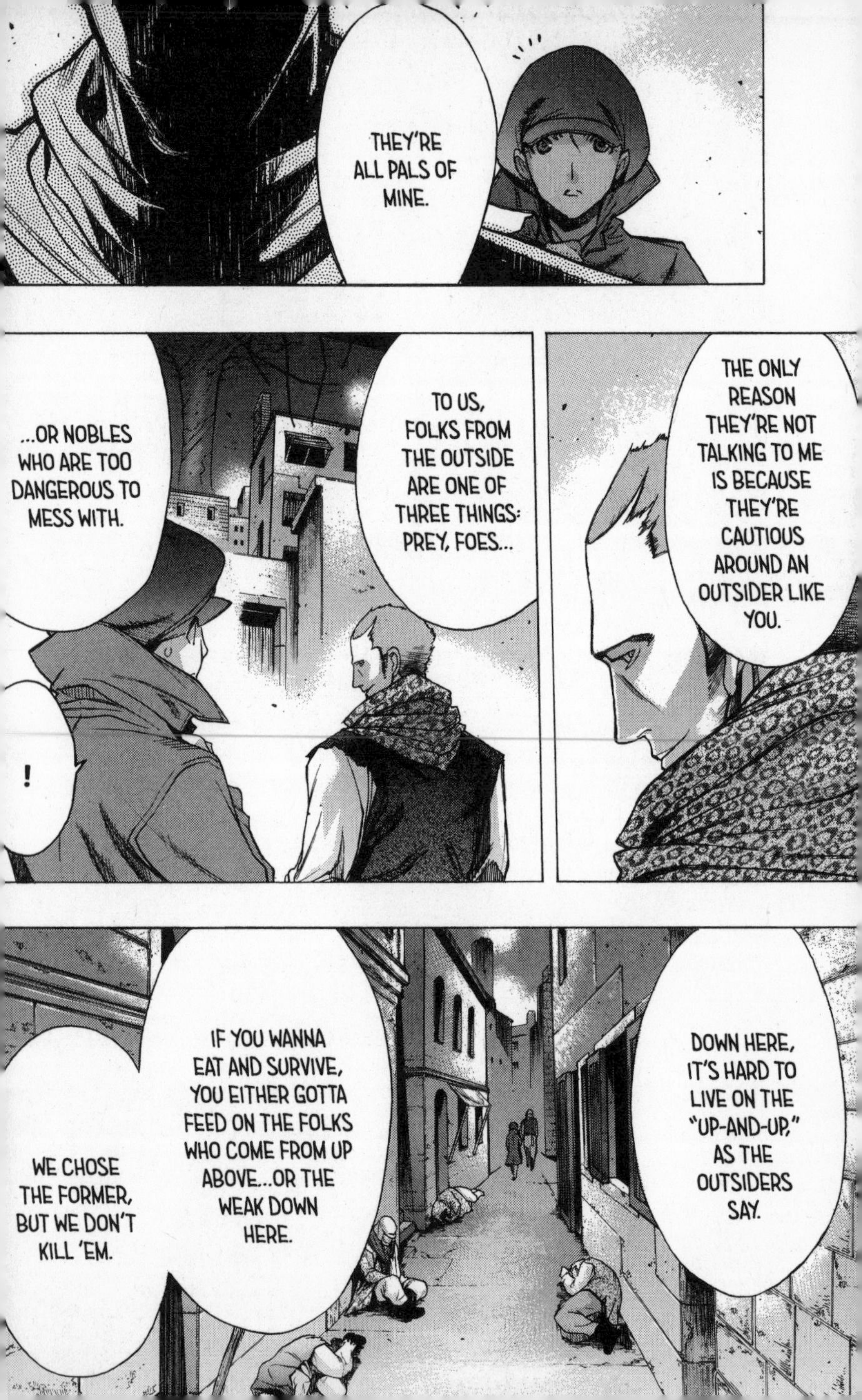
THEY'RE ALL PALS OF MINE.
THE ONLY REASON THEY'RE NOT TALKING TO ME IS BECAUSE THEY'RE CAUTIOUS AROUND AN OUTSIDER LIKE YOU.
TO US, FOLKS FROM THE OUTSIDE ARE ONE OF THREE THINGS: PREY, FOES...
...OR NOBLES WHO ARE TOO DANGEROUS TO MESS WITH.
!
DOWN HERE, IT'S HARD TO LIVE ON THE "UP-AND-UP," AS THE OUTSIDERS SAY.
IF YOU WANNA EAT AND SURVIVE, YOU EITHER GOTTA FEED ON THE FOLKS WHO COME FROM UP ABOVE...OR THE WEAK DOWN HERE.
WE CHOSE THE FORMER, BUT WE DON'T KILL 'EM.

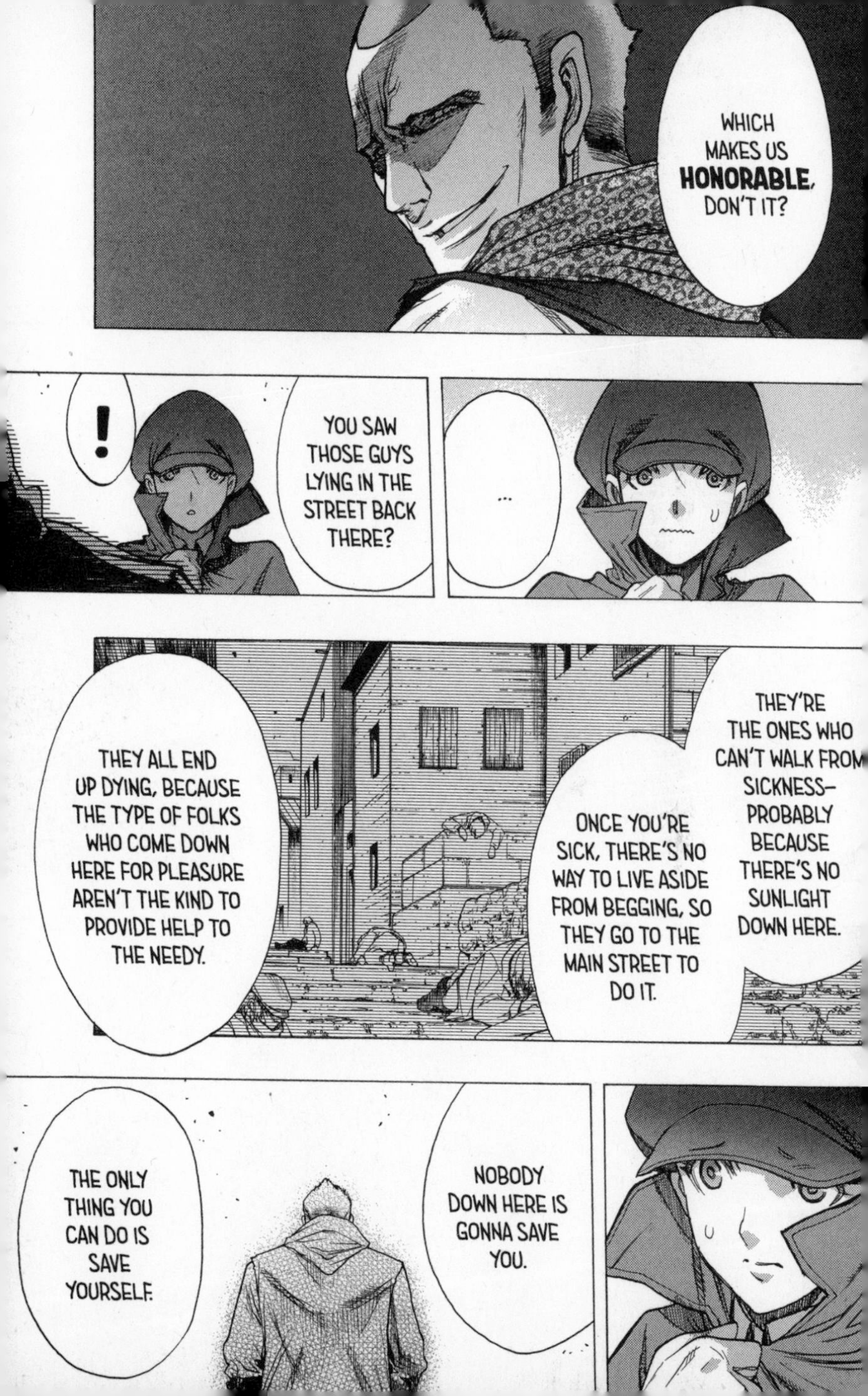
WHICH MAKES US **HONORABLE**, DON'T IT?
...
YOU SAW THOSE GUYS LYING IN THE STREET BACK THERE?
!
THEY'RE THE ONES WHO CAN'T WALK FROM SICKNESS— PROBABLY BECAUSE THERE'S NO SUNLIGHT DOWN HERE.
ONCE YOU'RE SICK, THERE'S NO WAY TO LIVE ASIDE FROM BEGGING, SO THEY GO TO THE MAIN STREET TO DO IT.
THEY ALL END UP DYING, BECAUSE THE TYPE OF FOLKS WHO COME DOWN HERE FOR PLEASURE AREN'T THE KIND TO PROVIDE HELP TO THE NEEDY.
NOBODY DOWN HERE IS GONNA SAVE YOU.
THE ONLY THING YOU CAN DO IS SAVE YOURSELF.

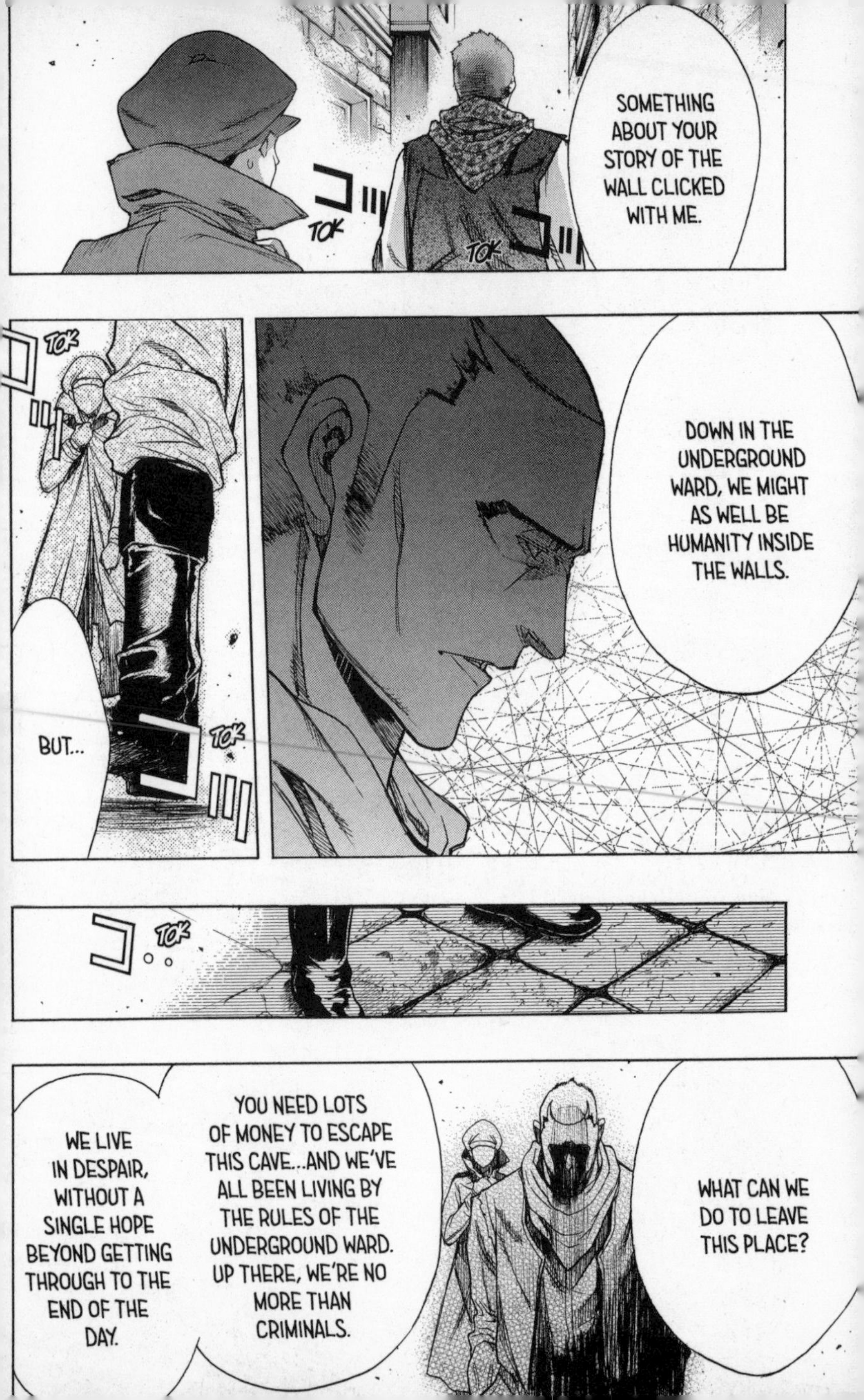
SOMETHING ABOUT YOUR STORY OF THE WALL CLICKED WITH ME.
TOK
TOK
DOWN IN THE UNDERGROUND WARD, WE MIGHT AS WELL BE HUMANITY INSIDE THE WALLS.
TOK
TOK
BUT...
TOK
WHAT CAN WE DO TO LEAVE THIS PLACE?
YOU NEED LOTS OF MONEY TO ESCAPE THIS CAVE...AND WE'VE ALL BEEN LIVING BY THE RULES OF THE UNDERGROUND WARD. UP THERE, WE'RE NO MORE THAN CRIMINALS.
WE LIVE IN DESPAIR, WITHOUT A SINGLE HOPE BEYOND GETTING THROUGH TO THE END OF THE DAY.

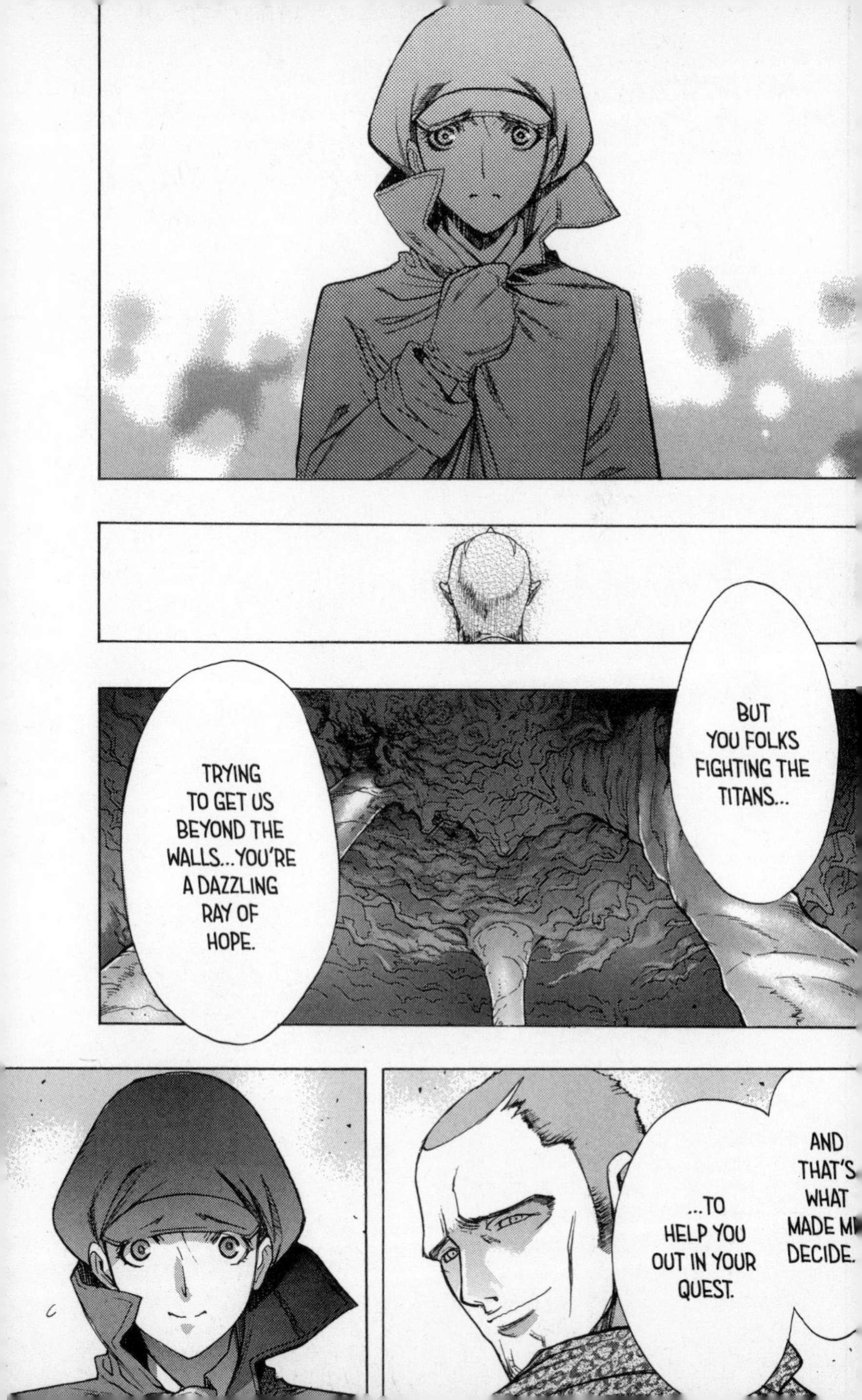
BUT YOU FOLKS FIGHTING THE TITANS...
TRYING TO GET US BEYOND THE WALLS...YOU'RE A DAZZLING RAY OF HOPE.
AND THAT'S WHAT MADE M DECIDE.
...TO HELP YOU OUT IN YOUR QUEST.

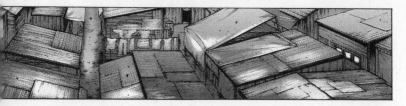

HA HA HA!

HEE HYA HYA!

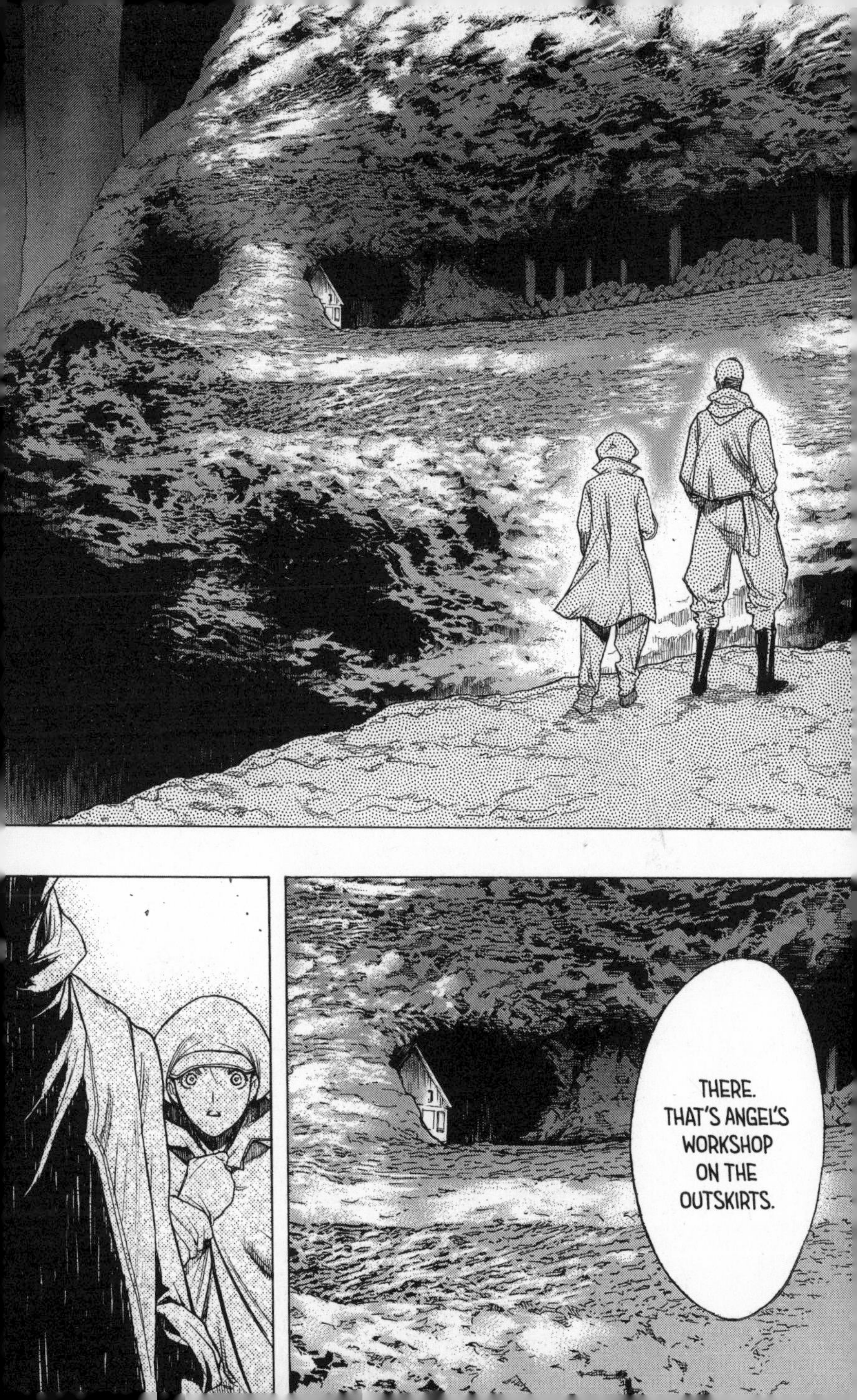
THERE. THAT'S ANGEL'S WORKSHOP ON THE OUTSKIRTS.

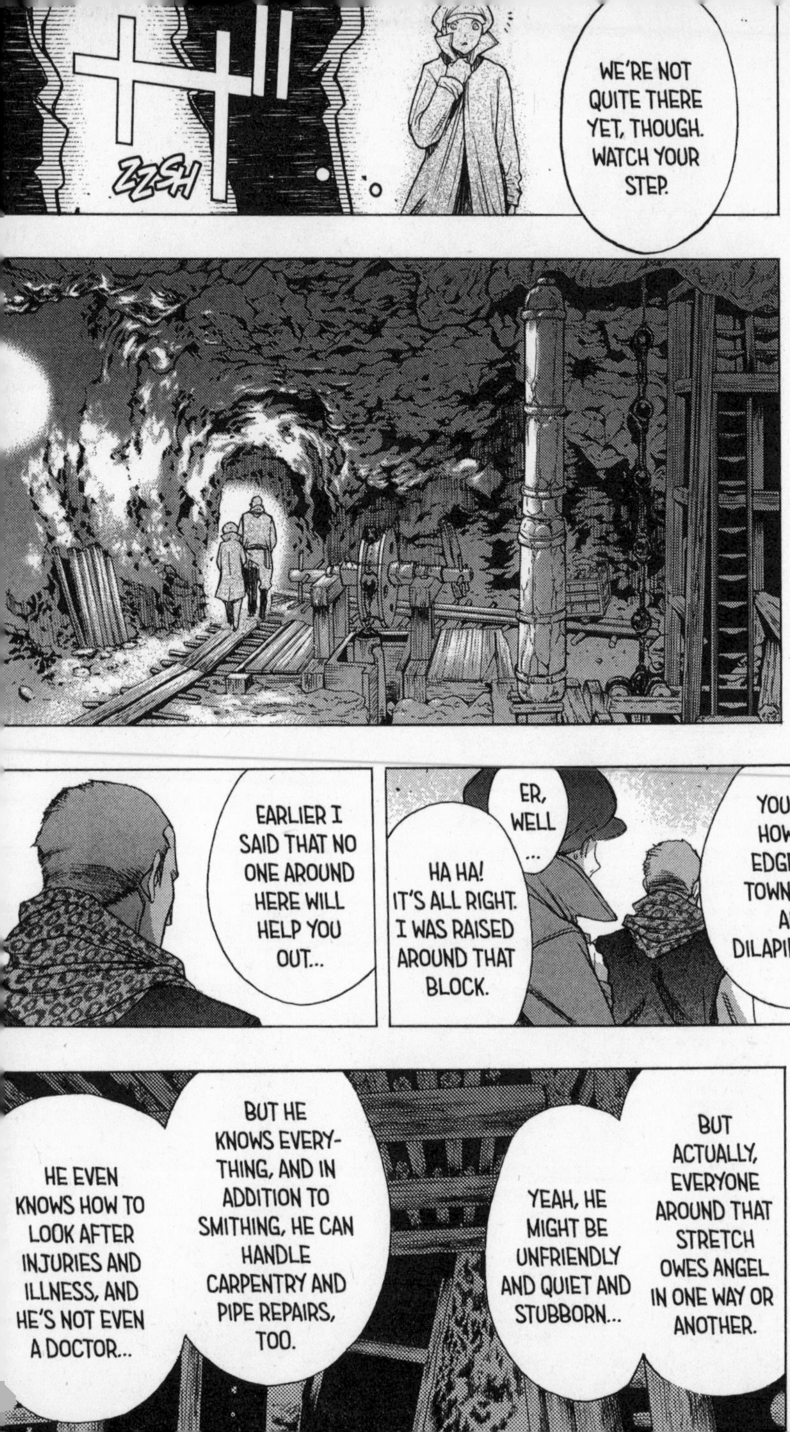
WE'RE NOT QUITE THERE YET, THOUGH. WATCH YOUR STEP.
ZZSH
YOU SAW HOW THE EDGES OF TOWN WERE ALL DILAPIDATED?
ER, WELL...
HA HA! IT'S ALL RIGHT. I WAS RAISED AROUND THAT BLOCK.
EARLIER I SAID THAT NO ONE AROUND HERE WILL HELP YOU OUT...
BUT ACTUALLY, EVERYONE AROUND THAT STRETCH OWES ANGEL IN ONE WAY OR ANOTHER.
YEAH, HE MIGHT BE UNFRIENDLY AND QUIET AND STUBBORN...
BUT HE KNOWS EVERY-THING, AND IN ADDITION TO SMITHING, HE CAN HANDLE CARPENTRY AND PIPE REPAIRS, TOO.
HE EVEN KNOWS HOW TO LOOK AFTER INJURIES AND ILLNESS, AND HE'S NOT EVEN A DOCTOR...

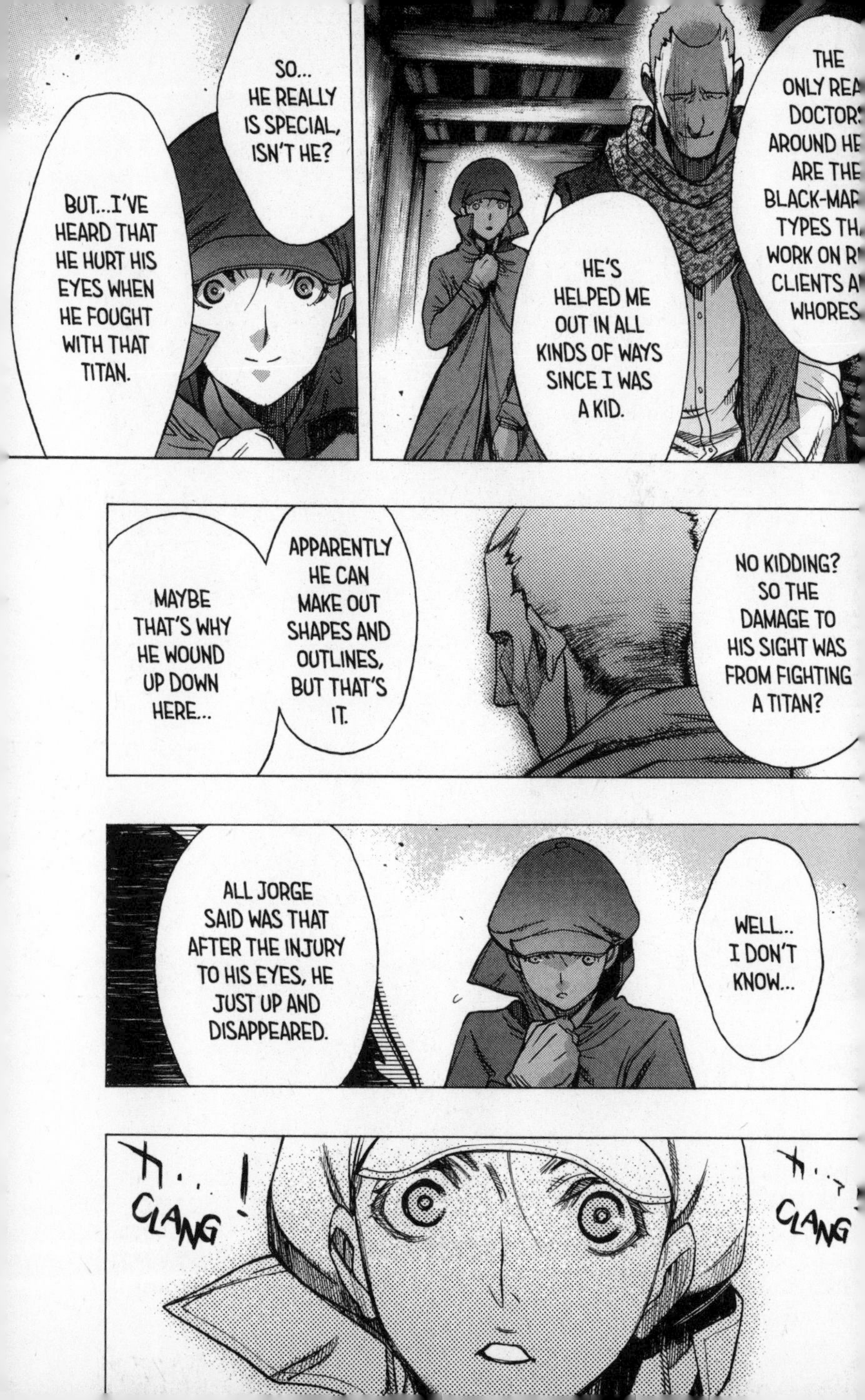

THE ONLY REA DOCTOR: AROUND HE ARE THE BLACK-MAR TYPES TH WORK ON R CLIENTS A WHORES
HE'S HELPED ME OUT IN ALL KINDS OF WAYS SINCE I WAS A KID.
SO... HE REALLY IS SPECIAL, ISN'T HE?
BUT...I'VE HEARD THAT HE HURT HIS EYES WHEN HE FOUGHT WITH THAT TITAN.
NO KIDDING? SO THE DAMAGE TO HIS SIGHT WAS FROM FIGHTING A TITAN?
APPARENTLY HE CAN MAKE OUT SHAPES AND OUTLINES, BUT THAT'S IT.
MAYBE THAT'S WHY HE WOUND UP DOWN HERE...
WELL... I DON'T KNOW...
ALL JORGE SAID WAS THAT AFTER THE INJURY TO HIS EYES, HE JUST UP AND DISAPPEARED.
CLANG
CLANG

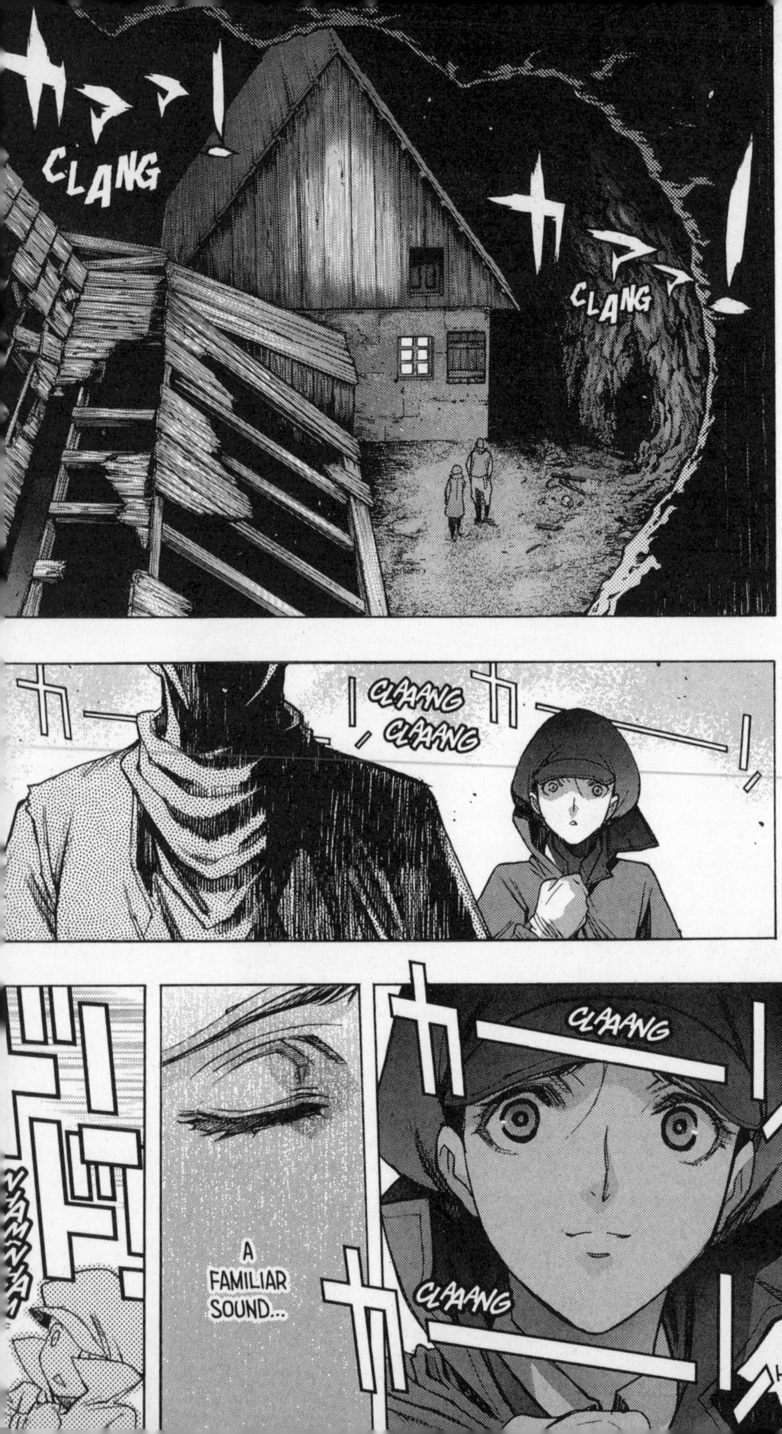
CLANG
CLANG
CLAAANG
CLAAANG
CLAAANG
CLAAANG
THAT'S A HAMMER...
A FAMILIAR SOUND...

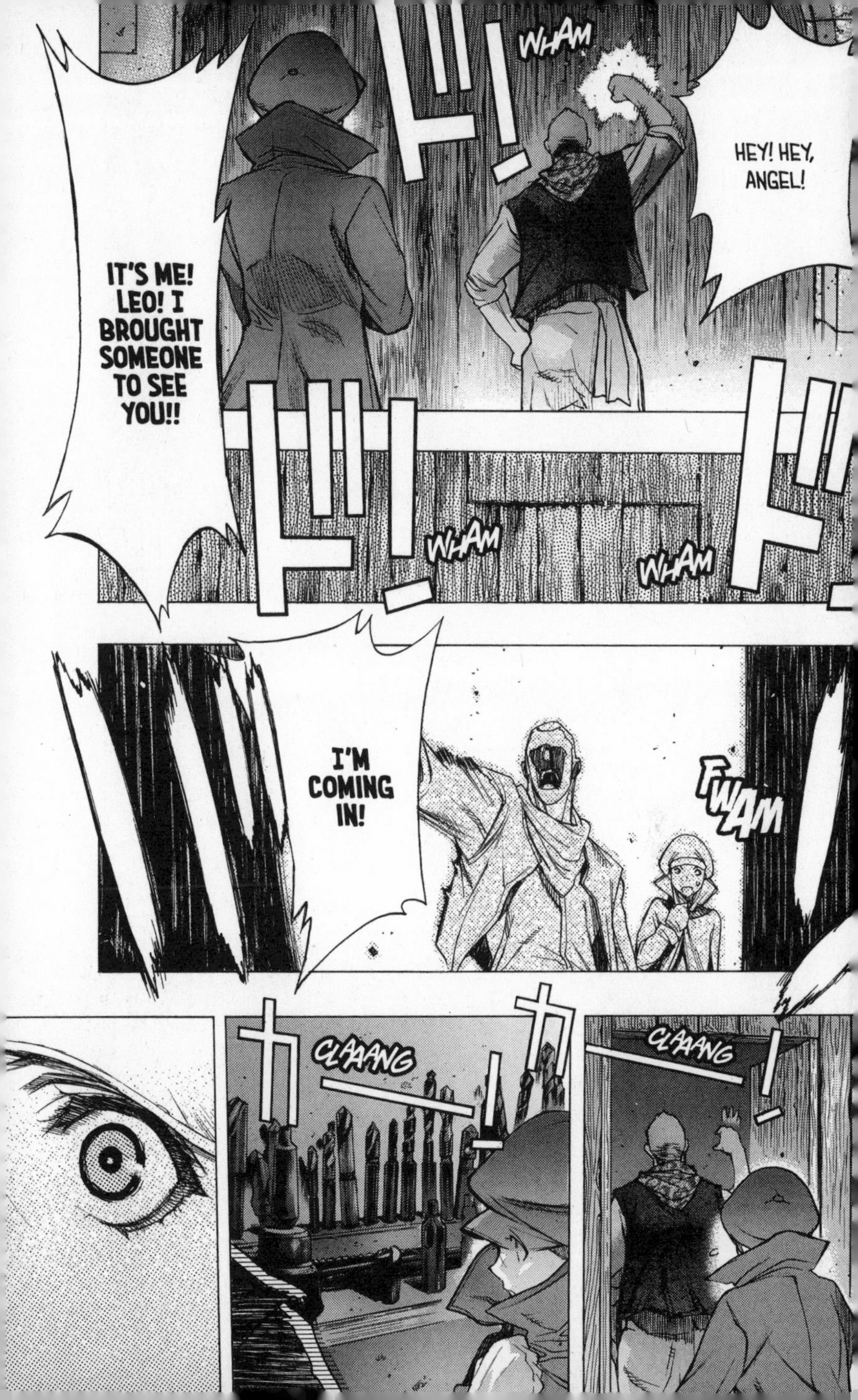
WHAM
HEY! HEY, ANGEL!
IT'S ME! LEO! I BROUGHT SOMEONE TO SEE YOU!!
WHAM
WHAM
FWAM
I'M COMING IN!
CLAAANG
CLAAANG

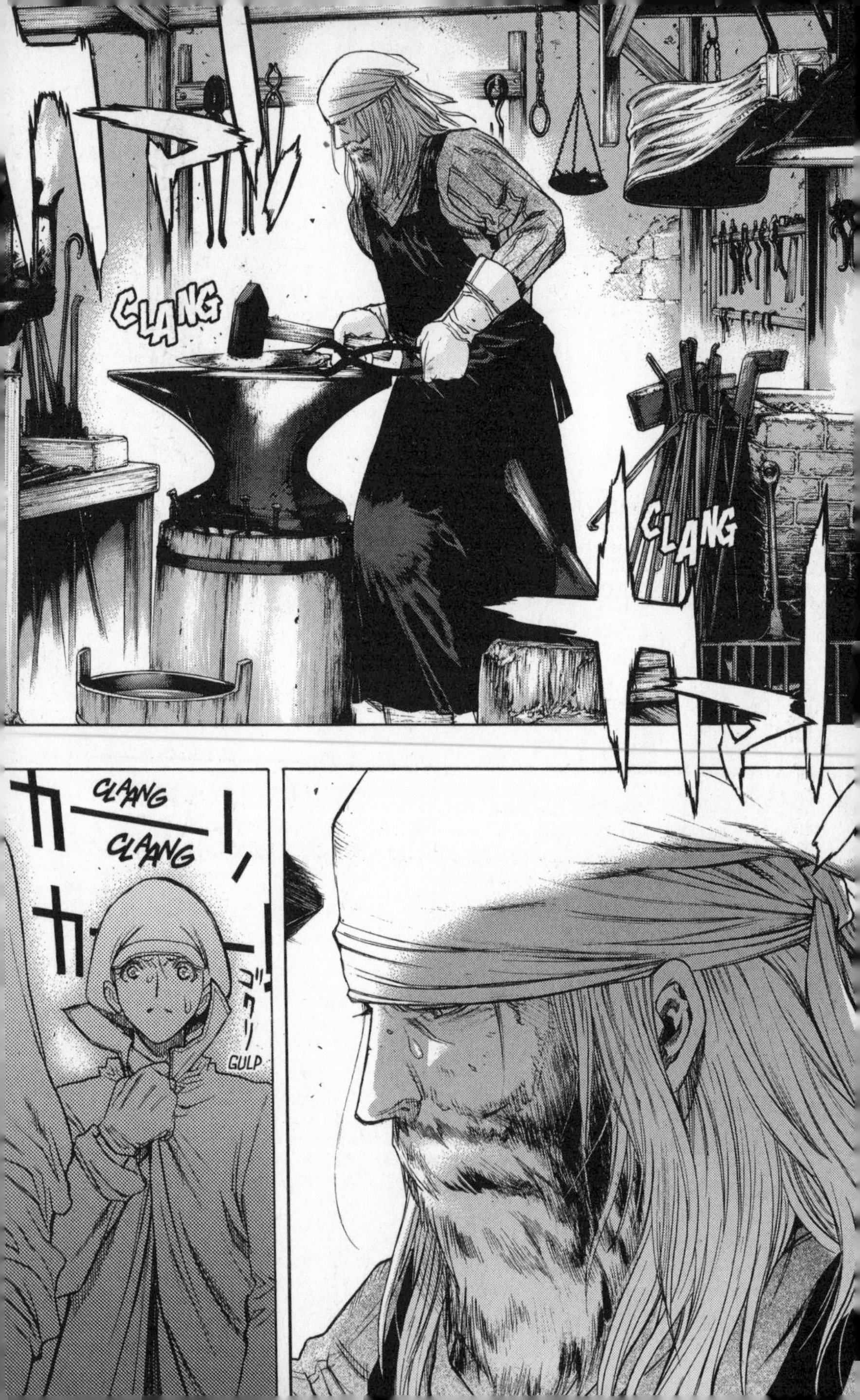
CLANG
CLANG
CLAANG
CLAANG
ゴクリ
GULP

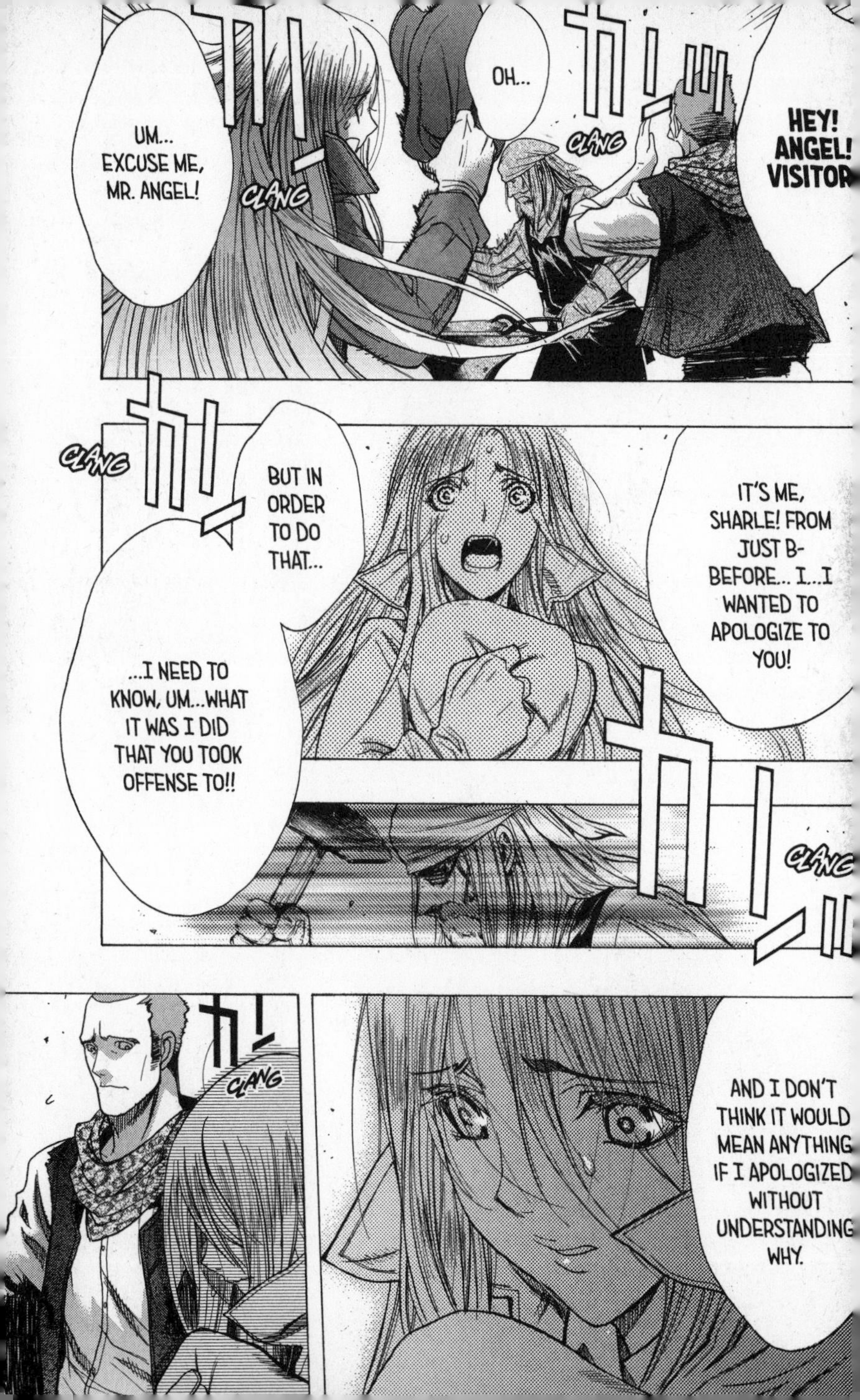
HEY! ANGEL! VISITOR
CLANG
OH...
UM... EXCUSE ME, MR. ANGEL!
CLANG
IT'S ME, SHARLE! FROM JUST B-BEFORE... I...I WANTED TO APOLOGIZE TO YOU!
BUT IN ORDER TO DO THAT...
CLANG
...I NEED TO KNOW, UM...WHAT IT WAS I DID THAT YOU TOOK OFFENSE TO!!
CLANG
AND I DON'T THINK IT WOULD MEAN ANYTHING IF I APOLOGIZED WITHOUT UNDERSTANDING WHY.
CLANG

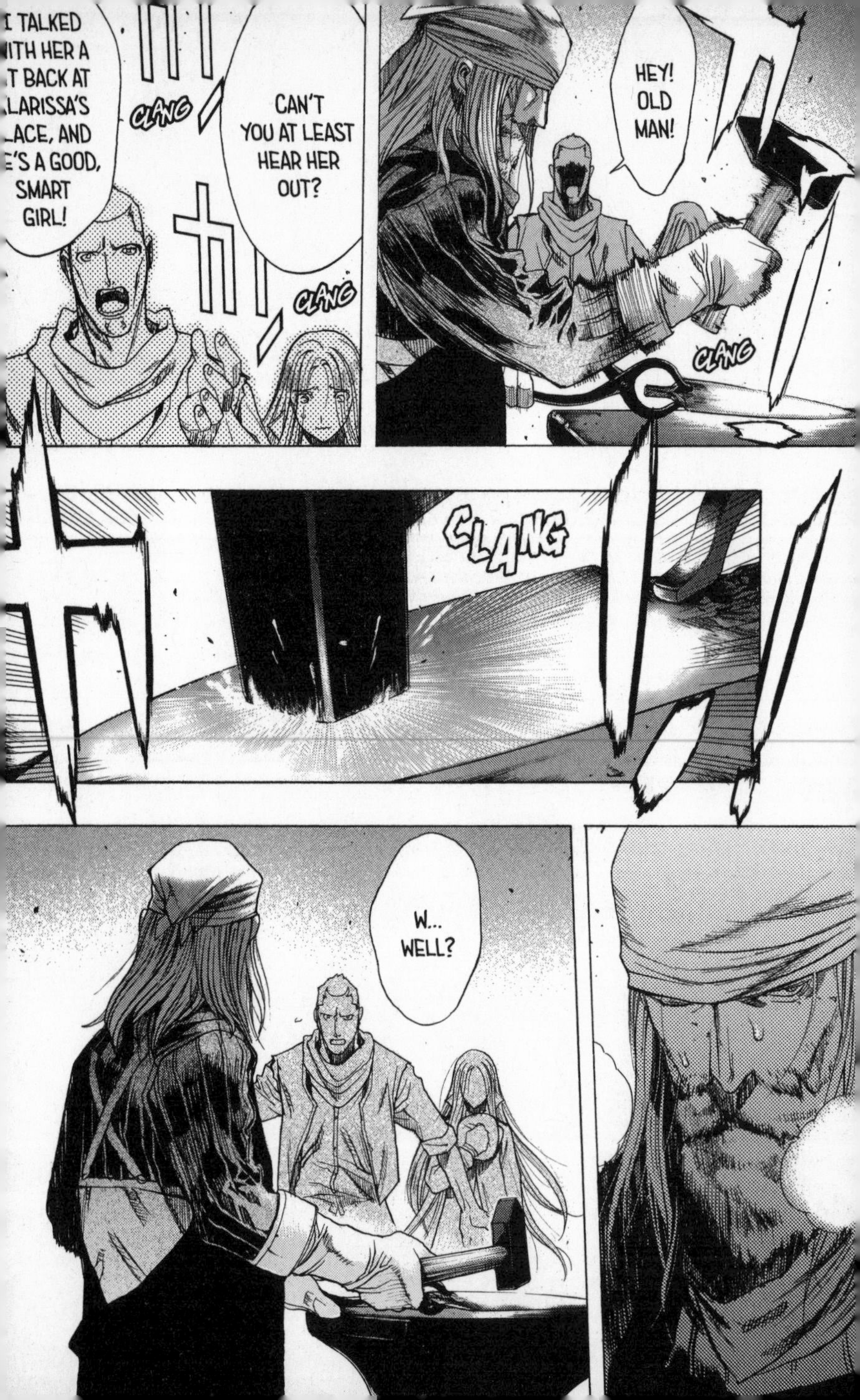
HEY! OLD MAN!
CLANG
CAN'T YOU AT LEAST HEAR HER OUT?
I TALKED ITH HER A T BACK AT LARISSA'S ACE, AND E'S A GOOD, SMART GIRL!
CLANG
CLANG
CLANG
W... WELL?

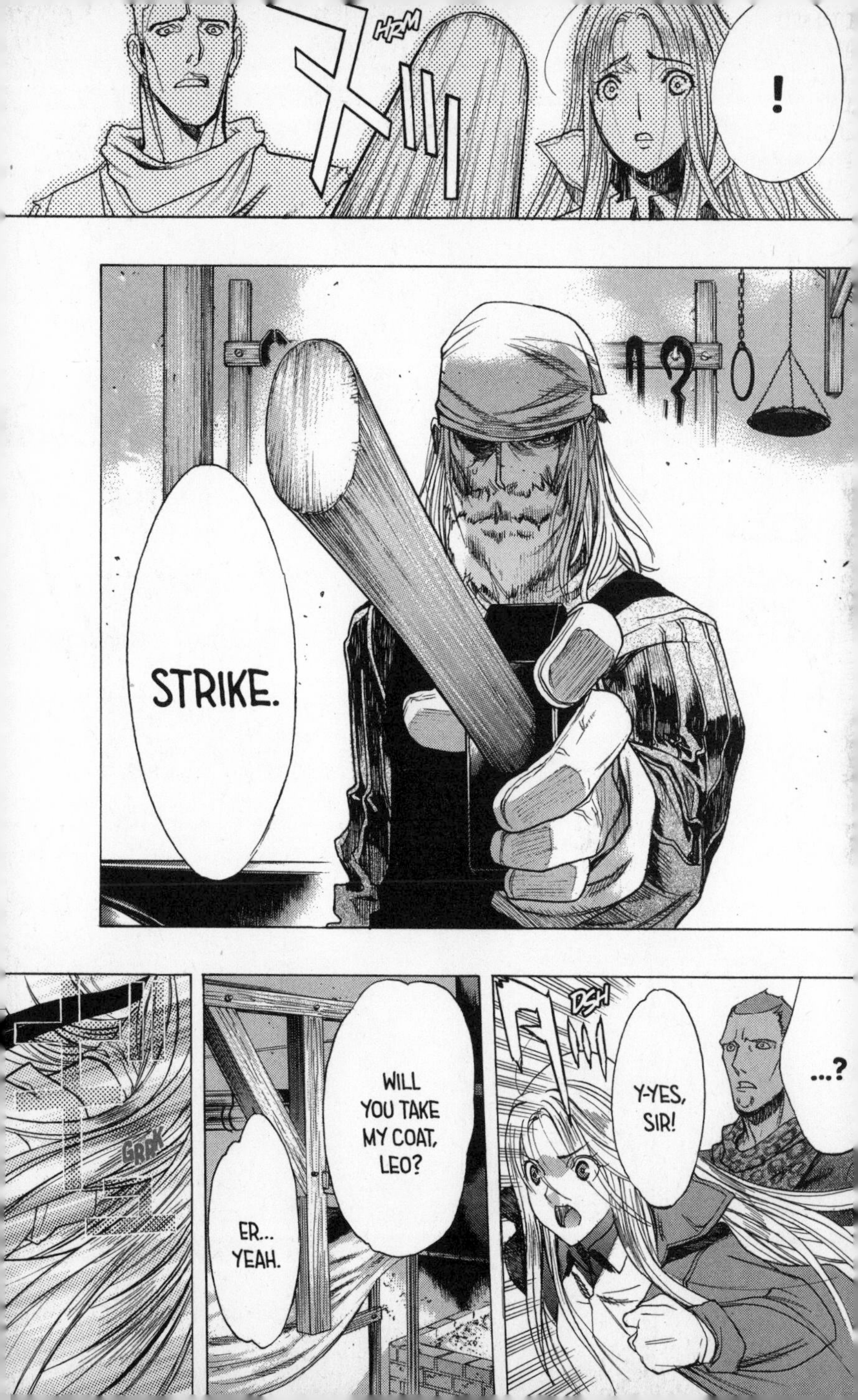
!
HRM
STRIKE.
...?
DSH
Y-YES, SIR!
WILL YOU TAKE MY COAT, LEO?
ER... YEAH.
GRRK

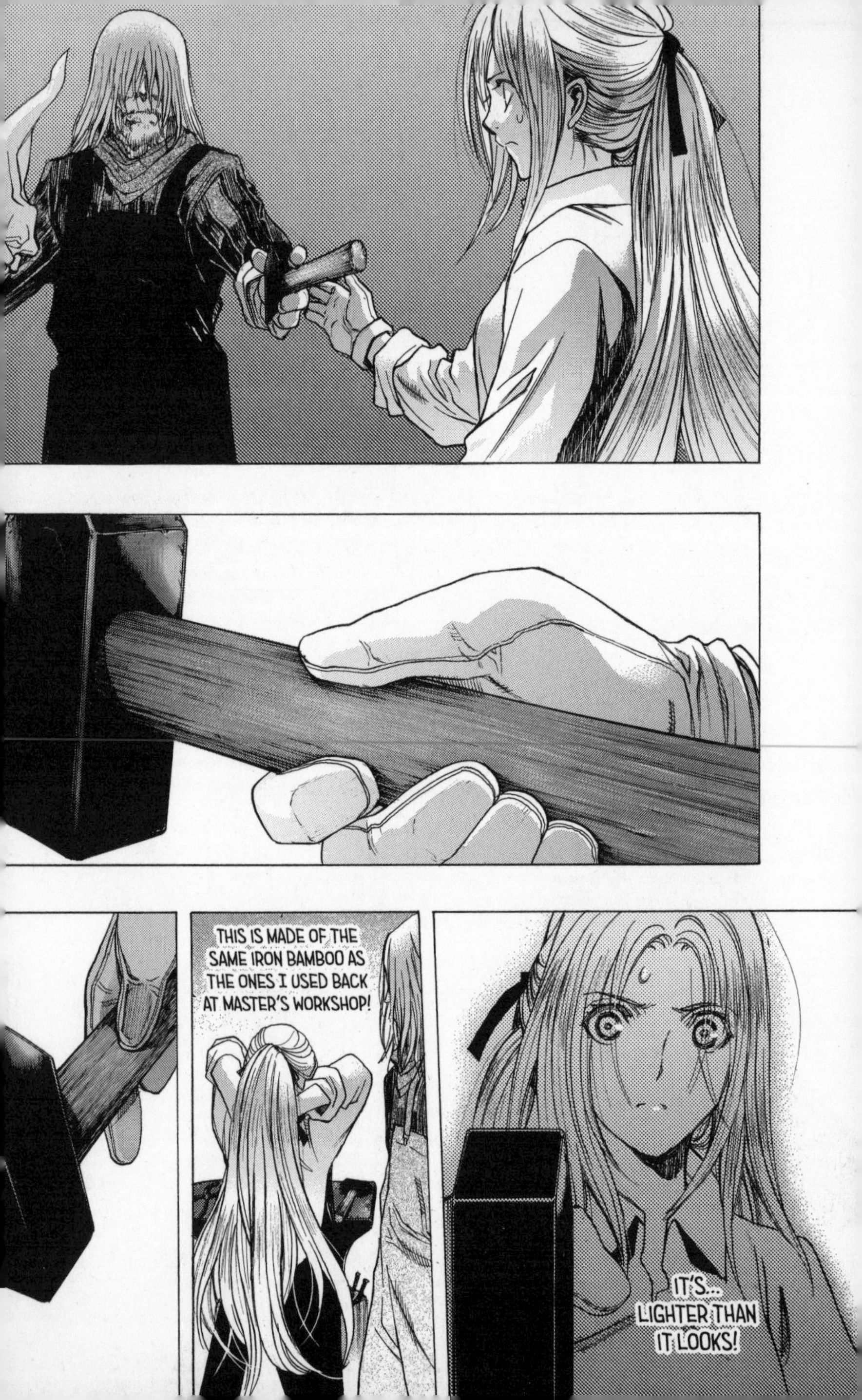
IT'S... LIGHTER THAN IT LOOKS!
THIS IS MADE OF THE SAME IRON BAMBOO AS THE ONES I USED BACK AT MASTER'S WORKSHOP!

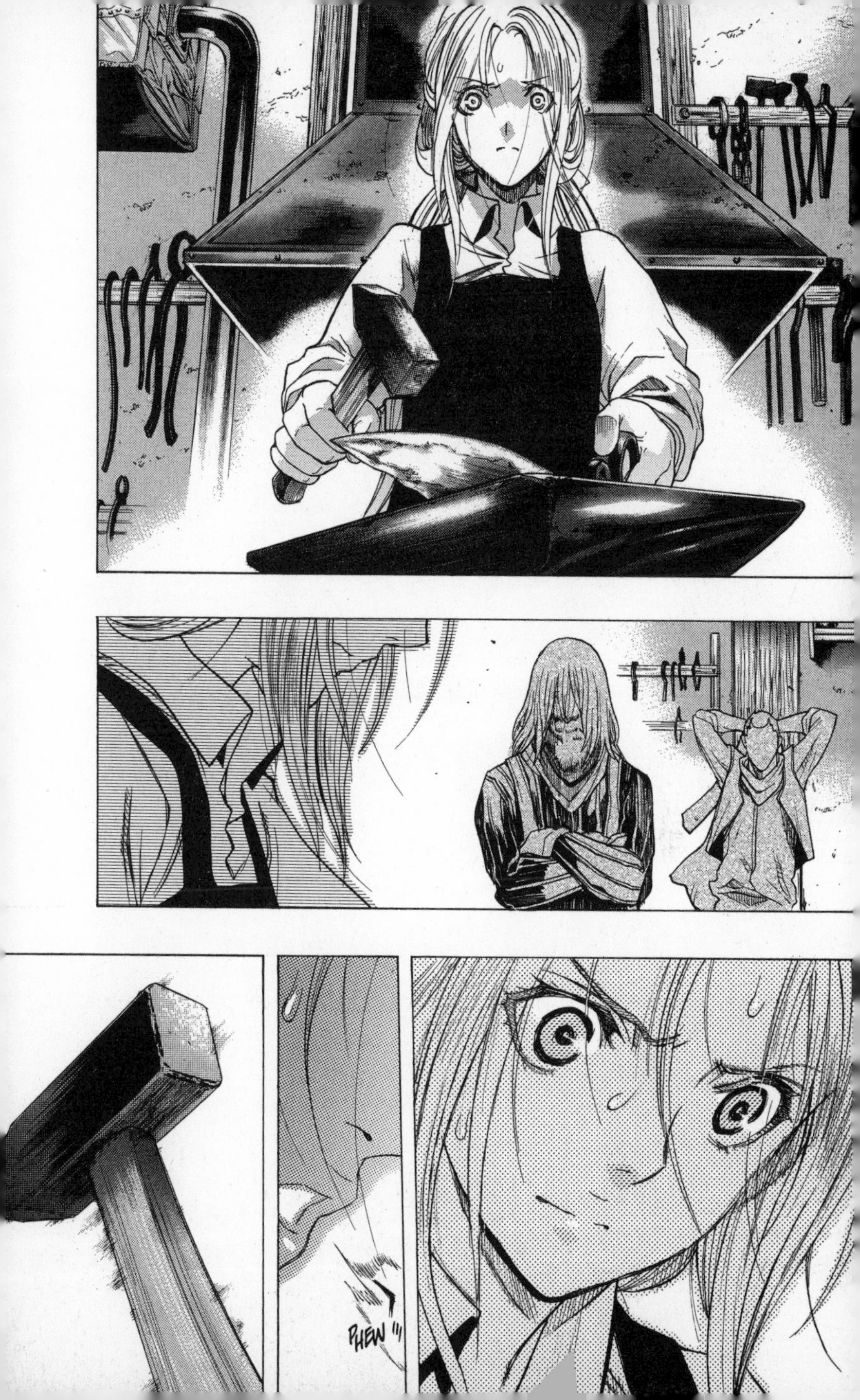
PHEW

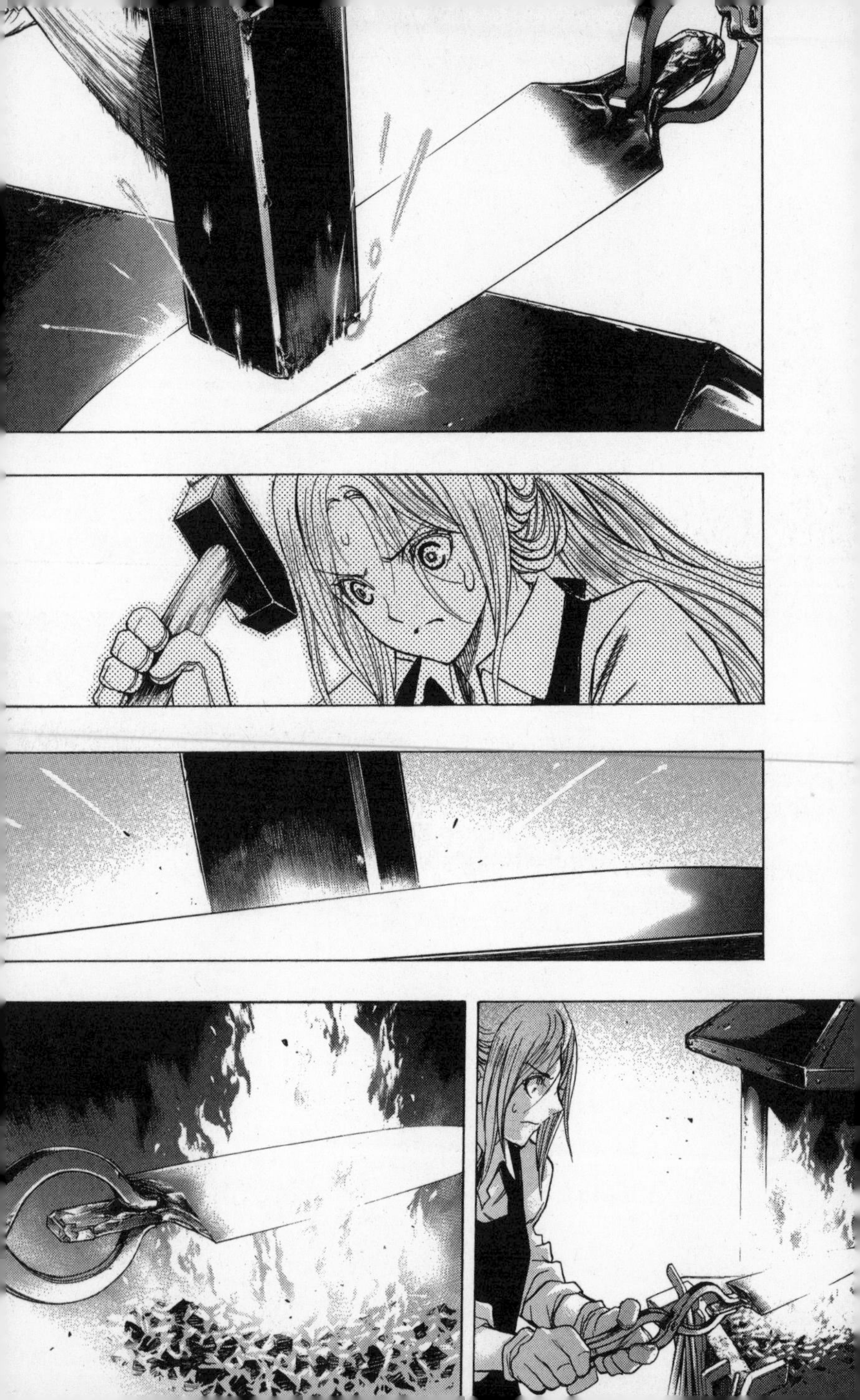

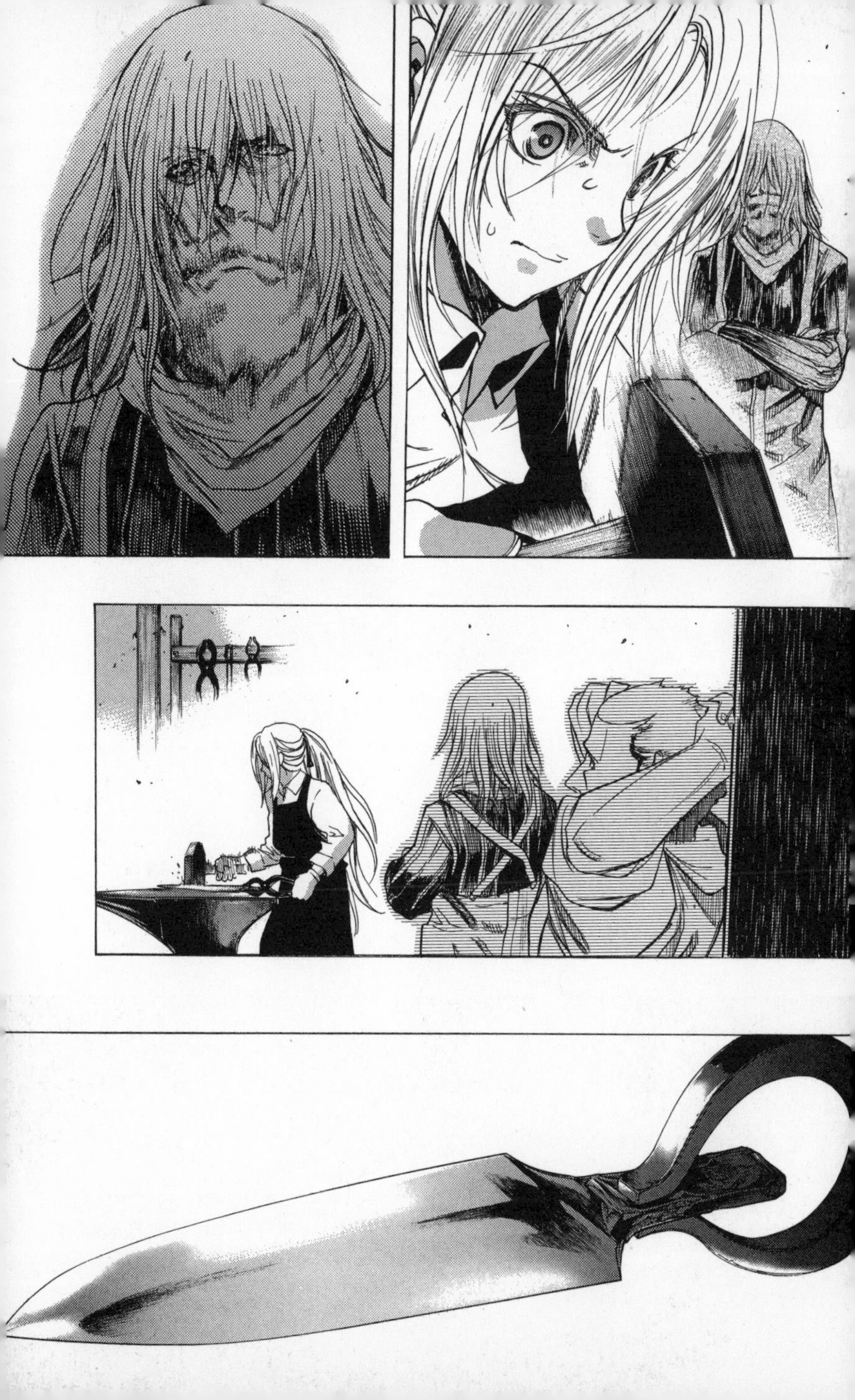

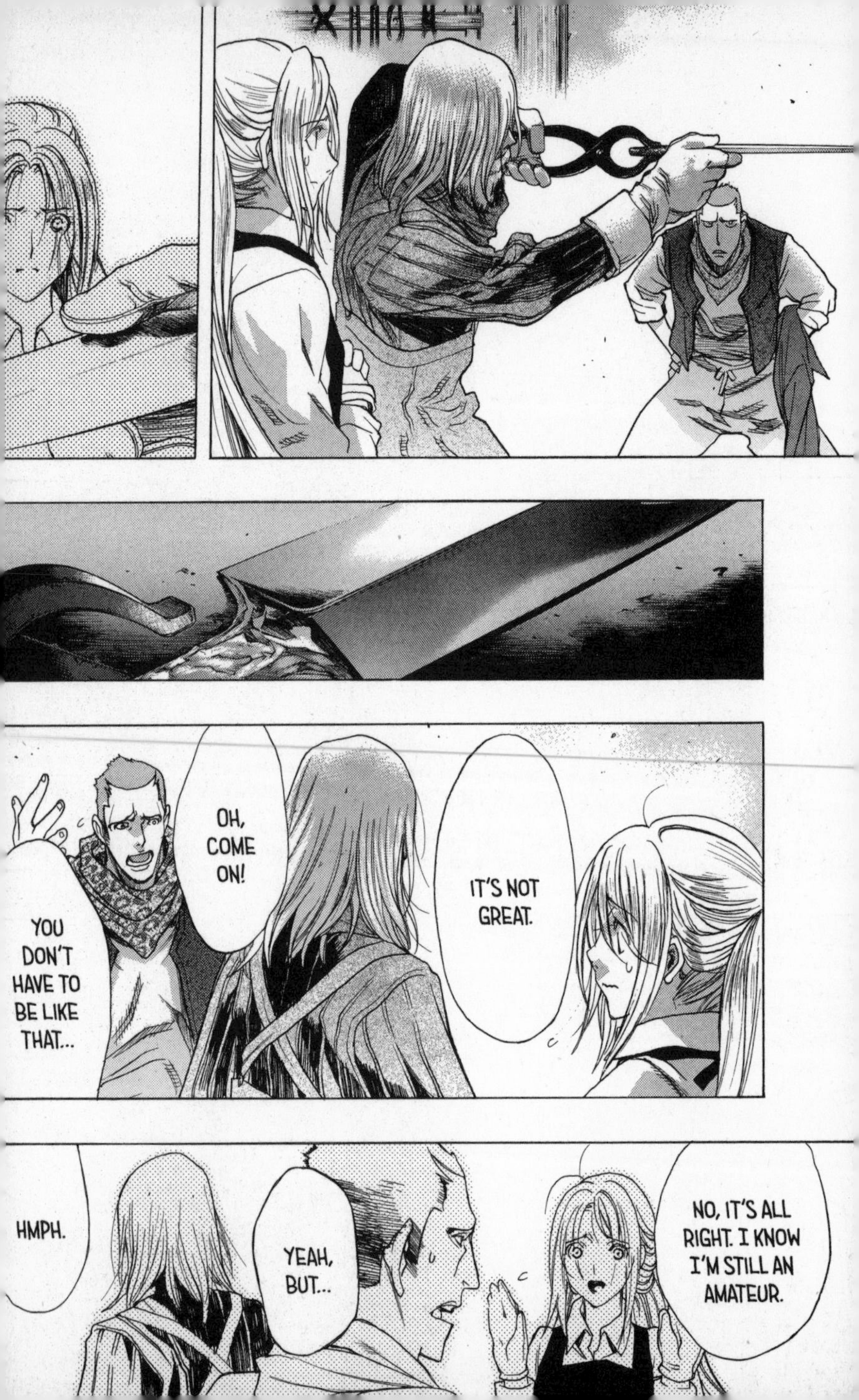
IT'S NOT GREAT.
OH, COME ON!
YOU DON'T HAVE TO BE LIKE THAT...
NO, IT'S ALL RIGHT. I KNOW I'M STILL AN AMATEUR.
YEAH, BUT...
HMPH.

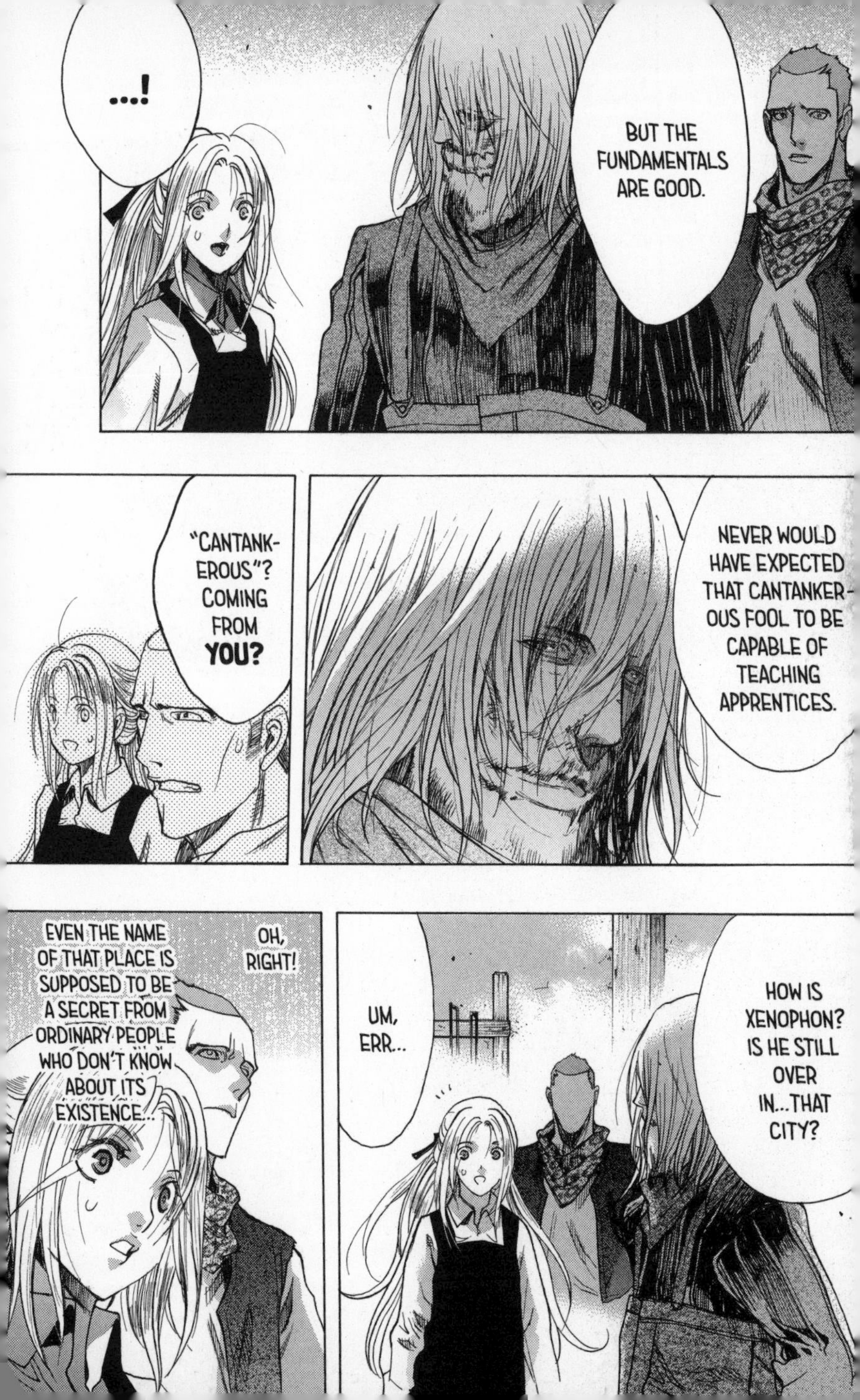
BUT THE FUNDAMENTALS ARE GOOD.
...!
NEVER WOULD HAVE EXPECTED THAT CANTANKER-OUS FOOL TO BE CAPABLE OF TEACHING APPRENTICES.
"CANTANK-EROUS"? COMING FROM **YOU?**
HOW IS XENOPHON? IS HE STILL OVER IN...THAT CITY?
UM, ERR...
OH, RIGHT!
EVEN THE NAME OF THAT PLACE IS SUPPOSED TO BE A SECRET FROM ORDINARY PEOPLE WHO DON'T KNOW ABOUT ITS EXISTENCE...

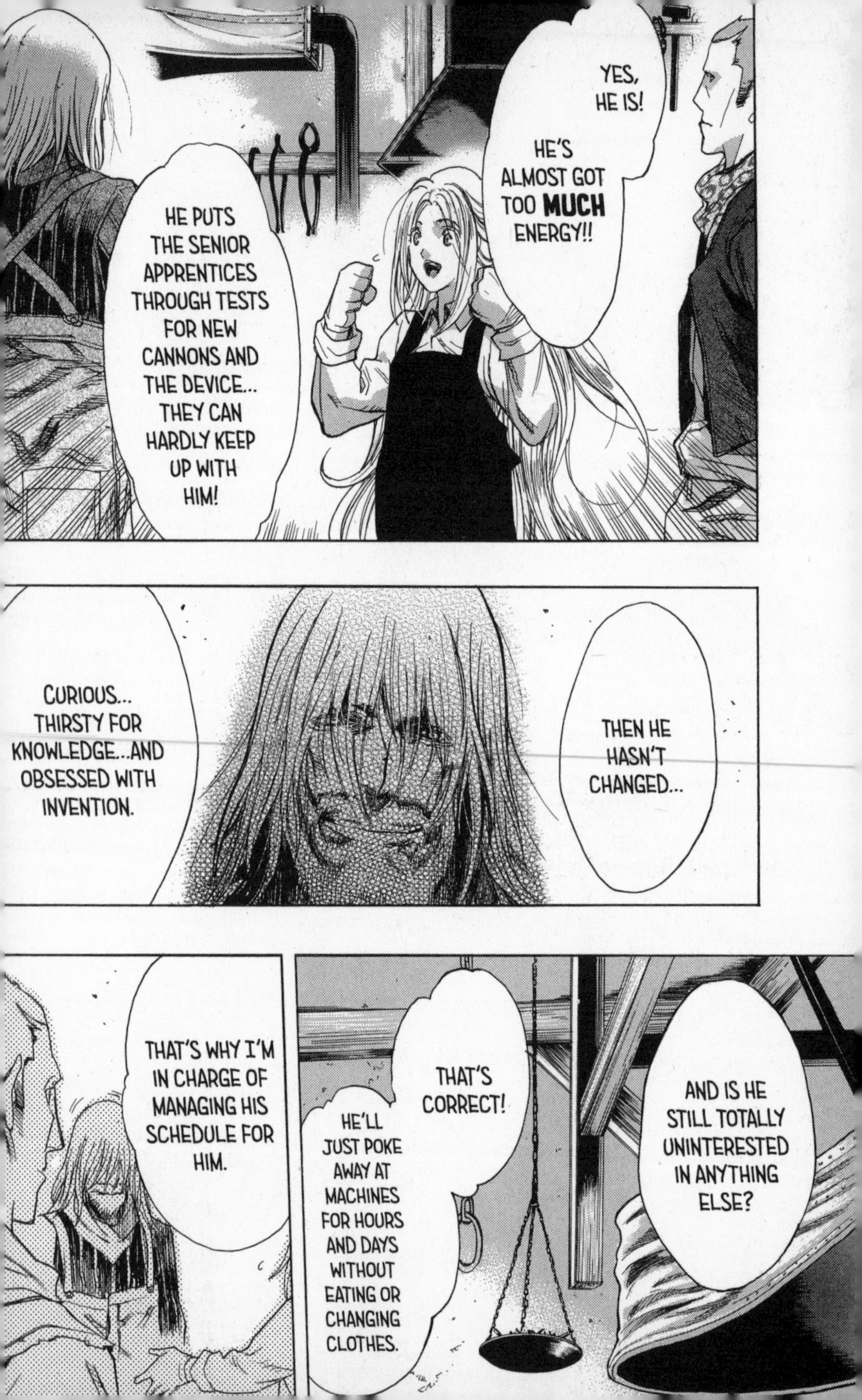
YES, HE IS!
HE'S ALMOST GOT TOO **MUCH** ENERGY!!
HE PUTS THE SENIOR APPRENTICES THROUGH TESTS FOR NEW CANNONS AND THE DEVICE... THEY CAN HARDLY KEEP UP WITH HIM!
THEN HE HASN'T CHANGED...
CURIOUS... THIRSTY FOR KNOWLEDGE...AND OBSESSED WITH INVENTION.
AND IS HE STILL TOTALLY UNINTERESTED IN ANYTHING ELSE?
THAT'S CORRECT!
HE'LL JUST POKE AWAY AT MACHINES FOR HOURS AND DAYS WITHOUT EATING OR CHANGING CLOTHES.
THAT'S WHY I'M IN CHARGE OF MANAGING HIS SCHEDULE FOR HIM.

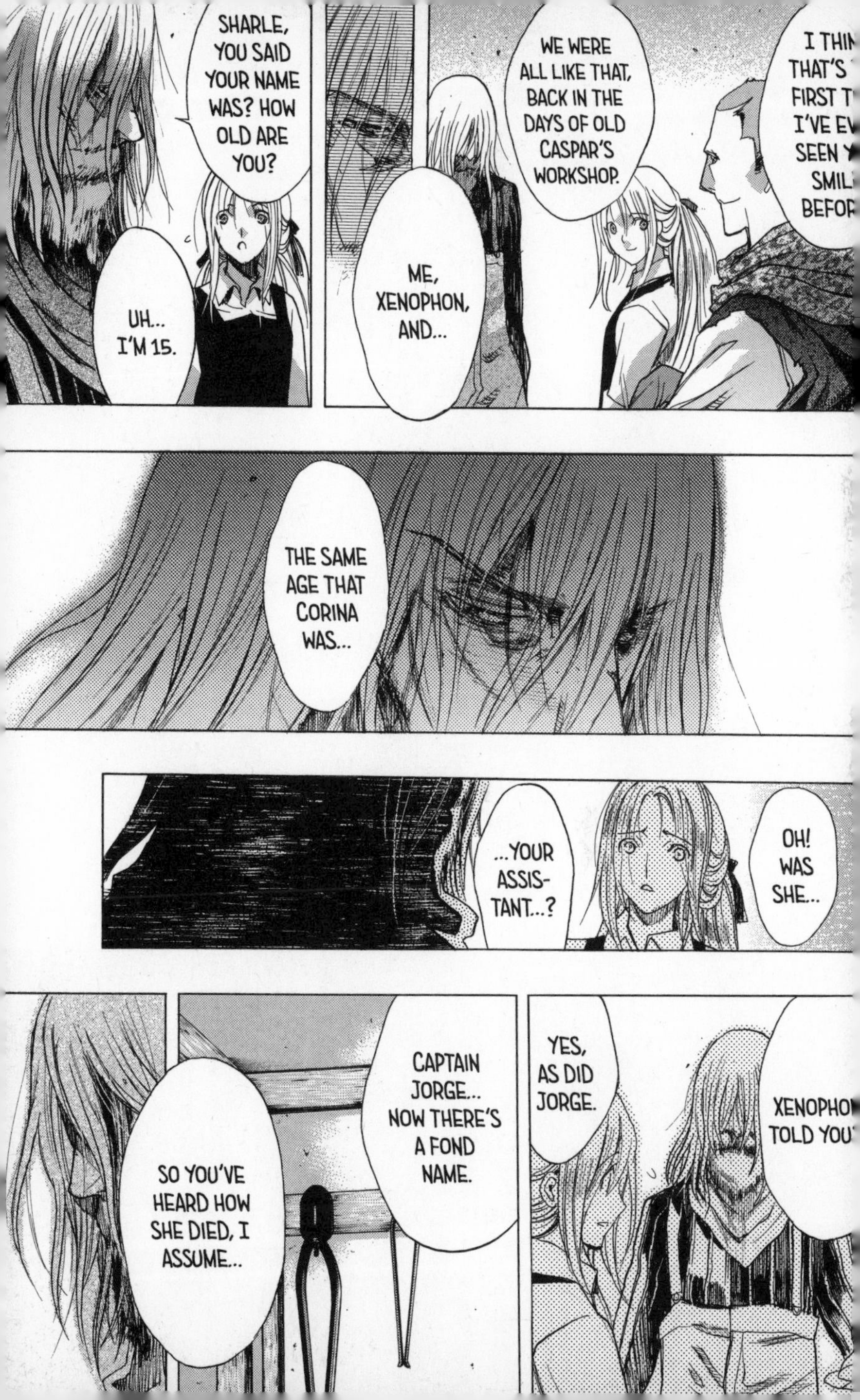
I THIN THAT'S FIRST T I'VE EV SEEN Y SMIL BEFOR
WE WERE ALL LIKE THAT, BACK IN THE DAYS OF OLD CASPAR'S WORKSHOP.
ME, XENOPHON, AND...
SHARLE, YOU SAID YOUR NAME WAS? HOW OLD ARE YOU?
UH... I'M 15.
THE SAME AGE THAT CORINA WAS...
OH! WAS SHE...
...YOUR ASSIS-TANT...?
XENOPHO TOLD YOU
YES, AS DID JORGE.
CAPTAIN JORGE... NOW THERE'S A FOND NAME.
SO YOU'VE HEARD HOW SHE DIED, I ASSUME...

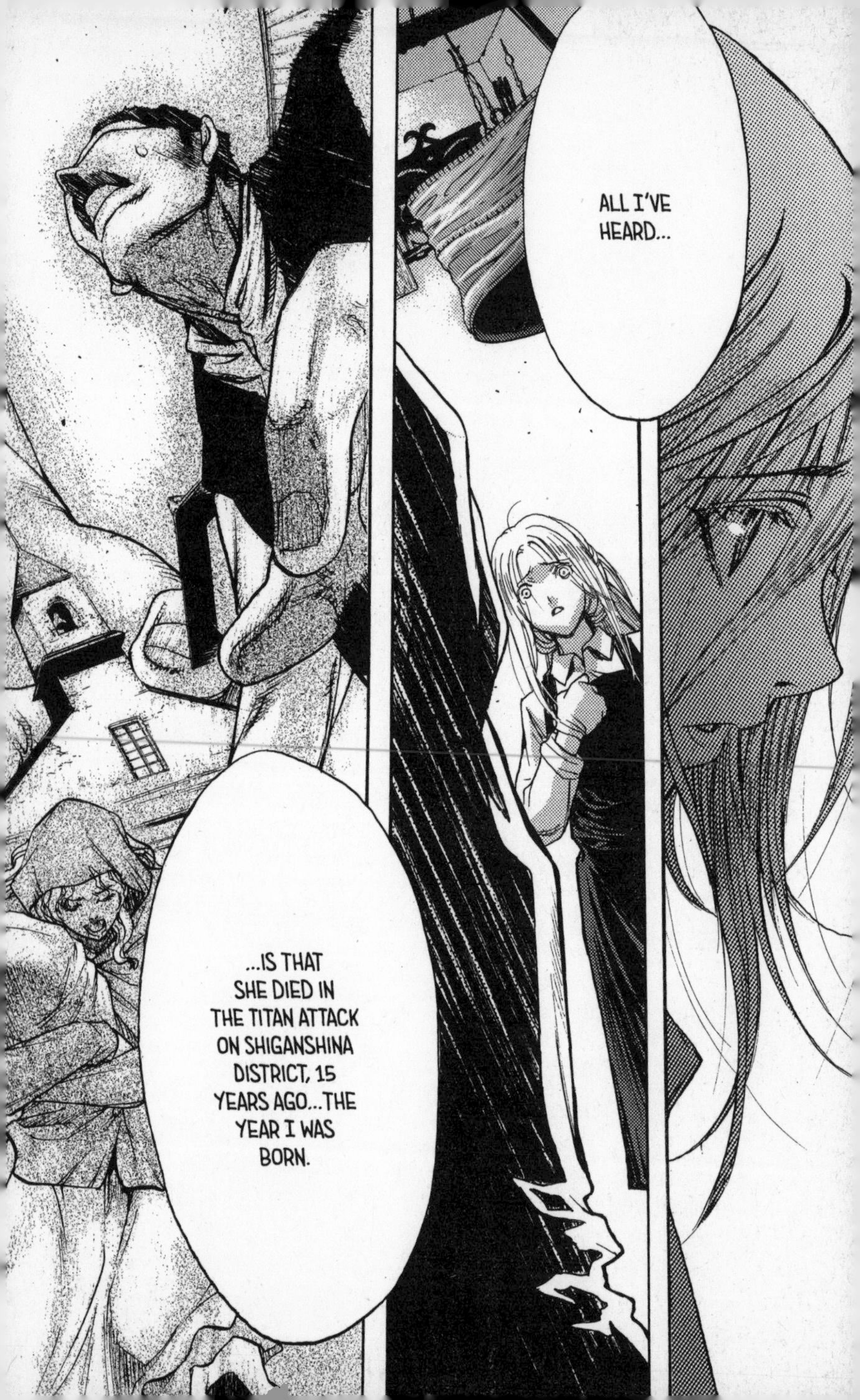
ALL I'VE HEARD...
...IS THAT SHE DIED IN THE TITAN ATTACK ON SHIGANSHINA DISTRICT, 15 YEARS AGO...THE YEAR I WAS BORN.

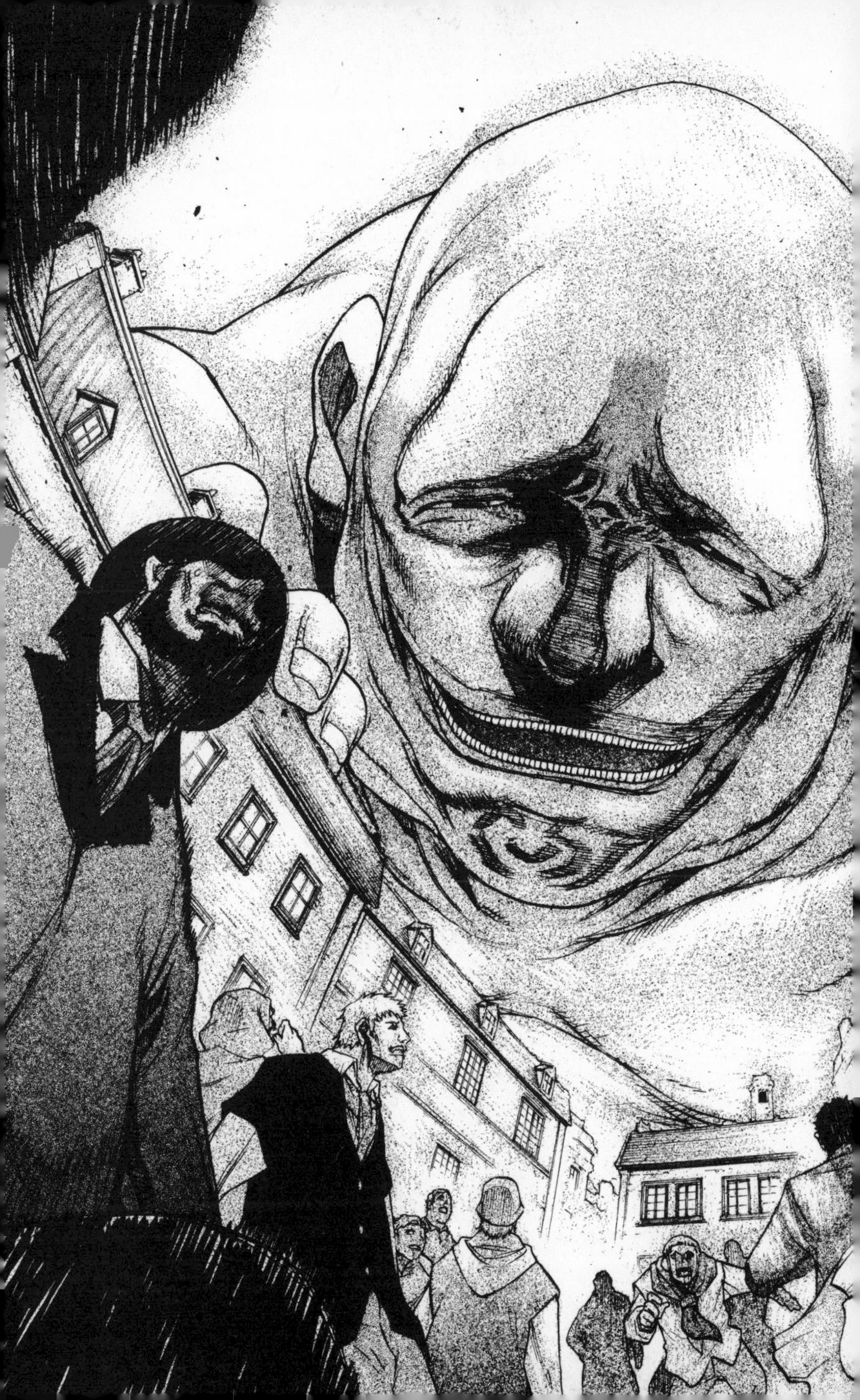

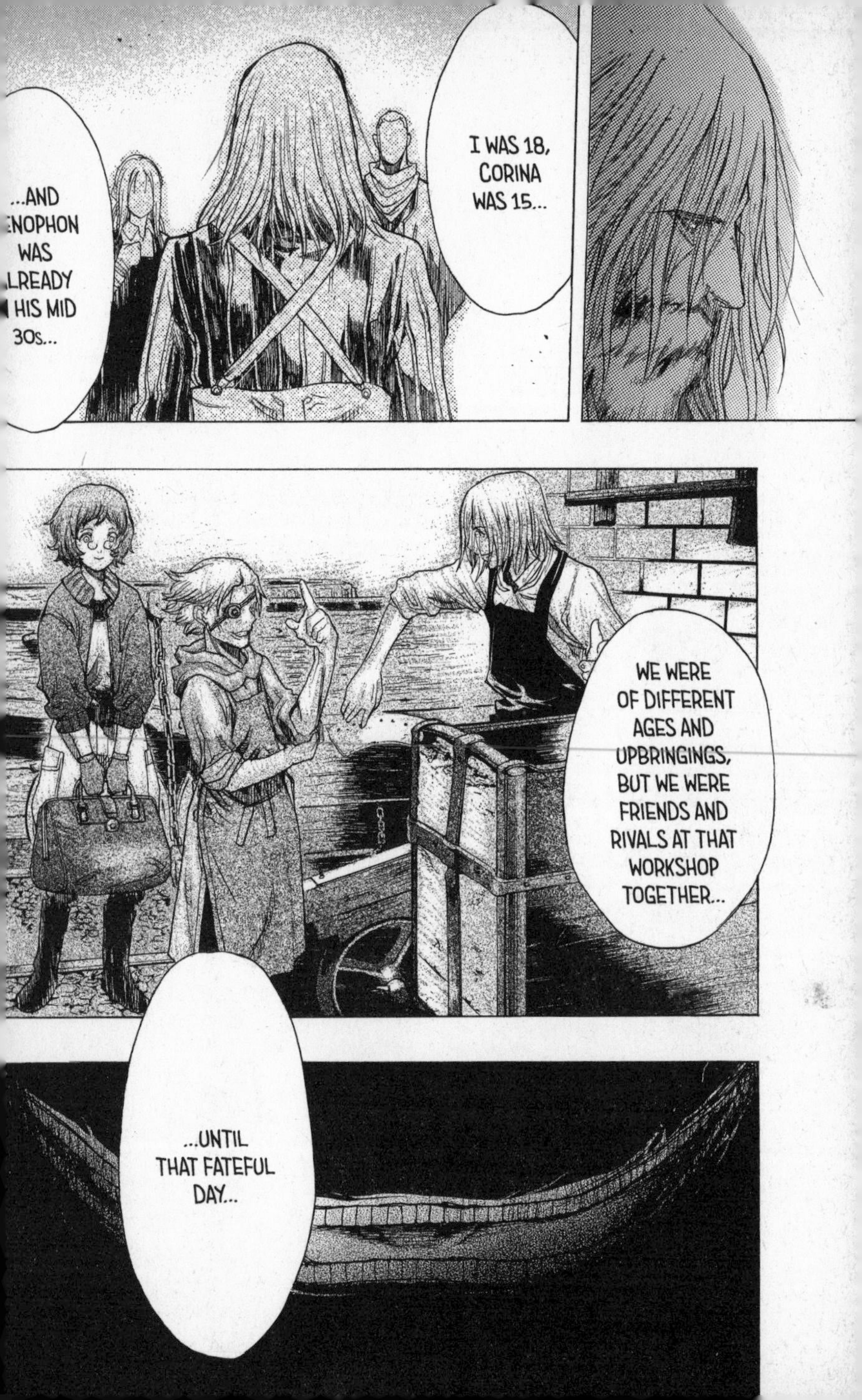
I WAS 18, CORINA WAS 15...
...AND ENOPHON WAS LREADY HIS MID 30s...
WE WERE OF DIFFERENT AGES AND UPBRINGINGS, BUT WE WERE FRIENDS AND RIVALS AT THAT WORKSHOP TOGETHER...
...UNTIL THAT FATEFUL DAY...

Chapter 35: Lone Shadow in the Town That Never Sleeps · E

ATTACK on TITAN

BEFORE THE FALL

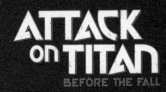

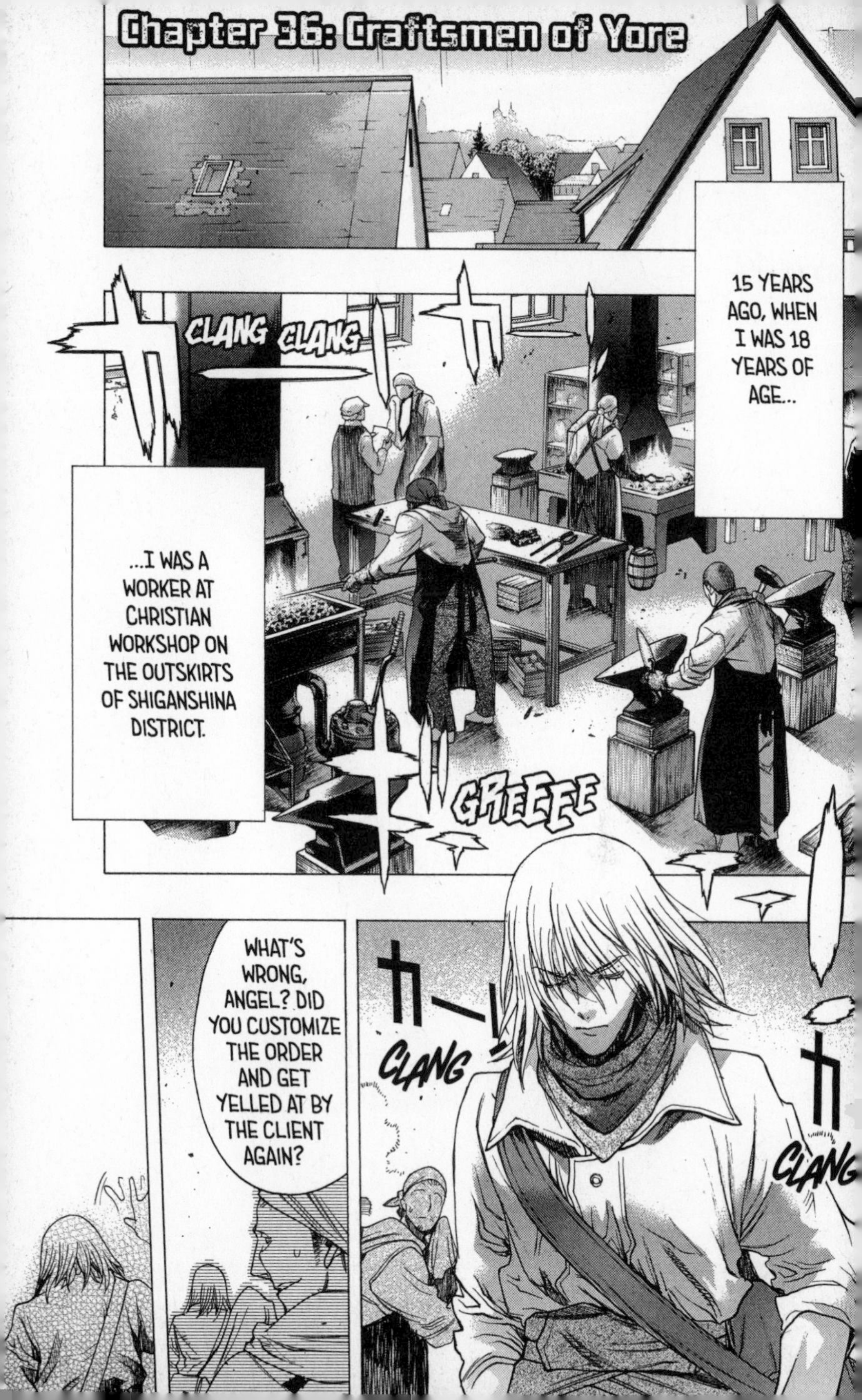
Chapter 36: Craftsmen of Yore
15 YEARS AGO, WHEN I WAS 18 YEARS OF AGE...
CLANG CLANG
...I WAS A WORKER AT CHRISTIAN WORKSHOP ON THE OUTSKIRTS OF SHIGANSHINA DISTRICT.
GREEEE
CLANG
CLANG
WHAT'S WRONG, ANGEL? DID YOU CUSTOMIZE THE ORDER AND GET YELLED AT BY THE CLIENT AGAIN?

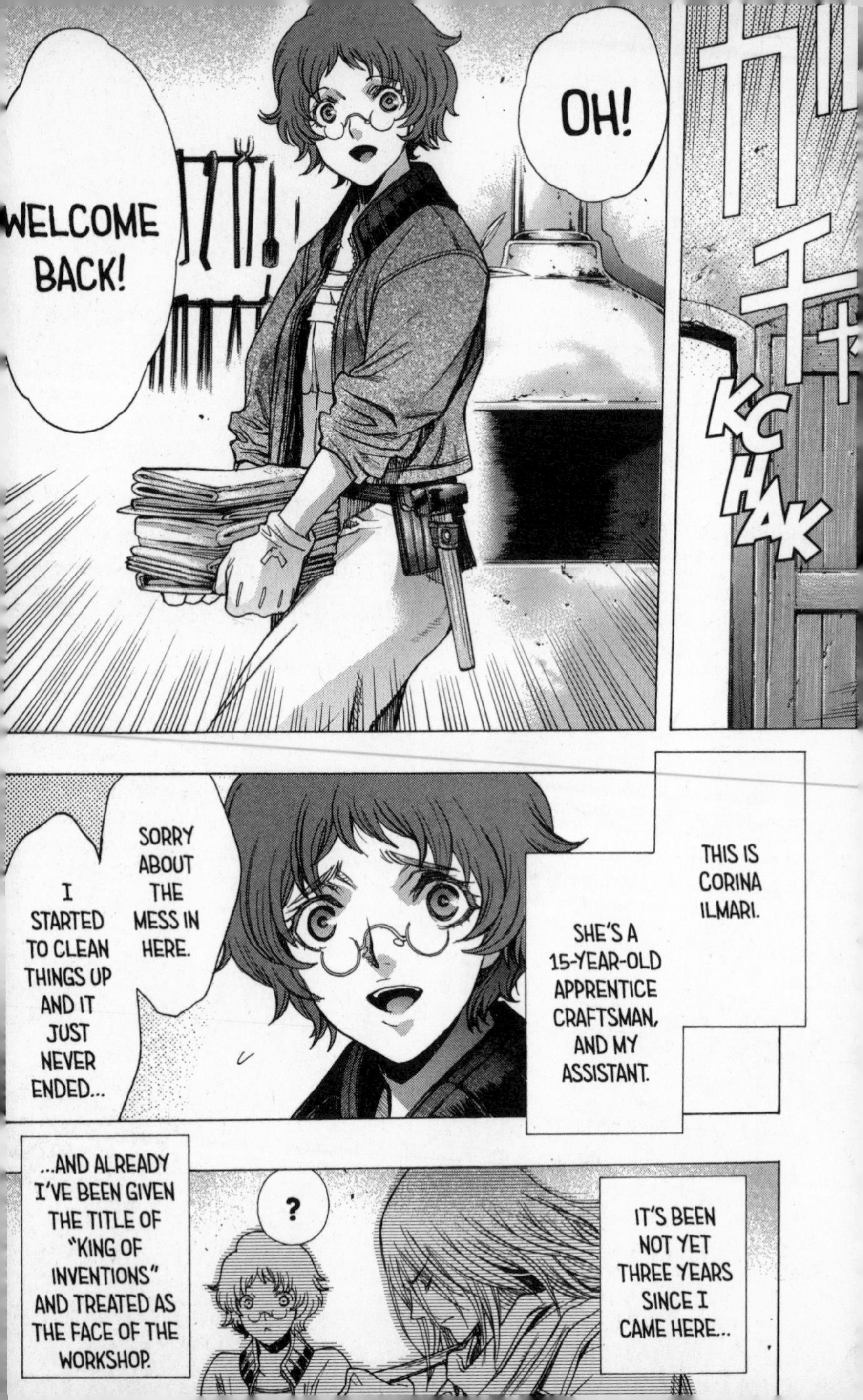
ガチャ
KCHAK
OH!
WELCOME BACK!
THIS IS CORINA ILMARI.
SHE'S A 15-YEAR-OLD APPRENTICE CRAFTSMAN, AND MY ASSISTANT.
SORRY ABOUT THE MESS IN HERE.
I STARTED TO CLEAN THINGS UP AND IT JUST NEVER ENDED...
IT'S BEEN NOT YET THREE YEARS SINCE I CAME HERE...
?
...AND ALREADY I'VE BEEN GIVEN THE TITLE OF "KING OF INVENTIONS" AND TREATED AS THE FACE OF THE WORKSHOP.

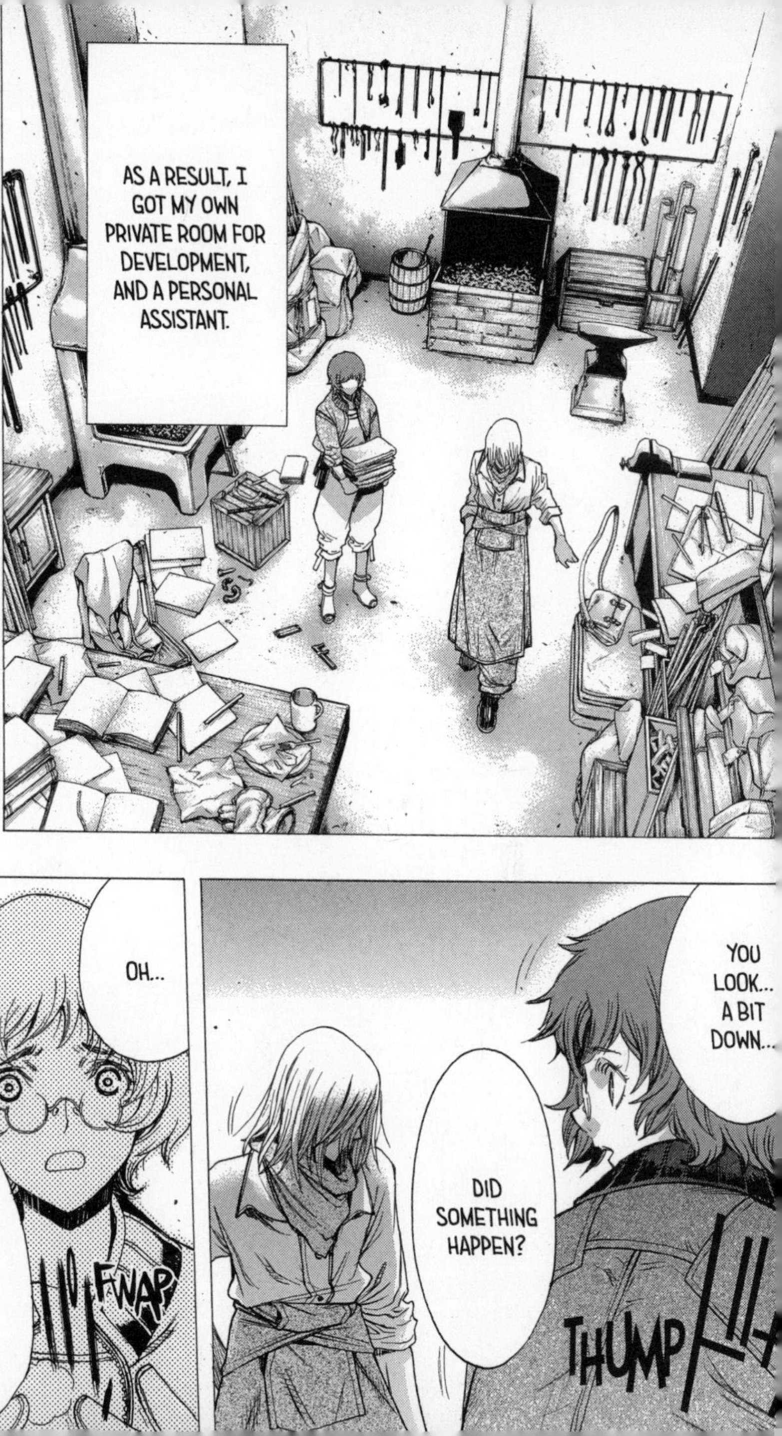
AS A RESULT, I GOT MY OWN PRIVATE ROOM FOR DEVELOPMENT, AND A PERSONAL ASSISTANT.
YOU LOOK... A BIT DOWN...
DID SOMETHING HAPPEN?
THUMP
OH...
FNAP
DID SORUM ...?

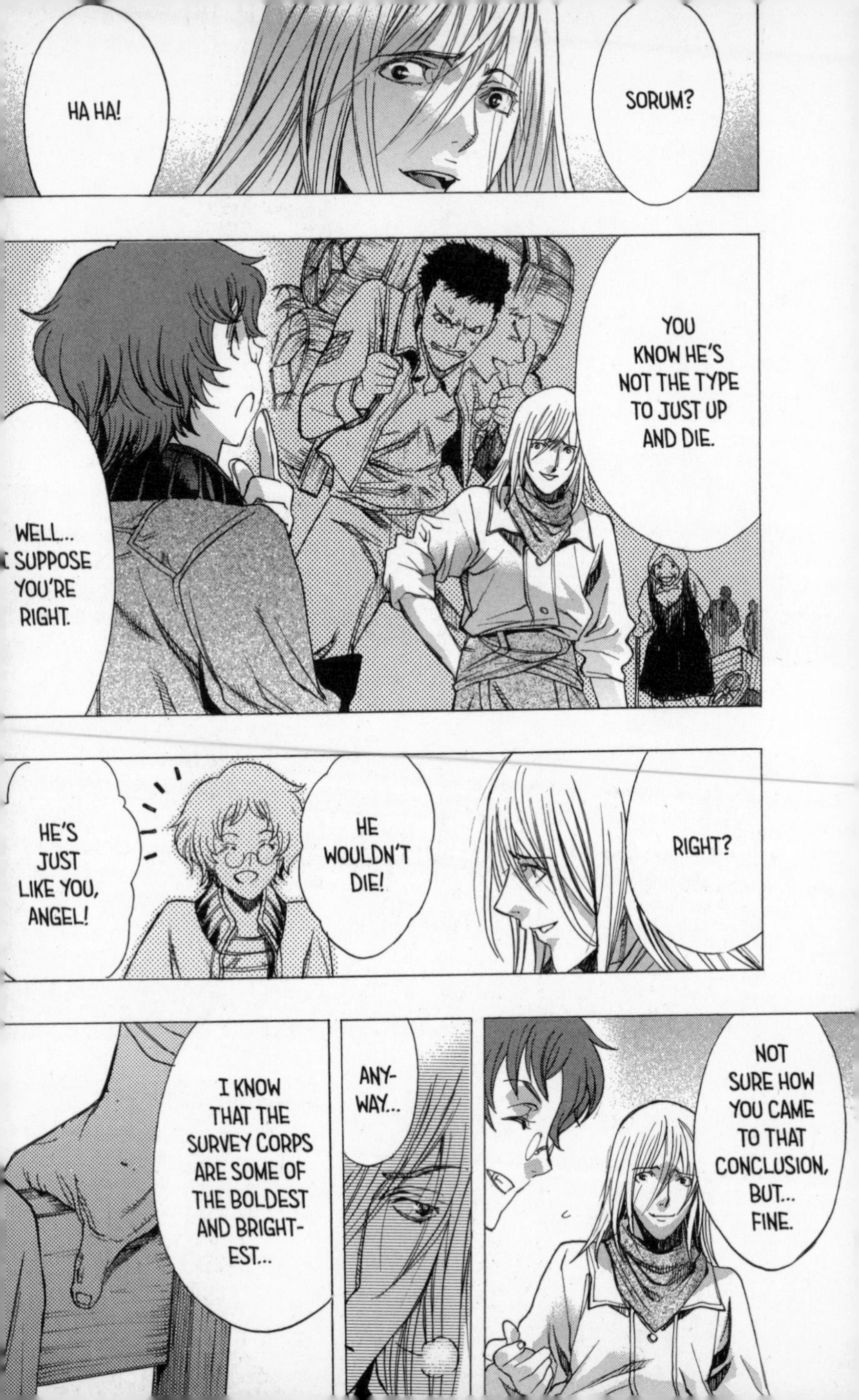
SORUM?
HA HA!
YOU KNOW HE'S NOT THE TYPE TO JUST UP AND DIE.
WELL... SUPPOSE YOU'RE RIGHT.
RIGHT?
HE WOULDN'T DIE!
HE'S JUST LIKE YOU, ANGEL!
NOT SURE HOW YOU CAME TO THAT CONCLUSION, BUT... FINE.
ANY-WAY...
I KNOW THAT THE SURVEY CORPS ARE SOME OF THE BOLDEST AND BRIGHT-EST...

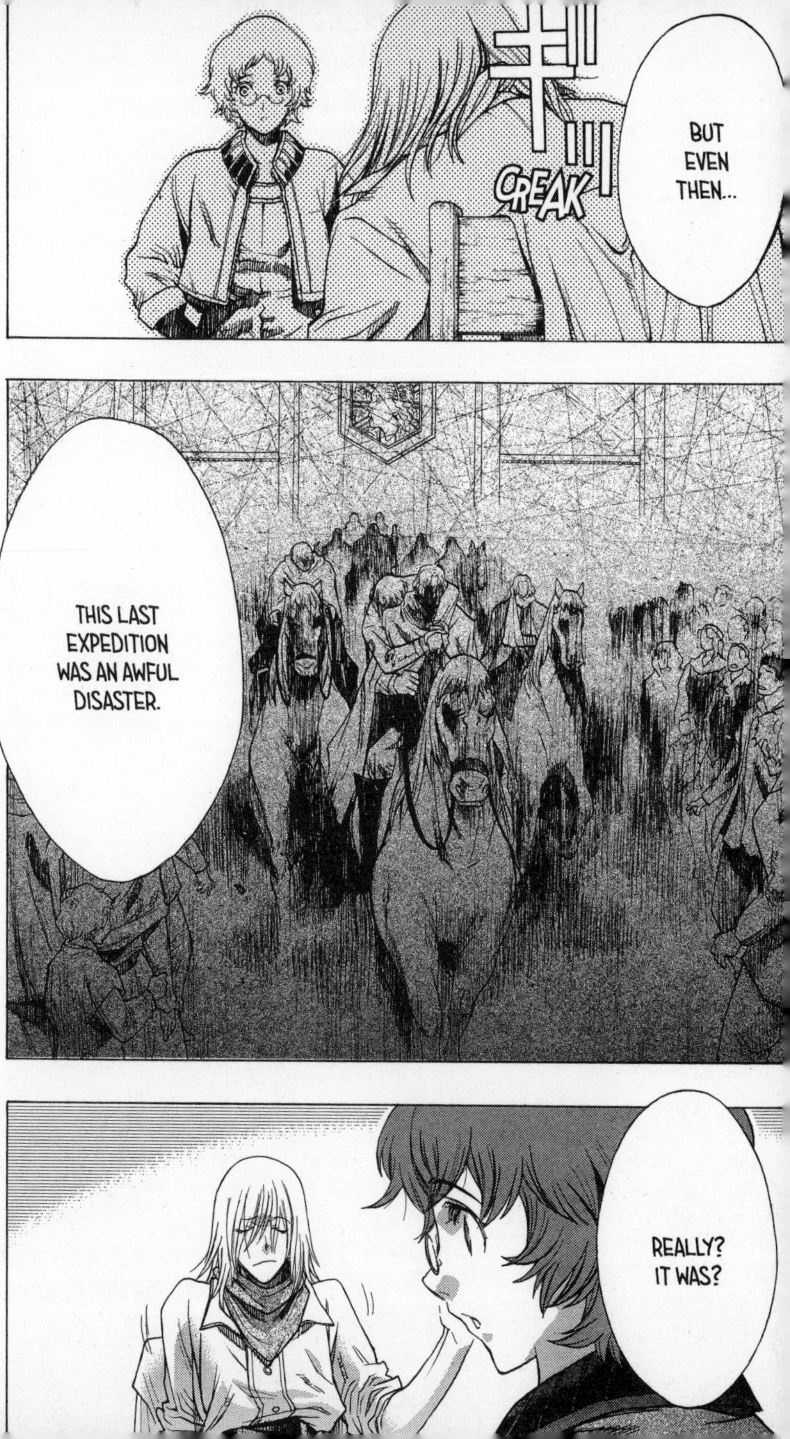
BUT EVEN THEN...
CREAK
THIS LAST EXPEDITION WAS AN AWFUL DISASTER.
REALLY? IT WAS?

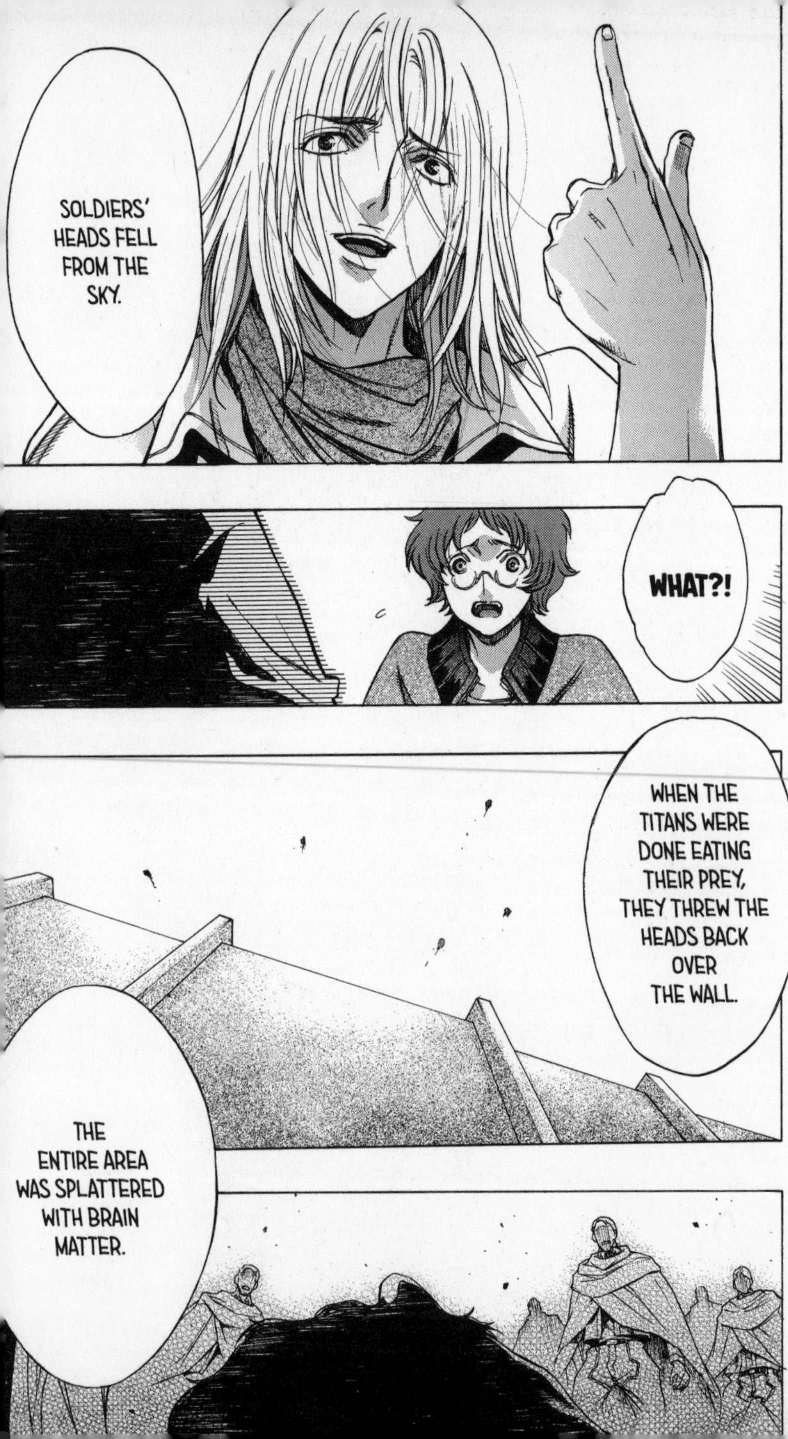
SOLDIERS' HEADS FELL FROM THE SKY.
WHAT?!
WHEN THE TITANS WERE DONE EATING THEIR PREY, THEY THREW THE HEADS BACK OVER THE WALL.
THE ENTIRE AREA WAS SPLATTERED WITH BRAIN MATTER.

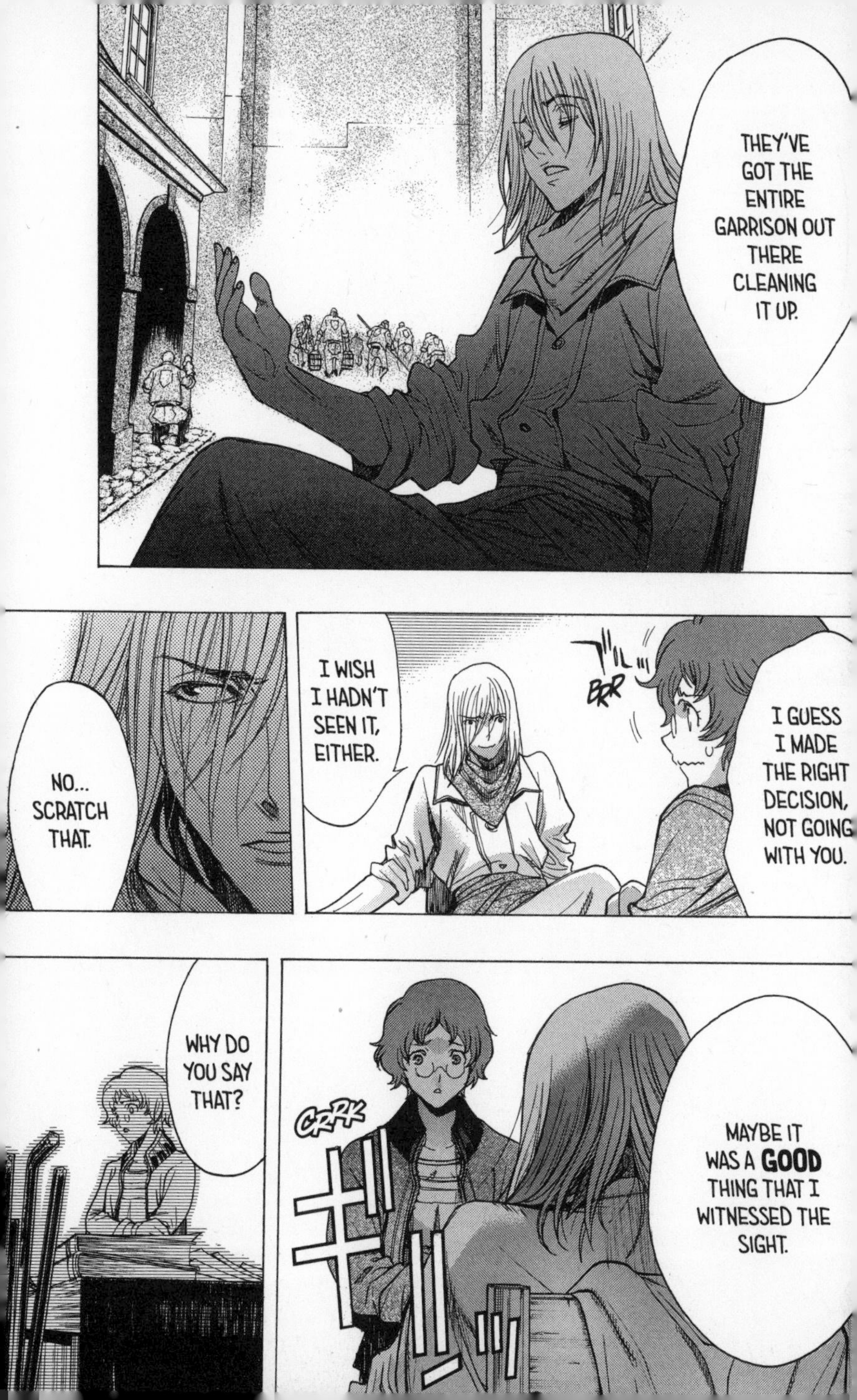
THEY'VE GOT THE ENTIRE GARRISON OUT THERE CLEANING IT UP.
BRR
I GUESS I MADE THE RIGHT DECISION, NOT GOING WITH YOU.
I WISH I HADN'T SEEN IT, EITHER.
NO... SCRATCH THAT.
MAYBE IT WAS A **GOOD** THING THAT I WITNESSED THE SIGHT.
CRRK
WHY DO YOU SAY THAT?

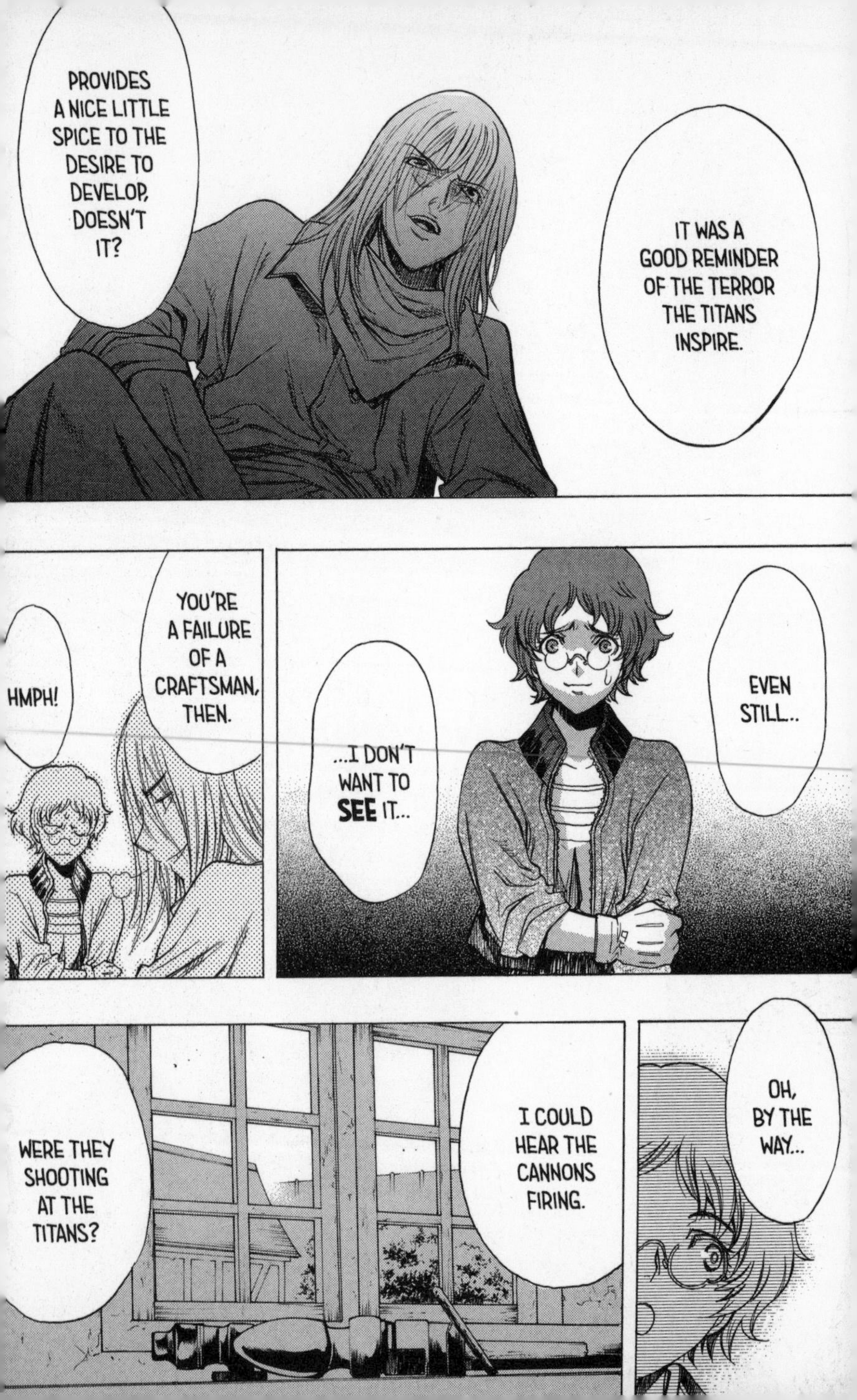
IT WAS A GOOD REMINDER OF THE TERROR THE TITANS INSPIRE.
PROVIDES A NICE LITTLE SPICE TO THE DESIRE TO DEVELOP, DOESN'T IT?
EVEN STILL...
...I DON'T WANT TO **SEE** IT...
YOU'RE A FAILURE OF A CRAFTSMAN, THEN.
HMPH!
OH, BY THE WAY...
I COULD HEAR THE CANNONS FIRING.
WERE THEY SHOOTING AT THE TITANS?

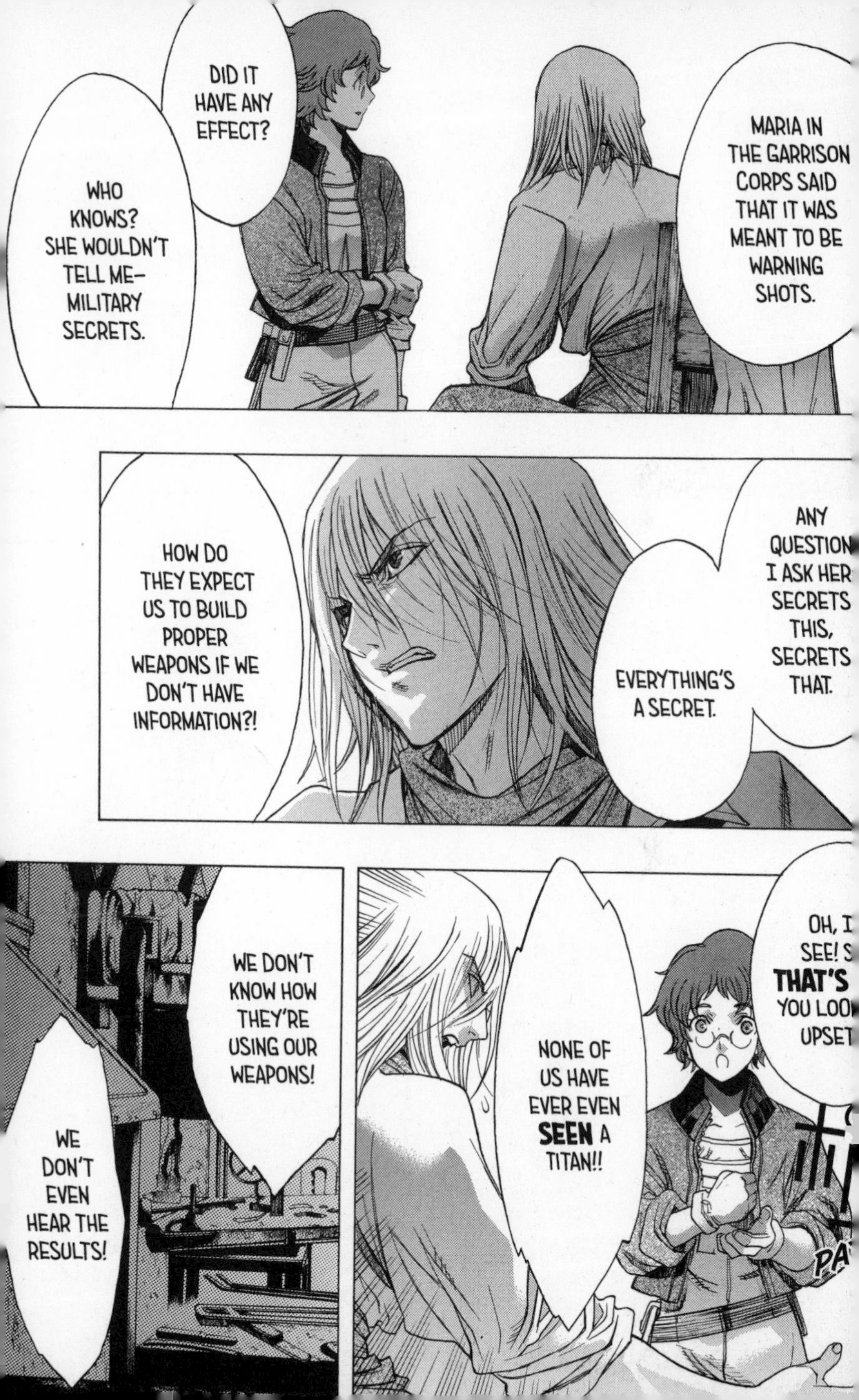
MARIA IN THE GARRISON CORPS SAID THAT IT WAS MEANT TO BE WARNING SHOTS.
DID IT HAVE ANY EFFECT?
WHO KNOWS? SHE WOULDN'T TELL ME— MILITARY SECRETS.
ANY QUESTION I ASK HER SECRETS THIS, SECRETS THAT.
EVERYTHING'S A SECRET.
HOW DO THEY EXPECT US TO BUILD PROPER WEAPONS IF WE DON'T HAVE INFORMATION?!
OH, I SEE! S **THAT'S** YOU LOO UPSET
NONE OF US HAVE EVER EVEN **SEEN** A TITAN!!
PA
WE DON'T KNOW HOW THEY'RE USING OUR WEAPONS!
WE DON'T EVEN HEAR THE RESULTS!

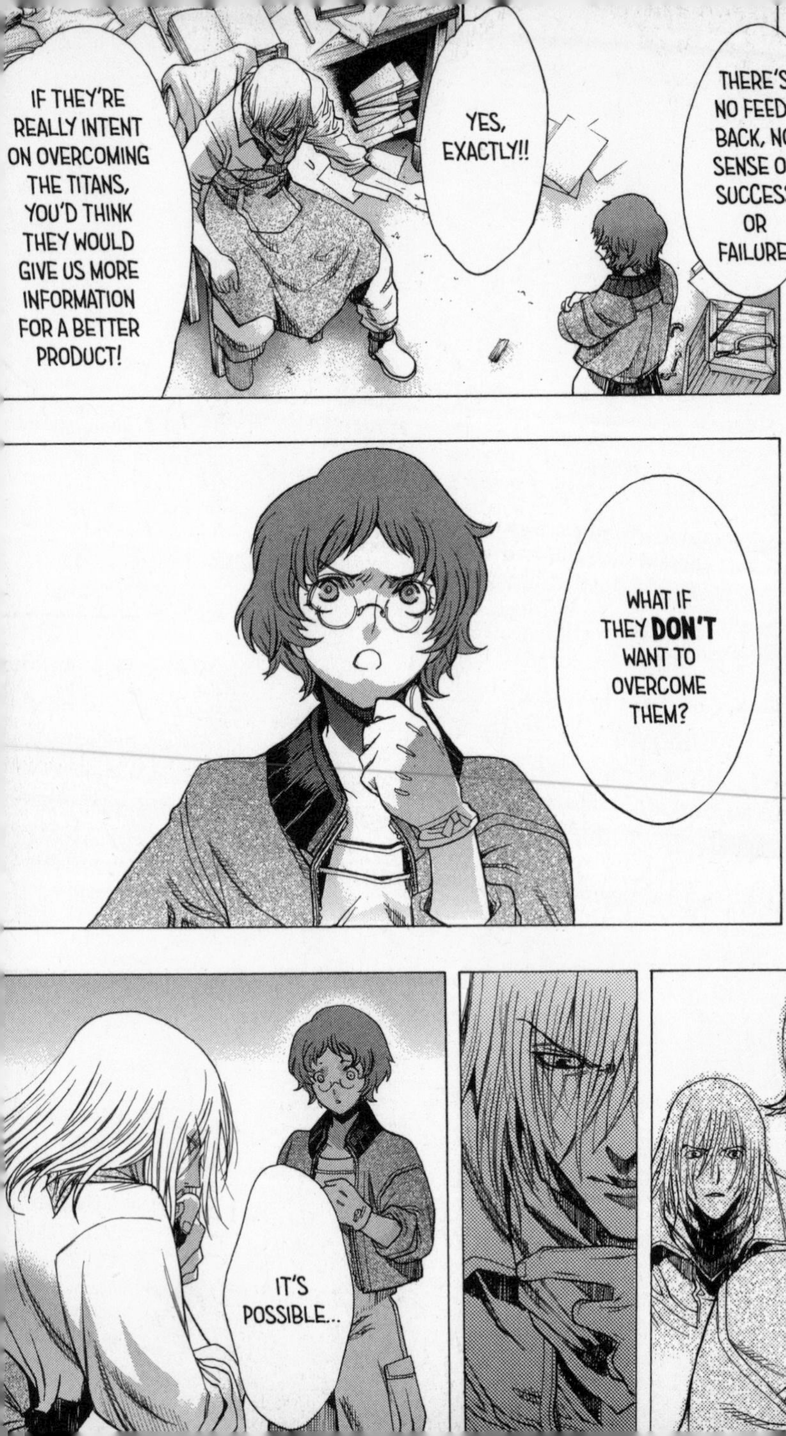
THERE'S NO FEED-BACK, NO SENSE OF SUCCESS OR FAILURE.
YES, EXACTLY!!
IF THEY'RE REALLY INTENT ON OVERCOMING THE TITANS, YOU'D THINK THEY WOULD GIVE US MORE INFORMATION FOR A BETTER PRODUCT!
WHAT IF THEY **DON'T** WANT TO OVERCOME THEM?
IT'S POSSIBLE...

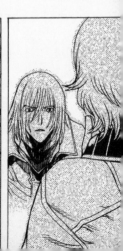

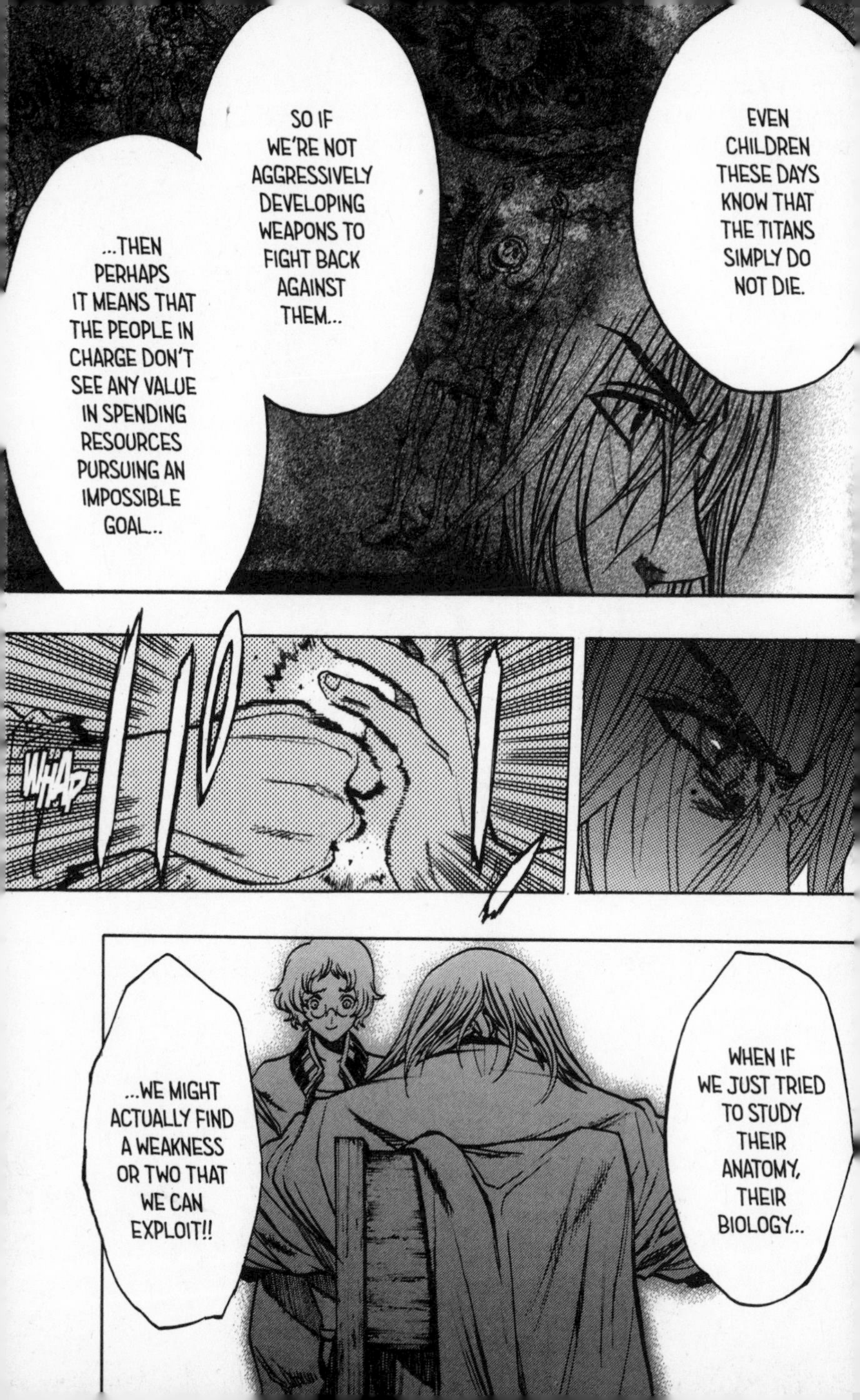
EVEN CHILDREN THESE DAYS KNOW THAT THE TITANS SIMPLY DO NOT DIE.
SO IF WE'RE NOT AGGRESSIVELY DEVELOPING WEAPONS TO FIGHT BACK AGAINST THEM...
...THEN PERHAPS IT MEANS THAT THE PEOPLE IN CHARGE DON'T SEE ANY VALUE IN SPENDING RESOURCES PURSUING AN IMPOSSIBLE GOAL...
WHAP
WHEN IF WE JUST TRIED TO STUDY THEIR ANATOMY, THEIR BIOLOGY...
...WE MIGHT ACTUALLY FIND A WEAKNESS OR TWO THAT WE CAN EXPLOIT!!

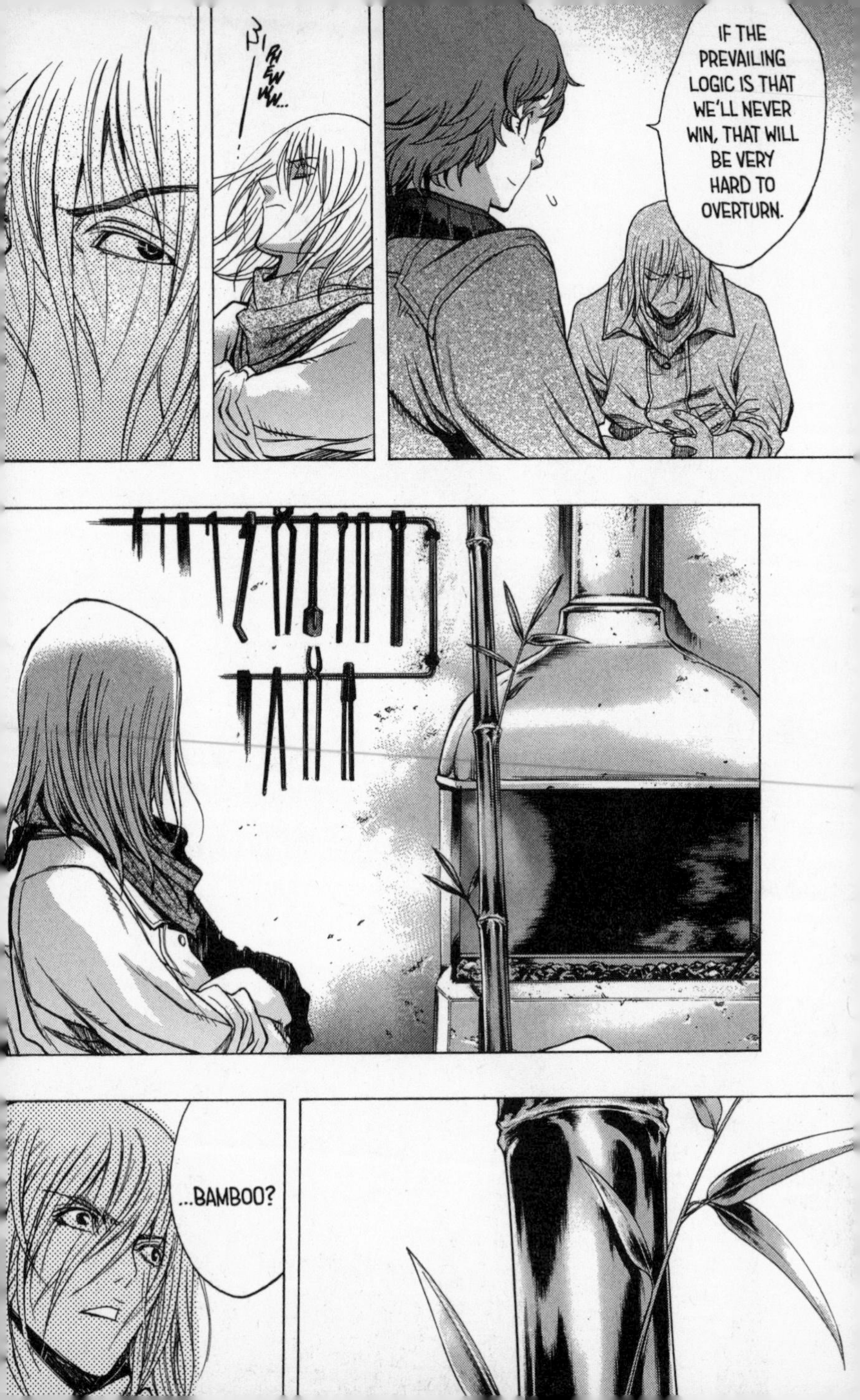
IF THE PREVAILING LOGIC IS THAT WE'LL NEVER WIN, THAT WILL BE VERY HARD TO OVERTURN.
PHEWWW...
...BAMBOO?

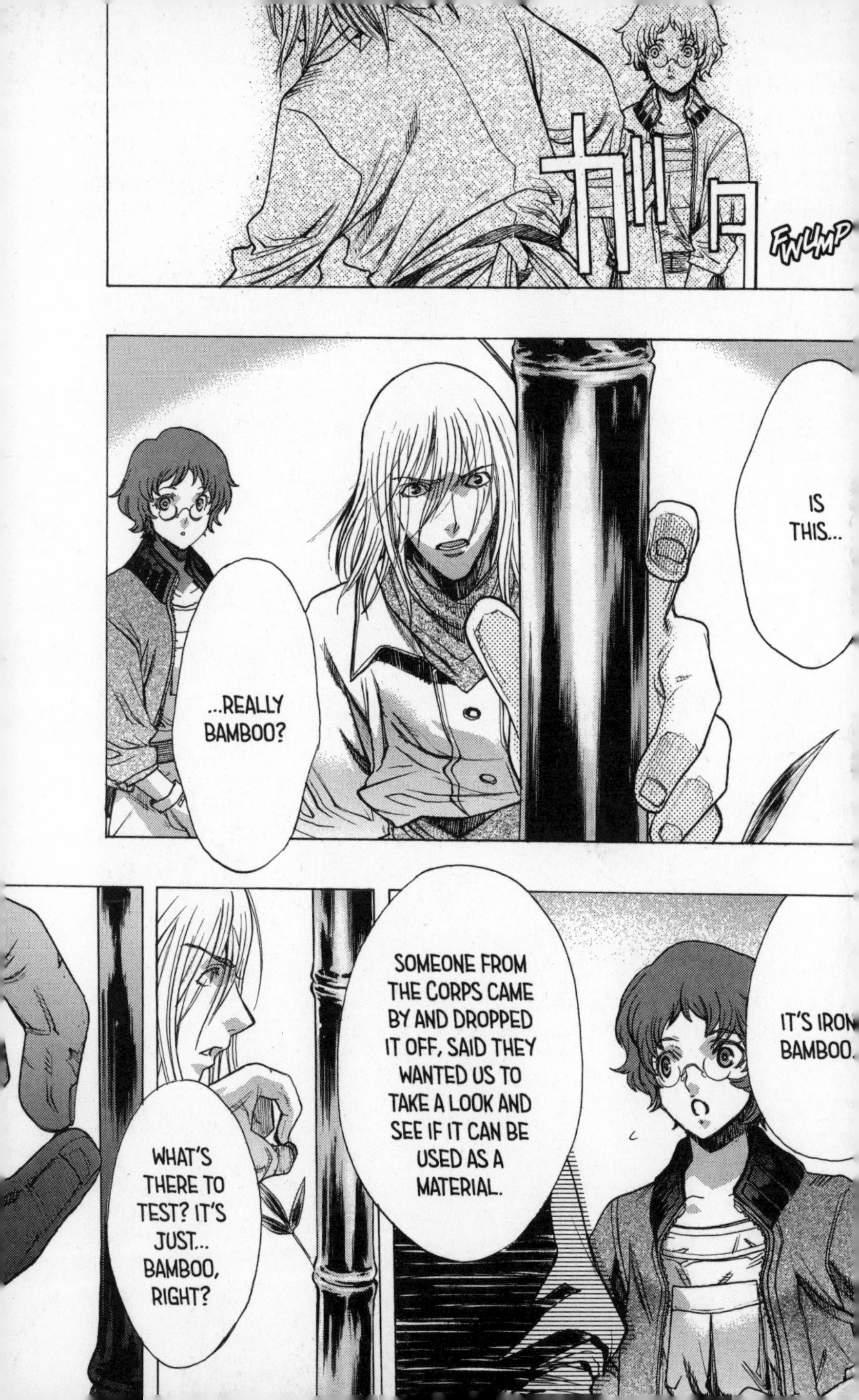
FWUMP
IS THIS...
...REALLY BAMBOO?
IT'S IRON BAMBOO.
SOMEONE FROM THE CORPS CAME BY AND DROPPED IT OFF, SAID THEY WANTED US TO TAKE A LOOK AND SEE IF IT CAN BE USED AS A MATERIAL.
WHAT'S THERE TO TEST? IT'S JUST... BAMBOO, RIGHT?

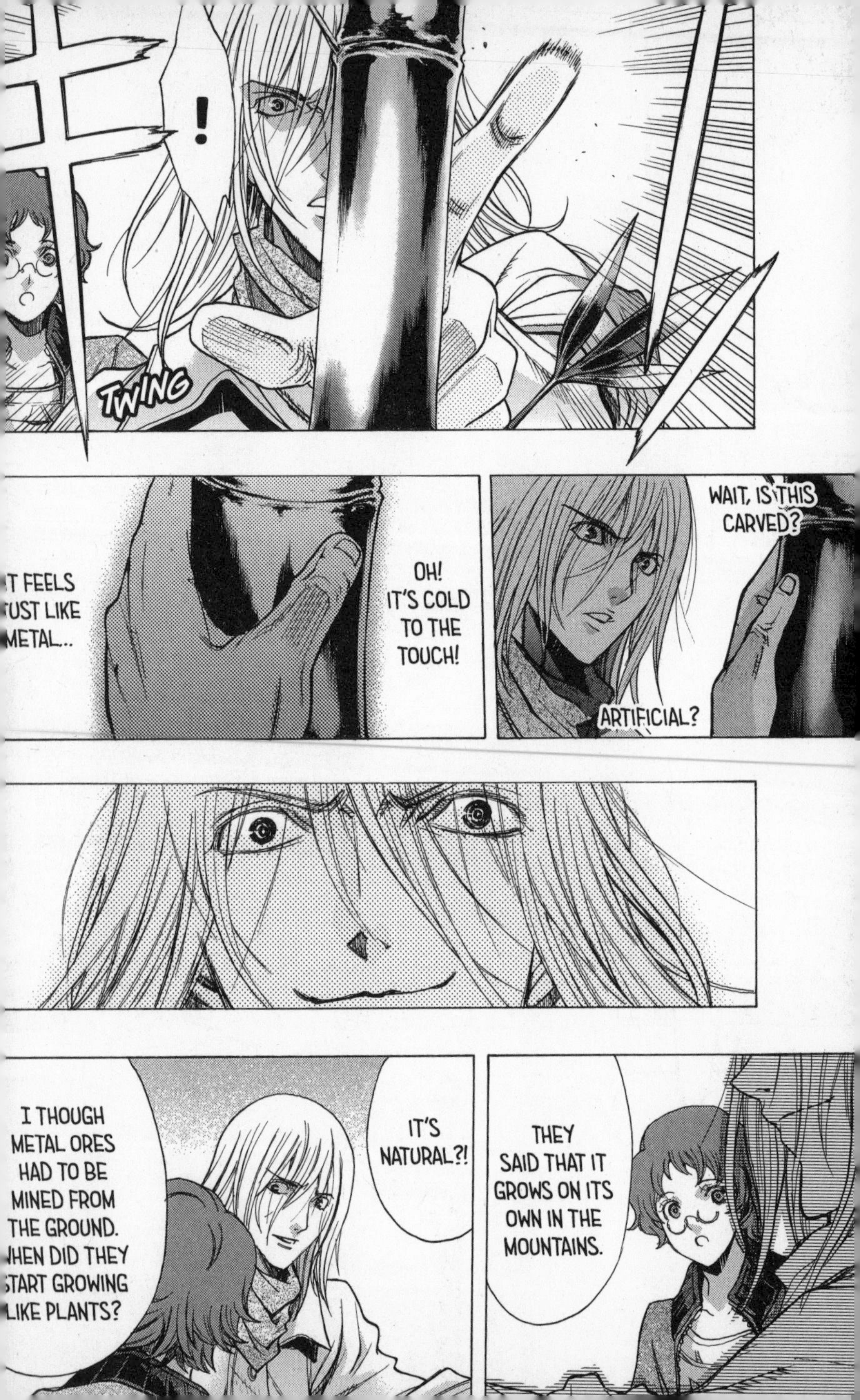
!
TWING
WAIT, IS THIS CARVED?
ARTIFICIAL?
OH! IT'S COLD TO THE TOUCH!
T FEELS JUST LIKE METAL...
THEY SAID THAT IT GROWS ON ITS OWN IN THE MOUNTAINS.
IT'S NATURAL?!
I THOUGH METAL ORES HAD TO BE MINED FROM THE GROUND. HEN DID THEY TART GROWING LIKE PLANTS?

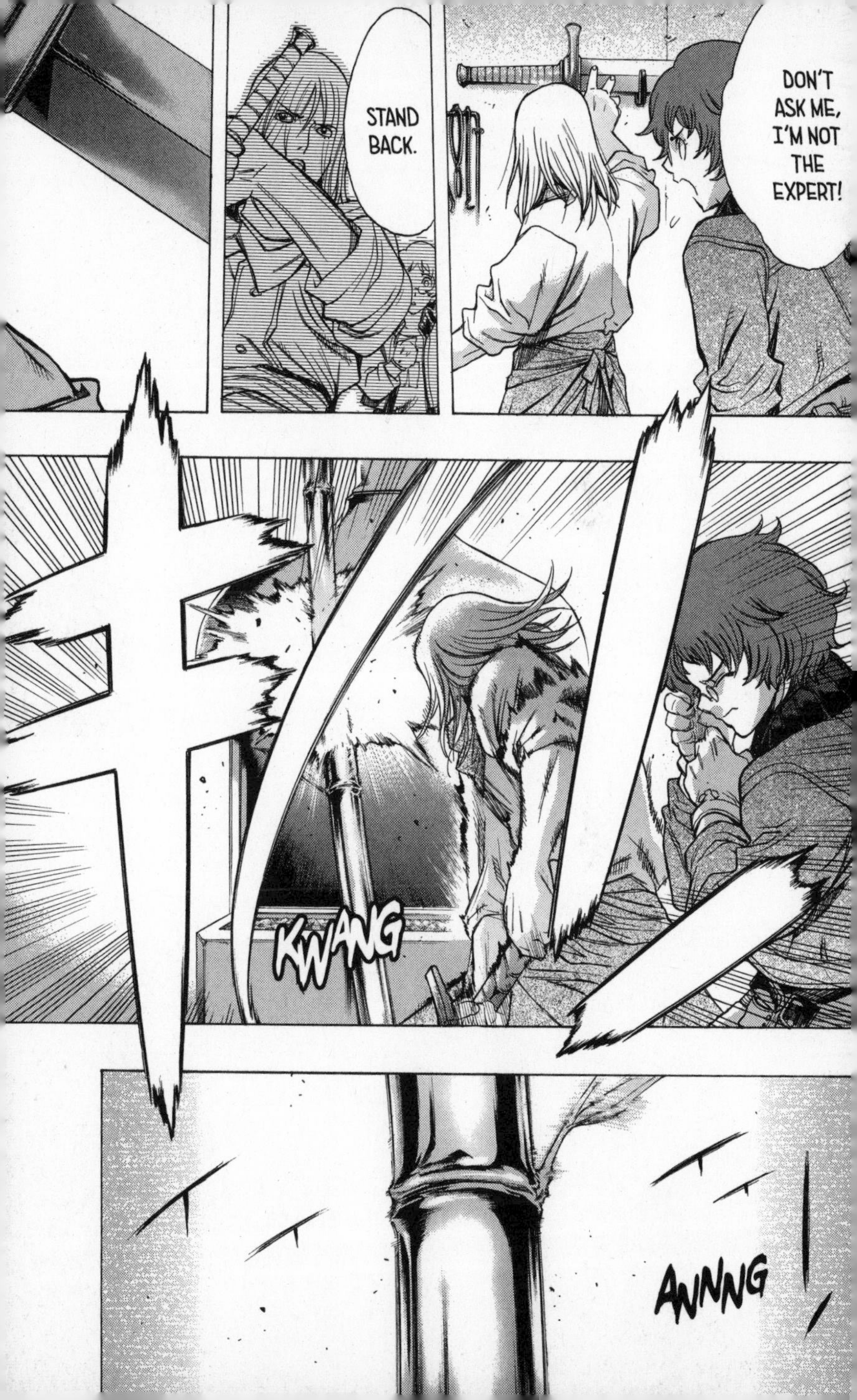
DON'T ASK ME, I'M NOT THE EXPERT!
STAND BACK.
KWANG
ANNNG

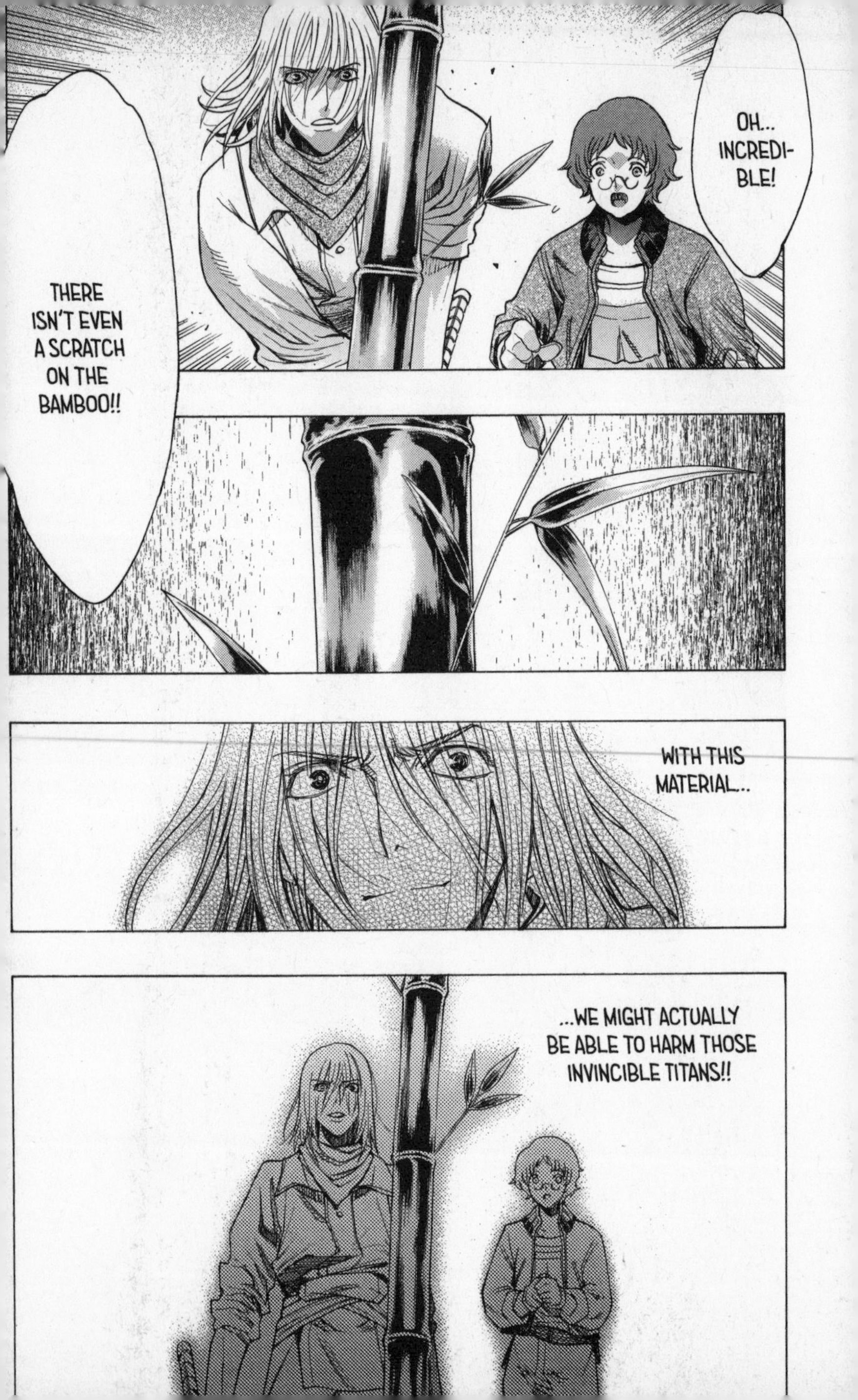
OH... INCREDI-BLE!
THERE ISN'T EVEN A SCRATCH ON THE BAMBOO!!
WITH THIS MATERIAL...
...WE MIGHT ACTUALLY BE ABLE TO HARM THOSE INVINCIBLE TITANS!!

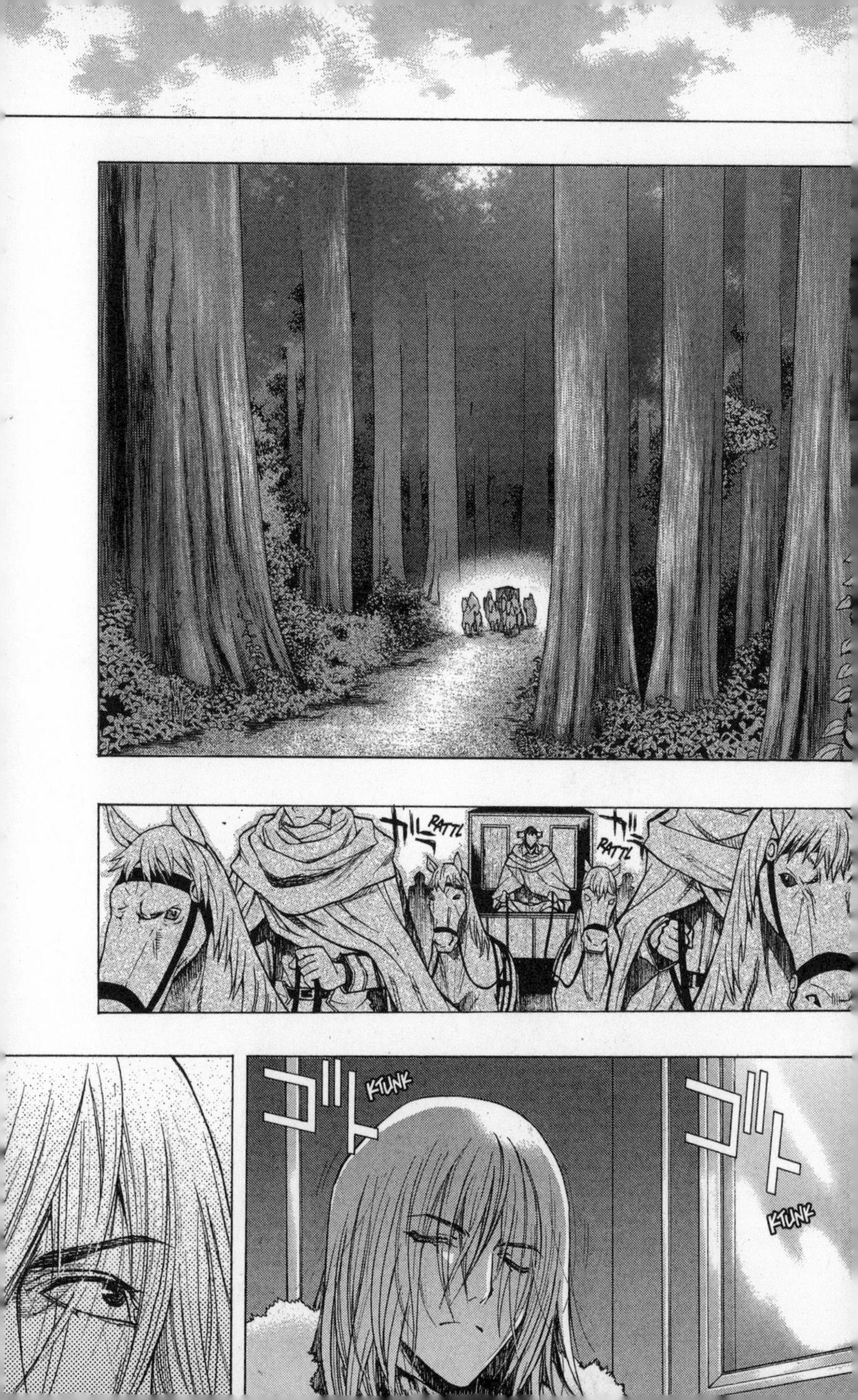
RATTL
RATTL
KTUNK
KTUNK

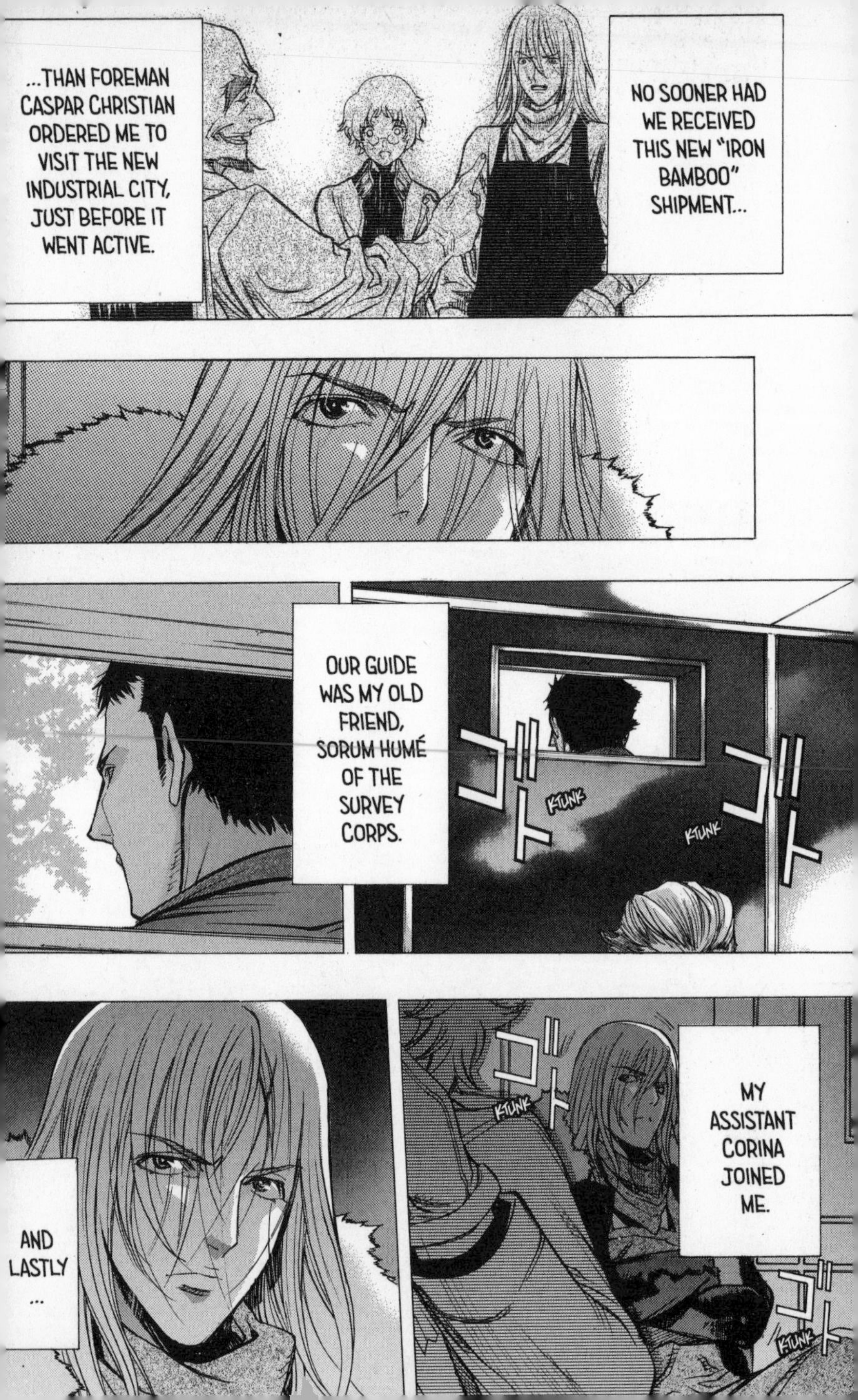
NO SOONER HAD WE RECEIVED THIS NEW "IRON BAMBOO" SHIPMENT...
...THAN FOREMAN CASPAR CHRISTIAN ORDERED ME TO VISIT THE NEW INDUSTRIAL CITY, JUST BEFORE IT WENT ACTIVE.
ゴト
KTUNK
ゴト
KTUNK
OUR GUIDE WAS MY OLD FRIEND, SORUM HUMÉ OF THE SURVEY CORPS.
MY ASSISTANT CORINA JOINED ME.
ゴト
KTUNK
ゴト
KTUNK
AND LASTLY ...

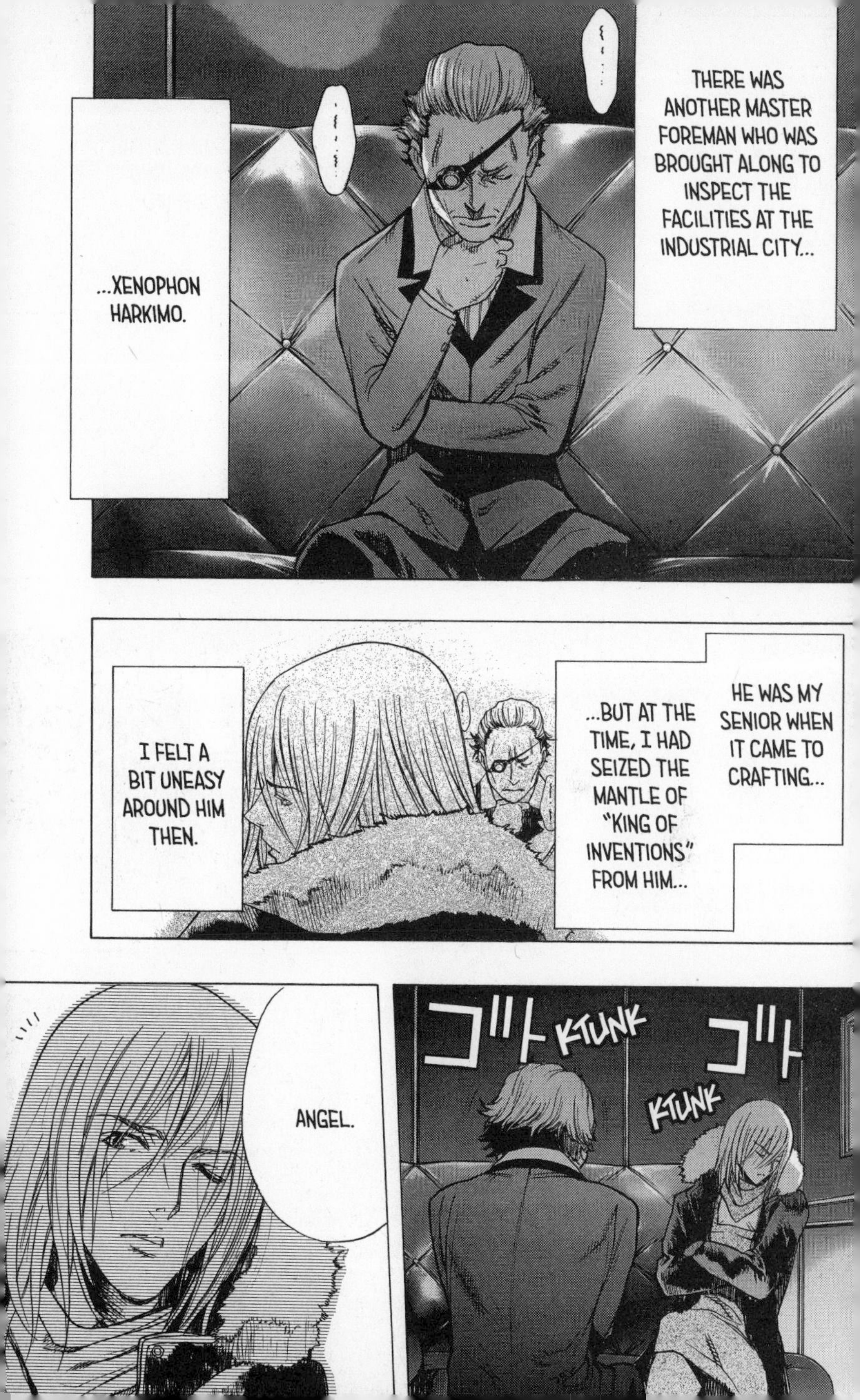
THERE WAS ANOTHER MASTER FOREMAN WHO WAS BROUGHT ALONG TO INSPECT THE FACILITIES AT THE INDUSTRIAL CITY...
...XENOPHON HARKIMO.
HE WAS MY SENIOR WHEN IT CAME TO CRAFTING...
...BUT AT THE TIME, I HAD SEIZED THE MANTLE OF "KING OF INVENTIONS" FROM HIM...
I FELT A BIT UNEASY AROUND HIM THEN.
ゴット
KTUNK
ゴット
KTUNK
ANGEL.

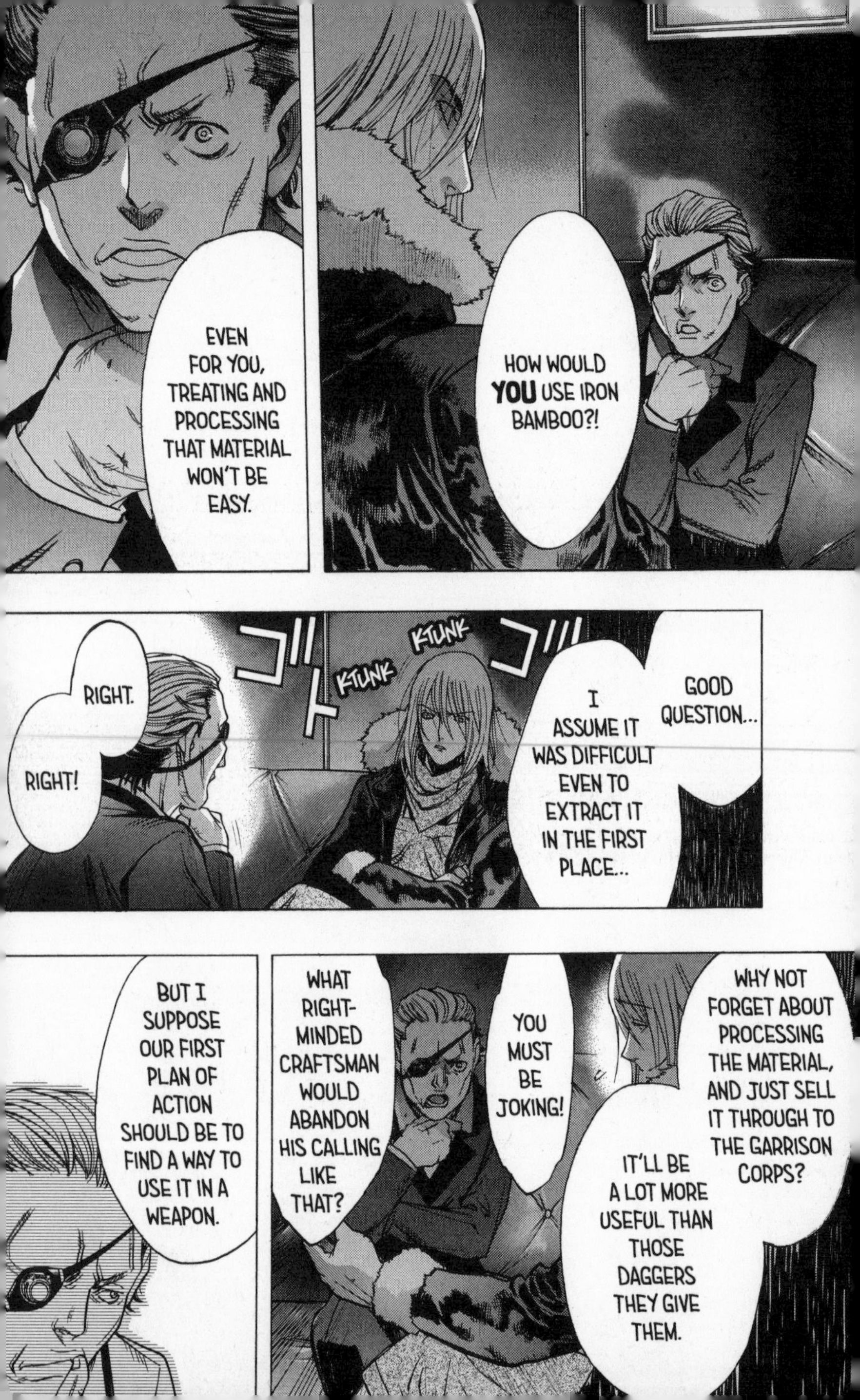
HOW WOULD YOU USE IRON BAMBOO?!
EVEN FOR YOU, TREATING AND PROCESSING THAT MATERIAL WON'T BE EASY.
GOOD QUESTION...
I ASSUME IT WAS DIFFICULT EVEN TO EXTRACT IT IN THE FIRST PLACE...
KTUNK
KTUNK
RIGHT.
RIGHT!
WHY NOT FORGET ABOUT PROCESSING THE MATERIAL, AND JUST SELL IT THROUGH TO THE GARRISON CORPS?
IT'LL BE A LOT MORE USEFUL THAN THOSE DAGGERS THEY GIVE THEM.
YOU MUST BE JOKING!
WHAT RIGHT-MINDED CRAFTSMAN WOULD ABANDON HIS CALLING LIKE THAT?
BUT I SUPPOSE OUR FIRST PLAN OF ACTION SHOULD BE TO FIND A WAY TO USE IT IN A WEAPON.

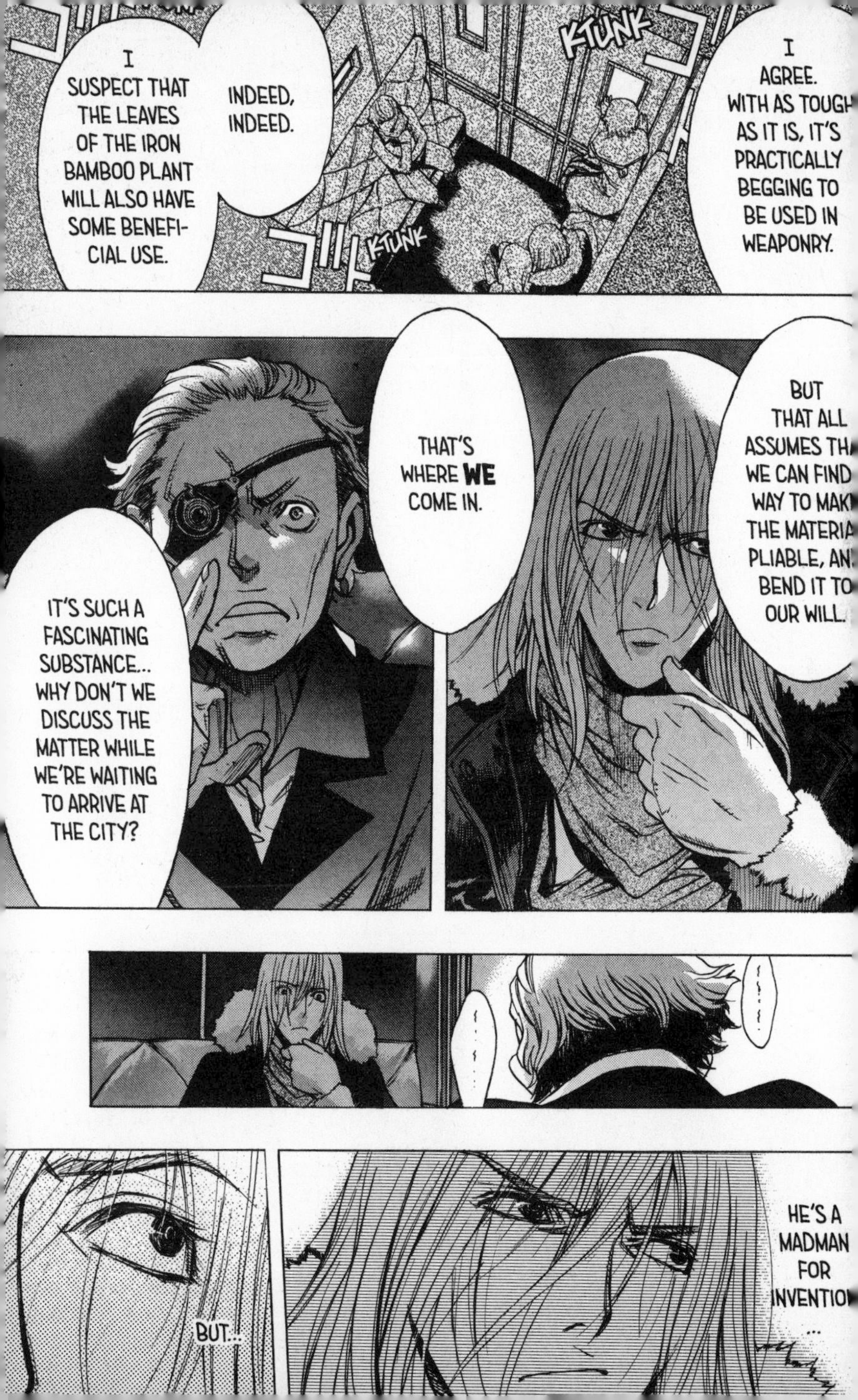
I AGREE. WITH AS TOUGH AS IT IS, IT'S PRACTICALLY BEGGING TO BE USED IN WEAPONRY.
KTUNK
INDEED, INDEED.
I SUSPECT THAT THE LEAVES OF THE IRON BAMBOO PLANT WILL ALSO HAVE SOME BENEFICIAL USE.
KTUNK
BUT THAT ALL ASSUMES THA WE CAN FIND WAY TO MAK THE MATERIA PLIABLE, AN BEND IT TO OUR WILL.
THAT'S WHERE **WE** COME IN.
IT'S SUCH A FASCINATING SUBSTANCE... WHY DON'T WE DISCUSS THE MATTER WHILE WE'RE WAITING TO ARRIVE AT THE CITY?
......
......
HE'S A MADMAN FOR INVENTIO ...
BUT...

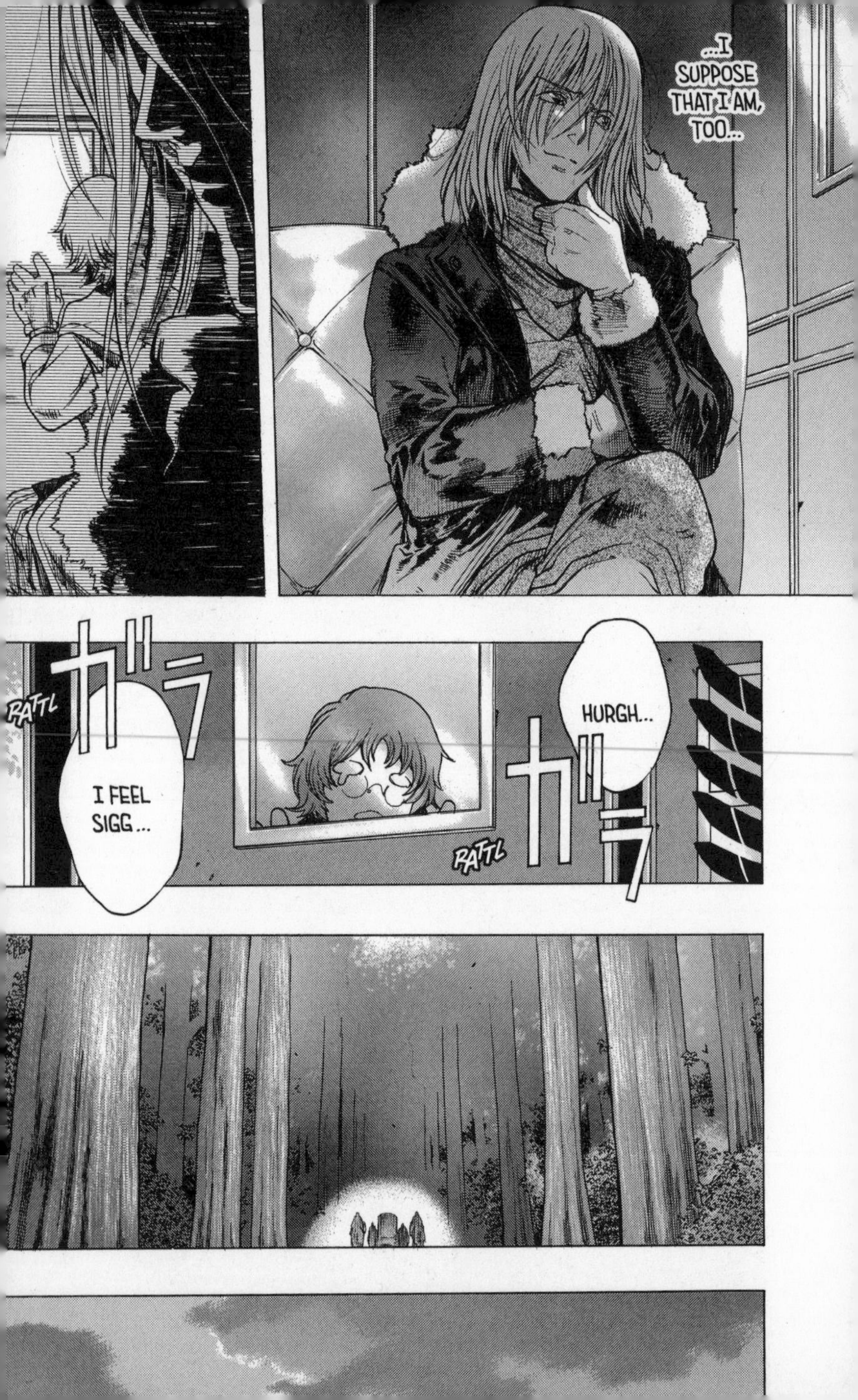
...I SUPPOSE THAT I AM, TOO...
HURGH...
ガラ
RATTL
ガラ
RATTL
I FEEL SIGG...

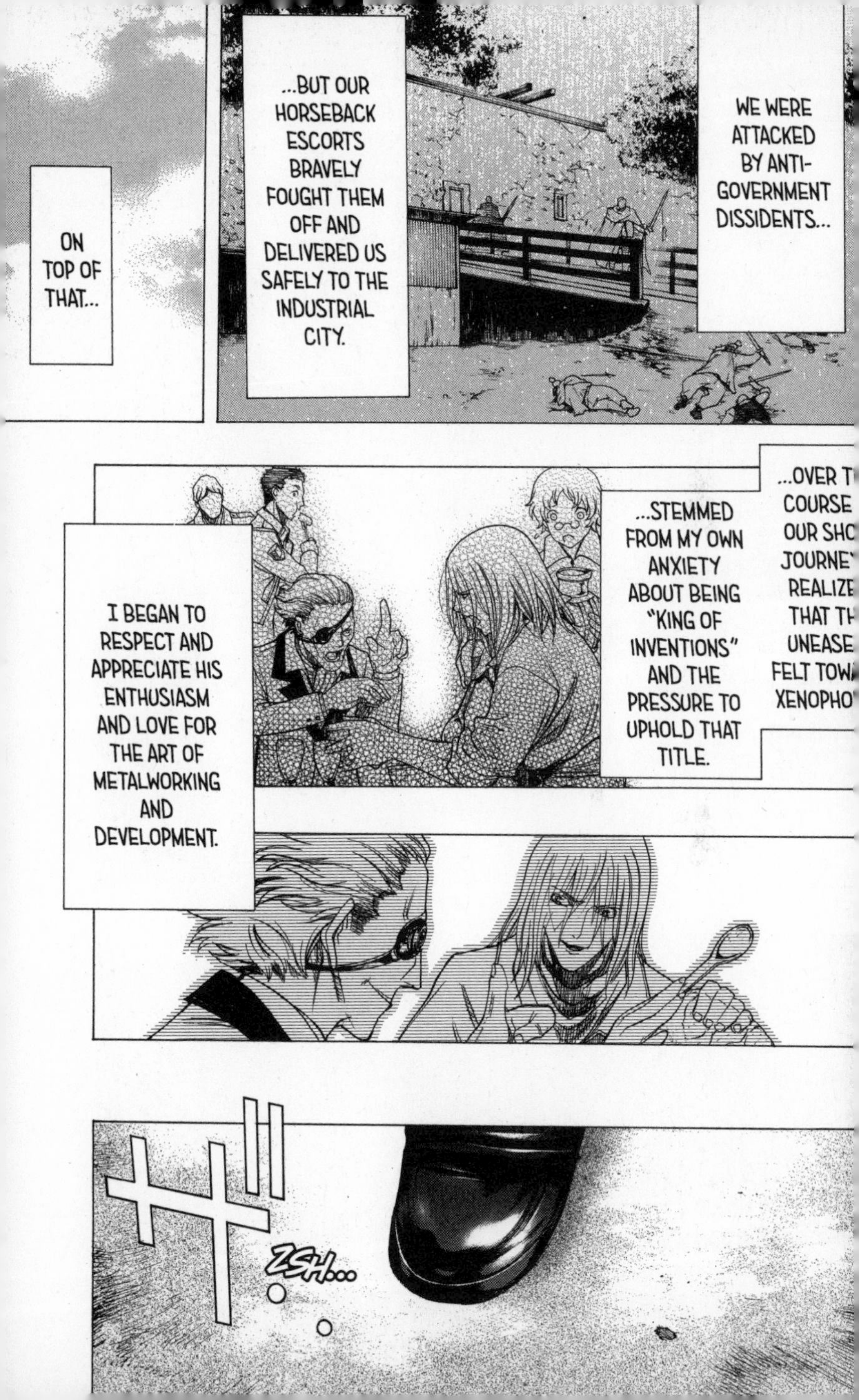
WE WERE ATTACKED BY ANTI-GOVERNMENT DISSIDENTS...
...BUT OUR HORSEBACK ESCORTS BRAVELY FOUGHT THEM OFF AND DELIVERED US SAFELY TO THE INDUSTRIAL CITY.
ON TOP OF THAT...
...OVER T COURSE OUR SHO JOURNE REALIZE THAT TH UNEASE FELT TOW XENOPHO
...STEMMED FROM MY OWN ANXIETY ABOUT BEING "KING OF INVENTIONS" AND THE PRESSURE TO UPHOLD THAT TITLE.
I BEGAN TO RESPECT AND APPRECIATE HIS ENTHUSIASM AND LOVE FOR THE ART OF METALWORKING AND DEVELOPMENT.
ZSHOOO

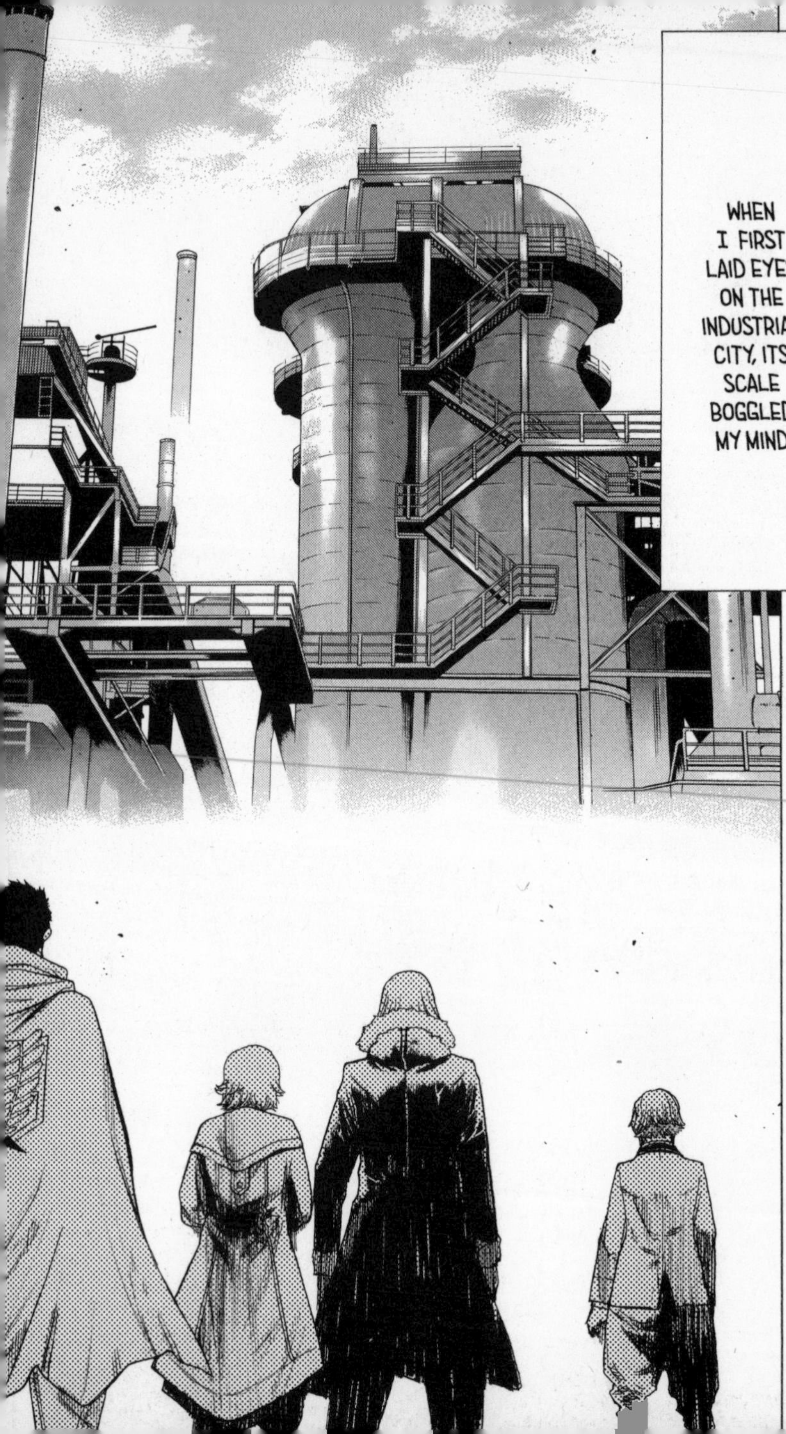
WHEN I FIRST LAID EYES ON THE INDUSTRIAL CITY, ITS SCALE BOGGLED MY MIND.

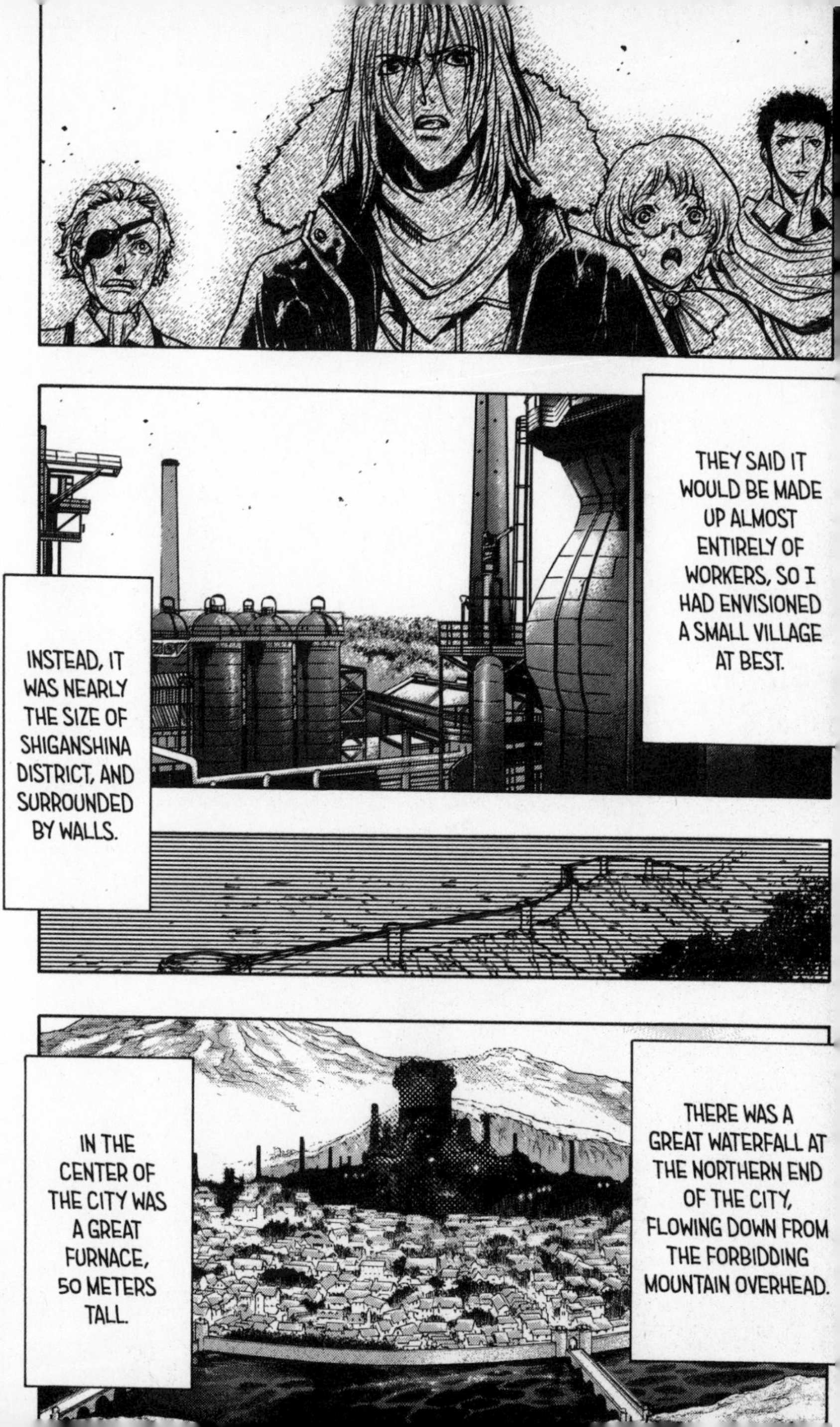
THEY SAID IT WOULD BE MADE UP ALMOST ENTIRELY OF WORKERS, SO I HAD ENVISIONED A SMALL VILLAGE AT BEST.
INSTEAD, IT WAS NEARLY THE SIZE OF SHIGANSHINA DISTRICT, AND SURROUNDED BY WALLS.
THERE WAS A GREAT WATERFALL AT THE NORTHERN END OF THE CITY, FLOWING DOWN FROM THE FORBIDDING MOUNTAIN OVERHEAD.
IN THE CENTER OF THE CITY WAS A GREAT FURNACE, 50 METERS TALL.

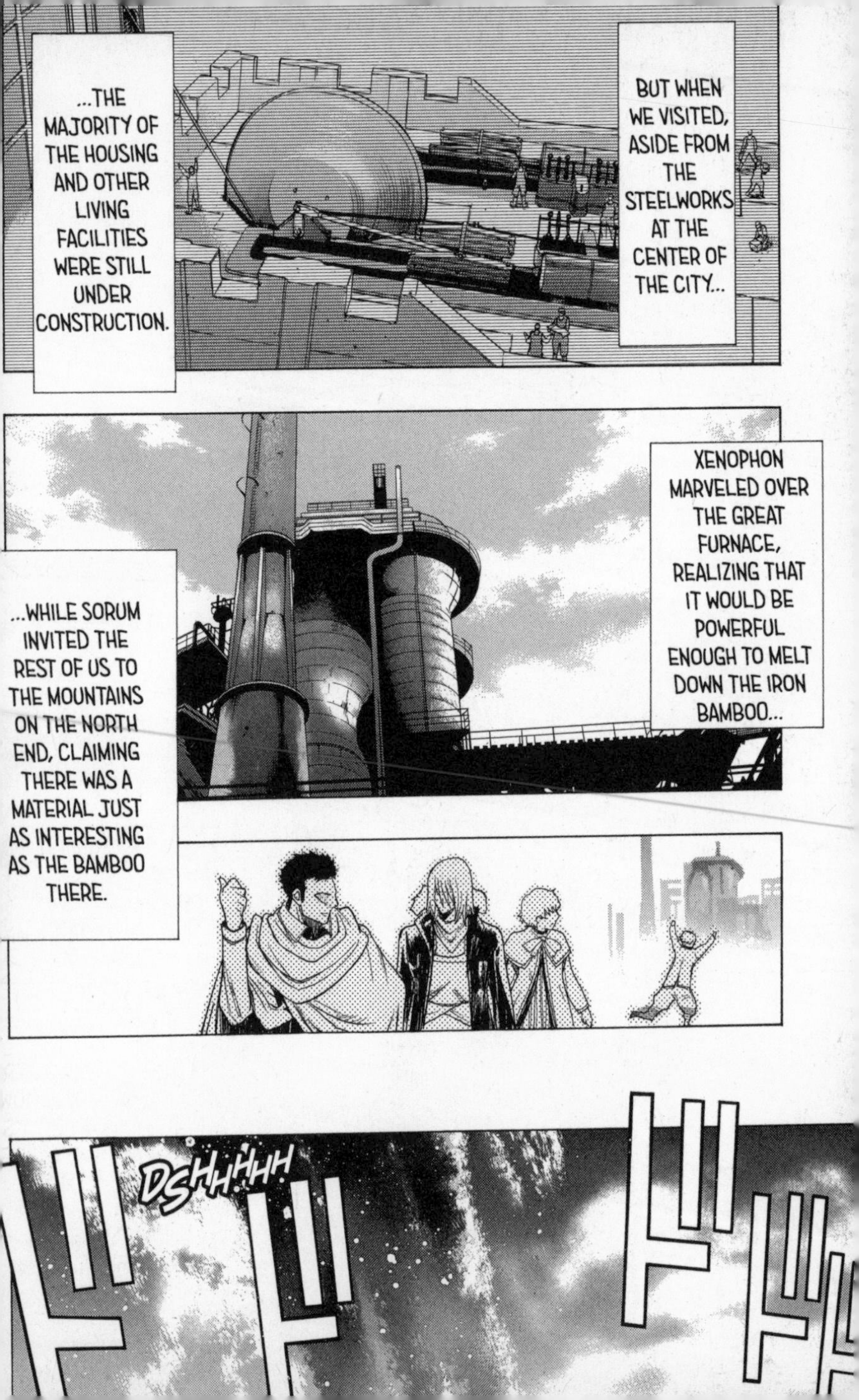
BUT WHEN WE VISITED, ASIDE FROM THE STEELWORKS AT THE CENTER OF THE CITY...
...THE MAJORITY OF THE HOUSING AND OTHER LIVING FACILITIES WERE STILL UNDER CONSTRUCTION.
XENOPHON MARVELED OVER THE GREAT FURNACE, REALIZING THAT IT WOULD BE POWERFUL ENOUGH TO MELT DOWN THE IRON BAMBOO...
...WHILE SORUM INVITED THE REST OF US TO THE MOUNTAINS ON THE NORTH END, CLAIMING THERE WAS A MATERIAL JUST AS INTERESTING AS THE BAMBOO THERE.
DSHHHHH

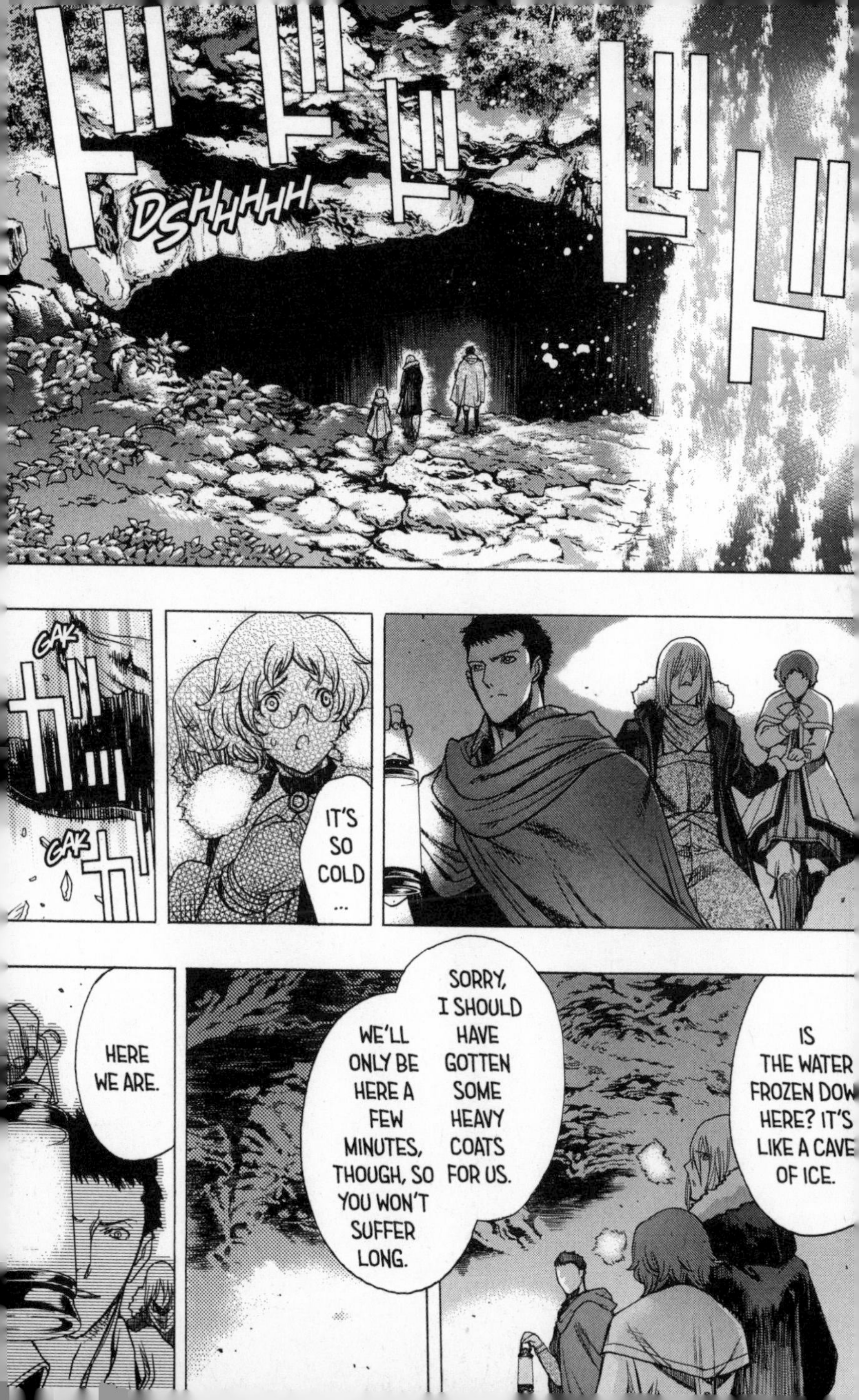
DSHHHHH
IT'S SO COLD ...
CAK
CAK
IS THE WATER FROZEN DOW HERE? IT'S LIKE A CAVE OF ICE.
SORRY, I SHOULD HAVE GOTTEN SOME HEAVY COATS FOR US.
WE'LL ONLY BE HERE A FEW MINUTES, THOUGH, SO YOU WON'T SUFFER LONG.
HERE WE ARE.

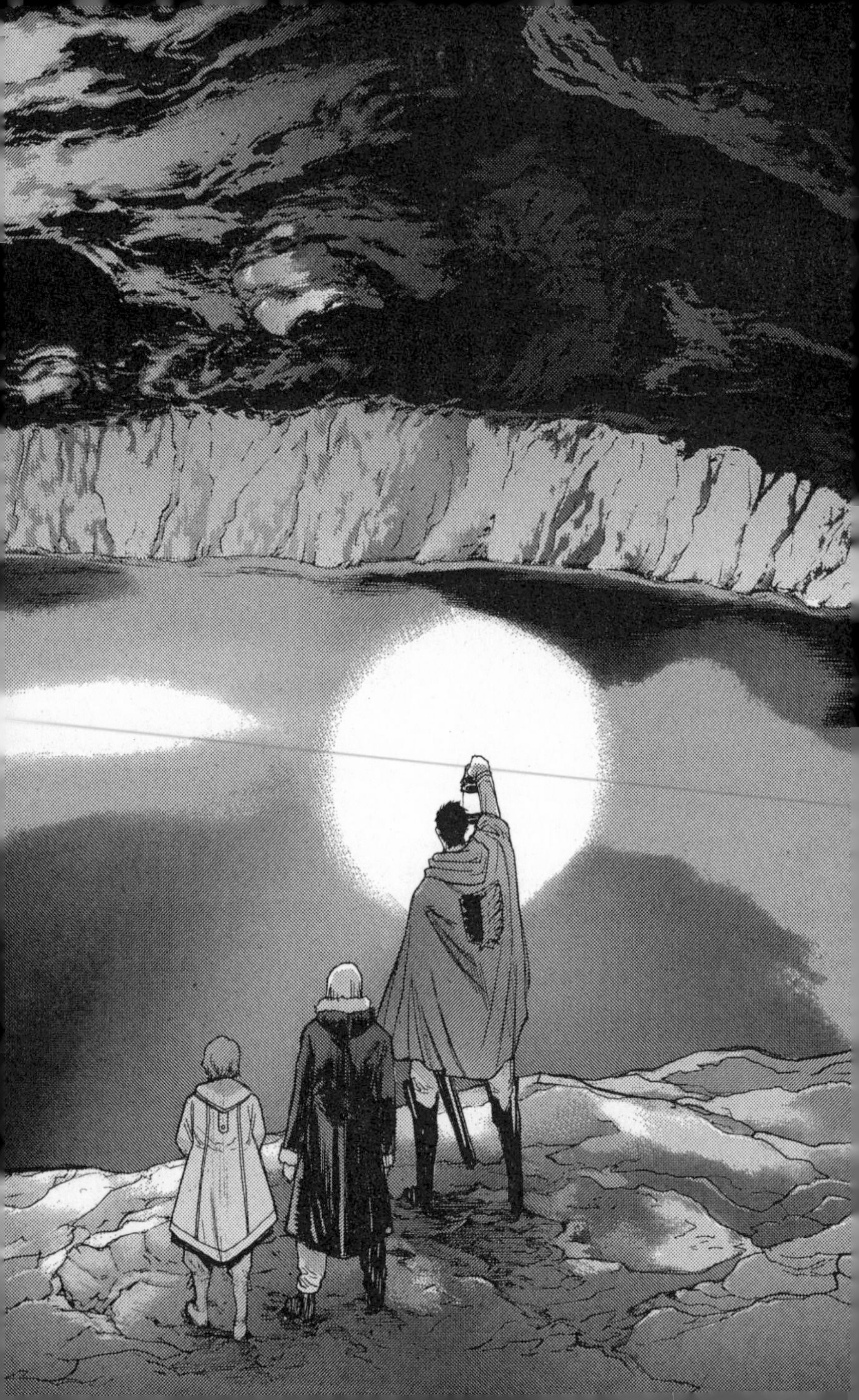

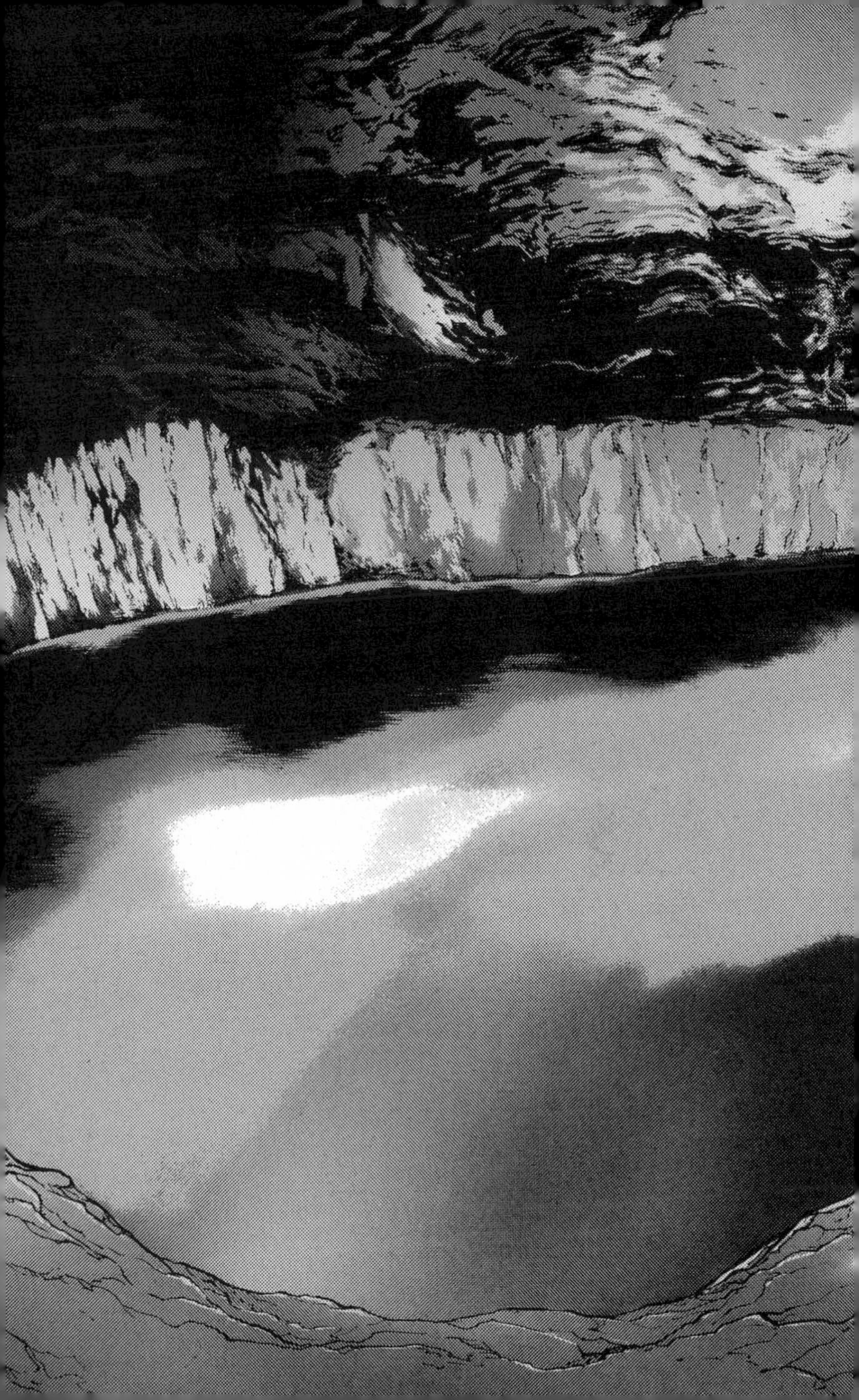

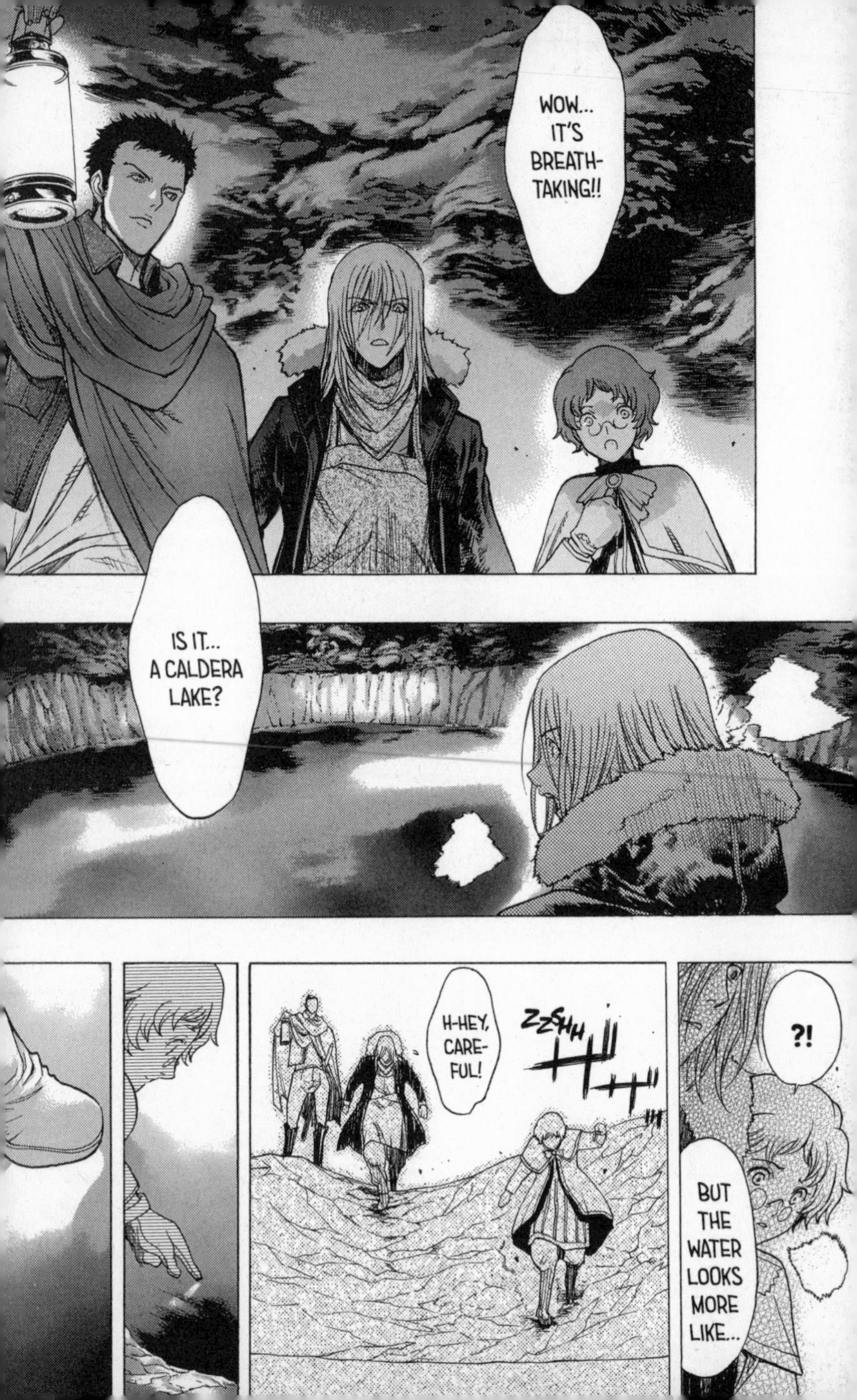
WOW... IT'S BREATH-TAKING!!
IS IT... A CALDERA LAKE?
?!
BUT THE WATER LOOKS MORE LIKE...
H-HEY, CARE-FUL!
ZZSHH

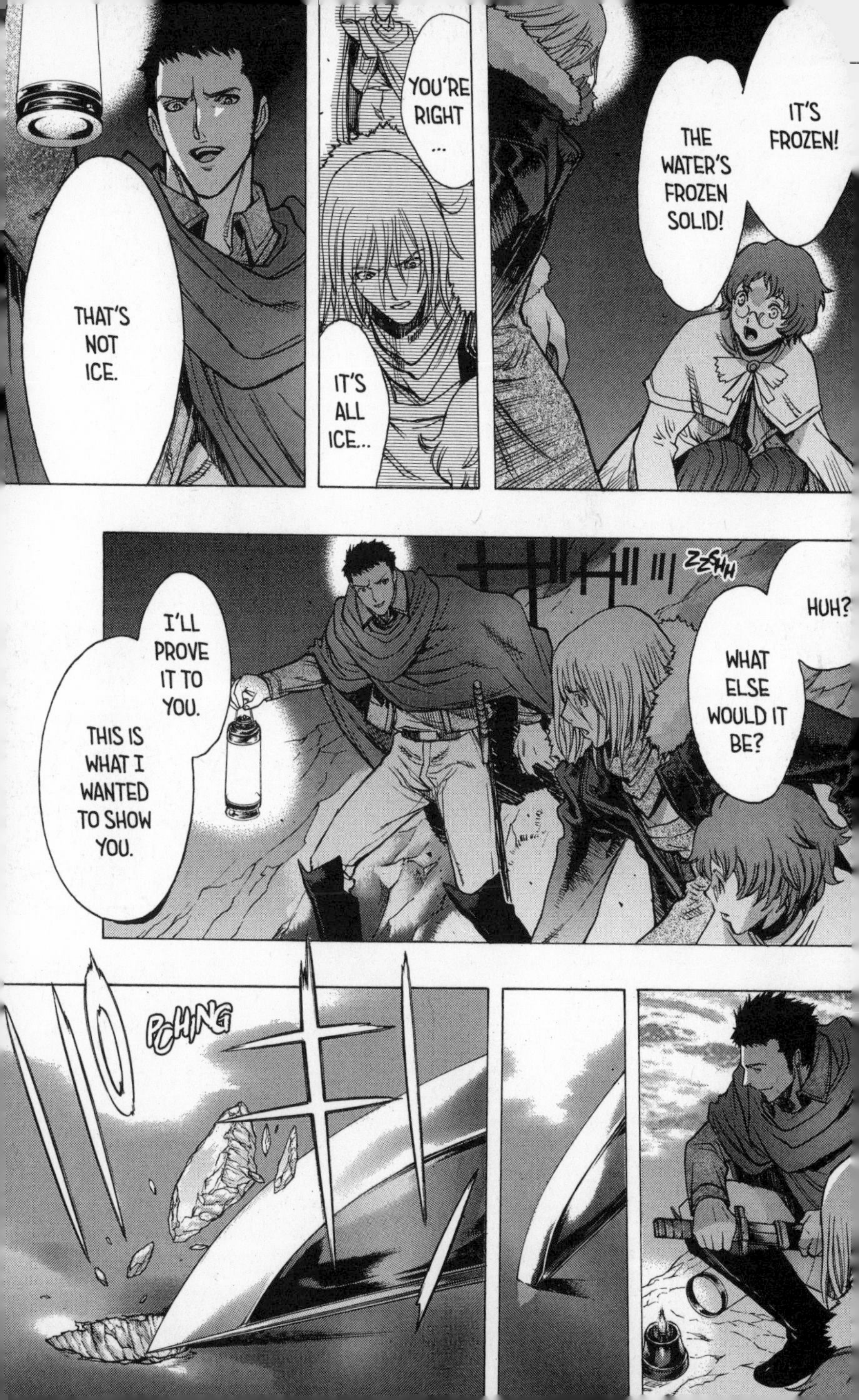
IT'S FROZEN!
THE WATER'S FROZEN SOLID!
YOU'RE RIGHT ...
IT'S ALL ICE...
THAT'S NOT ICE.
HUH?
WHAT ELSE WOULD IT BE?
ZZSHH
I'LL PROVE IT TO YOU.
THIS IS WHAT I WANTED TO SHOW YOU.
PCHING

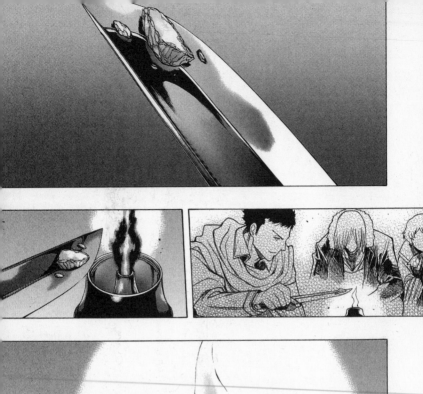

THE... THE ICE IS BURNING!

MY GOODNESS!!

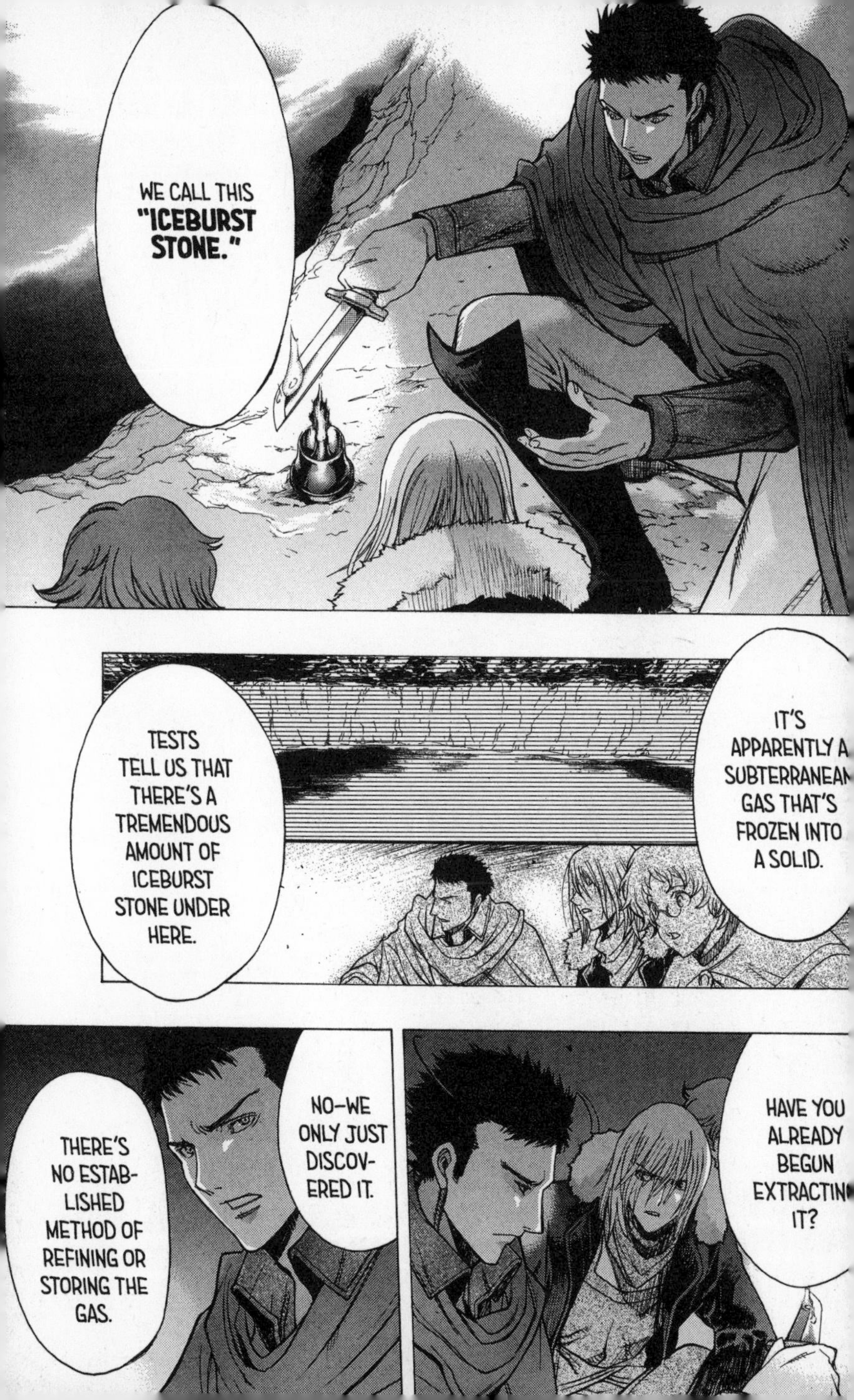
WE CALL THIS "ICEBURST STONE."
IT'S APPARENTLY A SUBTERRANEA GAS THAT'S FROZEN INTO A SOLID.
TESTS TELL US THAT THERE'S A TREMENDOUS AMOUNT OF ICEBURST STONE UNDER HERE.
HAVE YOU ALREADY BEGUN EXTRACTIN IT?
NO—WE ONLY JUST DISCOVERED IT.
THERE'S NO ESTABLISHED METHOD OF REFINING OR STORING THE GAS.

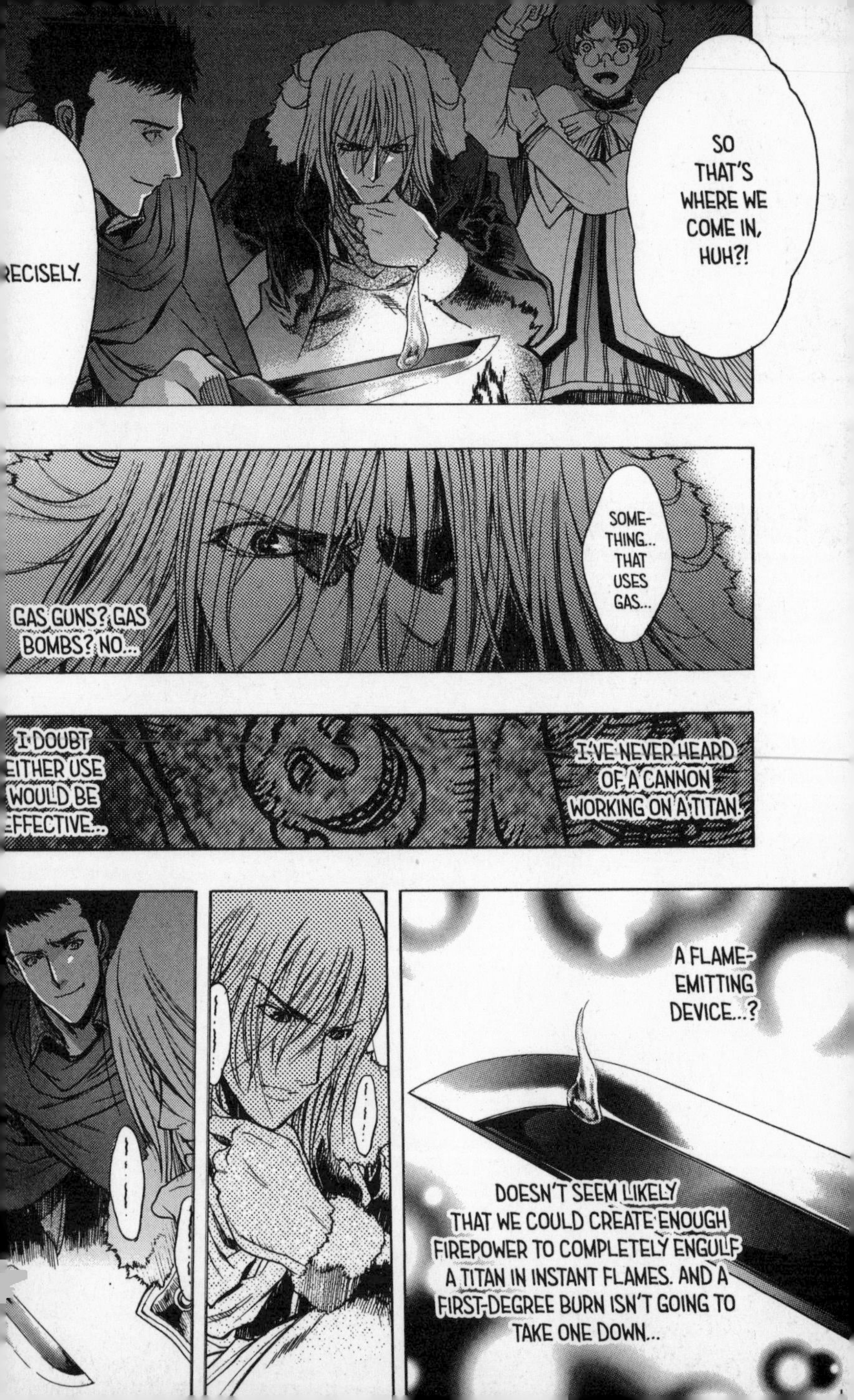
SO THAT'S WHERE WE COME IN, HUH?!
RECISELY.
SOME-THING... THAT USES GAS...
GAS GUNS? GAS BOMBS? NO...
I'VE NEVER HEARD OF A CANNON WORKING ON A TITAN.
I DOUBT EITHER USE WOULD BE EFFECTIVE...
A FLAME-EMITTING DEVICE...?
DOESN'T SEEM LIKELY THAT WE COULD CREATE ENOUGH FIREPOWER TO COMPLETELY ENGULF A TITAN IN INSTANT FLAMES. AND A FIRST-DEGREE BURN ISN'T GOING TO TAKE ONE DOWN...
......
......
......

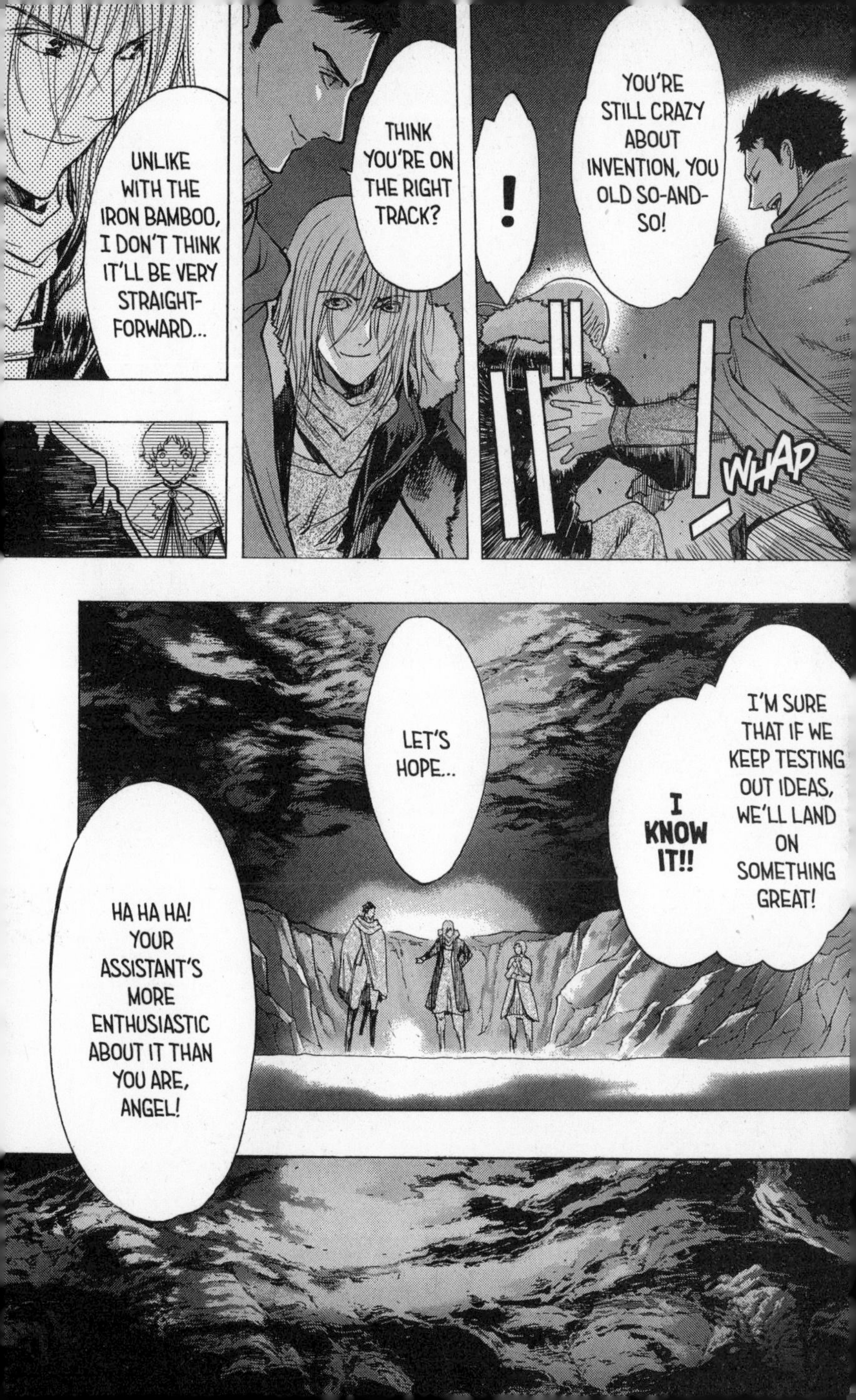
YOU'RE STILL CRAZY ABOUT INVENTION, YOU OLD SO-AND-SO!
!
WHAP
THINK YOU'RE ON THE RIGHT TRACK?
UNLIKE WITH THE IRON BAMBOO, I DON'T THINK IT'LL BE VERY STRAIGHT-FORWARD...
I'M SURE THAT IF WE KEEP TESTING OUT IDEAS, WE'LL LAND ON SOMETHING GREAT!
I KNOW IT!!
LET'S HOPE...
HA HA HA! YOUR ASSISTANT'S MORE ENTHUSIASTIC ABOUT IT THAN YOU ARE, ANGEL!

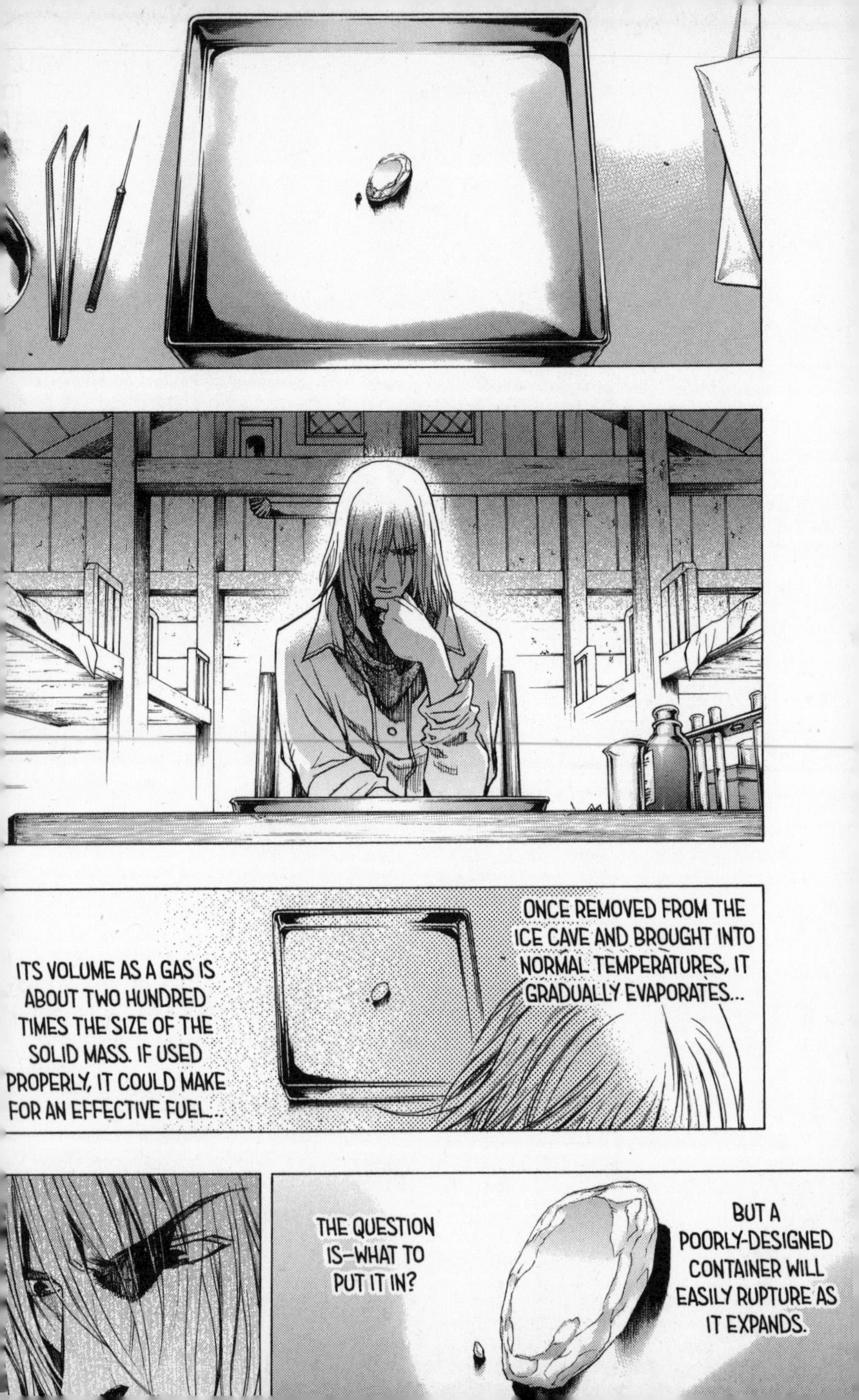
ONCE REMOVED FROM THE ICE CAVE AND BROUGHT INTO NORMAL TEMPERATURES, IT GRADUALLY EVAPORATES...
ITS VOLUME AS A GAS IS ABOUT TWO HUNDRED TIMES THE SIZE OF THE SOLID MASS. IF USED PROPERLY, IT COULD MAKE FOR AN EFFECTIVE FUEL...
BUT A POORLY-DESIGNED CONTAINER WILL EASILY RUPTURE AS IT EXPANDS.
THE QUESTION IS—WHAT TO PUT IT IN?

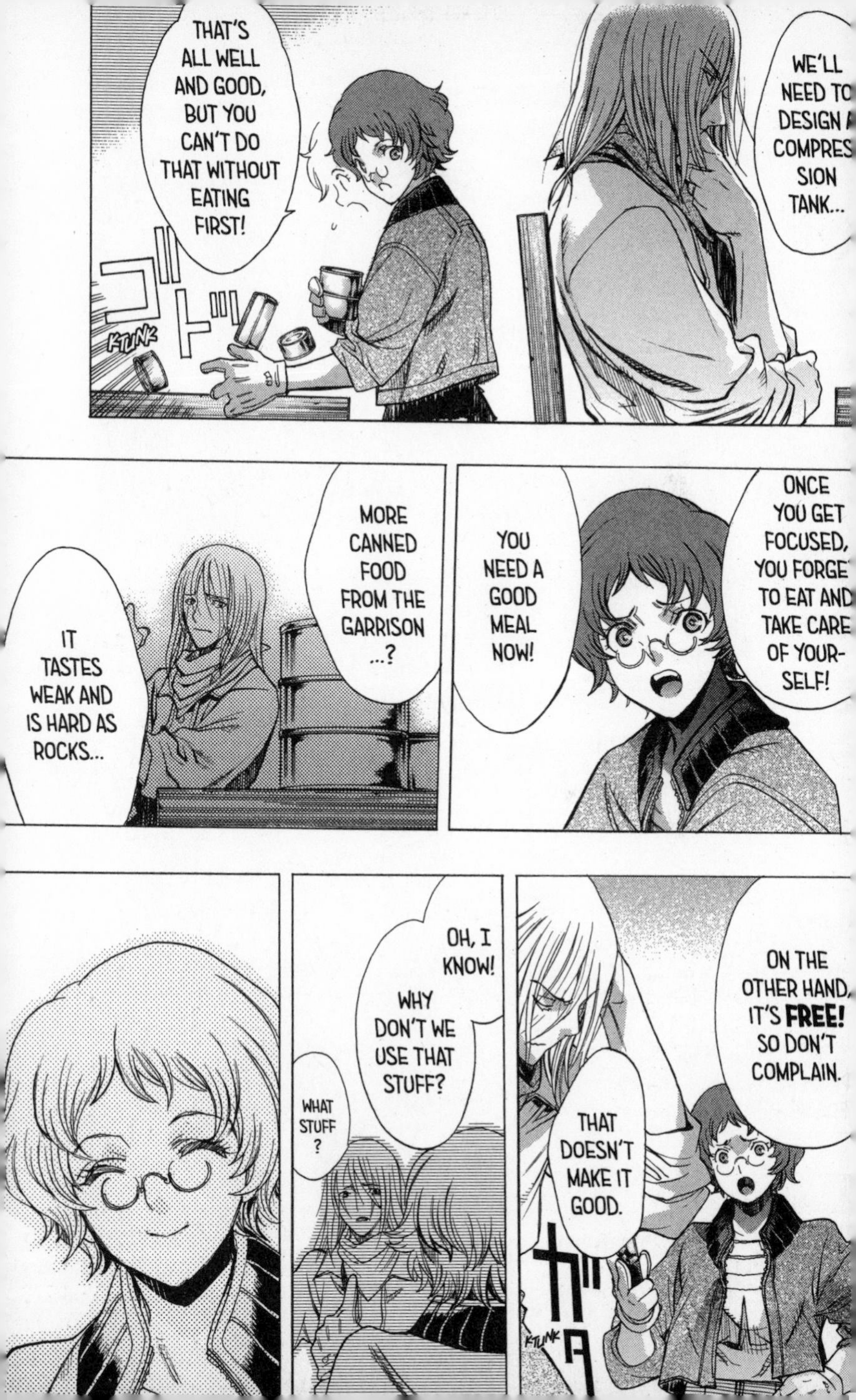
WE'LL NEED TO DESIGN A COMPRESSION TANK...
THAT'S ALL WELL AND GOOD, BUT YOU CAN'T DO THAT WITHOUT EATING FIRST!
KTUNK
ONCE YOU GET FOCUSED, YOU FORGET TO EAT AND TAKE CARE OF YOURSELF!
YOU NEED A GOOD MEAL NOW!
MORE CANNED FOOD FROM THE GARRISON ...?
IT TASTES WEAK AND IS HARD AS ROCKS...
ON THE OTHER HAND, IT'S **FREE!** SO DON'T COMPLAIN.
THAT DOESN'T MAKE IT GOOD.
KTUNK
OH, I KNOW!
WHY DON'T WE USE THAT STUFF?
WHAT STUFF?

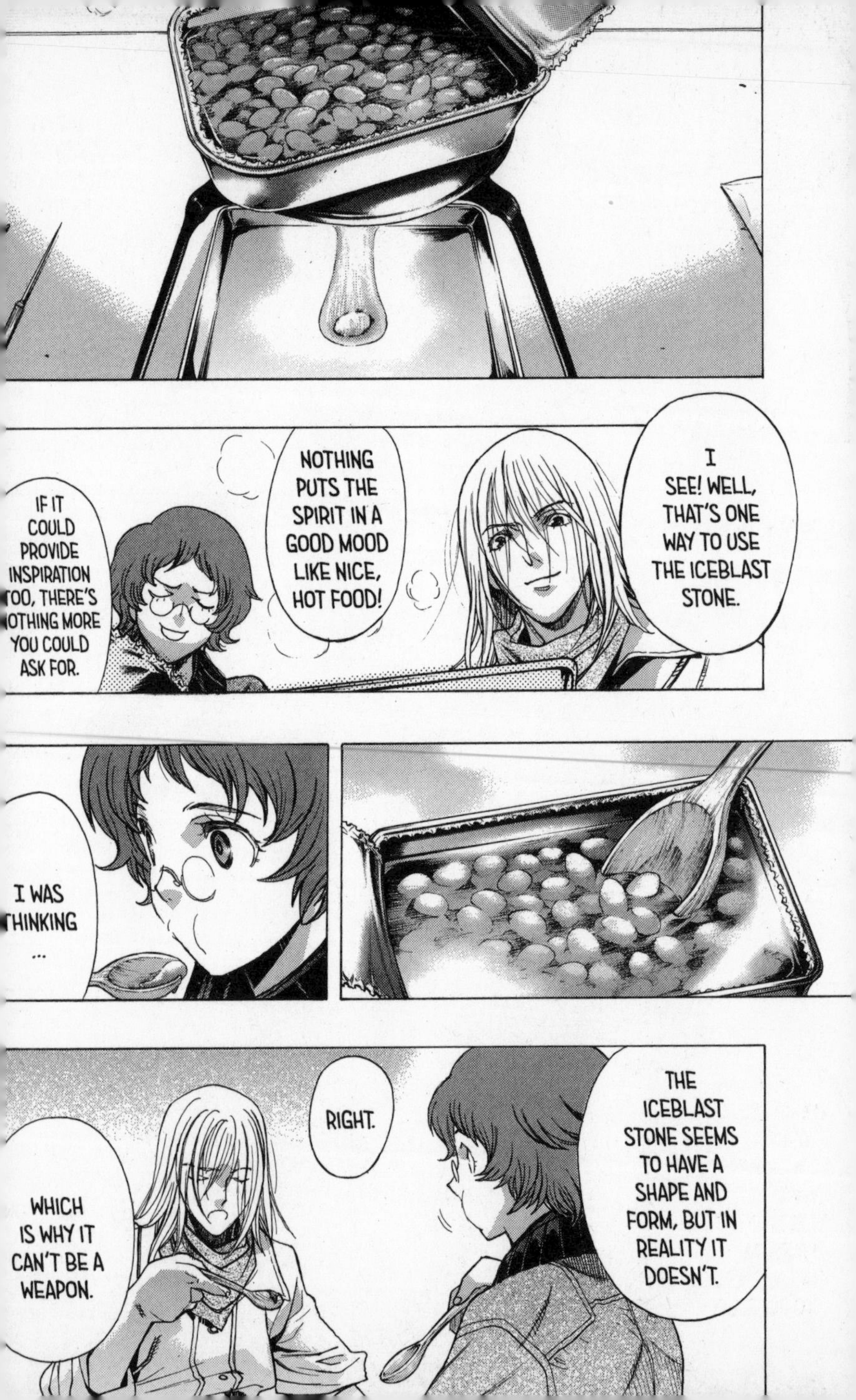
I SEE! WELL, THAT'S ONE WAY TO USE THE ICEBLAST STONE.
NOTHING PUTS THE SPIRIT IN A GOOD MOOD LIKE NICE, HOT FOOD!
IF IT COULD PROVIDE INSPIRATION TOO, THERE'S NOTHING MORE YOU COULD ASK FOR.
I WAS THINKING ...
THE ICEBLAST STONE SEEMS TO HAVE A SHAPE AND FORM, BUT IN REALITY IT DOESN'T.
RIGHT.
WHICH IS WHY IT CAN'T BE A WEAPON.

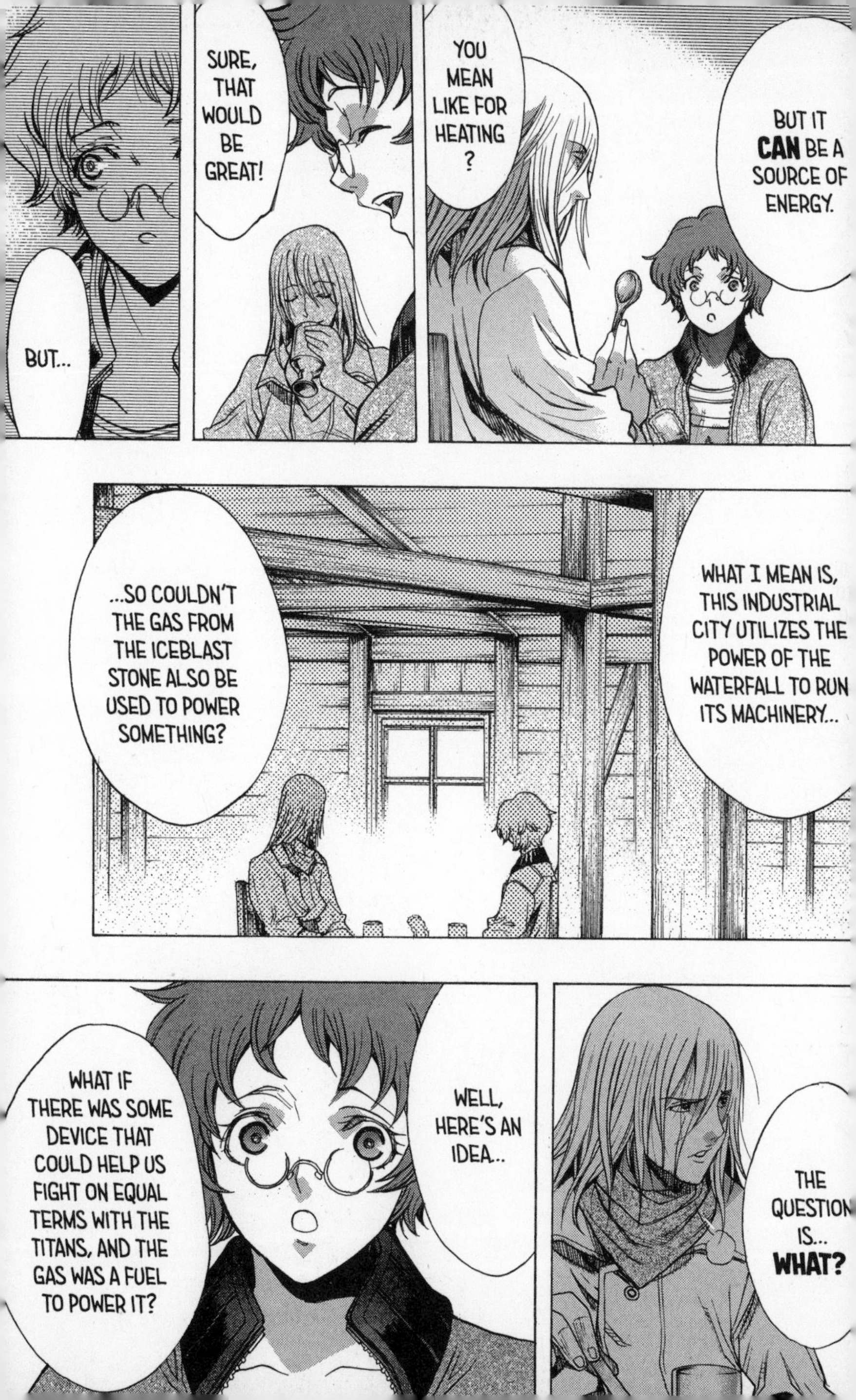
BUT IT CAN BE A SOURCE OF ENERGY.
YOU MEAN LIKE FOR HEATING?
SURE, THAT WOULD BE GREAT!
BUT...
WHAT I MEAN IS, THIS INDUSTRIAL CITY UTILIZES THE POWER OF THE WATERFALL TO RUN ITS MACHINERY...
...SO COULDN'T THE GAS FROM THE ICEBLAST STONE ALSO BE USED TO POWER SOMETHING?
THE QUESTION IS... WHAT?
WELL, HERE'S AN IDEA..
WHAT IF THERE WAS SOME DEVICE THAT COULD HELP US FIGHT ON EQUAL TERMS WITH THE TITANS, AND THE GAS WAS A FUEL TO POWER IT?

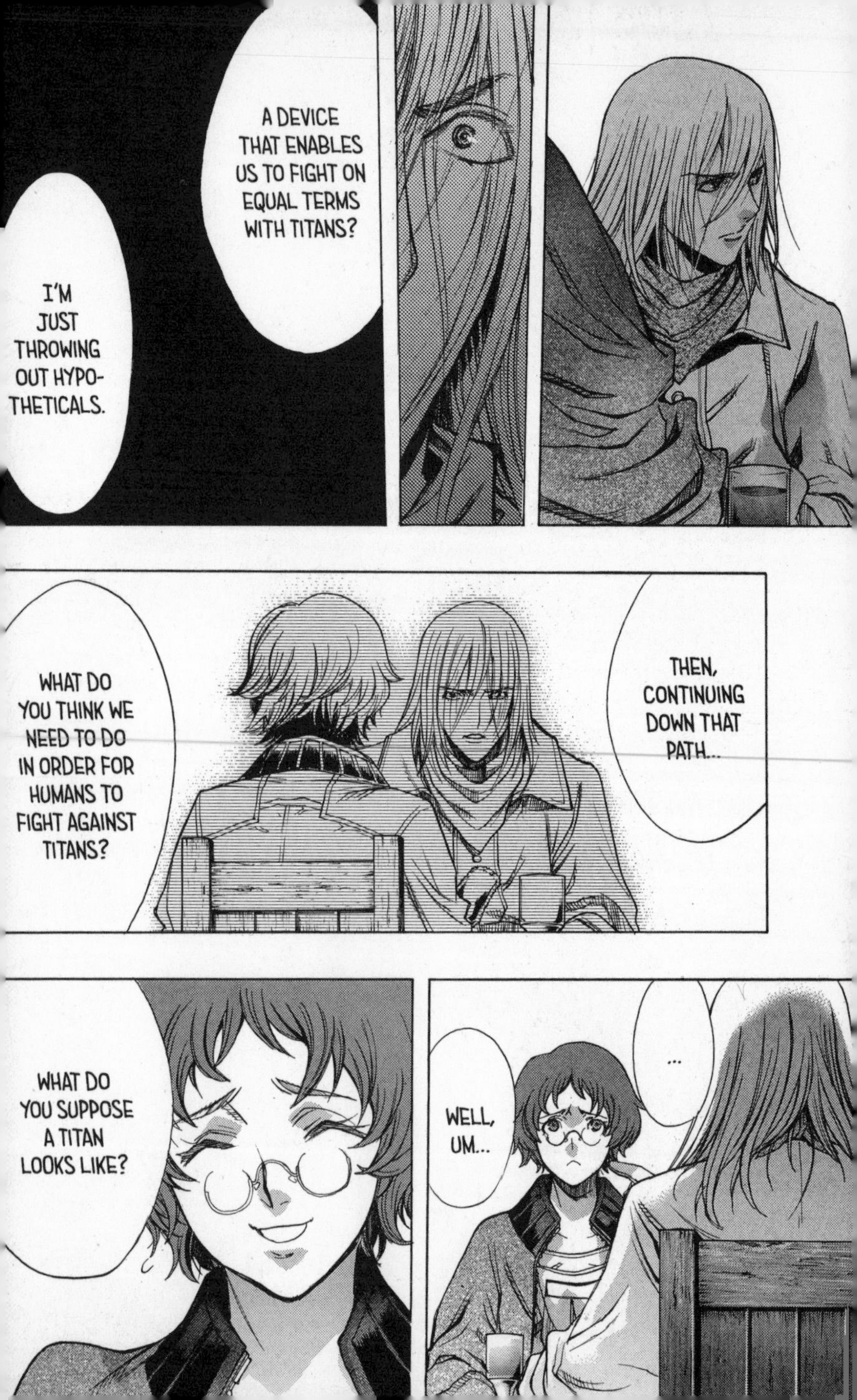
A DEVICE THAT ENABLES US TO FIGHT ON EQUAL TERMS WITH TITANS?
I'M JUST THROWING OUT HYPO-THETICALS.
THEN, CONTINUING DOWN THAT PATH...
WHAT DO YOU THINK WE NEED TO DO IN ORDER FOR HUMANS TO FIGHT AGAINST TITANS?
...
WELL, UM...
WHAT DO YOU SUPPOSE A TITAN LOOKS LIKE?

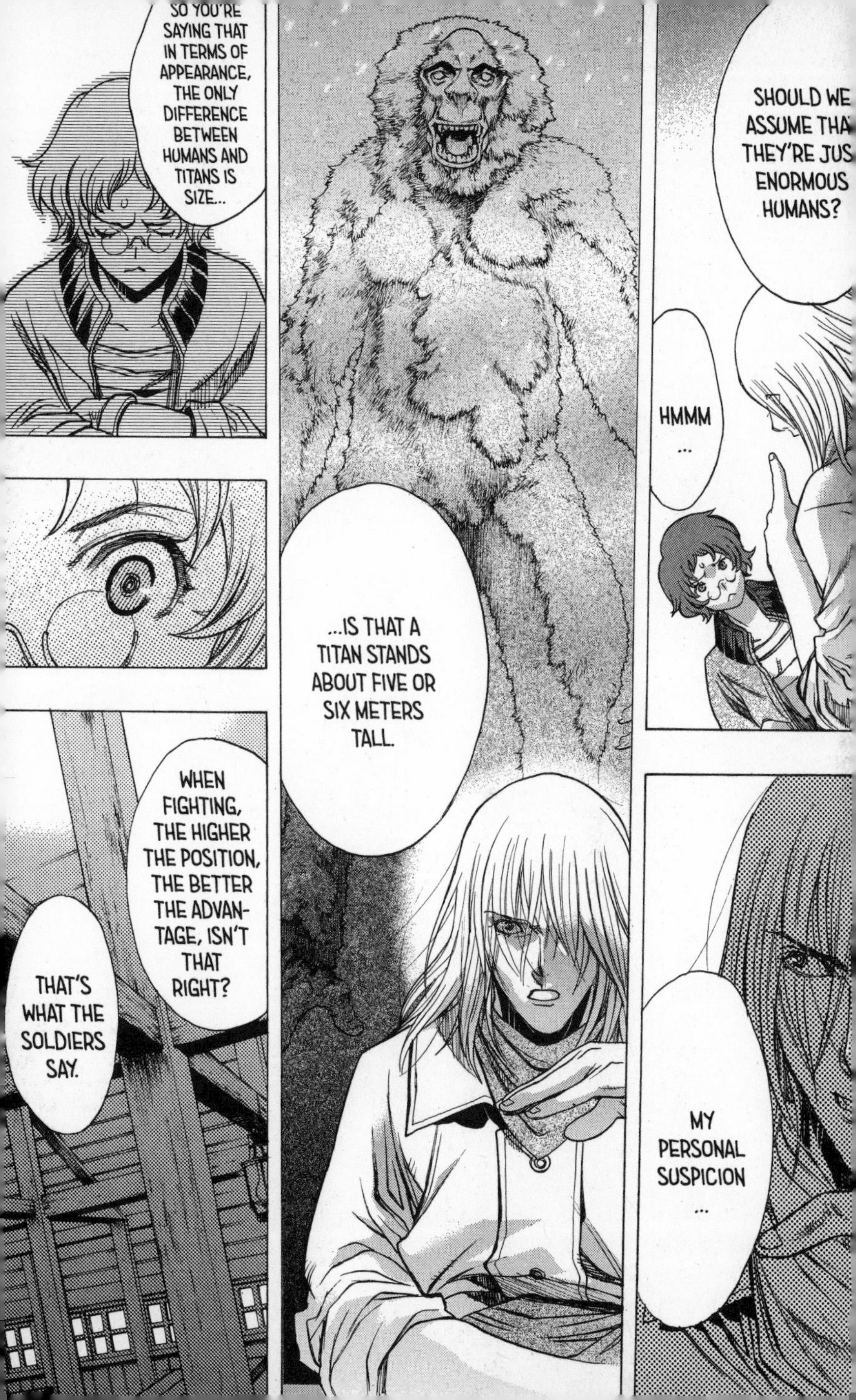

SHOULD WE ASSUME THA THEY'RE JUS ENORMOUS HUMANS?
HMMM ...
MY PERSONAL SUSPICION ...
...IS THAT A TITAN STANDS ABOUT FIVE OR SIX METERS TALL.
SO YOU'RE SAYING THAT IN TERMS OF APPEARANCE, THE ONLY DIFFERENCE BETWEEN HUMANS AND TITANS IS SIZE...
WHEN FIGHTING, THE HIGHER THE POSITION, THE BETTER THE ADVAN-TAGE, ISN'T THAT RIGHT?
THAT'S WHAT THE SOLDIERS SAY.

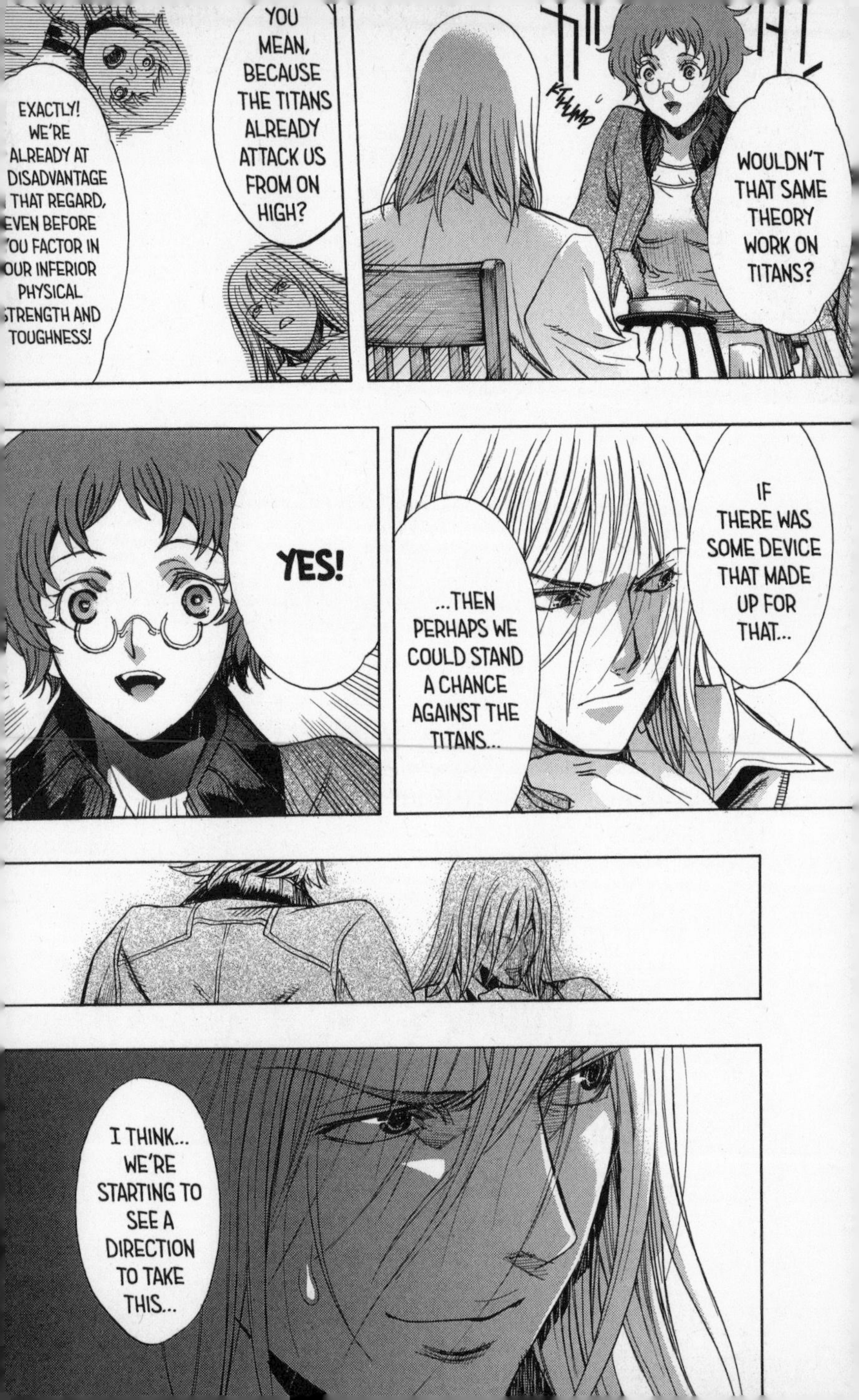
WOULDN'T THAT SAME THEORY WORK ON TITANS?
YOU MEAN, BECAUSE THE TITANS ALREADY ATTACK US FROM ON HIGH?
EXACTLY! WE'RE ALREADY AT DISADVANTAGE THAT REGARD, EVEN BEFORE YOU FACTOR IN OUR INFERIOR PHYSICAL STRENGTH AND TOUGHNESS!
IF THERE WAS SOME DEVICE THAT MADE UP FOR THAT...
...THEN PERHAPS WE COULD STAND A CHANCE AGAINST THE TITANS...
YES!
I THINK... WE'RE STARTING TO SEE A DIRECTION TO TAKE THIS...

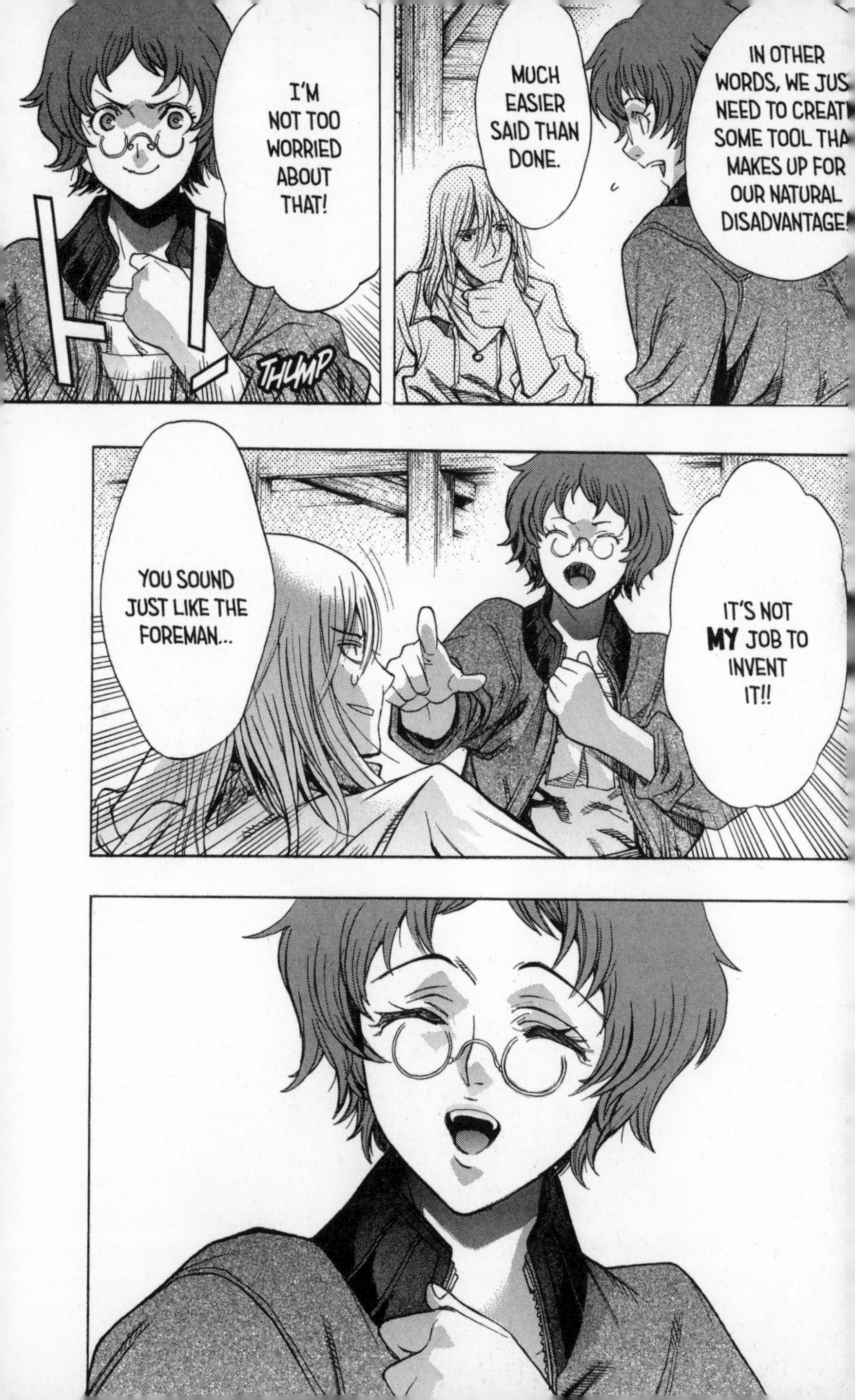
IN OTHER WORDS, WE JUS NEED TO CREAT SOME TOOL THA MAKES UP FOR OUR NATURAL DISADVANTAGE
MUCH EASIER SAID THAN DONE.
I'M NOT TOO WORRIED ABOUT THAT!
THUMP
IT'S NOT **MY** JOB TO INVENT IT!!
YOU SOUND JUST LIKE THE FOREMAN...

DURING THE
ONE-WEEK
STAY IN THE
INDUSTRIAL
CITY...

...WE WORKED
BREATHLESSLY,
SHORT ON
SLEEP, TO
DEVELOP NEW
TOOLS WITH
THE BOLD NEW
MATERIALS AND
FACILITIES AT
OUR DISPOSAL.

AND
ON THE
MORNING
WE WERE
TO
LEAVE...

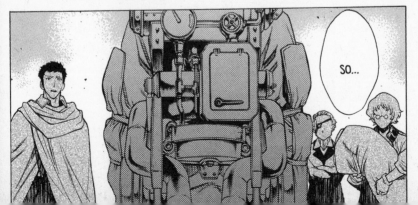

SO...

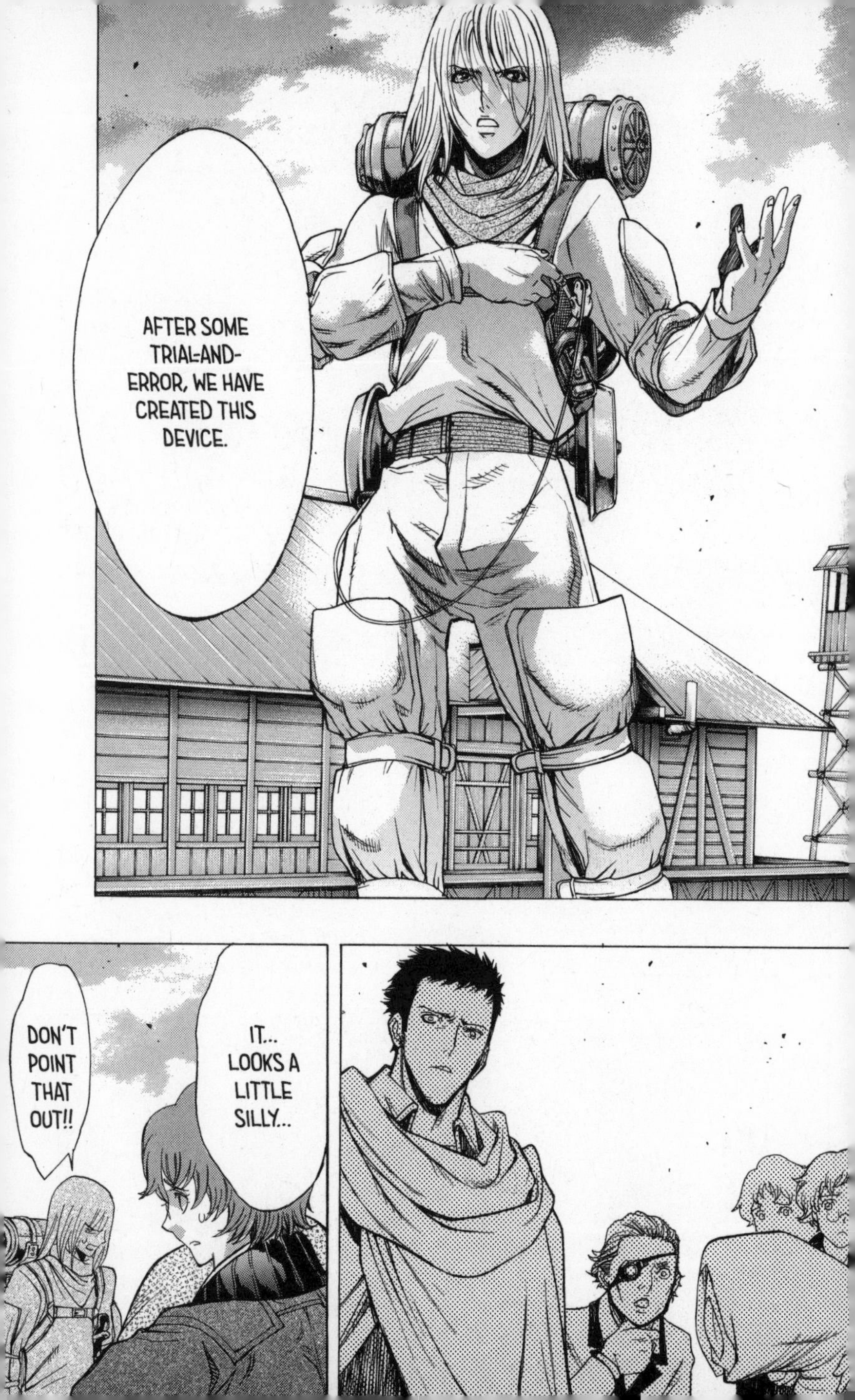
AFTER SOME TRIAL-AND-ERROR, WE HAVE CREATED THIS DEVICE.
IT... LOOKS A LITTLE SILLY...
DON'T POINT THAT OUT!!

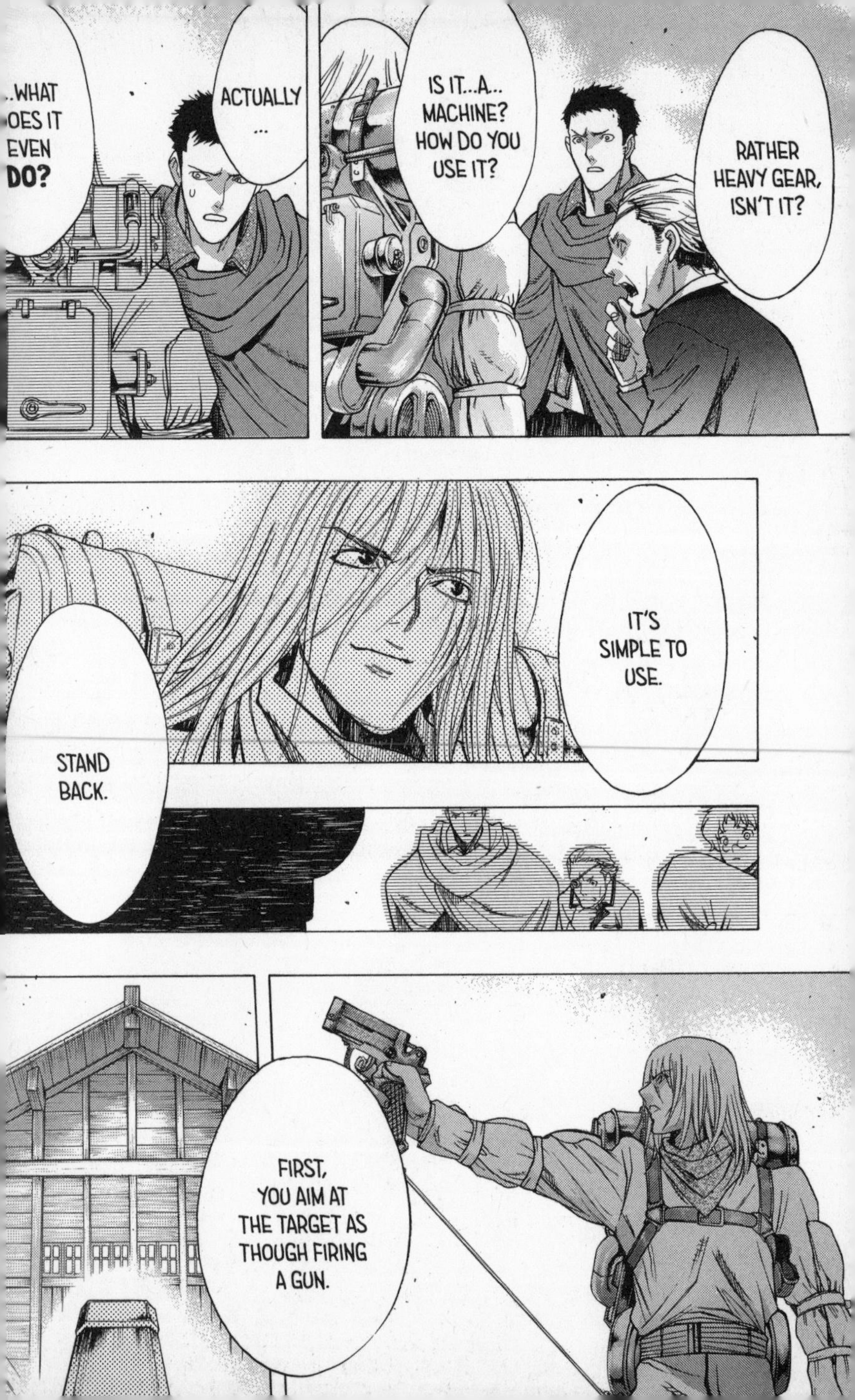
RATHER HEAVY GEAR, ISN'T IT?
IS IT...A... MACHINE? HOW DO YOU USE IT?
ACTUALLY ...
..WHAT OES IT EVEN DO?
IT'S SIMPLE TO USE.
STAND BACK.
FIRST, YOU AIM AT THE TARGET AS THOUGH FIRING A GUN.

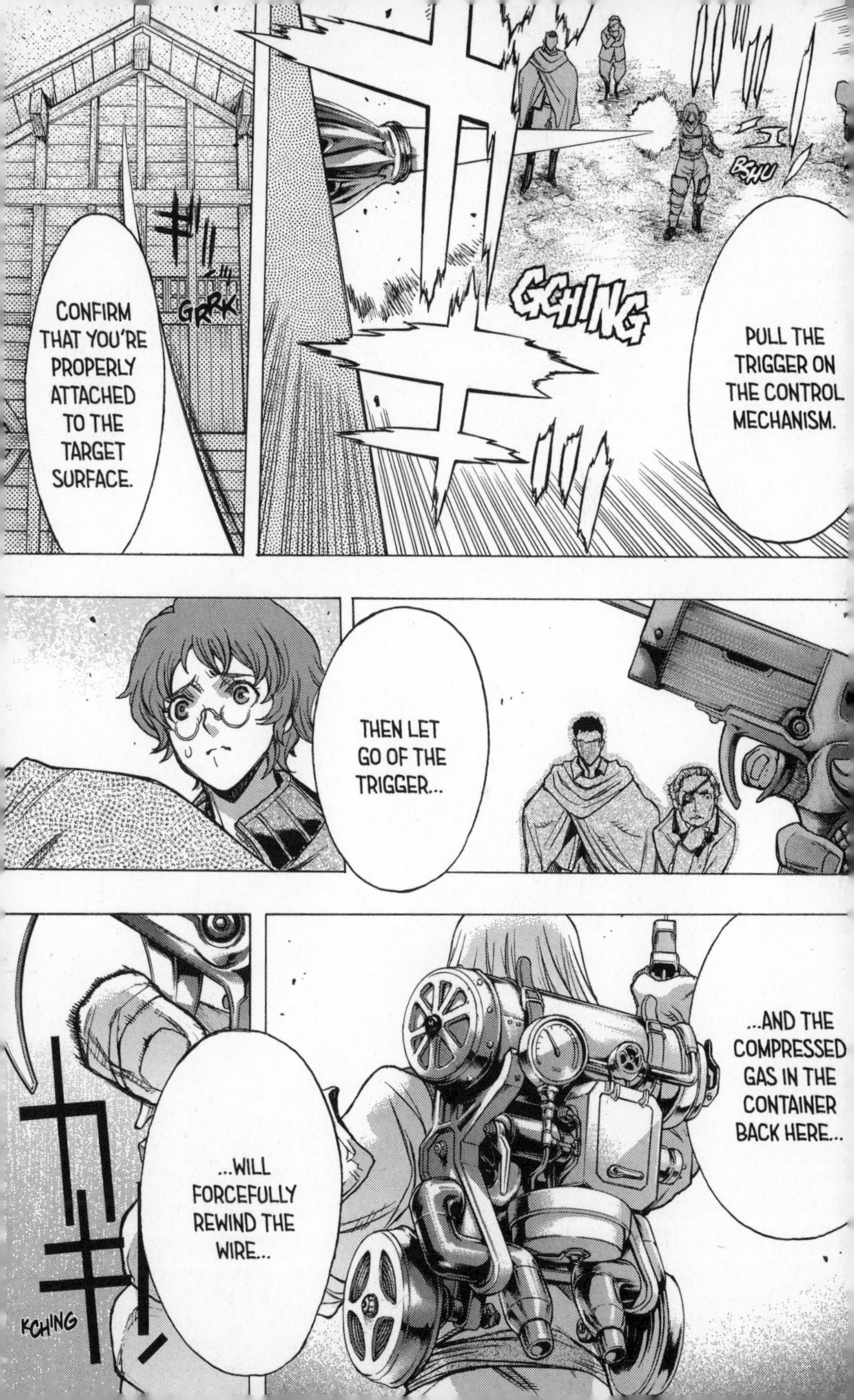
BSHU
PULL THE TRIGGER ON THE CONTROL MECHANISM.
GCHING
GRRK
CONFIRM THAT YOU'RE PROPERLY ATTACHED TO THE TARGET SURFACE.
...
THEN LET GO OF THE TRIGGER...
...AND THE COMPRESSED GAS IN THE CONTAINER BACK HERE...
...WILL FORCEFULLY REWIND THE WIRE...
KCHING

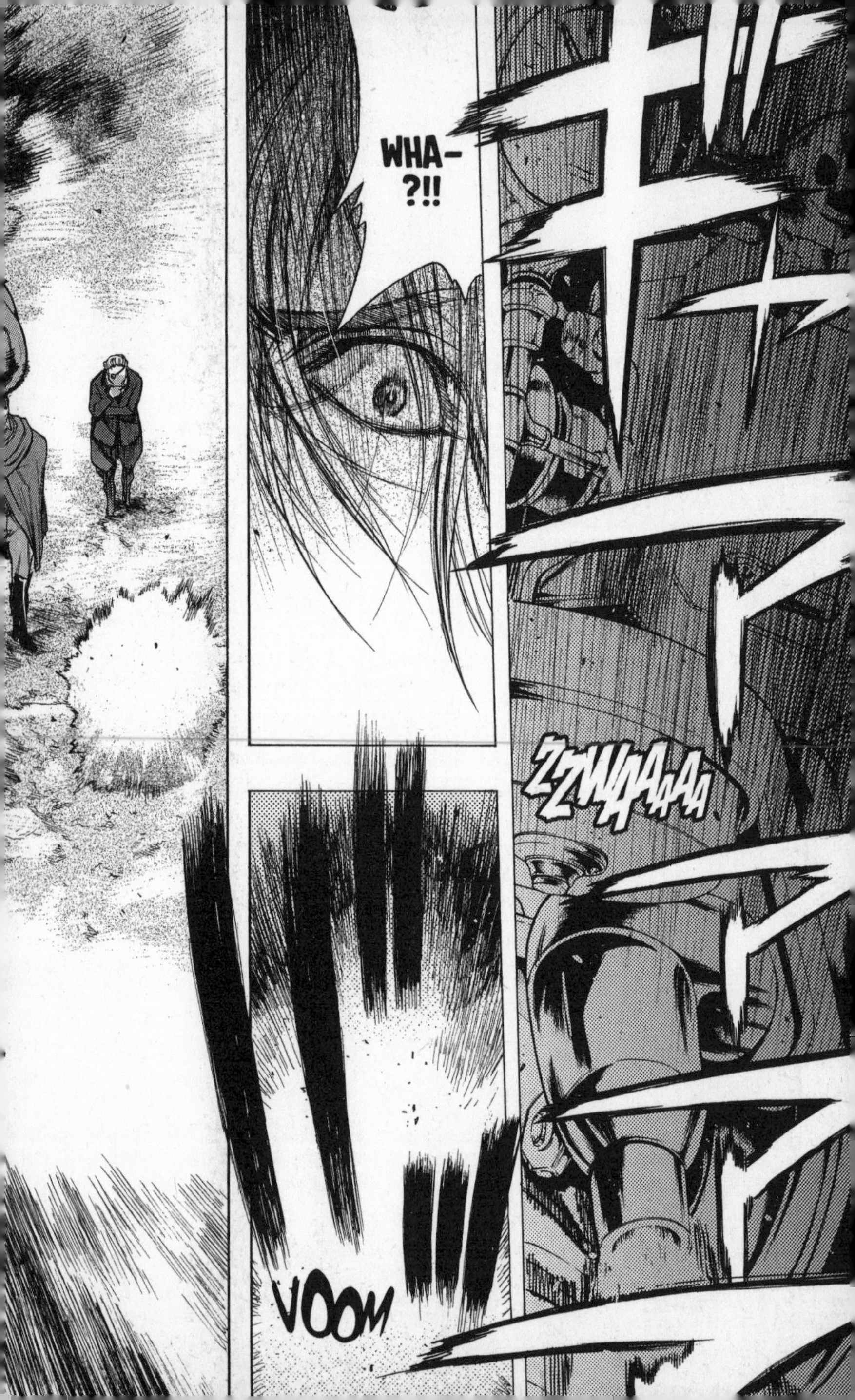
ZZWAAAAAA
WHA-?!!
VOOM

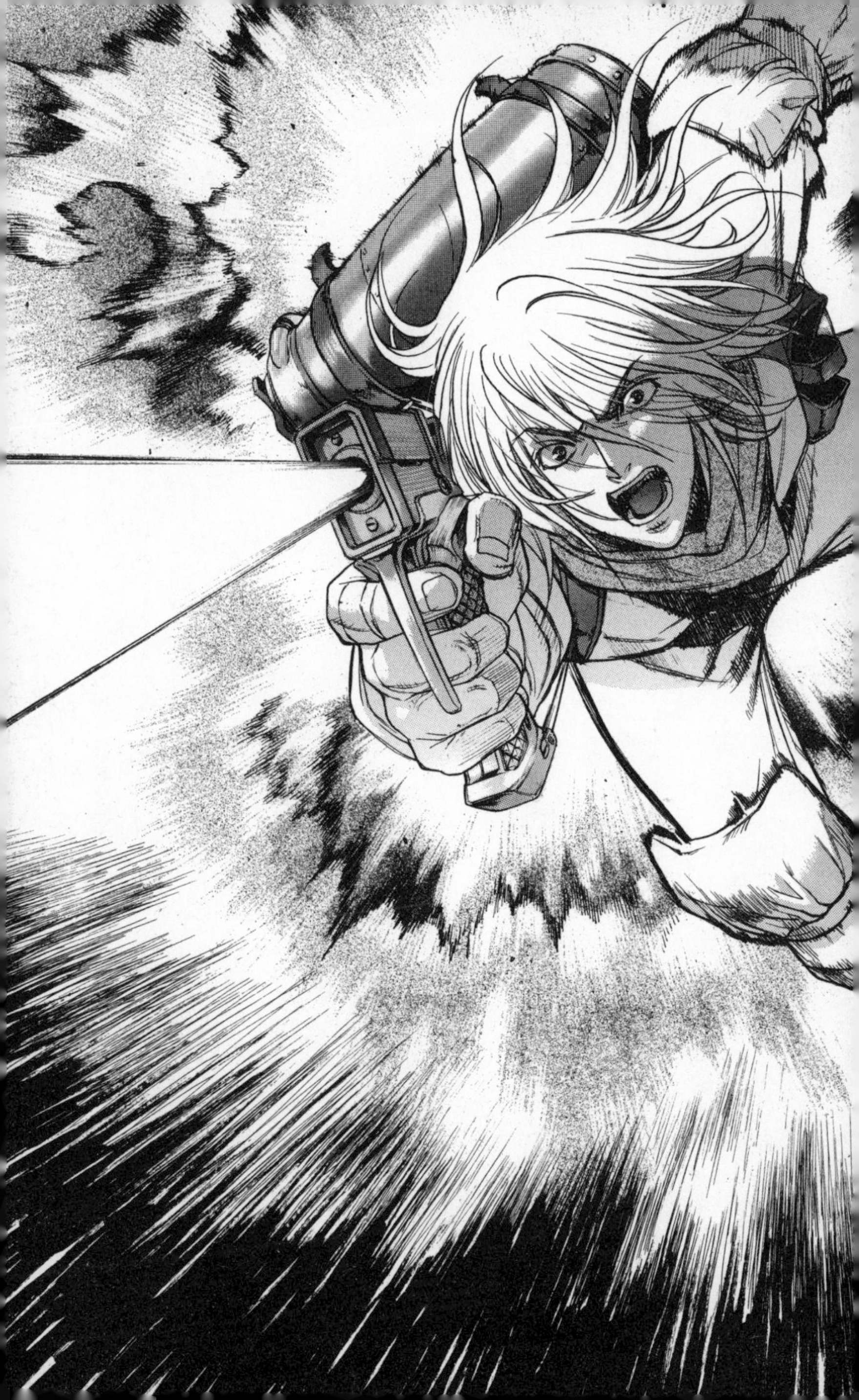

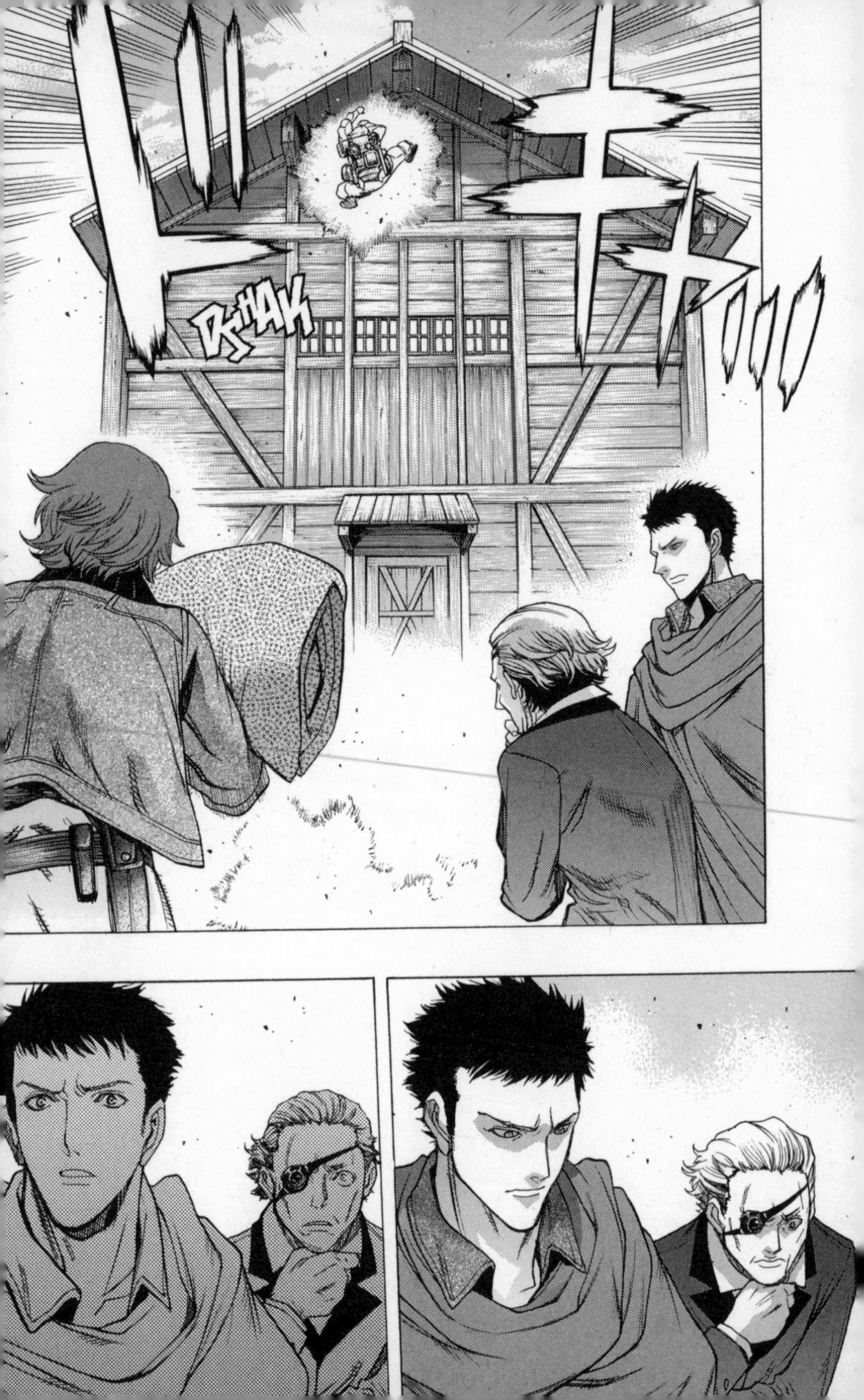
DSHAK

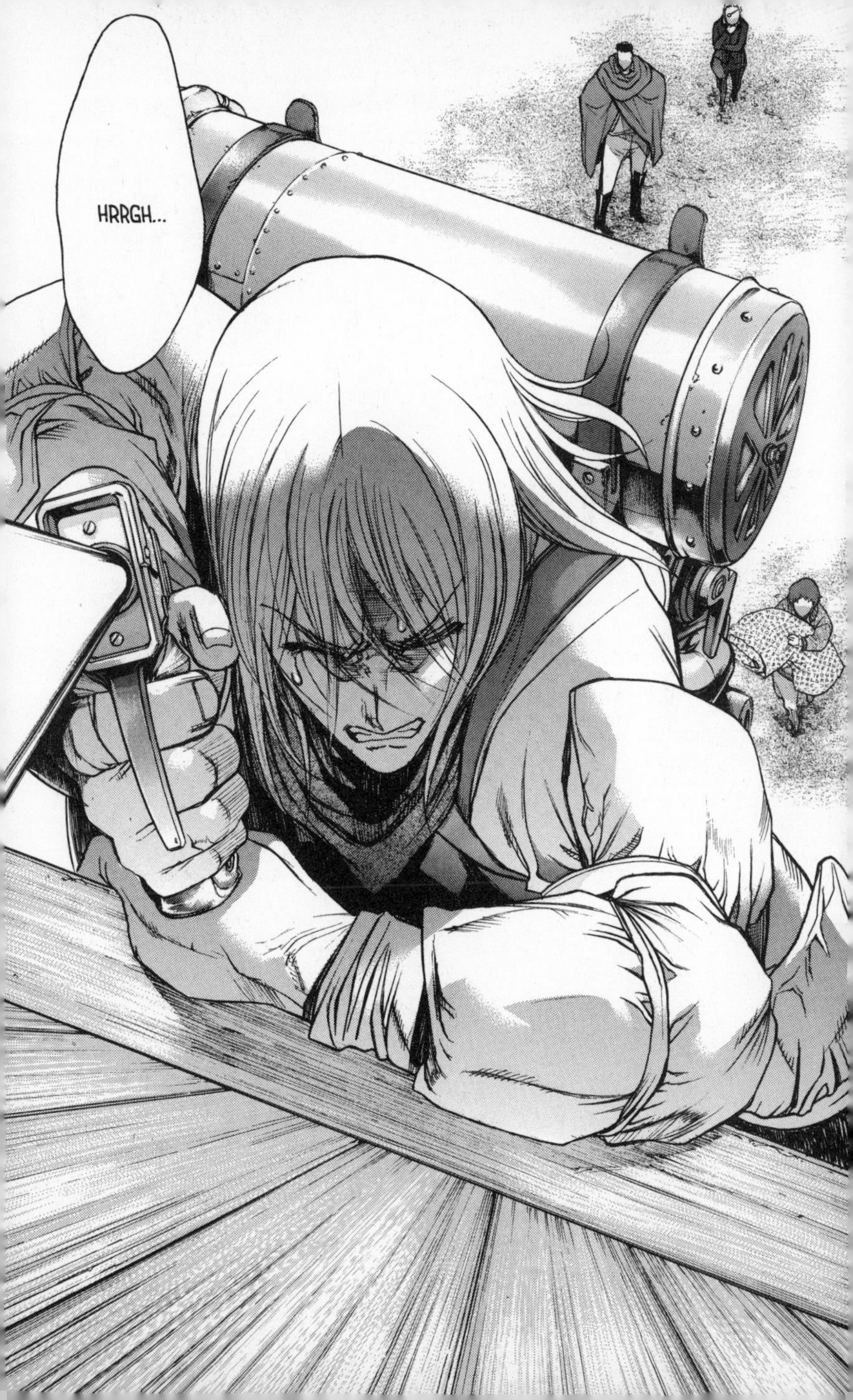
HRRGH...

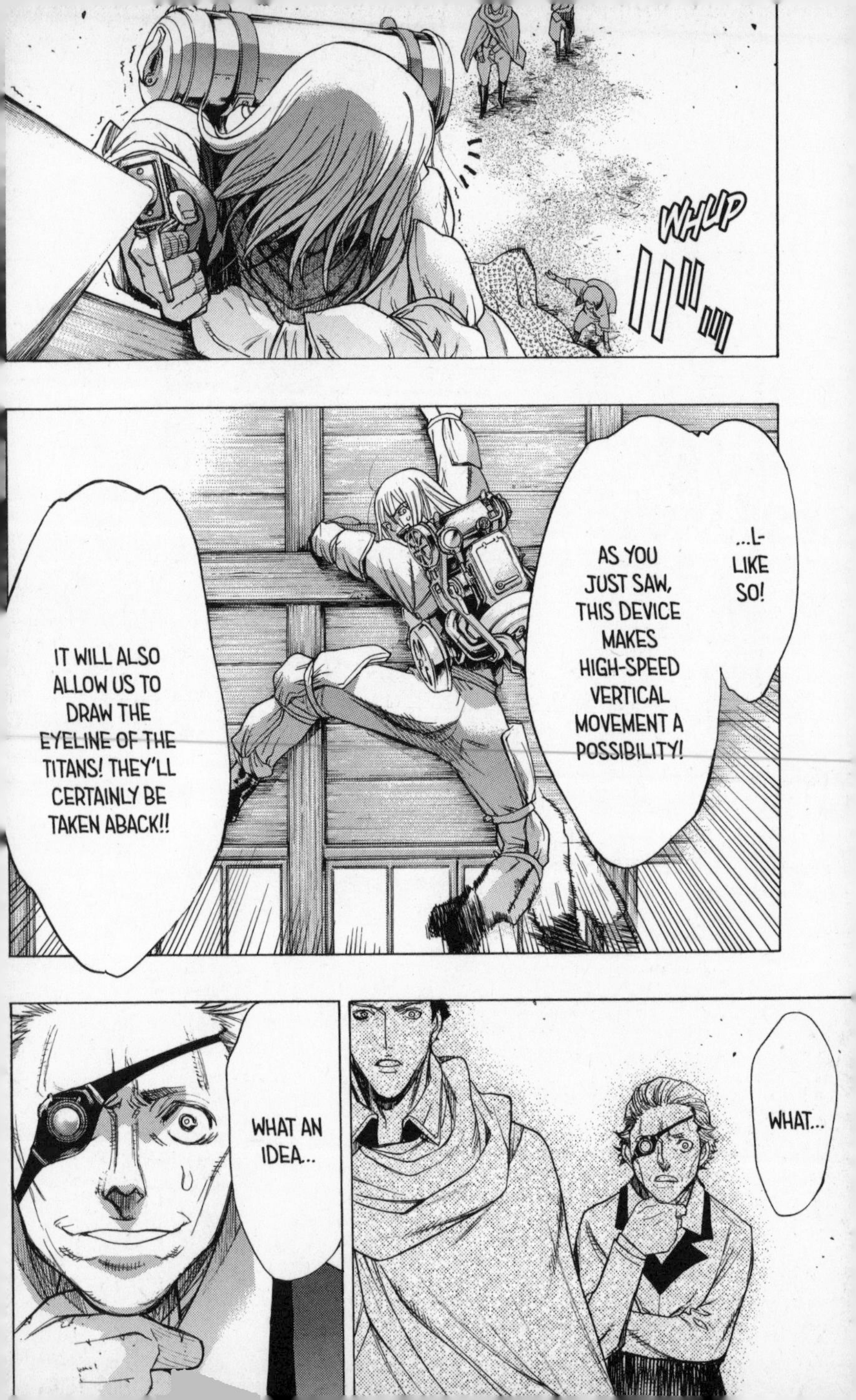
WHUP
...L- LIKE SO!
AS YOU JUST SAW, THIS DEVICE MAKES HIGH-SPEED VERTICAL MOVEMENT A POSSIBILITY!
IT WILL ALSO ALLOW US TO DRAW THE EYELINE OF THE TITANS! THEY'LL CERTAINLY BE TAKEN ABACK!!
WHAT...
WHAT AN IDEA...

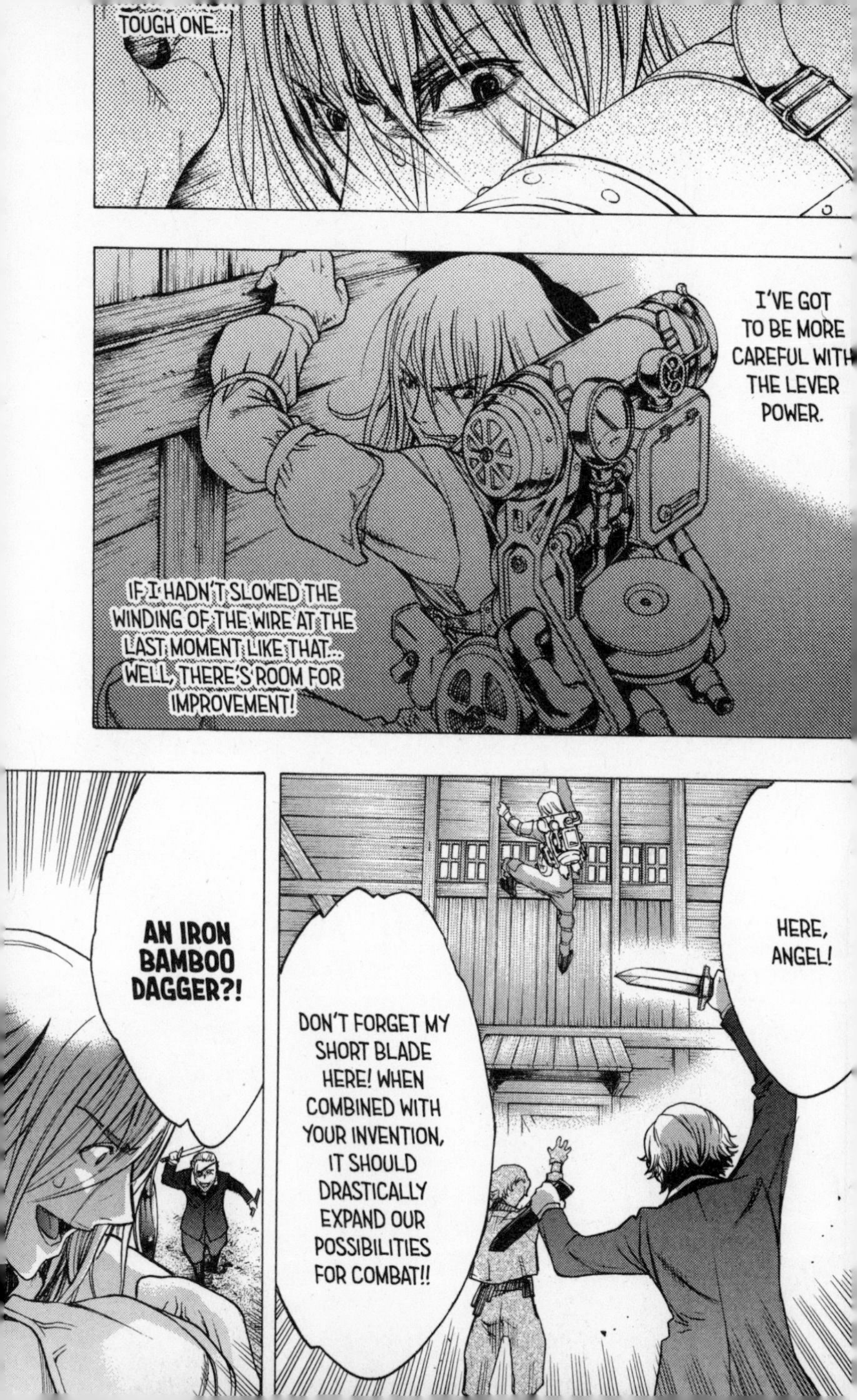
TOUGH ONE...
I'VE GOT TO BE MORE CAREFUL WITH THE LEVER POWER.
IF I HADN'T SLOWED THE WINDING OF THE WIRE AT THE LAST MOMENT LIKE THAT... WELL, THERE'S ROOM FOR IMPROVEMENT!
HERE, ANGEL!
DON'T FORGET MY SHORT BLADE HERE! WHEN COMBINED WITH YOUR INVENTION, IT SHOULD DRASTICALLY EXPAND OUR POSSIBILITIES FOR COMBAT!!
AN IRON BAMBOO DAGGER?!

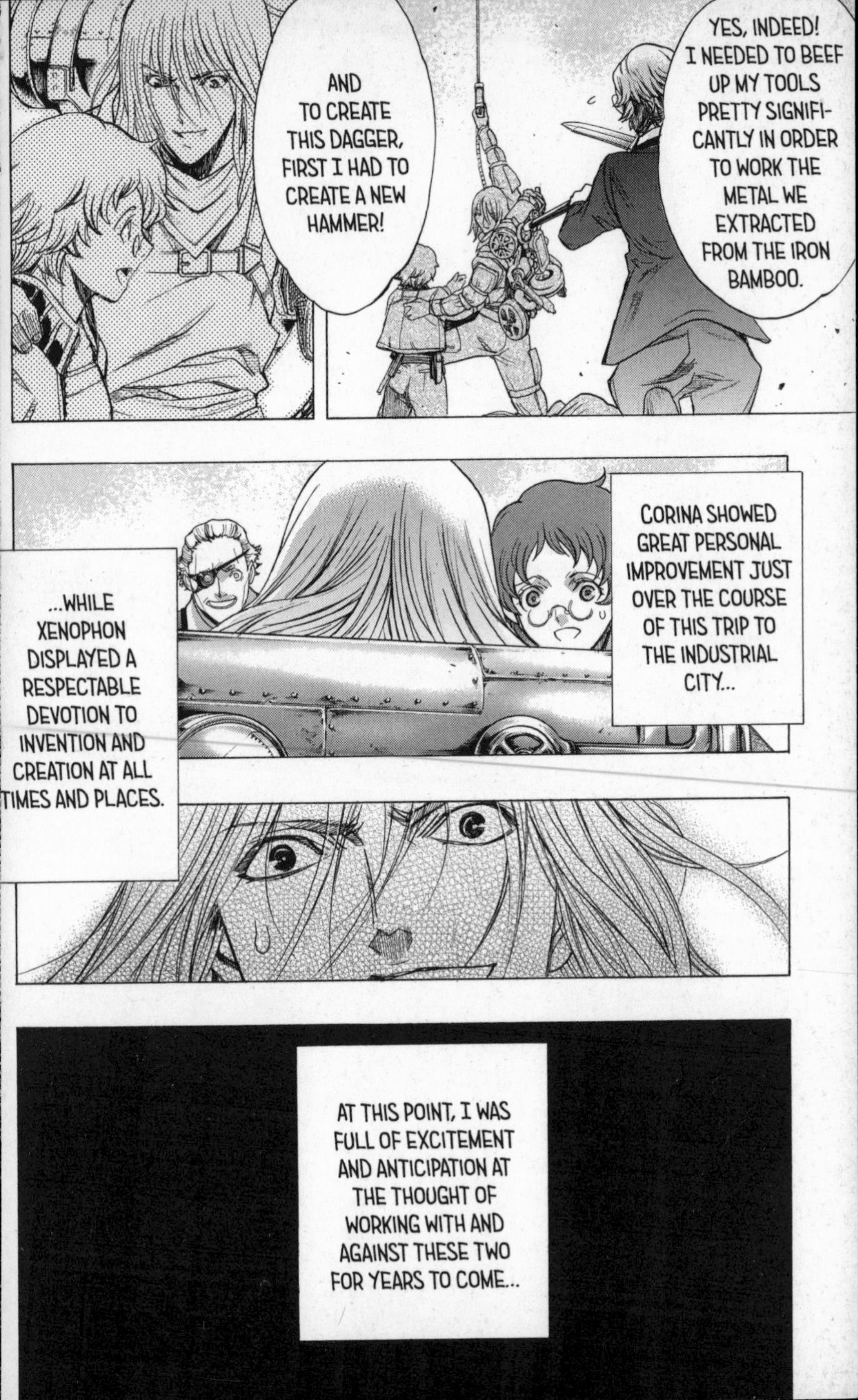
YES, INDEED! I NEEDED TO BEEF UP MY TOOLS PRETTY SIGNIFICANTLY IN ORDER TO WORK THE METAL WE EXTRACTED FROM THE IRON BAMBOO.
AND TO CREATE THIS DAGGER, FIRST I HAD TO CREATE A NEW HAMMER!
CORINA SHOWED GREAT PERSONAL IMPROVEMENT JUST OVER THE COURSE OF THIS TRIP TO THE INDUSTRIAL CITY...
...WHILE XENOPHON DISPLAYED A RESPECTABLE DEVOTION TO INVENTION AND CREATION AT ALL TIMES AND PLACES.
AT THIS POINT, I WAS FULL OF EXCITEMENT AND ANTICIPATION AT THE THOUGHT OF WORKING WITH AND AGAINST THESE TWO FOR YEARS TO COME...

ATTACK ON TITAN
BEFORE THE FALL

TO BE CONTINUED

GREATER INTIMACY THROUGH SELF-DEFENSE

A story of how Sharle learned the combat skills she exhibited against the rogue noblemen in this volume.

Originally published: *Bessatsu Shonen Magazine,* September 2016 issue

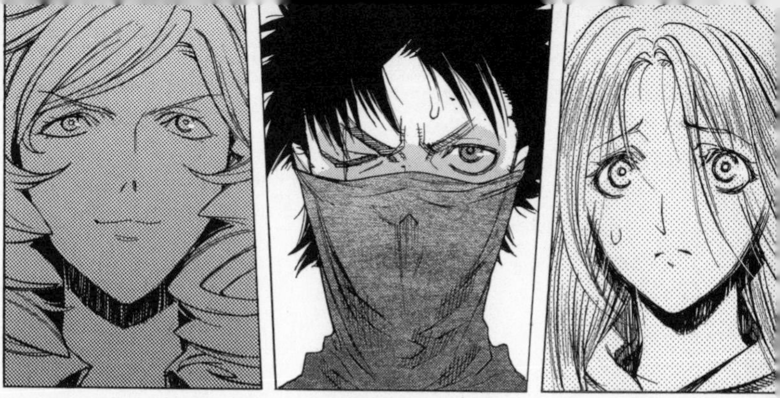

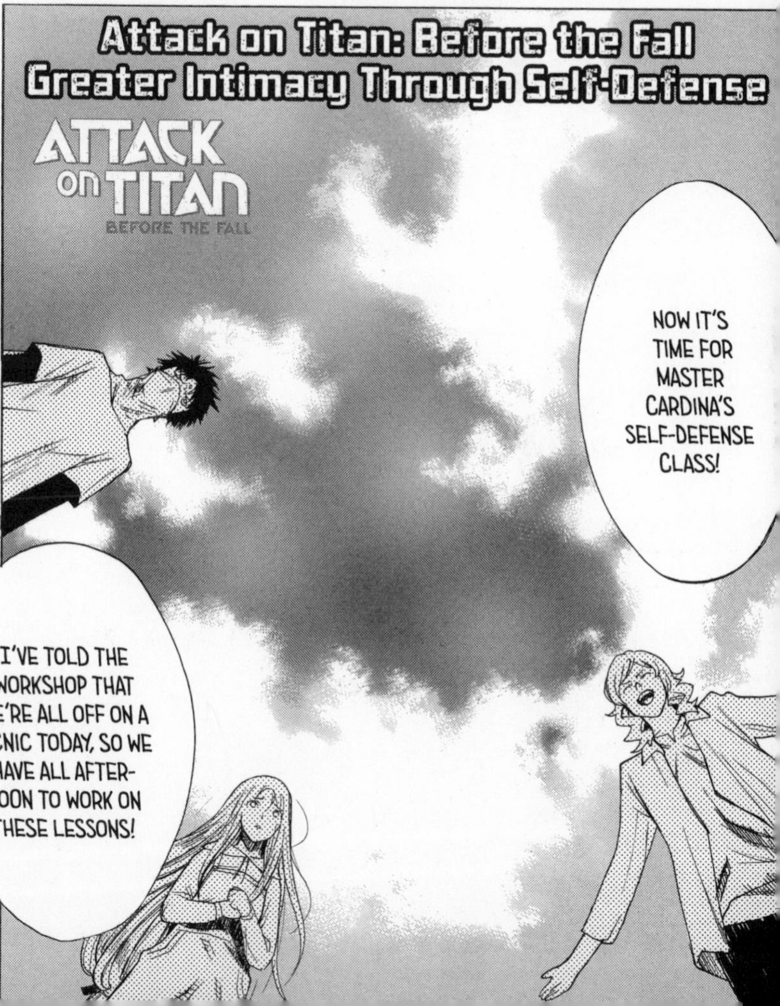
Attack on Titan: Before the Fall
Greater Intimacy Through Self-Defense
ATTACK on TITAN
BEFORE THE FALL
NOW IT'S TIME FOR MASTER CARDINA'S SELF-DEFENSE CLASS!
I'VE TOLD THE WORKSHOP THAT WE'RE ALL OFF ON A PICNIC TODAY, SO WE HAVE ALL AFTERNOON TO WORK ON THESE LESSONS!

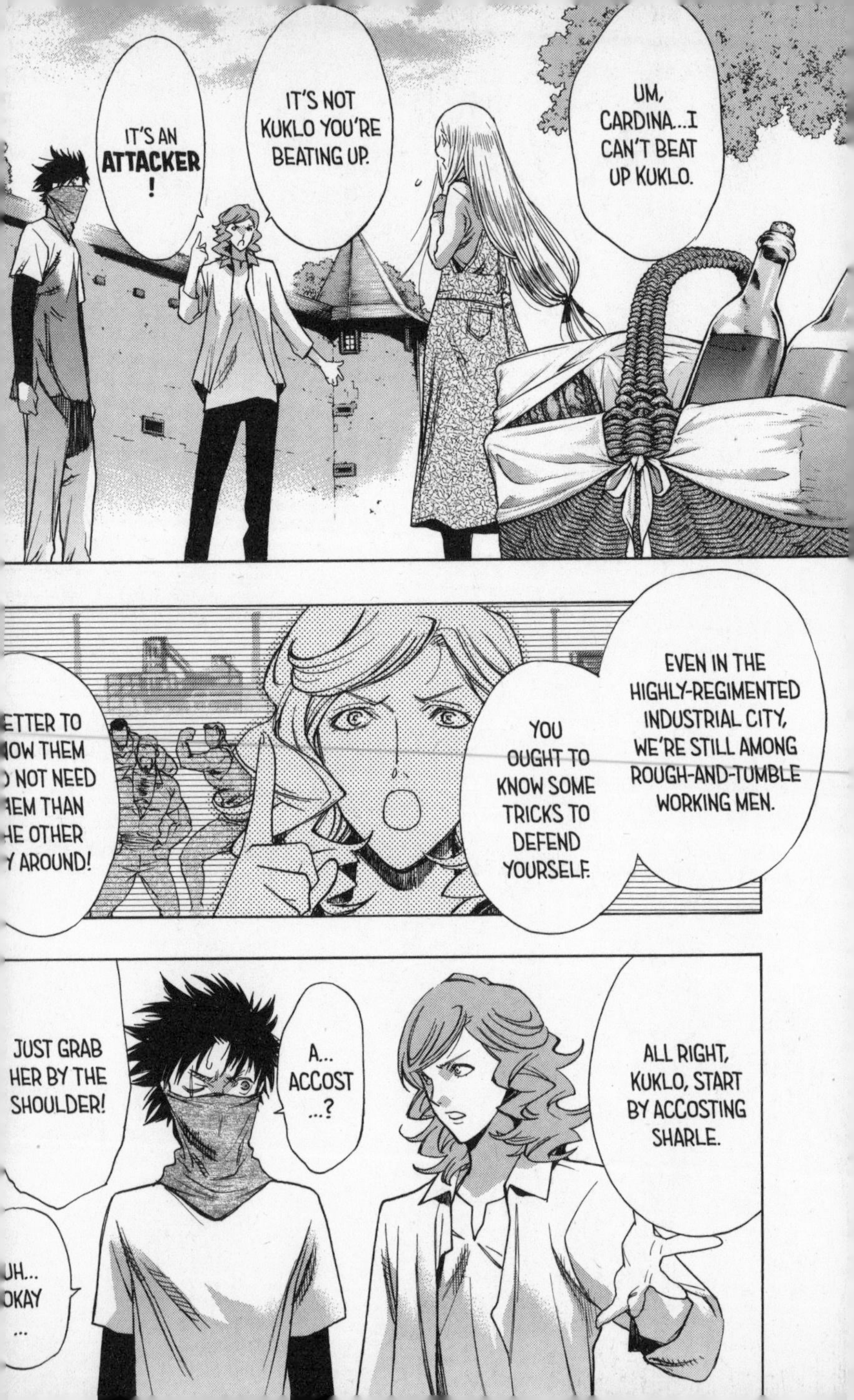
UM, CARDINA...I CAN'T BEAT UP KUKLO.
IT'S NOT KUKLO YOU'RE BEATING UP.
IT'S AN **ATTACKER** !
EVEN IN THE HIGHLY-REGIMENTED INDUSTRIAL CITY, WE'RE STILL AMONG ROUGH-AND-TUMBLE WORKING MEN.
YOU OUGHT TO KNOW SOME TRICKS TO DEFEND YOURSELF.
ETTER TO OW THEM NOT NEED EM THAN E OTHER AROUND!
ALL RIGHT, KUKLO, START BY ACCOSTING SHARLE.
A... ACCOST ...?
JUST GRAB HER BY THE SHOULDER!
H... OKAY ...

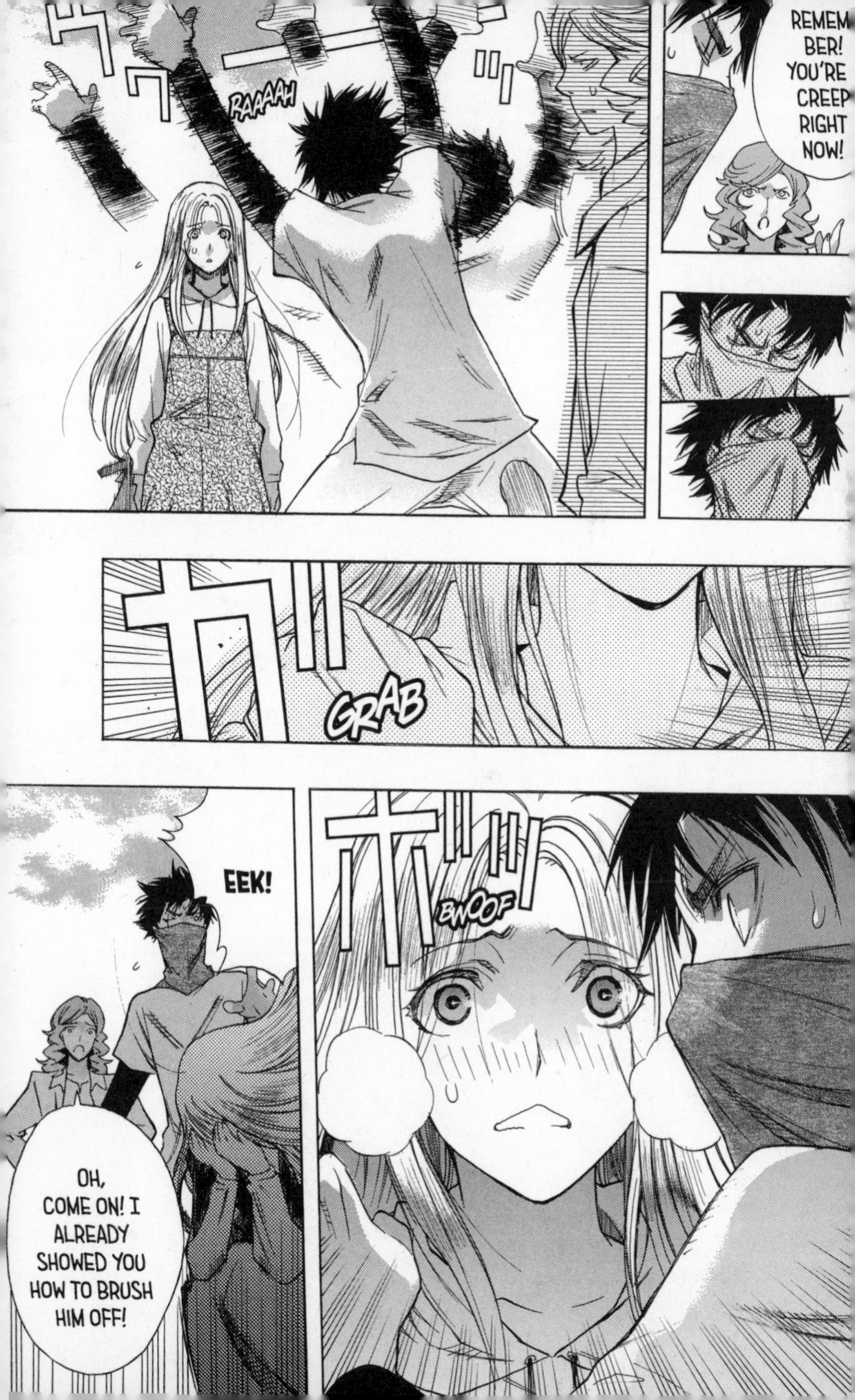
REMEM BER! YOU'RE CREEP RIGHT NOW!
RAAAAH
GRAB
BWOOF
EEK!
OH, COME ON! I ALREADY SHOWED YOU HOW TO BRUSH HIM OFF!

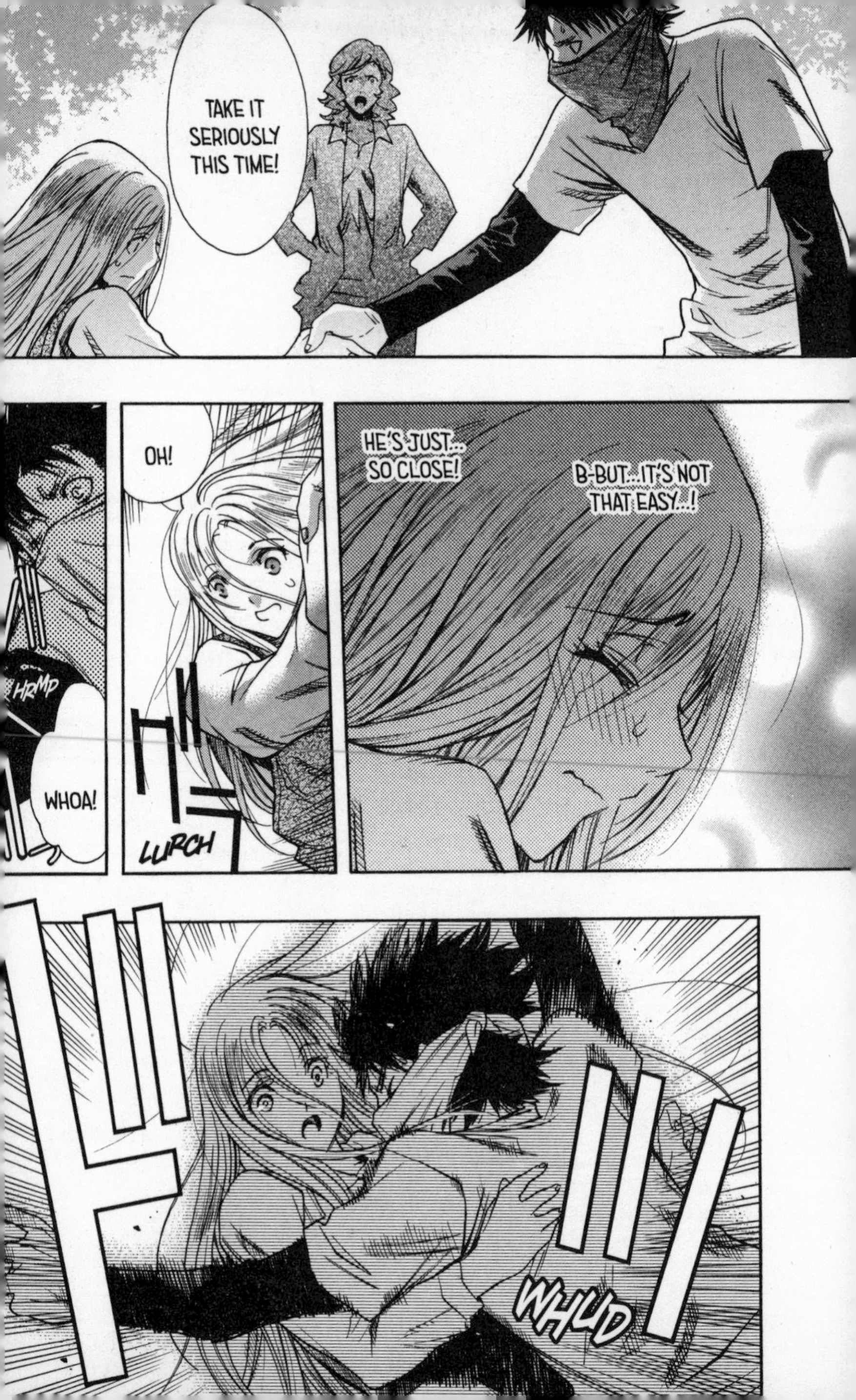
TAKE IT SERIOUSLY THIS TIME!
HE'S JUST... SO CLOSE!
B-BUT...IT'S NOT THAT EASY...!
OH!
LURCH
HRMP
WHOA!
WHUD

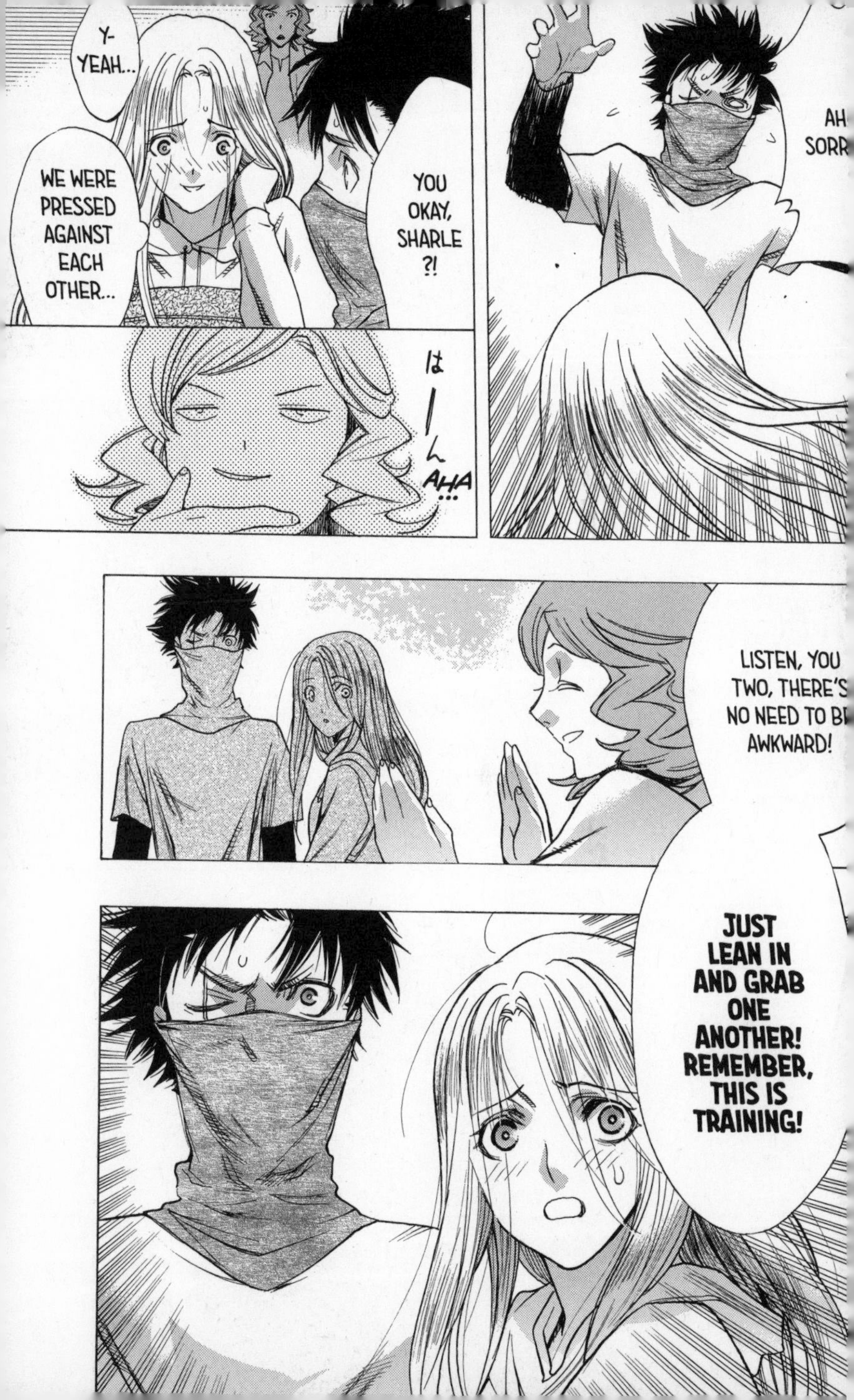
AH SORR
YOU OKAY, SHARLE?!
Y-YEAH...
WE WERE PRESSED AGAINST EACH OTHER...
はーん
AHA...
LISTEN, YOU TWO, THERE'S NO NEED TO B AWKWARD!
JUST LEAN IN AND GRAB ONE ANOTHER! REMEMBER, THIS IS TRAINING!

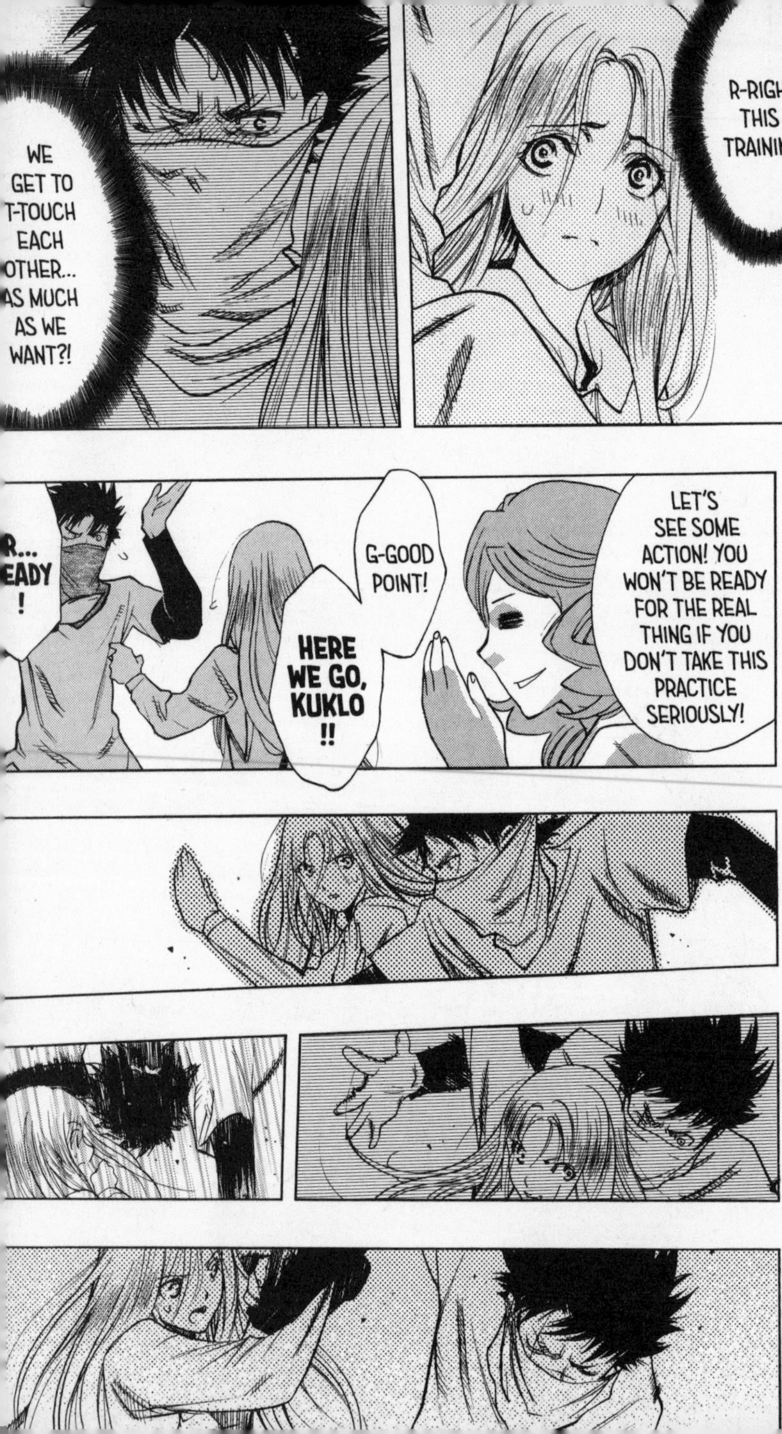
R-RIGHT... THIS IS TRAINING...
WE GET TO T-TOUCH EACH OTHER... AS MUCH AS WE WANT?!
LET'S SEE SOME ACTION! YOU WON'T BE READY FOR THE REAL THING IF YOU DON'T TAKE THIS PRACTICE SERIOUSLY!
G-GOOD POINT!
HERE WE GO, KUKLO !!
R... EADY !

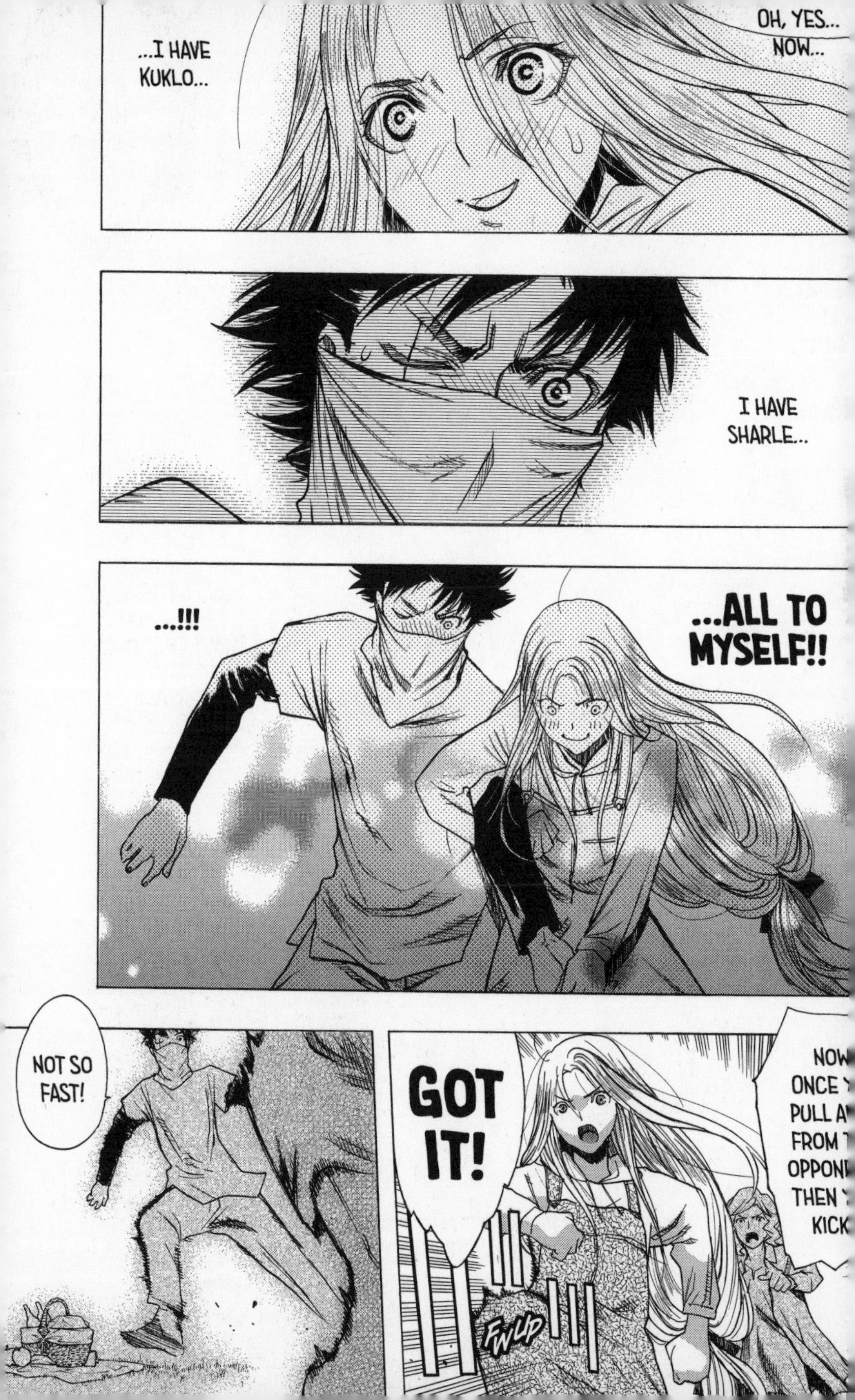
OH, YES... NOW...
...I HAVE KUKLO...
I HAVE SHARLE...
...ALL TO MYSELF!!
...!!!
NOW ONCE Y PULL A FROM T OPPON THEN Y KICK
GOT IT!
FWUP
NOT SO FAST!

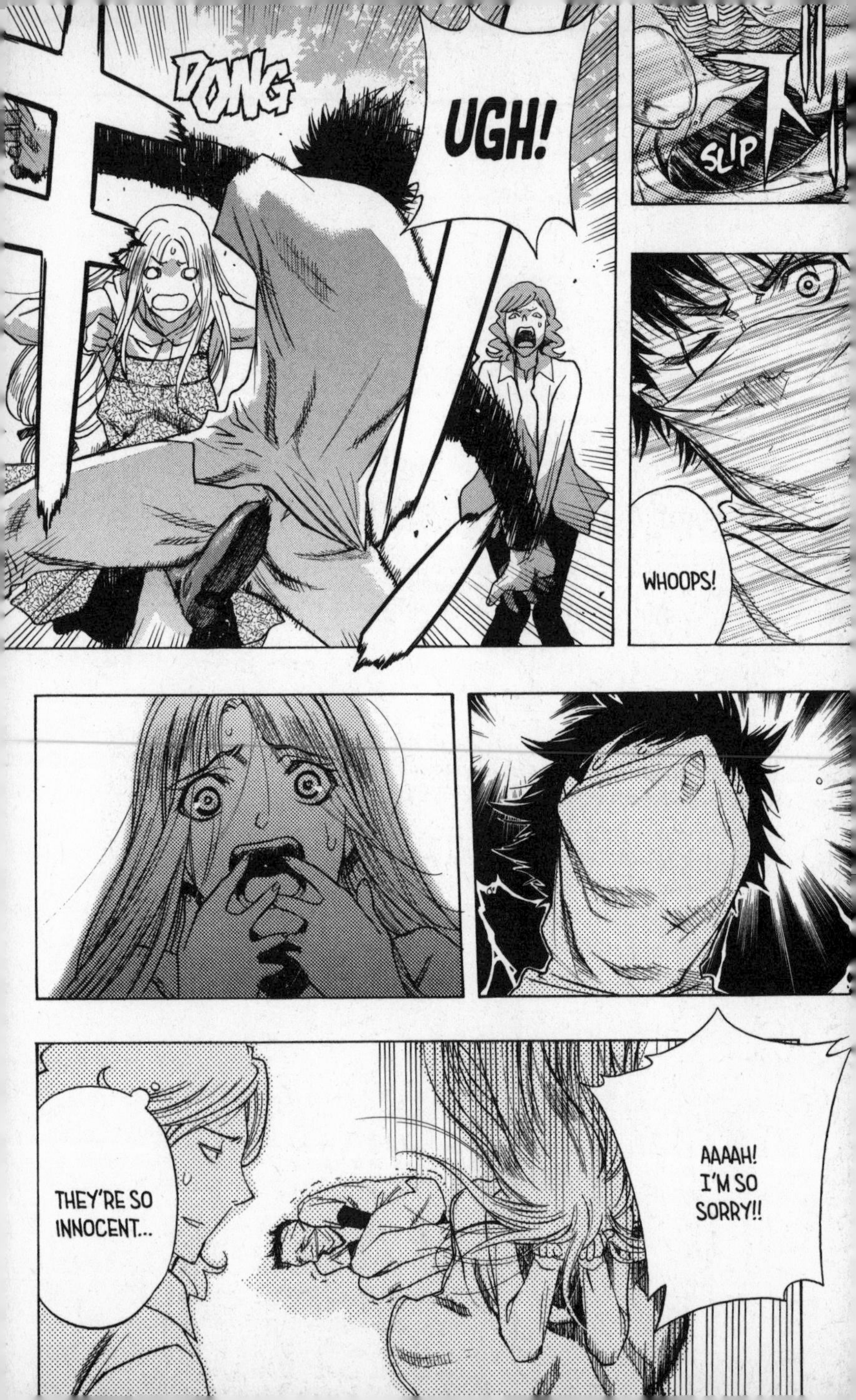
SLIP
WHOOPS!
UGH!
DONG
AAAAH! I'M SO SORRY!!
THEY'RE SO INNOCENT...

Greater Intimacy Through Self-Defense · En

INUYASHIKI

A superhero like none you've ever seen, from the creator of "Gantz"!

ICHIRO INUYASHIKI IS DOWN ON HIS LUCK. HE LOOKS MUCH OLDER THAN HIS 58 YEARS, HIS CHILDREN DESPISE HIM, AND HIS WIFE THINKS HE'S A USELESS COWARD. SO WHEN HE'S DIAGNOSED WITH STOMACH CANCER AND GIVEN THREE MONTHS TO LIVE, IT SEEMS THE ONLY ONE WHO'LL MISS HIM IS HIS DOG.

THEN A BLINDING LIGHT FILLS THE SKY, AND THE OLD MAN IS KILLED... ONLY TO WAKE UP LATER IN A BODY HE ALMOST RECOGNIZES AS HIS OWN. CAN IT BE THAT ICHIRO INUYASHIKI IS NO LONGER HUMAN?

COMES IN EXTRA-LARGE EDITIONS WITH COLOR PAGES!

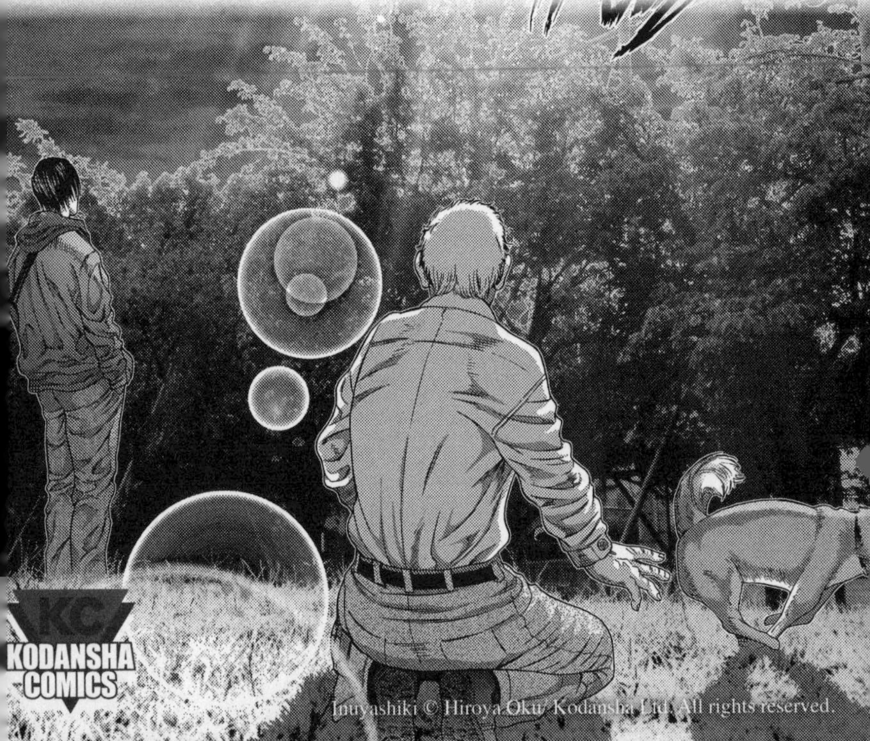

KC
KODANSHA COMICS

FINALLY, A LOWER-COST OMNIBUS EDITION OF FAIRY TAIL! CONTAINS VOLUMES 1-5. ONLY $39.99!

-NEARLY 1,000 PAGES!
-EXTRA LARGE 7"X10.5" TRIM SIZE
-HIGH-QUALITY PAPER!

Fairy Tail takes place in a world filled with magic. 17-year-old Lucy is a wizard-in-training who wants to join a magic guild so that she can become a full-fledged wizard. She dreams of joining the most famous guild, known as Fairy Tail. One day she meets Natsu, a boy raised by a dragon which vanished when he was young. Natsu has devoted his life to finding his dragon father. When Natsu helps Lucy out of a tricky situation, she discovers that he is a member of Fairy Tail, and our heroes' adventure together begins.

FAIRY TAIL

MASTER'S EDITION

SWAPPED WITH A KISS?!

Class troublemaker Ryu Yamada is already having a bad day when he stumbles down a staircase along with star student Urara Shiraishi. When he wakes up, he realizes they have switched bodies—and that Ryu has the power to trade places with anyone just by kissing them! Ryu and Urara take full advantage of the situation to improve their lives, but with such an oddly amazing power, just how long will they be able to keep their secret under wraps?

Available now in print and digitally!

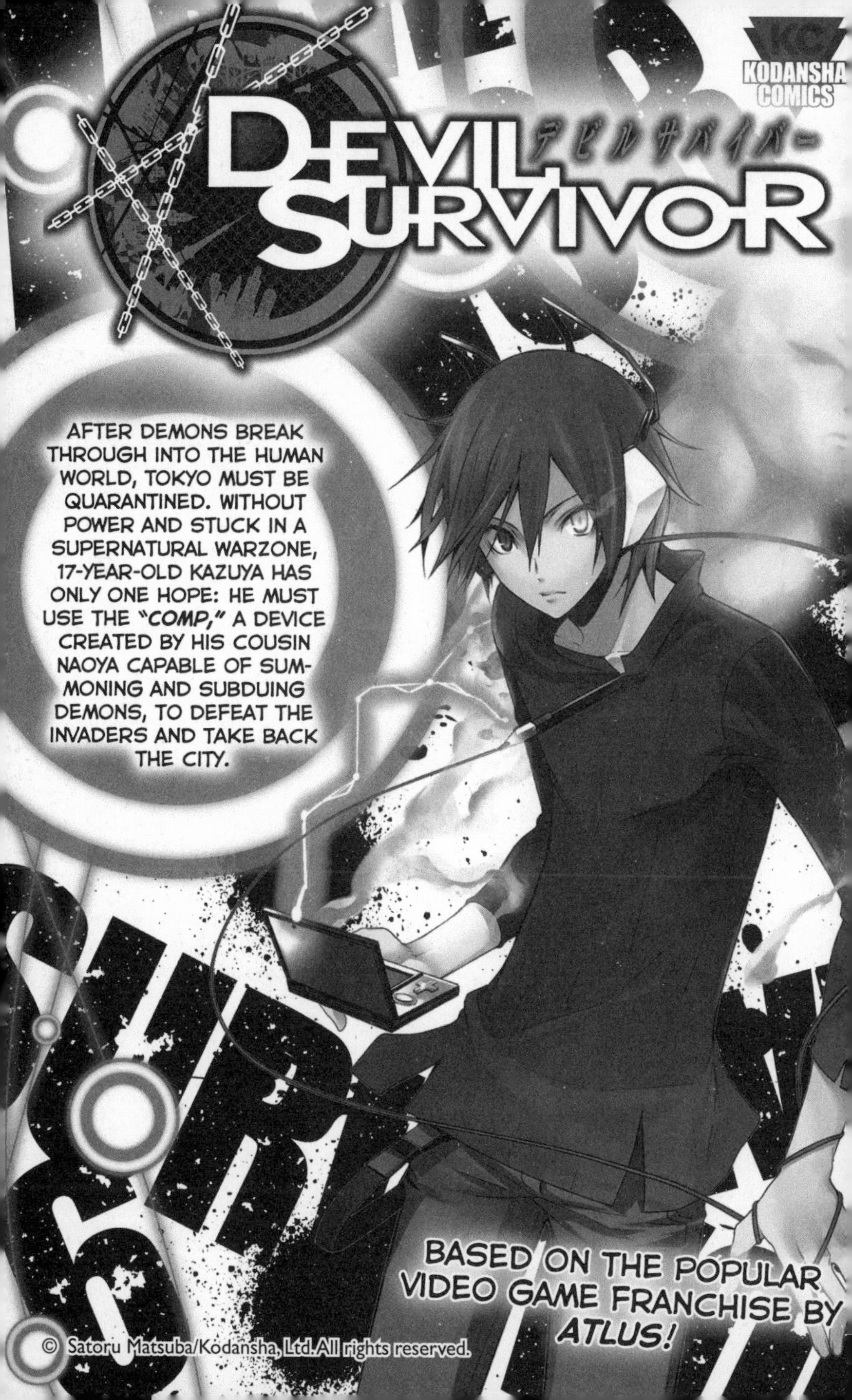
KODANSHA COMICS
DEVIL SURVIVOR
デビルサバイバー
AFTER DEMONS BREAK THROUGH INTO THE HUMAN WORLD, TOKYO MUST BE QUARANTINED. WITHOUT POWER AND STUCK IN A SUPERNATURAL WARZONE, 17-YEAR-OLD KAZUYA HAS ONLY ONE HOPE: HE MUST USE THE "COMP," A DEVICE CREATED BY HIS COUSIN NAOYA CAPABLE OF SUMMONING AND SUBDUING DEMONS, TO DEFEAT THE INVADERS AND TAKE BACK THE CITY.
BASED ON THE POPULAR VIDEO GAME FRANCHISE BY ATLUS!
© Satoru Matsuba/Kodansha, Ltd. All rights reserved.

Say I Love You.

KC
KODANSHA
COMICS

Mei Tachibana has no friends — and says she doesn't need them!
But everything changes when she accidentally roundhouse kicks the most popular boy in school! However, Yamato Kurosawa isn't angry in the slightest— in fact, he thinks his ordinary life could use an unusual girl like Mei. But winning Mei's trust will be a tough task. How long will she refuse to say, "I love you"?

"This series never fails to put a smile on my face."
-Dramatic Reviews

"A very funny look at what happens when two strange and strangely well-suited peop try to navigate the thorny path to true love together."

-Anime News Netwo

My Little Monster

OPPOSITES ATTRACT...MAYBE?

Haru Yoshida is feared as an unstable and violent "monster." Mizutani Shizuku is a grade-obsessed student with no friends. Fate brings these two together to form the most unlikely pair. Haru firmly believes he's in love with Mizutani and she firmly believes he's insane.

KC
KODANSHA
COMICS

Maria
THE VIRGIN WITCH

"Maria's brand of righteous
ustice, passion and plain talking
make for one of the freshest
nanga series of 2015. I dare any
other book to top it."
—UK Anime Network

PURITY AND POWER

As a war to determine the rightful ruler of
medieval France ravages the land, the witch
Maria decides she will not stand idly by as
men kill each other in the name of God and
glory. Using her powerful magic, she summons
various beasts and demons —even going as far
as using a succubus to seduce soldiers into sub-
mission under the veil of night— all to stop the
needless slaughter. However, after the Arch-
angel Michael puts an end to her meddling, he
curses her to lose her powers if she ever gives
up her virginity. Will she forgo the forbidden
fruit of adulthood in order to bring an end to
the merciless machine of war?
Available now in print and digitally!

KC
KODANSHA
COMICS

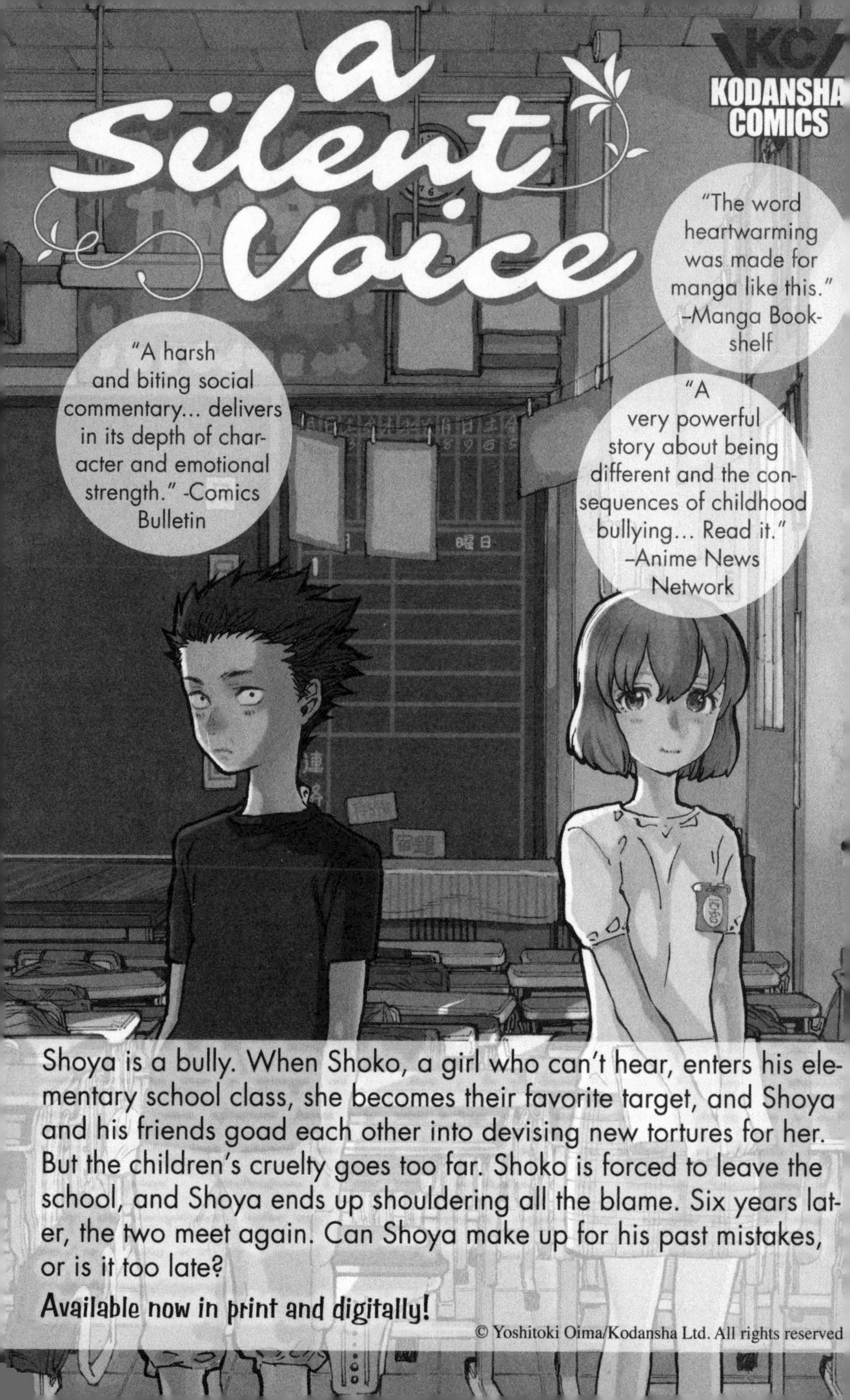
KODANSHA COMICS
a Silent Voice
"The word heartwarming was made for manga like this." –Manga Bookshelf
"A harsh and biting social commentary... delivers in its depth of character and emotional strength." -Comics Bulletin
"A very powerful story about being different and the consequences of childhood bullying… Read it." –Anime News Network
Shoya is a bully. When Shoko, a girl who can't hear, enters his elementary school class, she becomes their favorite target, and Shoya and his friends goad each other into devising new tortures for her. But the children's cruelty goes too far. Shoko is forced to leave the school, and Shoya ends up shouldering all the blame. Six years later, the two meet again. Can Shoya make up for his past mistakes, or is it too late?
Available now in print and digitally!
© Yoshitoki Oima/Kodansha Ltd. All rights reserved

SHERLOCK BONES

DEDUCTIVE DOG DETECTIVE

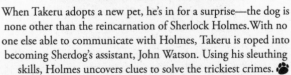

When Takeru adopts a new pet, he's in for a surprise—the dog is none other than the reincarnation of Sherlock Holmes. With no one else able to communicate with Holmes, Takeru is roped into becoming Sherdog's assistant, John Watson. Using his sleuthing skills, Holmes uncovers clues to solve the trickiest crimes. 🐾

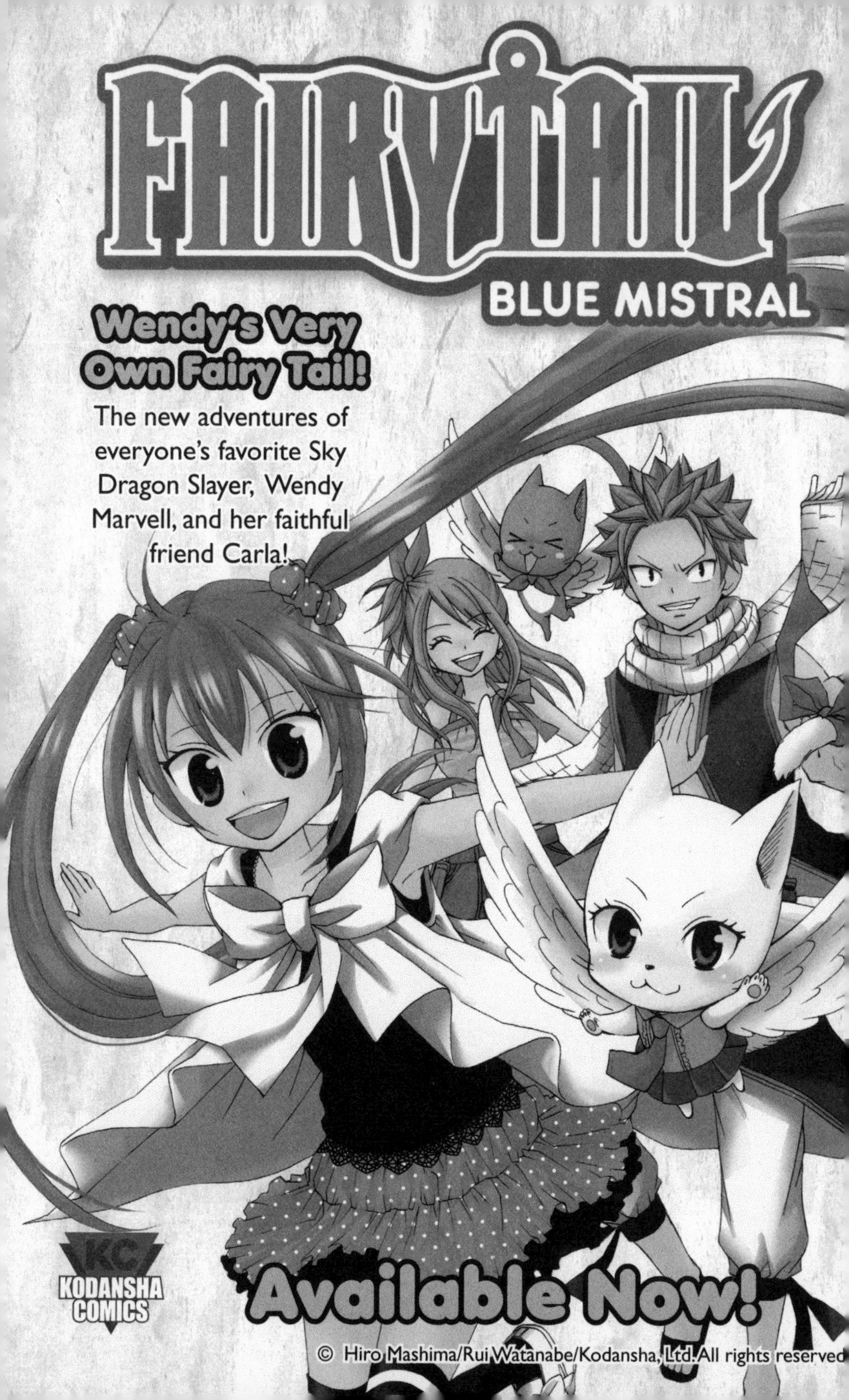
FAIRY TAIL
BLUE MISTRAL
Wendy's Very Own Fairy Tail!
The new adventures of everyone's favorite Sky Dragon Slayer, Wendy Marvell, and her faithful friend Carla!
KC KODANSHA COMICS
Available Now!
© Hiro Mashima/Rui Watanabe/Kodansha, Ltd. All rights reserved

ATTACK on TITAN
BEFORE THE FALL

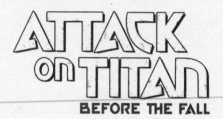

A Kodansha Comics Trade Paperback Original
Attack on Titan: Before the Fall volume 10 copyright © 2016 Hajime Isayama/
Ryo Suzukaze/Satoshi Shiki
English translation copyright © 2016 Hajime Isayama/Ryo Suzukaze/Satoshi Shiki

Published in the United States by Kodansha Comics, an imprint of
Kodansha USA Publishing, LLC, New York.

Publication rights for this English edition arranged through
Kodansha Ltd, Tokyo.

First published in Japan in 2016 by Kodansha Ltd., Tokyo
as *Shingeki no kyojin Before the fall*, volume 10.

ISBN 978-1-63236-381-7

Character designs by Thores Shibamoto
Original cover design by Takashi Shimoyama (Red Rooster)

Printed in the United States of America.

www.kodanshacomics.com

9 8 7 6 5 4 3 2 1
Translation: Stephen Paul
Lettering: Steve Wands
Editing: Lauren Scanlan
Kodansha Comics edition cover design by Phil Balsman

STOP!

You are going the *wrong way!*

Manga is a *completely* different type of reading experience.

To start at the *BEGINNING,* go to the *END!*

That's right! Authentic manga is read the traditional Japanese way—from right to left, exactly the opposite of how American books are read. It's easy to follow: just go to the other end of the book, and read each page—and each panel—from the right side to the left side, starting at the top right. Now you're experiencing manga as it was meant to be.

CPSIA information can be obtained
at www.ICGtesting.com
Printed in the USA
LVHW041515251119
638400LV00007B/1167/P